Also by CORNELIUS OSGOOD

The Koreans and Their Culture

Blue-and-White Chinese Porcelain
A Study of Form

VILLAGE LIFE
IN OLD CHINA

A COMMUNITY STUDY OF
KAO YAO, YÜNNAN

CORNELIUS OSGOOD

PROFESSOR OF ANTHROPOLOGY
YALE UNIVERSITY

THE RONALD PRESS COMPANY ⟋ NEW YORK

Library of Congress Catalog Card Number: 63–19749

PRINTED IN THE UNITED STATES OF AMERICA

For my friend

LI AN-CHE

PREFACE

This description of life in a Yünnan village is offered with some sadness and more humility since it presents the results of a disrupted period of research. The work was undertaken in southwestern China in 1938, a year during which that country was being invaded. Even for a young man whose ethnographic experience had then been limited only to non-literate people in the Far North, it would have been possible to accomplish significantly more had a longer period of time been available. Originally, in recognition of its incompleteness, the record of this scientific adventure was put aside with the hope that it would be possible to return and complete it. During a quarter of a century, that hope changed to dream, and the dream became vain. Now, were it possible to go back to the village, it would be useless insofar as one might expect to participate in the life of the people as it existed then. Even in 1938, the community presented an aspect of the traditional culture that was fast disappearing from China. Therefore, we invite indulgence for this attempt to save something of the excitement and the beauty of what now has gone.

CORNELIUS OSGOOD

Yale University
September, 1963

CONTENTS

MAPS AND TEXT FIGURES

MAPS AND TEXT FIGURES

PLATES

VILLAGE LIFE
IN OLD CHINA

1

JOURNEY TO YÜNNAN

MY APPOINTMENT was with a small French coastwise
steamer hidden among a hundred ships lying at anchor in the
harbor of Hong Kong. The bay, a basin of blue mercury, dazzled
the eyes in rippling reflections of the midday June sun. A few days
earlier I had come into the harbor lulled by the security of the simple
and familiar life on an ocean liner. For glamor and beauty there
was no need of going farther. It seemed so easy to remain motion-
less in the intimate heat with no thoughts beyond the quick change to
night, and the tart, cool refreshment of a gimlet with which to welcome again the flickering colored lights of the city as they moved
out over the water to lose themselves among the stars. A few miles
away was war, a tearing of flesh among a peaceful people, heartbreak
and starvation for a hundred million who saw only death in the sky.
My appointment was one which I could not afford to miss.

It would have been easy to take the ferry from Kowloon to the
city and then the company lighter out to the ship, but I preferred
the personal and incisive farewell to private pleasure which preserves
the imagery and leaves no sticky survivals stringing shoreward. The
whole psychological change was encompassed in an hour, all that
was mine on rickshas and down to the shore, bargaining with a
Chinese for a walla walla to reach my ship, a ride over the bay half-
hoping the motor would break down, and finally climbing the ship's
gangway. We seemed to sail immediately, but I observed an elderly
man, a sensitive oriental family, a blind woman talking to a young
Jew, and I drank a glass of champagne with two people in love.
Three nuns said good-by to a young girl, the two lovers kissed each
other passionately, a coolie selling soft drinks from a pail was kicked
by the captain who then went above to blow a last blast on his whistle.
It was all so sensuously French. I walked to my cabin and lay down.

Dinner was served in the small dining room amidships. The
French seemed to enjoy their food; the rest did not. My mind was

on other things, but I was charmed by being offered a cigar and good cognac in the little lounge with the compliments of the company, in my wanderings a unique experience which sealed the small ship among my affectionate memories of the sea. As the few passengers gradually retired, I became more conscious of the regular throb of the engine. The vessel commenced to roll gently and, when I was left alone, an irregular muffled wheeze suffused from its bowels. My thoughts tossed back and forth between the concisely contrived past and my precarious plans for maneuvering through a future as ominous of trouble as a mine field in a dark passage. My destiny bore the burden of a pertinacity and a beguiling imagination which, withal, might one day break my back.

For years I had made preparations to study a Chinese community in order to dissect from its weeping and laughter some of the secrets of human behavior and to bring to my own people a sense of sympathetic understanding for their superficially different fellow beings in a traditionally friendly nation. Plans had been quietly developed with my Chinese colleague to study his ancestral village in Hopei. He was to provide an articulate expression of the ideas and innate feelings of the people whom he so dearly loved, and to coagulate with his intuitive genius the configurations of their thoughts. To this, I offered the objectivity of an occidental who might draw on the intellectual heritage of brilliant teachers and a decade of technical experience among the semi-nomads in the far north. Then came war and destruction and death with regiments to rape the living, poison the helpless with heroin, and famish the remnants of fear-crazed families. Work in Hopei obviously would no longer gain for us the desired end. From communications received in Shanghai, I knew my colleague would try to join me as soon as he could escape from occupied territory. Hearing nothing more, I had set out for an uncertain rendezvous in Yünnan where the clouds drift down from Ta Hsüeh Shan over the plateau of southwest China. The place was only a misty fantasy in my mind, a mixture of legends from childhood, an altogether different prospect from living in the relatively sophisticated and familiar coastal region of Hopei. It was an uncertain future which would only become real in restrospect. I walked out on deck. In the distant darkness a ship was blinking signals. The Japanese were closing in on Kwangtung.

The hour for lunch was approaching when I arose the next day, relaxed by the deep sleep of mental exhaustion. My healthy appetite, contrasting with the absence of passengers who were making the seemingly inevitable adjustment to a second day at sea, calm though it was, sufficed as a subject of introductory comment to my tablemate. He had been one of the engineers in charge of the construction of the Indo-China and Yünnan railroad. He told of the thousands of Chinese brought from the high interior to labor in the tropical jungles and how the thousands died there in the fever-laden valleys. Malaria moved among the camps leaving few but the opium smokers to survive the transformation of millions of francs into a silver coil of narrow-gauge steel which fastened around the hills and glided across a hundred bridges to reach the cool plateau of Yünnan.* We drank our cognac, and I warmed to the challenge in this incident of man's conquest of his world. The journey would be recompense in itself, he said, but after a while my mind was distracted by other things and I became fatigued with the effort to follow in a foreign language his descriptions of the scenic beauty which lay ahead. Excusing myself, I went on deck to mingle with the other passengers.

A group of quiet Chinese attracted me. One, a young doctor who had come from Canton a few days before, was showing photographs of the horrors of the recent bombings, picture after picture one would hesitate to print, images of the suffering of innocent human beings which made me ache with anger. The prints passed from one Chinese to another, each viewing them with almost complete immobility of expression. A young woman whose tired face had the piquant beauty to be found among the central-east-coast provinces told of her escape from Shantung at the beginning of the war, an experience so harrowing that only after months in the hospital had she been able to continue her journey to the interior. Her ordeal had been paralleled by that of her sister who, shortly following their reunion in Shanghai, had been killed in the bombing at the Sincere store. The girl's eyes glistened slightly when she said that in Yünnan she expected to see her husband from whom she had been separated for more than a year. Yet these Chinese spoke calmly and

* It was not until ten years later that I was able to discover a satisfactory theory as to why few opium smokers died of malaria: mosquitoes avoid the drug-laden perspiration.

with seeming dispassionateness of the Japanese in a situation which could bring only hatred from a Westerner. Out of their suffering and sadness seemed to come something more like a profound pity for their enemy. When I walked away, my own anger was gone and I felt chastened. A feeling of humility had come over me as though I had experienced a mild religious ecstasy; I sorrowed for the exotic and beautiful Japan, for a certainty of a terrible and soul-rending defeat had descended upon me.

We passed through the Straits of Hainan in the late afternoon (Fig. 1, p. 7). The mainland looked like a barren sandy mass in the distance. Orange-tiled roofs, faintly contrasting with the yellow shore, showed the existence of a few villages but left the effect of a barren country. I watched dreamily until the supper gong announced the evening meal and the sudden descent of the darkness on the tropical sea.

Early the next morning, we steamed across the legendary and beautiful baie d'Along dotted with small fishing vessels skimming like porpoises over the light, foam-fringed waves. About nine we took on the pilot and proceeded slowly up a muddy stream bordered with unhealthy-looking mangrove trees toward the port of Haiphong at the confluence of the Cua-cam and Song-tam-bac rivers.

Haiphong was hot. A small group of passengers preferred to sit in the shade of a narrow niche of deck while the rest crowded down the gangplank. In the foreground of the docks stretched lines of very-narrow-gauge track with small flatcars for handling freight and baggage. Coolies piled trunks and suitcases on them, and I amused myself by trying to discover a free line to the customs house. The porters yelled at each other, but I could see from my vantage point that time would be needed to allay the confusion. We who waited were interested in the schedule of trains to Hanoi and the north. The war was taxing the capacities of the Indo-China and Yünnan railroad severely. An official of the China Travel Service graciously offered to smooth out some of the difficulties but then disappeared with some subordinates who had come to meet him. Sitting beside me was a representative of an American motion-picture company who, I discovered, was also traveling to Yünnan. We decided to venture ashore together and, after locating our baggage, found coolies to convey it across the tracks to the customs house. When we arrived with our safari, it was almost noon and the officer, perhaps in response to our unaggressive leisureliness, or more likely with a desire for his midday meal, passed our belongings with the minimum of inspection. Trusting to the oriental porter's deserved reputation for

Figure 1. Map of China (Showing Route of Journey and the Four Villages Compared)

honesty, we had the baggage loaded into rickshas and sent off to the railroad station to wait our arrival.

It was a relief to settle into rickshas ourselves and to be pulled over the wide, well-paved boulevards to the center of the city. The ricksha, or *pousse-pousse* as it was named in Indo-China, proved to be a very comfortable vehicle, for although not elaborate, the smoothness of the streets and the lack of congestion contributed to the ease of the ride. Haiphong was a city of approximately one hundred and ten thousand inhabitants of which about two per cent were Europeans. The impression on the visitor was one of spaciousness. Parkways and buildings had been developed to provide as much comfort as tropical temperatures would permit. Despite the large native population, the effect was that of a small town of rather imposing white or buff edifices laid out with the pleasant French gift for formal arrangement. Like Shanghai, Haiphong was practically a marsh when it was obtained by treaty from the Annamites in 1874 and, under Western influence, it had grown from a small fishing village into a city.

Our lunch in the café of one of the principal hotels, save for the Tonkinese waiters, was little different from that which one might have expected in a southern province of France. We managed to satisfy our appetites in time to take the one o'clock gasoline car to Hanoi. The *autorail,* as the French called it, was a small motorboat which operated on the railroad, making five trips each way daily between Haiphong and Hanoi, the capital of Tonkin. The journey consumed slightly less than two hours for the sixty-five miles. Despite the heat, I was fascinated by the tropical vegetation and by the little towns with their small, staring, brown-faced people who were dressed so gracefully. Three things would have impressed any traveler on his first visit: the crownlike hats of the women with a series of straight edges of cloth rising one above the other; their black-stained teeth; and the phonetically peculiar names of the Indo-Chinese towns, of which Ninh Binh, Cam Pha, and Ho Dong serve as examples.

Descending from the car in Hanoi, we were soon accosted by an agent of the sûreté who demanded our passports and immediately walked off with them. I began to feel as though we were under Russian surveillance, and then, that we had been tricked by an impostor. In a few minutes, however, the plainclothesman reappeared and nonchalantly returned those symbols of American freedom which in that day were the envy of world travelers.

At the exit of the station we found ourselves directly in the path of a large mob about to storm the building. Our baggage, which was quickly placed to form something of a barricade, was immediately dispersed in every direction, and our shock was hardly relieved by discovering that our belongings had been the object of attack. Our porters had become lost in the crowd of ricksha men, three or four of whom were trying to pull each bag away from another while the rest shouted advice. Intent on meeting one problem at a time, we paid our porters and then sat down to consider the situation. Our bags, of which I had a good number, were by then distributed intermittently along the broad front of vehicles. One would judge from the appearance that to conduct a *pousse-pousse* business was to set up an institution, for besides the puller of each vehicle, there seemed to be several subsidiary runners, agents, and guides. It was clear that to start off with such a caravan through the streets of Hanoi would be to take over the functions of a circus, if not to pay the cost of one. No amount of argument had any effect in ameliorating our predicament. Finally our wrangling came to a stalemate of exhaustion with everyone, including casual pedestrians, in smiles. It was a situation peculiar to the arrival of unsuspecting strangers, and the game was to find a solution with the least possible loss of face for everyone. We leisurely contemplated the problem in what shade the station portals afforded from the hot sun. We decided it was too complicated to ride in a *pousse-pousse* and telephoned to the principal hotel for a taxi and, when this luxury arrived, stepped into it as though we had never considered any other transportation. The driver had no difficulty in immediately collecting our belongings, and we drove to the hotel.

Hanoi offered commodious and comfortable accommodations for the traveler at a reasonable cost, as well as the gustatory pleasures of a French cuisine. Long-bladed ceiling fans stirred the hot air in both public and private rooms, but in the case of the latter, a small surcharge for the fans, which could be regulated at pleasure, appeared on the bill. Hanoi had the general appearance of Haiphong but was much more attractive, having a small lake surrounded by a park which extended to the intersection of the main business streets. Over the heads of the flower-sellers who gathered there, one could see a small pagoda built on a rock projecting above the water. The population of the capital of Tonkin was about one hundred and twenty thousand. Excellent stores attracted the residents, and there were a number of fine government buildings, as well as a museum and a college. In visiting the shops, an American enjoyed a sense of luxury because of the cheapness of excellent perfumes and champagnes, and because of the display of finely illustrated books.

We soon tired of moving about and wished for less-active diversion. Having forty-eight hours to wait before taking the fast weekly train to Kunming, we were at a loss to decide how we could spend our time profitably. We needed someone who was familiar with the city but were without friends to help us. Thirsty, we sat down to have a cool drink in the sidewalk café facing the lake. We had just been served when a gentleman at a nearby table, hearing a conversation in English, invited us to join him. We soon discovered that our new acquaintance, the Saigon representative of an American oil company, was also on his way to Kunming in order to survey the possibilities of business there. He was going to the Yünnan capital early the next morning on a plane of the recently established Eurasia airline. My friend saw the advantage of flying, but I was unable to go because of my heavy equipment. By arranging an exchange of Hong Kong dollars for Indo-Chinese piastres among ourselves, we were able to procure his accommodation. This financial transaction was necessitated because the German airline would not accept the fluctuating Hong Kong dollars and, by that hour, all the banks had closed.

After dinner at the hotel, our new acquaintance offered to show me the native quarter. We set out by means of the familiar *pousse-pousse,* eventually leaving the broad boulevards behind us. We seemed to be in the country except for the closely built two-story houses along the street and the increased population, for the most part resting in the evening heat. At a small restaurant we stopped and, walking through a passage, came out in a garden with winding stone paths lacing the grass. Tables and chairs were provided for guests and at one side was a polished-stone dance floor about twenty feet wide and thirty feet long. Ten or twelve Tonkinese girls who could be engaged as dancing partners sat along one edge of the floor. The evening seemed somewhat cooler under the clear sky and, as we drank, we watched the dancers turning to the music. I saw no Europeans, but many of the guests seemed of mixed parentage. The white-silk costume of the Tonkinese women had an appealing simplicity. It consisted of a full-sleeved, high-necked tunic flaring slightly from the waist to just below the knees, partly covering white-silk trousers which in turn almost hid the shoes. Payment to the hostesses appeared to be made clandestinely, and the behavior of the whole company left the impression of gentleness and quiet. I do not remember ever visiting a more relaxing and peaceful place to dance.

My friends left before dawn and I returned to sleep. My companion of the previous evening in good heart had given me his card to a young French banker whom he had recently met. I called on this resident of Hanoi in the forenoon and, after a pleasant chat, he invited me to go swimming with him that evening and later to dine at his home, hospitality which I was happy to accept.

He came for me at six-thirty, bringing a companion who was an artist, and after a drink we set out in the latter's small car. The artist's driving might be described conservatively as impetuous, and I began to recall tales of Frenchmen staying in Indo-China who had gone mad from the heat. Our manner of stopping was no less provocative than the ride, for the man on arriving at his apartment purposefully ran into a *pousse-pousse* parked at the curb because he was irritated by its being there. The native puller was first frightened and then crestfallen. Our driver stepped out of the car and proceeded to berate him vociferously. The brown man's eyes flashed once or twice, then filled with fear. A Tonkinese woman, perhaps a half caste, came from a house and entered into the argument with bitterness. As in the case of most ricksha men, the pousse-pousse was a rented vehicle. I could see helplessness in his face and a sense of the tragedy of being born a native as he looked at the crushed wheel. A wordless anger rose inside me and an understanding of something more about the country than printed books had explained. In the twilight sky, I could see the word revolution burning itself into those brown skins, though Devil's Island was the destiny for those who dared speak it.

The *Cercle Sportif de Hanoi* on a warm evening was an idyllic place. A large rectangular building bordered a swimming pool with ladies in brightly colored summer dress and gentlemen in white sitting in friendly parties at tables on the second-story verandah overlooking the water in which the bathers dove and splashed, sending up resplendent spray to catch the gleam of the incandescent lights. We joined a family party for a cocktail and then indulged in a cool but exhausting swim. On the far side of the pool, tables for the bathers extended back under a protected arcade. From them one saw the silhouettes of women on the balcony passing in front of the deep-blue lights of the bar beyond. I thought of the dancing girls I had watched the night before dressed in their exotic white-silk costumes. The image became superimposed against the setting of clean, traditionless, modern architecture, creating an entrancing fantasy of what life might become in Indo-China.

We had to go on to our dinner party and my vision was lost as we returned to the dark mass of people crouching in the shadows of the world outside. Neither excellent food nor the champagne and laughter of charming people at the *Bagatelle* could completely dispel my memory of the unhappy *pousse-pousse* puller.

The next day was divorced from the interlude of pleasant French society by concern for problems which had little in common with the life of the Tonkinese capital. The weekly express for Yünnan was scheduled to leave at eight-thirty that evening. Having renewed an acquaintance with a Chinese businessman with whom I had conversed on the boat coming from Hong Kong, we attended to the necessary arrangements together. He had changed from a European suit to a long white-silk gown so ideally suited to the country that I wished that I might have done likewise without attracting attention. His piquant and realistic comments on the life about us somehow suffused me with a sense of complete security. He evinced a feeling of being close to home in a way which must always be alien to a European in the Far East. Also, his sense of humor was endearing. We individually had difficulty in having our accounts made up properly—a frequent problem with some hotels—and proceeded to the *gare* by *pousse-pousse*. There we were called upon for our passports by the sûreté.

The platform was crowded with people making their farewells. The train was full. Our two-place compartment in the old *wagon-lit* was comfortable enough to satisfy the seasoned traveler insensitive to sticky grime. The engine puffed eastward over the Red River which flowed by Hanoi and soon stopped at the first of the series of small stations between which we jerked hour after hour. In the dim light, one could discern thatched houses and people moving to and fro. Vendors of various kinds solicited the passengers at each stop. Still weary from the night before, I retired in the scantiest costume possible, undisturbed by the proximity of people familiar with the intimacies of a hot country. Quickly there dropped from my mind even the penetrating tones of the train's whistle as we rattled on toward the Chinese border which we were scheduled to reach early in the morning.

When I awakened it was still dark. The noises of the train had ceased and we were obviously not moving. Other passengers, apparently disturbed by the unusual quiet, commenced shuffling about, and soon the provocative chatter put a final end to sleep. Throwing a gown over my shorts, I walked out into the passage. A steady rain was falling and the little I could see of the country showed it to be covered with a thick verdure of tropical plants. I watched the rain dripping from the palms and then my eyes fell to the ground beneath the windows. A dog stretched his neck in order to look up at me. My first impression was that he was in a dangerous position straddling the rail, but as I looked lengthwise of the train, I saw another dog sheltering himself in the same fashion. I said nothing, not wishing to disturb the customs of dogs. My fellow passengers did not know the cause of our delay, but finally a passing trainman conveyed the information that the track had been undermined by water and that we were a long way from Lao K'ai, the border station.

Hour after hour passed while the rain made music by pattering on the roof, swishing from leaf to leaf in the palms, tinkling on pools of water, and gulping through the gutters. But time weakened my avidness in separating the sounds and the dread monotony of a single chord of unceasing, changeless tropical rain descended. We arrived at Lao K'ai at noon and, after a brief respite for lunch at a nearby hotel, took our places in a large new *autorail* car, a gleaming, streamlined, French fabrication, and a pulsing symbol of a modern technical world in the hinterland of China. This sleek white car, popularly called the *Micheline* after its builders, was divided into four sections. The glassed-in, airplane-like front was reserved for a pair of Chinese pilots who sat with each hand on a large vertical lever which controlled the brakes. My first impression of surplus mechanism was soon to be changed to the wish that each passenger also had brake levers. Behind the operators was the first-class compartment with its comfortably cushioned blue-leather seats and its windows protected from the sun. A swinging door connected a smaller, third-class section with wooden seats. Behind all was a narrow baggage compartment. The car set off with a shriek of its whistle and coasted over a bridge into Yünnan to stop at the customs station for a perfunctory and courteous inspection of our baggage.

The first few hours of the journey to Kunming consisted of climbing from the low tropical country to the plateau of Yünnan several thousand feet above sea level. The course of the narrow-gauge track as it wound higher and higher created a scenic railway which can seldom have been surpassed in the history of engineering. The rails shone in the sun like some mythical silver snake coiling around the hills and trying desperately to hang on in the attempt to reach the world above. The rivers with their luxurious vegetation dropped away gradually, the trees thinned out, and as each tunnel was left behind, a new and more startling vista fascinated the eyes. Ribbons of water rushed down the mountainsides until they disappeared, seemingly transpired into mist by the endlessness of their fall. From the gorges, one came upon wider valleys of terraced rice fields creating their own peculiar designs in colorings of green and brown, glazed with a sheen of sparkling water.

The pilots performed their work unperturbedly, one spending the greater part of his time sounding the whistle and turning the lights on and off as we passed through a hundred tunnels. Progress would have been simpler if the people of the country had not adopted the railroad as a highway so that the big white car sneaked up on them unawares, forcing the drivers to pull back on all their brake levers with sudden animation. Perhaps, however, the constant practice had its reward, for shooting out from a tunnel through a projecting cliff in the darkness, we were faced with a tremendous boulder, a menace that had fallen from the rain-washed slopes above. The pilots, spontaneously rising from their seats, swung their weight on the brakes and averted a crash. The relief expressed on their faces precipitated a general good humor, and the boulder was pried to the side of the roadbed.

Once the plateau was reached, the journey became faster (Fig. 2, p. 15). Periodically we stopped at a small village with houses of sundried brick so typical of China. Some of the bridges were guarded against sabotage by sentries, but the threat of bombing seemed secondary to the danger of the line's being tied up by washouts. From time to time we passed companies of soldiers better equipped than any previously observed in the East. Their new machine guns, divided among the men, appeared mobile and effective armament; their blue steel helmets and blue shorts striped with red gave smartness to their

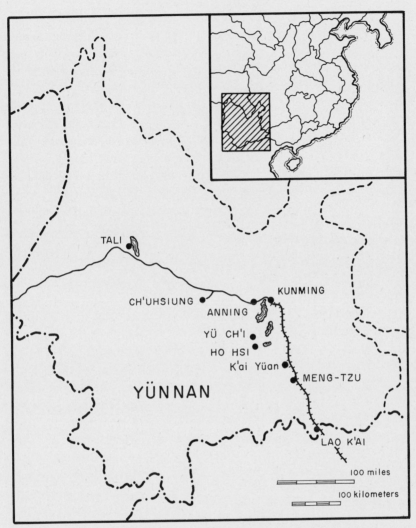

Figure 2. Map of Yünnan

dress. But of their training and leadership there was no way to judge.

We arrived at K'ai Yûan, some thirty miles beyond Meng-tzu, about six-thirty in the evening. The French manager of the hotel, or bungalow as it was called, was suffering from a frenzy apparently induced by having to accommodate passengers for the night who had been scheduled to stop only for luncheon. It was evident that there was a shortage of rooms. A few of the travelers were being directed to temporary quarters at some distance in a hospital, while others were left to shift for themselves in the Chinese city. Things having quieted down, I engaged the manager with my predicament and he graciously furnished a very excellent and convenient room. At dinner I learned that the official of the China Travel Service, aware of the situation, had wired ahead for accommodations but had been able to obtain none on his arrival. I could appreciate his irritation. The French concession was merely an enlarged section of the right of way enclosed by a wall. After eating, I walked through the narrow main street of the adjoining town which, in the darkness, seemed overrun with people. Actually Yünnan, covering some three hundred and twenty thousand square kilometers, the third largest of the eighteen provinces, had but twelve million inhabitants, thus ranking last save Kansu in density of population. Of these people, more than two-thirds were non-Chinese Tai or Shan, and an additional half million were of Tibeto-Burmese stock. More than a third of the Yünnanese professed the Mohammedan religion.

The *Micheline* departed early in the morning through a pouring rain, and I was glad that my somewhat excessive baggage had been near at hand. About sixty kilometers from Kunming, a French driver took the place of the Chinese and we proceeded at a faster speed. His attention to his business was a notable contrast to the easy fearlessness of the Chinese. There were more hills and gorges but none with the awe-inspiring quality of those near the Indo-China border. At last we spied the high radio towers of the capital and sped past the Kunming airport, then one of the important Chinese aviation schools. As we pulled into the station I felt that whatever else was to come, I had experienced an unforgettable railroad journey.

2

KUNMING THE CAPITAL

MY NEWLY found friends who had flown on ahead from Hanoi greeted me at the station in high spirits and immediately informed me of the great difficulty of finding a place to sleep in the city. The capital, normally containing about one hundred and fifty thousand people was overflowing from an endless stream of émigrés from the war area. The small French hotel had long been filled to capacity, and extra space in the hospitals had been taken up by the more important visitors, while the remainder squeezed in everywhere, bulging out the warehouses or any shelter which could be temporarily adapted as a habitation. Fortunately my companions had obtained excellent quarters on one of the landings in the tower of the modern building of the Green Youth Association, or Chinese YMCA. Since my equipment contained the necessary modicum of furnishings, there would be no problem but a little further crowding.

My first perception of Kunming as a whole was the smell. It was sometimes uncouthly said by sailors that one could detect the odor of the East a hundred miles offshore, and it could not be denied that the lack of sanitation facilities often provided oriental cities with an aroma of their own, but from Kunming on that warm midday there spread an indescribable stench! The odor entered inside one until smell and taste could scarcely be distinguished. It was a liquid engulfing each newcomer, a baptism in old China befouled by war. But Kunming was alive, and exciting, and the smell was already forgotten as I looked into the animated faces of the ricksha coolies who conveyed us from the railroad concession at the edge of the city.

Once outside we turned left on a narrow, roughly cobbled street crowded with oxcarts and people. Many men carried burdens on shoulder poles, many women were pregnant. There were no imposing buildings and scarcely any that did not conform to the ancient two-story pattern. The outside world seemed to have made little effect, and I could easily imagine what wholesale death would be inflicted by a well-placed bomb.

After a short ride we arrived at the Green Youth Association and climbed to the fourth floor in the tower. A cot had been set up, and a mattress spread on eight small benches had provided another bed. My belongings were quickly disposed of and we returned to the railroad concession to have lunch at the French hotel. Despite excellent food and pleasant surroundings, I did not feel comfortable. My work, with its pleasures and its griefs, for better or for worse was with the Chinese, and moving back and forth from one cultural milieu to another merely added to the strain. I never returned to the hotel.

On our return, we walked through the outlying section of the city which impressed one with squalor and poverty. At one place where water had been diverted from a small canal, women were pounding clothes on the stones. We bought an old coin from a boy and examined a pagoda which was one of the few artistic landmarks of the city. Then we sauntered home as my companions had business engagements which had to be fulfilled in the few days of their visit. For myself, I knew no one. I could not understand the language and I had discovered that interpreters were almost nonexistent. My task was to locate a suitable Chinese village and to make a study of it within the weeks available. Obviously, other difficulties relegated themselves to petty annoyances.

My companions having left on their separate missions, I had about settled into a serious survey of my prospects when one returned to say that he had obtained from his host an invitation for me to a banquet given by the directors of one of the two cinemas in Kunming. Not only was I pleased by the anticipation of so gala a first evening in the city, but I was grateful for the sense of well-being engendered by the gesture of my friend in arranging to include me.

With our host's son at the wheel, we set out in a Ford car, one of the relatively few private automobiles in the city. As is usual when one has been unaccustomed to driving on narrow streets, it seemed that we were traveling at a ferocious speed, leaving the dead and injured piled up in the darkness behind us. Actually, we wriggled through the excited crowd for a few blocks and drew up before the Hsin Yah Restaurant. We entered a narrow room which save for its exotic appearance looked like a dive on the American water front. We climbed a narrow, rickety staircase over the railing of which I could see flashes of fire from the open hearths of the kitchen in the rear. In a private room had gathered a number of Chinese gentlemen to whom we were introduced.

The civility and character of these people immediately diminished all sense of deficiency in the physical surroundings, and I soon realized that good fortune had brought me into contact with business and cultural representatives of the old city, a conservative group who were reserved in their reception of sophisticated newcomers from the coastal centers. I was delighted, and my appetite increased apace as we sat down at a large oval table and waiters brought dish after dish of the most delectable food. In usual Chinese style, we helped ourselves with chopsticks, eating from the common bowls. I was charmed by one old man who, holding up the end of the right sleeve of his silken gown with his left hand, would reach for a morsel of food, his eyes making a clear inquiry of permission to all with scarcely a move of his head, before deftly lifting a choice bit with the extending chopsticks. The rhythm of his movement, his gentle grace, transposed the commonplace ritual of everyday life into the art of the ballet dancer. The food was not only excellent to the taste but beautiful to the eyes, and I was delighted with the evenly cut, creamy-colored bamboo shoots relished for their texture.

In our honor, the host served cognac. He would raise his cup periodically and say *kan-pei* and we would drain our portions only to have the containers immediately refilled. The dinner lasted for several hours, waiters intermittently bringing new dishes, often made with the mushrooms or ham for which Yünnan was famous. After the meal, we retired to the adjoining front room where we were served with steaming perfumed towels to remove any stickiness from our hands. This ceremony over, fruit and cigarettes were pressed upon us.

A little after nine we set out for the Cosmopolitan cinema in our host's car. The journey was a short one and we descended at the side door which led to the directors' office. My first impression was of being in a dark basement room of an old house, but the feeling was soon displaced by friendliness when tea was served. About ten, we all went into the theater to see the picture, a box with comfortable overstuffed arm chairs of the European type being reserved for us. The building itself was originally a temple famous for its great red columns of a celebrated hard wood notably used for expensive coffins.

We sat in a reserved section of the left wing of a balcony, the central part of which extended some distance to the rear. All quarters of the house were crowded with Chinese and, as the picture began, someone started shouting at the other side of the balcony creating a din which made the English sound track of the film, already somewhat muted, completely inaudible. I expected the man who was yelling to have vented his feeling after a while, but when he continued with no sign of stopping, I discovered that he was the *speaker,* and that he was paid to convey the theme of the film to the audience who could not understand English nor, for the most part, read the Chinese characters customarily added to a foreign production. My companion informed me that Kunming was one of the few cities in China where the custom of having a *speaker* still existed. I regretted not being able to understand for, from what I could comprehend of the picture, it could not have helped from being considerably improved by an oriental commentary.

After the performance was over, our host put us in rickshas with considerable ceremony, having paid the pullers in advance and given them the directions to our abode. We set off speedily down dark cobblestone streets and I was soon separated from my companion. I shall probably never forget that ride as I was completely lost, for in the few hours I had been in the city, I had not even learned my own address. We seemed to bump along interminably through empty byways with only occasional lights showing through the colored paper windows of some balcony. All I could think of was a story told me many times as a boy by my grandmother who had suffered a similar experience. When I thought back at my childish contempt for her fears, I laughed and laughed, for I realized that the charming and in many ways unsophisticated lady must have been frightened nearly to death. In any event I owed her an apology and realized that I was only laughing from nervousness. When the coolie set me down at my destination, he wiped his face with a dirty towel and grinned.

My companion of the previous night left on the plane for Chengtu at five in the morning, having arranged with his ricksha coolie to return for him in time to take him to the airport. It seemed a casual way to make certain of keeping an important appointment but, as I learned in the course of time, an adequate one. My own problem commenced to loom ahead of me. I had to find some way to integrate into Chinese life and I had no time to waste. I needed an interpreter, and I had already discovered that such a person was extremely hard to find, since English-speaking natives were rare in Yünnan, and most of the émigrés could not understand the local dialect themselves. In two days my remaining acquaintance, the only person I knew in Kunming, was flying back to Indo-China and there would not even be companionship left.

On the floor below our landing in the tower I found a lavatory with four or five washbasins and three showers. In one corner was a urinal which intermittently failed to drain. At the other end of the room were two charcoal braziers on which were heating large pitcher-like kettles of water. At first I was conscious of the slop beneath my feet, but I discovered that by using a pair of Cantonese wood shoes I could avail myself of a reasonably high standard of living, providing the Japanese did not bomb my new home out of existence.

The first floor of the Green Youth Association consisted of offices, several game rooms, shower baths for the non-resident members, a barber shop, an adjoining restaurant, and a small tearoom in the court. I had my breakfast, consisting of hot cocoa and chocolate cake, in the latter place. Both were in evidence, so I had ordered them and found the combination very satisfying. The cost was about five American cents.

After my meal I set out to orient myself as much as possible in my new environment. I went to the Banque d'Indochine which had modern, tube-steel furniture, and there I opened an account, converting a small amount of money into Chinese currency. The exchange at the time was about eighteen American cents for the National, or Shanghai, dollar. This rate was extremely favorable and made life for the foreigner in Yünnan incredibly cheap if he lived in Chinese style. This was true because Yünnan was relatively inexpensive normally and, except for housing costs, there had not been much advance in prices as a result of the war. To complicate matters, however, there were two other types of currency in use. The first of these was the old Yünnan money and the second the New Yünnan, or Fu Tien, money which took its name from a bank. One dollar of the Chinese National currency was worth nominally ten old Yünnan dollars or two New Yünnan dollars. Actually, the relative values fluctuated slightly. The National money had the greatest prestige apparently, but old Yünnan paper bills were the recognized medium of exchange, at least among the common people of the province. For my purposes, National money was the easiest to handle, and I carried a pack of ten- and twenty-cent bills in one pocket and a pack of one-dollar bills in another. Occasionally a fifty-cent note appeared, and less often a twenty-five-cent one. Copper half-cent pieces of National currency came as change, and at night I piled them up on the window sill to keep them from making holes in my pockets. To give some idea of the value these coppers had, one may compute that ten were worth less than an American penny, and for twice that many one could hire a ricksha to go from one end of the city to the other. One hundred would purchase a small bottle of Szechuan rose wine; fourteen hundred, a fifth of Martell cognac. Foreign business had also introduced the French Indo-Chinese *piastre* into the upper stratum of financial life of Kunming, while if one went into the country, one encountered several more types of Chinese money varying downward in value to the brass *cash* of which approximately a thousand equaled a Fu Tien dollar.

With the money situation in hand, I set out on foot to familiarize myself with the city. I wanted to buy a map but soon discovered that their sale was prohibited because of the war. Having good visual memory, I made up for this deficiency by walking, first in one direction and then another, to the great brick wall which almost completely surrounded the city, returning to my starting point by ricksha. The ancient walled city was nearly square except for the southwest corner which was cut off diagonally, the distance east and west being perhaps slightly under two miles, the distance north to south, a little more. The eastern end of the south wall had been torn down and the city extended an additional mile in the south and east. Here were located most of the foreign agencies, the French railway concession, and the Green Youth Association.

Walking around Kunming excited the senses of a stranger jostling along in the crowd. Only a few streets had sidewalks of adequate capacity for the moving populace and some had none at all. The streets swarmed with people and the fastest movement was in the center of the road from which constantly came sharp cries of every conceivable pitch as warnings from conveyors of goods or from trotting ricksha pullers. Along the way were open shops selling food, clothing, hardware, and all varieties of local merchandise. The most modern establishments faced one of the chief thoroughfares of the city which extended a half mile or so north from the south gate, an elaborate brick structure mounting with a series of upward flaring roof corners in classic Chinese style to overlook all other buildings. This thoroughfare was popularily known as Silk Street. Included on it were two department stores and a drugstore which were apparently the best in the city and had superficial resemblance to those that might have been found in a country town in America during the early part of the twentieth century. Such cosmopolitan conceptions as the bar, or the soda fountain, were still unborn in the second largest province of China.

Visiting the shops was easy and pleasant. Sales people of both sexes received customers with courtesy and reserve, and an average American with the good sense to act toward other human beings as he would have been forced to do at home soon found himself the object of traditional good will. I developed a smiling acquaintance with Kunming tradespeople and manufacturers, many of whom had their workrooms projecting from their open shops. On the side streets I stopped to watch them making cheap furniture, putting items down in my memory for future needs. Near the south gate one workshop was overflowing onto the sidewalk so as to almost block the street. At first I thought they were constructing large skyrockets from old gasoline cans; then a cold chill went down my back. These rusty containers with tail fins would bring death quicker than ptomaine; they were homemade aerial bombs. A worker with tin shears sitting on the curbstone leaned back his close-shaven head and smiled with a glint in his eye. Then he looked skyward. The skin on my face tightened, and I walked on home.

At the Green Youth Association I met a worker named Lee who had recently returned from the front and who spoke English. I told him I wanted to live in a Chinese village which had not been influenced by Europeans, that I wanted to describe life there so that Americans would better understand it. He was a little incredulous that I would put up with the living conditions which such villages afforded, but he finally realized that I was absolutely serious and not to be diverted from my purpose. He agreed to see if he could hire a car with which to make a reconnaissance of the countryside, but he was extremely discouraging about the prospects of obtaining an interpreter. We also sent off messages to some Chinese scientists whose names I had been given to see whether they could help.

Lee and I had supper in the adjoining restaurant, a room about thirty feet square with tables seating four people and one or two larger ones. The room was conspicuously clean and completely without accessory decoration. Some Chinese said that it was so clean that they did not like to eat there, although I suspect it was the unbroken plainness which was the disturbing factor. Also, no alcoholic drinks were served. A long menu written out in Chinese was brought by the waiter, as well as brush, ink, and paper with which to write the order. The food was of such quality as to rank the restaurant as one of the better places to eat in the capital. Most of the patrons belonged to the younger, educated group of men. Sometimes families appeared with their children. There was a definite campaign against spitting on the floor and the management had supplied brass spittoons. The only time I can remember seeing one used, however, was when a young woman left her meal momentarily to permit her baby to relieve itself in one. The baby sat there like a cherub, a perfect fit.

The next day I proceeded with the plan of finding a village in which to live. Lee had managed to hire a car for the afternoon to take us around the end of the lake and to the temples of the Western Hill (Fig. 3, p. 25). We drove through the north gate of Kunming and turned onto the road which led to Tali and ultimately Burma. A short distance outside the city we stopped for a brief interrogation at the military control, and then we sped on to the west over a gravel-surfaced road. Warm, clean air blew down from the green hills and the whole country seemed fresh and colorful. Suddenly I felt a deep antipathy toward returning to the narrow dark streets of Kunming. Soon we began to pass terraced rice fields in the flood basin of a very large lake. Curving against the horizon were the ever bending backs of the weed pullers, while water buffalo stood nearby as though to give the signature of genuineness to the picture. We passed by one village after another, all characterized by the clay color of the sun-dried bricks of their interlocked houses and connecting walls. Here was no overcrowding of people, and the distant hills looked wild. The individuals we passed on the road appeared to wear typical Chinese dress except for an occasional woman with jacket and trousers varying from twilight pink to the brightest scarlet, but always creat-

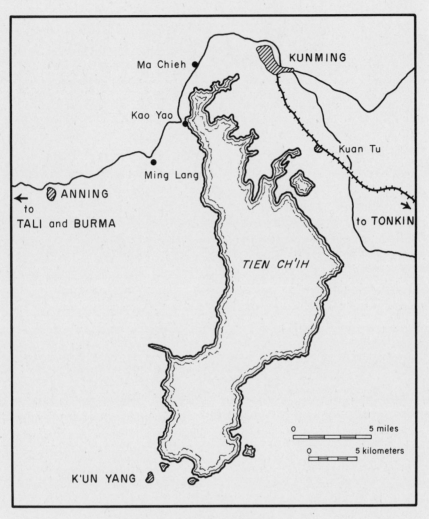

Figure 3. Map of the Kunming Area

ing a piquant contrast to the commonplace blue. As we began to climb into the hills, we turned off the main road and followed a new one which led to the famous temples. The first at which we stopped was a Buddhist monastery. The sculptures were impressive and especially the grandiose figures of the Four Guardians, but the grass in the courtyard was sorely in need of attention, a fact which emphasized the languid dispassionateness of the priests. We drove part way to a second monastery and then continued up the mountain on foot as the road had not been finished. There the buildings were more uniform and the multiple perquisites of religious ceremonialism crowded ornament upon ornament. The priests were friendly and charitable toward intrusion. We continued our walk toward the promontory of the hill, ascending a steep trail until we came to the most remarkable of the structures devoted to the gods, a Taoist temple cut into the rock. Here was an inspiring sight. The great lake lay hundreds of feet beneath, an aquamarine set into the plateau of Yünnan. The sun poured golden bubbles onto the water, creating an illusory surface like a glass of freshly poured champagne. Toy brown boats with square mat sails were plying between the west shore and the canals leading to the city on the other side. Faintly, in the distance, the capital was discernible on a hill shining in a mist reflected from the lake. We took tea on a balcony from which we watched the view, and then, having rested, descended to the car. Along the shore I observed several villages and one in particular which extended out on a peninsula not unlike the tip of an arrow (Pl. 1, p. 27). Seen from our vantage point, the community looked quietly secure, and I asked whether it was Chinese or Lolo. On learning the occupants were the former, I suddenly desired to live there. Since it was a Chinese village of the approximate size I was seeking, it seemed unreasonable to waste more days searching the countryside. With a scarcity of time, a convenient place beckoned which, from the distance, appeared esthetically pleasing, if nothing else. Lee suggested renting a small villa nearby on the shore of the lake, a proposal from which it was evident that he had yet to comprehend the plan in my mind. We went to see the villa which had been built as a summer residence by a doctor in Kunming. It was a delightful little place, but so much better suited for a rendezvous with a mistress that I laughed. I tried to explain to Lee that I did not want to study a village and live in luxury apart from the people. It was impractical to walk back and forth. I would always be a visitor and never really participate in the group. I wanted to live with the Chinese, not overlook them as did foreign dignitaries. I wanted to share in their daily work, drink with them in the tea shops, pass among them as one come humbly, not to preach, but to learn. I could see that Lee was not convinced, and when we walked on to the village and down its single street to the little jetty at the end, I realized that he had grounds for wonder. This was no idyllic spot

1. VIEW OF KAO YAO VILLAGE

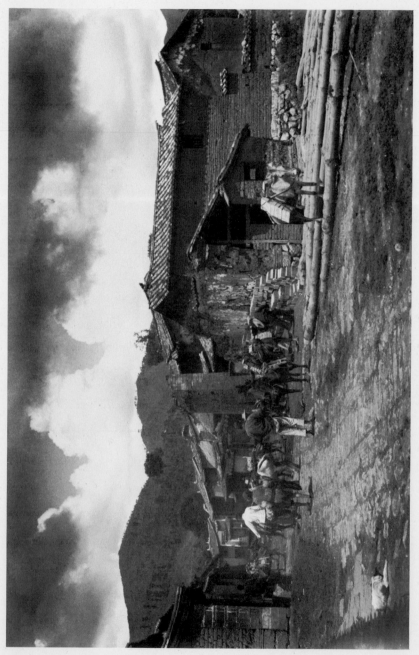

2. PORTERS AT END OF VILLAGE STREET

in the hills but a small port where carriers from the west brought their goods to be ferried to the city, where they stopped and ate and drank, and then took new loads to the hills.   Dozens of strange craft were tied to the stone embankment, and dogs and pigs milled around in the mud.   About a third of the population lived on tiny boats.   I could see the signs of disease, the open toilet in the street above the principal well.   As we walked back through the crowd, I noticed that many of the people had huge goitres.   When we returned to the road, the hills were above us; beneath us, my chosen abode projected into the lake which had turned blue in the late afternoon.   One either despised such a place or felt as I did—I wanted to live there.

We returned to Kunming and after supper, for lack of something better to do, went to call on the owner of the villa.   He received us courteously and said his house was engaged for the summer but suggested that a former president of the University of Yünnan had a residence in the village itself which might be rented.

The next morning I felt lonely and went out into the street and sat down on a box at the corner of the marketplace.   A motley throng of people were gathered at the temporary stalls examining the collection of articles for sale which included vegetables, secondhand clothing, dishes, and junk of all kinds.   Many of the vendors laid their wares out in squares and rectangles on the ground.   The contents of some looked as though they had been collected by boys from the refuse of Chicago's alleys—dilapidated metal flashlight casings, pieces of wire, broken insulators, rusty screws and nails, with a mixture of odd bits of foreign manufactures.   There were few things to tempt the traveler in quest of the exotic—but there were also few, if any, travelers.   At several places in the crowd, professional gamblers had put down squares of cloth with the zodiac-like markings of a game. The players added their coppers to the points at the edges and won or lost on the toss of a bundle of straws.

Most of the people were obviously poor, both sexes being dressed in jackets and trousers of differing shades of blue, the color depending on how often they had been washed.   The men wore black skullcaps with a button of either black or red in the center, while women, as well as girls and boys, were usually bareheaded.   The great majority of people wore the black cloth slipper typical of China.   From this standard dress, I began to pick out the variations, chief of which was a yellow straw hat about two feet in diameter.   Most of them had the shape of an inverted shallow bowl with a depression for the head, but others were broad-based cones. Both men and women wore them, but since the day was pleasant, many hats had slipped off to be held against the shoulders by cords which passed around the necks of the owners. Some women had black cloth hats tight fitting like an aviator's helmet, but not extending under the chin. Also, I observed a large number of the people wearing straw sandals.

Tired of sitting on my box, I moved off up the street but still watching for peculiarities in the dress of the people. Occasionally I encountered some Indo-Chinese women in their long flaring shirts and tight trousers, but the cloth was black instead of the cool white seen in tropical Tonkin. Also, near the city gate, I saw pink-trousered country girls and tribespeople in costumes suggestive of Tibet. Some men distinguished themselves by adopting felt hats with high brims pulled out on one side like those of the medieval Italians. Rumor has it that the style was set by Marco Polo, but more likely it had descended from the highlands of the Himalayas. Everyone was pressing about their business, but when I stopped to sit down, children gathered and stared, and then a second row of adult stragglers grouped around us. I had never felt myself such a curiosity before.

Cutting across the poorer section of the city on my way to Silk Street, I saw a small child whose blind eyes were open sores placed outside a wall to beg and, even more unusual, a woman so ragged that her breasts protruded from her garments. Although one frequently confronted mothers suckling their children, the Chinese women seldom appeared unclothed between their neck and their knees. Babies were carried astraddle of the back with a strap under the legs, and it was a genre sight to behold a mother unconsciously cupping her hands under the child's exposed buttocks as a safeguard against a wetting.

On reaching Silk Street, I went to the principal tea shop which had balcony tables from which one could overlook the thoroughfare. From there it was easy to observe the passers-by while imbibing hot tea and practicing the gentle art of cracking melon seeds between the teeth. Here the newcomer noticed gentlemen of the upper class in long gowns, generally blue or black but sometimes gray, and almost always wearing European-style felt hats which were the one really intrusive article of European clothing. Quite characteristic of the street, I saw a dignified man stroll by in a blue gown and a brown fedora holding a typical black English umbrella over his head as a protection from the sun while cooling himself gently with his unfolded fan. The day was not hot and the fan seemed to function as a symbol of gentility like an Englishman's cane.

The better-dressed women resorted to silk jackets and long, full trousers of quiet colors. Footwear with red or other bright embroidery occasionally flashed from beneath their garments, or more rarely, imported high-heeled shoes. A married woman did her black hair into a bun at the back of the head with a bar pin of green jade, whereas girls let their hair hang in braids, the only suggestion of the nonexistent queues traditional among Chinese men. A totally European costume on an adult was a rarity and, if one accepted the high standards of Shantung and Anhwei, so was a beautiful woman. A stranger soon learned that a pretty girl on Silk Street was almost surely an émigré from the east. On my way home I stopped to buy a snuff bottle from a street peddlar, and I watched an old woman picking lice out of a girl's hair.

In the afternoon I went with Lee to call on the first president of the university who had been succeeded some years past. He lived in a small house in the northern section of the city. It was my first opportunity to visit the interior of a Yünnanese home, and I wondered what my impression would be. We entered the gate, a porter having come to open it for us. A square two-story house of the inevitable clay color appeared in the center of a small courtyard created by the surrounding walls. A few plants grew up from large pottery jars, but any sensation of lush green was lacking. Perhaps it was the absence of formal lawns which made any other setting for a house look unfinished to an American. But there was also the echo of the dry dustiness of the high Yünnan plateau which threatened mud and yellow puddles under the feet. Highland China had strength and rugged, precipitous beauty, but it could not be considered pretty.

We were invited into the reception room and sat down after the usual exchange of courtesies. At first the room seemed cold and stiff, but as the personality of our host emerged through his conversation, one felt the need of substituting the words simplicity and clarity to describe the room. I began to be conscious of a series of scrolls on the walls, and of the musical, laughing voices of children in other parts of the building. Unfortunately we were not able to obtain the house in the village which was said to be occupied for the summer. It was raining when we left, and the family had gathered on the porch. In our short visit, I had gained a sense of friendliness and was sorry to leave.

We went on up the hill to the university itself which was an institution founded by the provincial government in 1917 with its large main building finished in 1920. The campus was spacious and attractive with room beyond the city wall for the expansion which seemed inevitable as the result of the influx of people emigrating from the disrupted culture centers of the east. The school had practically closed down for the summer, but it was said that there were about four hundred students there during the academic year. We found a place to climb the old city wall which at that point was about twenty feet high and faced with heavy bricks, some baked and some sun dried. The section between the facings had originally been filled with rubble and was wide enough for a cart. Open country spread northward up into the hills. In the foreground men were digging long trenches for the construction of bomb-proof shelters.

After returning home, I went to the post office to inquire for mail and was rewarded for the first time. A letter had been flown from New York to San Francisco, and then by Pan American clipper to Hong Kong. Finally a plane had carried it to Hankow and another to Chengtu and down to Kunming. It bore seventy American cents in postage and more stamps had been added in Hong Kong, but it had come through in seventeen days despite the war which was the record for dispatch during my stay in the province. A second letter from the same source with five cents postage had required a little over five weeks. The post office, like a hundred others over the world, had the cold official atmosphere of a completely unfinished room with a series of grilled windows. Generally there were queues of people waiting from ten minutes to half an hour. Most of the customers were servants or minor business officials, but I enjoyed going there as the crowd was friendly. Once I met the son of a missionary just arrived from a station near the Tibetan border. Also, behind one window was a Chinese girl who knew some English. We never spoke except about stamps, but despite the iron bars in front and the line of waiting people behind, it was a warming contact which made me realize how much I was alone.

I had a rather unsuccessful dinner and wandered through the streets until I was weary. Once I stopped to buy a half-catty of peanut candy at a shop. The streets were still crowded although it was dark. The man selling the candy weighed it on a little hand scale which he held up before him and then asked an additional two coppers for the sample I had taken. On the way home I saw a man who obviously had drunk too much wine. I went to bed, but mosquitoes kept me awake. It began to rain, and I heard a child shrieking in the street. I looked out the window and saw that a crowd had gathered. It was impossible to judge what had happened so I went back to my cot while sudden bursts of thunder eliminated all other sounds. Presently the strange Chinese who lived in the top room of the tower above me came stumbling through my landing in the darkness. I slept momentarily, dreaming of a bombing raid, only to be awakened by terrific peals of thunder and flashes of lightning. I lay there trying somewhat desperately to coordinate my plans for action in the next few days. It was the darkest night of my journey, but I tried to relax, smiling over the richness of my experience. Presently the thunder diminished as rapidly as it had come, and in the onrush of returning commonplace sounds I heard the Chinese émigrés who were occupying the space below me talking with great spirit. How strange the tones of their language seemed to my ears. Suddenly I heard something which startled me so that I jumped out of bed and stood trembling with excitement. But I could again only hear the sing-song of Chinese voices. I walked over to the stair well from which I could see the light below. Then I heard it again. Someone said, "God damn, you're crazy," almost without an accent. I put my head over the railing and yelled. A large, moon-faced Chinese appeared beneath me and shouted, "Hello up there," drawing out the vowels like a trombone. Then he added, "Come on down here."

I descended the stairs and a huge, pleasant-faced fellow in pyjamas extended his hand. "I am Ssu—University of Michigan. That's Mr. Wang—Cornell," and then they all laughed. Soon I had met the six men sleeping in the room and, as each was introduced with the name of his university, the fat man laughed louder, and we all laughed in turn. All the men had attended American schools except one who had studied in France. Chance seemed to have brought them together in Kunming from various Japanese-dominated cities on the coast. In a few minutes I had taken some measure of these men and the spirit of their intentions filled me with enthusiasm. They were disgusted with Kunming as they found it and were intent on building it anew, each within the field of his interest. A new suburb was going to rise from the marsh outside the west wall with modern streets and sanitation facilities. Their excitement passed from one to another and on to me like electricity. Here was something, a new China rising from the ashes of the old; not simply a rebuilding, but a rebirth. I felt with absolute certainty that nothing could suppress their accomplishments, and I went back to my room elated and slept with perfect confidence.

3

PLEASURE IN THE CITY

I MET my new friends in the morning eating cake in the breakfast room and they asked me to join their clublike table, an invitation which I promised to accept at the first opportunity. A boy from Changsha had come to see me, having been sent by one of the secretaries of the institution, but although I found him unsatisfactory as an interpreter, there was no discouragement left in me. I went to the barber shop in the building which was surprisingly modern. Despite my protests, the operator insisted on cutting off more of my hair than I wished, he being accustomed to close clipping in the usual Chinese style. Then he finished with a quick shampoo poorly rinsed with a hand sprinkler, and added a few drops of scent and some pink hair grease before I could stop him. This experience cost me approximately seven American cents. I had discovered the United States consulate in Kunming where a big red chop had been put in my passport with my Chinese name for purposes of identification. My visit there I had presumed would be my last. Consequently the invitation to lunch which followed came as a surprise, and I was momentarily annoyed at the thought of having to unpack my luggage to find a suitable costume. The passing of days had brought me to the point of being unconscious of the standards of living which I had adopted, and the thought of laying out good clothes in the environment of my sleeping quarters made me dissatisfied. I read the invitation again. The style and freshness of the wording gave clear indications of an interesting person. I wiped off a bench with a dirty sock that someone had left on the floor and proceeded to spread out my meager choice of clean linen.

The consulate was in the north section of the city near the university, at least twenty minutes ride by ricksha. I tried to wrap the cuffs of my trousers tightly around my ankles to keep the fleas on the floor boards of the vehicle where one inevitably found them. By the time I had arrived at my destination, I had given up the attempt and

felt more comfortable. I rang the bell at the big gate and was bowed
into an elaborate compound with a large fountain and potted plants
bearing beautiful red flowers. On the street side of the garden was
a one-story building which stretched along the wall and provided
attractive rooms for the consular offices, while on the other side, set
off by a slight rise in the paved court, stood a large, square, two-
story house with a small reception porch. There was a second-floor
screened veranda at the rear of the house which extended in two balconies over the yard to join symmetrically placed rectangular wings
of two-story height flanking the side walls of the compound. In the
rear, a pleasant garden sloped up a steep hill to the remainder of the
estate which belonged to one of the former war lords of Yünnan.

My hostess greeted me on a porch which was comfortably furnished for sitting out of doors. She was a tall, striking-looking
woman with sky-blue eyes and slightly reddish-blonde hair which
curled vibrantly. I liked her immediately. Her husband was also
tall, somewhat thin, and with a pleasant objective attitude. He came
from the Middle West of the United States and had a hesitancy in his
gestures vaguely akin to shyness. He had spent a long time in China,
and I made a mental note that he might be one of those men whose
youthful good looks and nervous personality could hide far more
knowledge and experience than might ordinarily be expected. There
were other guests, a young woman painter from New Zealand who
was staying at the house, a Chinese architect who had studied at Yale,
and later, which was more interesting, with Frank Lloyd Wright at
Taliesin. As though this were not enough to distinguish him, he was
accompanied by his wife, one of those exquisitely beautiful things
which flower in the eastern provinces. A tall Chinese servant with
an intelligent face dressed in a pale-green figured jacket and white
skirt brought out iced gimlets made by adding first gin and then ice
water to the top of lime juice, the famous hot-weather drink of the
sophisticated orient. Such servants did not originate in Yünnan,
and I learned that he was an old retainer brought from Peiping.

The conversation was cosmopolitan but soon drifted around to
the future of Yünnan and the projected railroad to Burma. We went
in to lunch in a dining room with silver-papered walls having a
border of blue stars about a foot high under the ceiling. The table
was perfectly ordered with delightful food and more servants in pale
green pouring cold champagne. When we had finished eating, we re-

tired to a living room extending through the house in the middle of the second floor. The dominant note in the decoration was a wood *k'ang* along one wall with a table in the center and blue cushions laid out to form seats that functioned as a chaise longues. On the floor was a pale salmon-colored rug which matched the walls. My admiration went out to a woman who could create such a home in the hinterland of China. This exquisite environment had an inordinate appeal to me, but I felt a conflict between this return to luxurious living and my predestined descent into the simple culture of the common Yünnanese. As I left, gladly promising to come again, I noticed that the war lord had furnished his fountain with the statues of two European females pouring water from Italian pitchers—to my eyes, ugliness brought from a far distance at great expense. After the big gates closed behind me, I walked a long way down the narrow street, at first deeply depressed, and then, becoming more and more conscious of the surging life around me, I was excited by it until the luncheon became a memory lost in some distant past. I hailed a ricksha and went home and repacked my clothes.

In the restaurant I found my Chinese friends sitting around a large table ordering their food. It was a great advantage to belong to such a group as then each participant could order one or two specialities which, placed together, made a feast for all. Once finished we drew matches, the custom of the table being that he who pulled the short one paid for the meal.

After dinner I found a companion who was willing to go to one of the two old Chinese theaters with me. We found rickshas and were soon speeding along to the south gate of the city. Directly after passing through it, we turned west along a narrow street abutting its inner face. Gradually the way became narrower until, when it was necessary for us to pass rickshas coming from the opposite direction, there was danger of entangling the wheels. The street was extremely uneven, and I became disturbed by the arguments almost constantly incurred as the result of the impassable traffic. Also, when we stopped suddenly, there was the danger of being thrown backwards out of the ricksha onto the cobblestones which, if causing no serious injury, was almost certain to land one in the mud. Arriving in front of the theater at last, we discharged our rickshas and walked up to the box office. The ticket seller had a printed plan of the seating in front of him so that a purchaser could put his fingers on the seats desired.

We purchased two of the best for seventy cents each in National currency (thirty cents less than the most expensive at the cinema). They were then checked off the plan with a red pencil.

The theater itself consisted of an orchestra pit with settees made of wood covered with cotton pads too thin to alleviate much of their hardness. The settees were arranged in rows parallel to the stage, not perpendicular to it, as was the old Chinese custom. On the back of each extended a wood tray about six inches wide to serve the people sitting in the row behind. On it, for each customer, was placed a small teapot, cakes of various kinds, edible seeds, and roasted beans. Accepting these things as we did, we had to pay a few coppers to the vendor who continually passed up and down the aisle to refill the teapots with hot water at no additional charge. Practically all the occupants of the orchestra indulged. At the sides of the theater, balconies ran at right angles to the stage. The one on the left hand side was for men only, and the one on the right for women. The orchestra section served for both sexes, however, and the seats became less expensive farther back. The theater was open to its gabled roof, the rafters being visible from the inside. The stage looked similar to its European counterpart, except that it projected more into the theater and that the front portion had open wings to accommodate theatrical furniture and the stage hands.

To a foreigner, unquestionably the most noticeable thing about the theater was the first onrush of smells which made one think of a large cesspool pervaded by the sweetish, sickening odor of sewer gas. I never knew anything equal to it until I visited the second opera in Kunming which had an open drain between the stage and the orchestra seats. Such inconsequential matters, however, soon disappeared from mind as one became more and more imbued with the spirit of the audience. The patrons did not behave as do those in the American theater where everyone sits quietly in the dark, but rather like people at a circus. There was quite sufficient illumination to see about, and the opportunity was taken to talk when one could be heard above the clanging of cymbals which filled the interims between the speeches of the actors. Everyone seemed to be eating seeds or beans and spitting out the shells. When I was distracted by the hot water seller, my first thought was always that he was going to offer me a soft drink. Directly in front of us was a family with children of various ages, the small ones turning around to eye me with furtive amazement. Underfoot the floor had become a thin layer of mud mixed with the refuse of food. All about one heard the clearing of throats—a long, deep, drawn-out process which ended in a peculiar gurgle in the mouth and fulsome expectoration.

The drama in process had its story laid in the Sung dynasty (960–1127). The course of the action was evident enough even if one did not understand Chinese. Presented at its minimum, it was the tale of two high officials at the court, each of whom had supplied a daughter as a wife for the Emperor. The son of one of the officials killed the son of the other for attempting to seduce a girl, a circumstance which started a chain of melodramatic events including the revenge of the afflicted father and eventually the final triumph of justice. This is a very brief summary of a play which lasted about four hours.

One of the most distinctive things about the Chinese theater was the role of the stagehands who lingered among a pile of chairs stacked up at the sides of the platform on which the show was being performed. When needed, one of these assistants in ordinary dress carried a chair into the midst of the performers. Then he backed up against his supply with a cigarette hanging from the corner of his mouth, never bothering to remove it during the course of his duties. Sometimes children belonging to members of the company climbed on top of the pile to view the performance. Whether this was the regular custom I did not learn, but they seemed to disturb no one except once when late in the evening a little girl fell asleep and toppled off onto the floor, apparently irritating the tall custodian of the furniture, but perhaps he was merely startled as was I. The stage had a back drop which was changed occasionally and also served to exclude the rear section of the platform which was used as a sort of waiting room as well as for storing various theatrical properties. The wings were also shifted once in a while, a change in scene being indicated by two stagehands drawing together a pair of dirty green curtains with large black characters on them. The curtains were drawn at the back of the stage, not in front of it.

An essential accompaniment of the play was the music supplied by an orchestra sitting at the stage end of one of the balconies, at the distance above the performers that they themselves were above the main floor. The orchestra consisted of half a dozen musicians of whom perhaps the most important was the player of the *pan,* a kind of clapper made of three pieces of hard wood which produced a resonant, monotonous sound. This instrument provided the timing for the music. Hence the *pan* player paralleled in part the conductor of an orchestra in the West. There were also two players of stringed instruments which looked like *hu-ch'in,* or two-stringed violins, but perhaps they were some other forms of *hu* which I could not distinguish. Also, I saw no moon guitar. Two men performed on an assortment of percussion instruments—drums, gongs, bells, and cymbals. When one appeared not to be making a sufficient din by himself, the other joined in with a pair of large cymbals which annihilated all other sounds in the house. Actually, the actors indicated the beginning and end of the musical accompaniment which was all quite formalized, and pleasing to one who knew what to expect. It may be that foreigners' nerves were frazzled, not so much by the volume of the sound as by their constantly being surprised by its sudden and unexpected intrusion. To attend a play performed in an unknown language usually tends to put one to sleep, but in China one enjoys the performance or leaves.

The embroidered costumes of the actors and actresses, even in this poor theater, were extraordinarily elaborate, the headdresses differing particularly from anything seen in ordinary life. The traditional forms of dramatic dress went back to ancient times and represented the principal investment of theatrical producers. For the habitué, the style and decoration of the robes and the various accessories told much about the characters presented, and when the whiskers and face-painting were added, the cultured man could be certain of what followed.

There were a number of other notable things about the opera. The actors introduced themselves at the beginning of the play and recited some verse when entering and leaving. They made asides to explain the private feelings of the character to the audience. Also quite unforgettable was the unnaturally high, nasal pitch of the singing which, as much as anything else, produced what has been frequently termed the "indescribable" quality of the Chinese theater. What most readily appealed to the esthetic sense of the visitor from the western world was the ritualized behavior, or pantomime, that represented the essence of Chinese acting, and which at times rose almost to the heights of a formalized dance. Each step, each turn could be an art in itself. The slight swaying of the heroine's hips

might make an audience ecstatic. And then there were the multi-
tude of special movements such as the often-parodied opening and
closing of a nonexistent door, the conventional fighting, the drinking
of tea with the face turned behind a full-hanging sleeve, the manipula-
tions of which formed the principal routine of the gesturing throughout the play. What effrontery or what sorrow could be expressed by
a simple turn of a sleeve. Sometimes the performers seemed to
become bored, and I was startled to see the principal actress sitting
on a chair in the middle of the stage stop her performance while she
cleared her throat and expectorated in a long drawn-out fashion
without turning her head.

When the play was over, we went home down the same dark
streets in the rain. I was thoroughly tired and glad to find a room
boy still up to bring me a pitcher of water. I took a large swallow
and burned myself painfully, which was one way of learning that all
drinking water in Kunming was normally boiled.

The official who lived in the top room of the tower moved away,
so I ascended to the relative privacy of his quarters which had windows overlooking the city in all directions. The view brought an
escape from the feeling of being enclosed by the narrow streets and
tumultuous masses of people which constitute congested China. From
my five-storied height, I looked down on the tile roofs of Kunming.
The typical building had two floors. The end walls seemed to be
of unbaked brick with stone reinforcements to hold the latter in place.
Sometimes there was a light plaster over the brick, with a clay wash
of gray or tan. The fronts and probably the interiors were almost
wholly of wood, and there were second-story balconies a few feet
wide normally projecting over the street. The walls of the first floor
of business establishments in almost every case consisted of removable panels about one and a half feet wide, reaching from a baseboard
to within a few inches of the ceiling. These were taken away during
the daytime, exposing the shops; then replaced at night. The railings
of the balconies had turned wood columns like an elaborate, old-
fashioned American porch. The front panels of the second story,
which separated the balcony from the rooms behind, in many instances
looked like those on the ground, but they were hinged fixtures rather
than removable sections. Others had larger panels with fancy grill-
ing covered from behind with colored paper. It was through these
grills that came the picturesque illumination of flickering blue or red

lights one saw when looking up from a ricksha on an evening ride. The roof tiles of the buildings were about eighty-five per cent gray and the remainder, flatter red ones. The latter were apparently more modern as they generally appeared on roofs lacking the old-style turned-up eves and corners which arced skyward. The fronts of the buildings also had some color, many being painted a brick red, but green and other hues intermingled, all dulled by weather. Above the first-floor paneling the shops had a rectangular sign board, typically red or black with four characters in gold.

I could see many houses with interior courts from which smoke emanated, there being no chimneys visible, but the better homes with enclosed gardens were situated too distantly to be distinguished. Some modern buildings caught the eyes in the newer quarters of the city. One rose four floors, the first of stone with some carving, and the other three of orange brick. Another in process of construction near the French concession was made of white concrete, rectangular and simple in design. The only structures taller than my vantage point were two pagodas and three gatehouses of the city wall, elaborate ancient works of brick reminiscent of Peiping, standing in exquisite silhouette against the background of hills and cloudy heavens. These gave a relief from drabness, for despite a spotting of cedar-like green trees, the view overlooking Kunming in other respects left an image of grayness and weather-streaked, colorless clay.

Inactivity made me uncertain about the future of my plans, so I persuaded Lee to drive to my chosen village again to see if I could not find a house without further delay. The journey was familiar and quickly passed. We had to stop some distance outside because rain had washed away the road, but a short walk over sticky clay brought us to our destination. We sat down in a tea shop facing the small marketplace and ordered tea and a plateful of roasted beans. The establishment, a small room about fifteen feet square, was run by a widow with a kindly, humorous face. She told us that there were no vacant houses but, on looking around, we discovered a large stage above the entrance to the courtyard of the school. We entered it by climbing a ladder leading through an aperture in the floor. The stage was entirely open on its long interior side except for one end which had been partitioned by pasting old newspapers over a lattice work of split bamboo. There were also three dingy rooms lighted by two small open windows looking out on the marketplace and down the main street beyond which one could see the lake. This vantage point struck me as ideal for my work since on one side I could observe unnoticed the coming and going of people through the village while on the other were the unclosed doors of the school and the courtyard in which the children played during recess. Also, I liked the openness of the stage looking out on forested hills rising high against the near horizon. I asked Lee if I could rent this place, but he refused to believe that I found it desirable. The rooms were littered with refuse and were occupied by some chickens which were enjoying the remnants of grain that had been scattered on the floor from a past season. Acquiring the stage seemed a simple solution to my problem and I urged him to see what could be done, so he consulted our hostess of the tea room. She said it was a poor place, that the roof leaked, and seemed to think it a very queer residence to be sought after by a foreigner, who, from her viewpoint, must have been tremendously wealthy. The more I considered the location, the more it pleased me, and I encouraged my companion to action.

The building, a part of the school compound, was not private property, and permission to occupy it rested in the hands of the school manager, a village official. We sent the old lady off to find him which she fortunately succeeded in doing after a short delay. As it was certain that he would be curious about my purpose in living in the village, it seemed best to explain that I was anxious to remove from the city to escape the anticipated bombing raids. This was a fortunate thought, for it afforded a rationalization completely understandable by everyone which would set aside the inevitable suspicion as to why I was there. By undertaking my mission at a time which had been regarded most unlikely for success, I had gained an unexpected advantage of tremendous significance. The school manager, who joined us at tea, promised to discuss the arrangement with the members of the village council and come to the city on the following day with their decision. Lee, with his wisdom of the ways of the East, wisely suggested giving him a present of two dollars Shanghai which was accepted after polite protestations of refusal. The teahouse woman was equally courteous in her manner of receiving payment for her services and, when we had left, I found that my short contact with Kao Yao and its people had more deeply attracted me to my newly found village.

Driving back to the city, I noticed a peculiar custom of the natives walking along the road. Just before we reached them, they would usually cross to the opposite side in front of the car, thus forcing the driver to put on his brakes with uncomfortable alacrity. I had never before been conscious of this type of behavior and could find no explanation for it, although other drivers confirmed my observation.

That evening, I was honored by an invitation to dinner from two of China's leading archaeologists, Li Chi and Liang Ssu-yung, who as members of the Academia Sinica had recently come with that organization from Nanking. Their working quarters was a converted house in the university section of the city, a ramshackle sort of place at best. If they missed the comfortable modern laboratories taken by the Japanese, they gave no outward sign. The real tragedy was the dispersal of their libraries and collections, leaving a burden of bitterness for the lost years which had gone into their making. They were beginning over again in the new China.

We went to one of the outstanding restaurants of a city justly famous for its food. Like Hsin Yah's, it was on Silk Street, but a short distance outside the city gate. Hsin Yah's, where I had gone on the evening of my arrival in Kunming, had a Cantonese-style cuisine, whereas this other eating place specialized in northern dishes. Walking through the kitchen, I had to pick my steps among a dozen slabs of ham lying on a floor so encrusted with dirt that I could not tell if there were cobblestones or planks beneath. Piles of magnificent big cabbages, melons, and a host of other vegetables struck the eye, besides herbs and spices spread out on basket trays. Green jugs filled with sauces lined the walls, faintly reflecting the open fires in small clay stoves. Numerous cooks and their helpers moved unceasingly from one place to another, taking a portion of condiment here and a slice of meat there. It seemed like an ancient alchemist's shop in whose smoky interior, genii of the darkness conspired to turn out the most wonderful tasting stuff. I cannot imagine such a kitchen being clean, for it was almost as though the good odors had of necessity to permeate everything, soaking into the grime, until no room was left except for aromatic smells. A clean dish towel would have been a white flag in the battle for flavor.

We had our meal in the rear room of the second floor, the waiter immediately placing handleless teacups on the table and filling them. Then he inserted small saucers upside down on the top, not to wash them, but to keep the tea hot. He finished setting the table by dealing out a pair of bone chopsticks to each guest, matching them first for size, and then adding a porcelain soup spoon and a small dish. My hosts insisted on a bowl of hot water being brought to the table and proceeded to wash the implements of our meal, but whether to satisfy their own standards or out of deference to me, I was not quite certain. It was the only time I enjoyed such an opportunity which I am sure the Yünnanese considered an affectation of the effete.

A bottle of Kweichow wine had been brought along which, with the product of Chekiang, ranked as the most famous in China. It came in a stone jug like Holland gin. Each of our small cups was filled with the liquid crystal, and when we drank, fire floated down our throats, for the best wine in China was a distilled spirit, the union of exotic spices with alcohol. Our dinner was ordered from a seemingly endless menu with the additional discussions which distinguish the gourmet. Soon the dishes began to arrive—chicken broiled in oil, delicious Yünnan mushrooms, strips of fresh bamboo which looked like the ivory keys of a piano dissolved into edible fibers, local ham broiled with onions, chicken served in its special steaming pot, pickled eggs which the foreigners say are a thousand years old, all this and more brightened with many colors the table before us. The waiter brought rice, the common food of Yünnan, which was said to be harder than that of other provinces, but people who were accustomed to the softer variety often came to prefer the former. Also, we had the white, spongy, steamed wheat bread which was northern food. Our banquet lasted long and our conversation turned to the intellectual problems which confronted us. Gradually the food was forgotten and the room seemed to disappear in the smoke of our cigarettes. The imminence of space and time was lost in the interchange of ideas. I had the singular feeling of an all-embracing commonality which transcended the categories of age or status or nationality. Nothing was strange, the exotic was gone, I felt as though I had lived all my life in Kunming and was not going elsewhere. Somehow the superficialities of life which stamped the world into segments had been tossed aside before the onrush of common ideals. I went home with the feeling of having had an evening of the good life which symbolizes the desire of the truly urbane.

Lee told me the next morning that the old man from the village had come to see me and offered to rent me either the stage or two rooms which he would make available in his own house. I was greatly pleased by both his gesture of hospitality and by the opportunity to settle down to work. I took the stage as it seemed best suited to my requirements and gave him some money to have the leaking roof repaired, as well as the interior cleaned.

One piece of good fortune followed another when a student arrived, sent to me from the university by an acquaintance on the faculty. He was a short, round-faced youth with sharp brown eyes and a quizzical smile which sometimes spread to a grin showing his gleaming white teeth. His name was Ho Chia-ping. He had been born in Shanghai twenty years before, but his family had moved to Fuchow in Fukien when he was eight years old. At the age of seventeen, he had returned to the former city and attended St. John's School for one term. During the previous year of war, he had been gradually moving westward to Kunming. Since his arrival, time had just been sufficient for him to spend one semester at the University of Yünnan and to attain a degree of familiarity with the dialect of the province. He was shy at first and spoke English hesitatingly, but I considered myself fortunate to have found him. After I had presented my purpose briefly, he agreed to work with me, and I was glad to discover that he did not hesitate in facing the problem of making a home on a village stage.

We went out to purchase furniture and other necessary equipment for our new residence—tables, chairs, dishes, and scores of various things which we would require. When we arrived at Silk Street, flags were flying and there was a general air of excitement. I had lost track of dates in my concentration on my own problems and had to inquire concerning the cause for the celebration. The day was July 7, 1938, the first anniversary of the beginning of the war. As we walked along, a marching column of children approached, singing in unison. We stopped at a convenient point of observation to watch them pass, but they came on endlessly—boys and girls in scout uniform followed by soldiers, then some little tots so small one wondered if their legs would not fail them. When they stopped their singing, the marchers broke into yells against the invading Japanese. As time passed, a sense of change in the populace struck me. The Yünnanese, usually so dispassionate and provincial in their traditional isolation, seemed to have become conscious of each other as people with a common cause against an encroaching conqueror. In front of my eyes I could observe the birth of a new nationalism such as had never before existed in the history of China. Perhaps the patriots who prophesied that war would bring this wished-for change were right, that only such a catastrophe could unify the nation and shake it out of a hundred years of lethargy until, like a waking giant, it stretched the resourceful strength of its great arms to sweep aside annoying intruders. Hour upon hour the people passed with banners waving, and I realized there was little time in which to take a measure of the old life before it would be overwhelmed by the marching spirit of China's millions.

4

FAREWELL TO FOREIGNERS

WHEN WE returned to the Green Youth Association, loaded with bundles, I was exhausted, as much from excitement as from our labors. I looked forward to an engagement during the evening with some acquaintances I had met in the foreign colony, for I was certain of finding among them the relief of a sharp contrast in values. Of approximately three hundred Europeans in Kunming, about one-half were French, one-quarter German, and the larger share of the remainder English and American. This number included the consular authorities of these countries and the missionaries, the rest being principally business agents of one kind or another.

The Germans formed a group somewhat apart, intense in their belief in the coming of a new day in the status of the fatherland. Outstanding among them were the operators of the Eurasia airline which had recently opened an effective extension to Hanoi in Indo-China. The fares were cheap, and I was told that they were willing to operate at a loss until a shift in power made possible a through service to the homeland. The Germans' sometimes arrogance was disagreeable, yet I could understand it in view of what they had suffered in loss of prestige. In the face of it, their courage, unity, and efficiency attracted admiration.

The few British I saw had that restrained self-esteem which irritated most Americans, but I could not help respecting their faith in the cultural standards which they struggled to uphold. One felt in them a sense of honor which, with all its possible deficiencies, seemed to suggest a search for a satisfactory symbol of justice with which to demand respect from the whole world. If such an ideal could remain steadfast in times of peril, history should mark its greatness.

The French had enjoyed considerable influence in Yünnan since building the railroad from Tonkin. They had a bank, a hospital, a

48

hotel, and many of the principal business agencies. The head of the Chinese customs was French. Somehow one gained the impression that these people idolized their native country more than did other exiles, but at the same time they were given to very practical compromises with an alien culture, or at least did not stand apart from it. Like other Latins, they expressed their emotions and did not freeze one with reserve. Best of all, I liked their feeling for drollery which made me think that he who had not affection for the French had no sense of humor.

I went to visit a charming but temperamental gentleman who had a comfortable house in the suburbs guarded by three dogs, one a monster from Tibet, which roamed the grassy court within the walls. My host found solace in smoking opium and invited me to share the intimacy of his den, a gray-walled room eight feet wide and fifteen long. Dim illumination suffused from green and blue lights hidden above the door. Against one wall stood a table on which rested an electric victrola with a radio amplifier, the controls being within easy reach of a softly upholstered lounging chair. Over more than half the room extended from wall to wall a k'ang, or divan-like platform, a super bed a foot and a half high covered with a beautiful robe of Chinese fox skins. Above it close to the ceiling had been suspended a great, open, red parasol with a carved ball beneath its center. A magnificent silver tray with smoking utensils of ingenious Indo-Chinese craftsmanship glistened from a low Chinese table placed in the middle of the k'ang. Like a little shrine, a small opium lamp with a silver base was burning in the center of the tray. It had a characteristic glass cover in the shape of an inverted cup with a hole in the top a half inch in diameter and, as an added delicacy, a carved silver insect served to shade the oil flames from the front. Nearby rested a jade box filled with opium which looked like dark, thick molasses. Several smaller utensils, all chased with the same figures suggesting the carvings on the *vats* of Angkor, added an intriguing complexity to the general ensemble. Among the utensils was a small oil container and a silver opium needle with a grotesque silver fish to rest on. Along each side of the tray lay an opium pipe with a knoblike projecting bowl. My host resumed his position among the pillows at the rear while across from him reclined one of the charming and sophisticated female members of the French colony who came up to the plateau of Yünnan to escape the inordinate heat of France's tropical empire. The effect of the scene was so seductive that it would have made an American director of oriental melodramas suffer with envy.

Glamor was actually pushed back into its reasonable place after a few minutes of adjustment to the unusual décor, and the conversation ranged from business and politics to prognostications concerning the course of the Japanese invasion, the whole pleasantly spiced with a mixture of gossip and amusing stories.

There was a considerable difference of opinion among the foreigners in Kunming about the matter of smoking opium, some holding it in horror while others championed the practice as one in which a moderate indulgence had much to recommend it over the use of alcohol. At least in Yünnan, with reputedly the best and cheapest opium in the East, a slight addiction did not make one déclassé. Unfortunately, as with alcohol, some smokers demonstrated a tendency toward increasing the quantity used. Apart from the direct result on the physiological system, indulgence in opium consumed both time and money which the majority of people could ill afford. This was perhaps the most noticeable misfortune as it brought many to economic ruin. Further, it displaced the normal appetite for food, and the absence of the latter naturally weakened resistance against disease. Although, like alcohol and tobacco, it was habit forming, it had the further dread danger of leading to the use of derivatives such as morphine and heroin which, when thrust upon an unresisting people, becomes one of the most insidious horrors perpetrated by man upon his fellow human beings.

For a number of years the growing of opium poppies had been illegal, but the production had gained such proportions that complete suppression could be brought about only by an annual reduction of the crop. That year, 1938, was the last in which the growing was tolerated in Yünnan. Whatever may be said of the roles of individuals, the history of the national government's campaign against opium as a social evil deserved the highest praise. The authorities had fought with unceasing energy against intrenched interests, meting out the death penalty to thousands, and propagandizing the dangers of the practice until responsible Chinese had come to recognize the use of the drug as a national shame which it was almost taboo to discuss. Without invasion or foreign influence, it seems certain that the problem would have long since been brought under control.

Furnishing a house, even when it was such a poor one as a village stage, became an intriguing procedure. There were some furniture-makers who worked on the same narrow street along the inside of the south wall where I had seen men fashioning bombs, and we went there to buy tables. The craftsmanship undoubtedly was of the poorer kind but, since our ends were wholly practical, we were content after some shopping around to purchase two at five National dollars apiece. Something to serve as writing desks was a necessity, and these standardized products, freshly painted black, had an appealing simplicity. Chairs caused some uncertainty as the common Chinese solid variety were distinctly uncomfortable. Then Ho recalled the rattan weavers on the road leading to the unversity. As was customary in China, the shops of one trade tended to cluster together, and we found several making woven splint chairs of foreign design. A little bargaining soon brought us to the base price of three and a half dollars—fifty-four cents of American money—for as satisfactory a chair as one could wish. The freshly interlaced cane even smelled nice, the seat was soft, and the back extended into two luxurious arms. Having acquired four of them, I felt we were well on our way to becoming settled members of the community although not until we had conveyed them to a suitable storage place, for Ho took seriously his role as financial adviser and suggested that for the sake of efficiency we transport them on our rickshas, one on the shafts and another on top of our heads. Somehow our real friendship began then and there, for we could not waste time in needless consideration for one's dignity. On Silk Street outside the walls we found the mat makers with great bundles of straw rugs about four by seven feet in size. The price was fifty-five cents a mat, and Ho went from one shop to another, discussing the purchase. His face appeared expressionless and there was a sharp note of finality in his voice each time he moved on. I felt certain he was not getting anywhere, and I uttered a sign of relief when he said I should pay for four. But the seller counted out five and rolled them up. I looked at my companion with renewed admiration and his eye unmistakably twinkled.

In the two days we devoted to acquiring our necessities, we visited many strange little shops, some of which had nothing we needed, but I liked to stop and record things in my memory for the future pleasure of thinking about them. My companion found it illuminating too, and he continually pointed out things that people did or said which were strange from the background of an East China person. A portable bed or cot demanded one of our longest searches, for I wanted my companion to share the same degree of comfort which I myself enjoyed. Finally we found a secondhand folding cot of European manufacture with a mosquito net attached. It was our greatest extravagance, unless I include our cook. Since I had anticipated scheduling our time with complete devotion to my work, I determined to take advantage of one outstanding available luxury in that cheapest of all countries—a master cook—and the gods favored us with a tall, gaunt, neurotic-looking individual who, whatever his faults, I still think of longingly as a genius in his art.

At times we repaired to one of the main department stores for small utensils, or we went to the paper-sellers, waiting while they counted out piece after piece of their product, for in such fashion it was sold. I remembered the bamboo lattice work of the open stage, and I determined to pull off the old newspapers which served as a windbreak and repaper everything freshly as some salve to our self-respect. When all the equipment for the opening of our residence had been purchased, we made the following list. The prices are in National, or Shanghai, dollars, which will be the currency used throughout this study unless otherwise indicated.

6 wine cups (porcelain)	$ .50
4 spoons (tin) at .08	.32
4 spoons (plastic) at .10	.40
4 bowls (plastic) at .60	2.40
4 cups and saucers (enamel) at .40	1.60
1 large teapot (porcelain)	3.70
2 small teapots (porcelain) at .80	1.60
10 pr. chopsticks (wood)	.35
4 large plates (enamel) and 4 small plates (enamel)	4.40
1 teakettle (aluminum)	6.30
1 frying pan (aluminum)	2.80
1 steam kettle (aluminum)	2.20
1 ladle (aluminum)	.25
1 water bucket (wood)	.50
1 dish pan (tin)	1.20
1 stove (clay)	.40
3 fly protectors for food at 1.00	3.00
160 sheets paper at .26 per 80	.52
50 sheets paper at .03 ½	1.75

1 cot with mosquito net	16.00
2 tables (wood) at 5.00	10.00
1 cook's table (wood)	4.50
4 chairs (rattan) at 3.50	14.00
5 mats (straw) at .55 (one free)	2.20
5 oil lamps at .60	3.00
10 lamp glasses at .05	.50
7½ catties of kerosene at .60	4.50
1 mosquito net	6.00
1 can Flit (pint)	2.60
1 pump for Flit	2.00
1 wash basin (enamel)	4.40
1 mirror	.80
6 towels	2.30
1 soap dish (enamel)	.70
4 coat hooks at .25	1.00
2 fly swatters at .20	.40
1 thermos bottle (pint)	3.50
1 thermometer	1.20
1 flashlight	2.50
	$116.29

The total came to approximately twenty American dollars. The outlay was not extravagant and other items were added from time to time. Our cook received the munificent sum of thirty dollars a month which was undoubtedly increased by the customary percentage on a generous budget for food which he himself purchased.

We left Kunming very early one Sunday morning hoping that it would not rain, for we had a veritable caravan of rickshas loaded with all our furnishings and private possessions. Ho and I were in the lead with the cook at the end of the procession, he having been given orders to shout when any of our belongings fell off of the vehicles. The chairs proved our particular bane in this respect as they had been insecurely added to the tops of the loads. I felt that we should have had runners ahead with lanterns to announce the coming of dignitaries of the first rank, for it was easy to play at being Manchu ambassadors when jouncing through the narrow, uneven street along the curving south wall. Of course we should then have had chairs carried on the shoulders of perspiring coolies, but the ancient palanquins were already practically outmoded except for marriages and funerals, and we saw only three or four during our stay in Yünnan. In about twenty minutes we reached the west gate and emerged onto a wider thoroughfare which led to the canals running in from the lake.

The street was already busy, and faster moving rickshas speeded by bearing parties bound for holiday picnics, some spending the day on small sailing craft available for the purpose, while others were destined for the temples in the hills. We passed heavy, solid-wheeled, flat carts with oxen straining to pull loads of cut stone brought from the quarries across the lake. Shops of all kinds lined the road and we could see men bent over in the sawing of great logs while others, as though geared into a machine, rhythmically pushed heavy planes to smooth the wood. They were making coffins, one of the principal crafts of the country. Nearby was a vendor of firecrackers which served for numerous kinds of celebrations and ceremonies. A whole crowd of coolies were conveying a heavy log, yelling for the travelers to give way. In order to bear the weight, they cleverly distributed it among their number by putting the middle of one carrying pole under the end of another until there resulted such a zigzag of supporting members, it became a puzzle to trace them.

At last we reached the port, merely a bulbous root of the narrow canal which stemmed from the lake. One edge of the bank was lined perpendicularly with sampans, all practically uniform in size and shape, while farther along were the larger junks, mostly engaged in transporting stone. As our caravan came into view, the women of the sampans swarmed down on us, gesticulating for our trade like a flutter of bluebirds after a handful of grain. The boats were remarkably clean. One old woman with a wizened face like a walnut had little to say, but there was a twinkle in her eyes and we agreed to pay two dollars for the journey across the lake. The ricksha coolies loaded our miscellaneous assortment of furniture onto the craft which was about thirty feet long. Bed nets, spreading their white gauze from round hoops were piled on bags, baskets of vegetables, pieces of meat, sausages of various shapes and sizes. Tables and chairs stood on end wedged between the gunwales. We had just dismissed the coolies and managed to climb aboard ourselves when the cook announced that he had forgotten to buy rice and charcoal, so there was nothing to do but wait while he procured them. He set off in a stilted walk up the dusty street while I tried to find a soft place to recline since I felt drowsy in the increasing heat of the morning.

The old woman was shy and said nothing, but her daughter, a girl of about twelve, smiled at me from the stern of the boat. The child was not yet married, as I could see from the pigtails hanging down her back. She was dressed in the red jacket of the west country, while extending from the bottoms of her trousers her bare feet, large and clean, gripped the planks with the appearance of being rooted there. Her lower garment was turning pink and I pondered if it was so because she washed only half her costume. From her ears hung ornaments of green jade set with imitation rubies making a flash of color against the blackness of her hair. In the next sampan an old lady was soaking rice in the canal, unmindful of the soapy water drifting out from the shore where a woman pounded a garment turned almost white from continued washing. Suddenly a furor broke out among a group of females because another wished room for her incoming sampan. When they had beaten her down verbally, the newcomer was a picture of crestfallen desperation, but it was only for a moment until she began her complaints again. I could tell by the diminishing animosity that she would win if she kept trying, and I occupied myself by making mental wagers on her success. Then a boat pulled out leaving adequate space, so I was forced to concede that the dispute was a draw.

Before the cook returned, I had become tired of waiting. Then he appeared empty handed, a coolie having been detailed to follow with the load. This further delay obviously angered me—to the cook's surprise. His eyes popped open; his jaw dropped, pulling the skin of the sides of his face to drumhead tautness; and he pursed his mouth as though about to speak, but he was too frightened. I could see that I had hurt his feelings, so I smiled. He sat down, intermittently pouting and looking up at me from the corners of his eyes. Presently the rice and charcoal arrived and we set off down the canal.

The girl and her mother leaned back and forth against the sweeps with an easy rhythm and we made steady progress under a leafy avenue of overhanging trees that threw spotted shadows on the yellow water. A dirt road paralleled the right bank. A number of people went by us on bicycles which were common enough in Kunming to attract no particular attention. I also saw a peculiar-looking boxlike vehicle with two little wheels in front and two large ones in the rear, the whole being surmounted by a flat, tasseled top like a surrey and drawn by a pony driven by one of two gentlemen apparently out for a Sunday airing.

We passed a few junks bound for the city and, after a time, came to the stone abutments of a footbridge which consisted of two planks. I could see that the mat housing in the center of our boat would not pass underneath. We pulled into the adjacent bank and the old woman went ashore and lifted the planks about a foot so we could slide under, then replaced them and jumped on the stern. I wondered, since this process was repeated by scores of sampans all day long, whether there would come a time when someone would build that bridge a few inches higher, or whether the old process would go on for years as a vestige of changeless China.

Some distance down the canal we pulled up to the left bank where there was a small mud hut with a mat lean-to adjoining. Here the husband of the woman from whom we had engaged the boat came aboard with a square mat sail with bamboo yards. He had a sympathetic face and seemed glad to be moving on his boat again. We had quite a discussion about the problems of his trade. I asked him if his storehouse on the bank of the canal was safe from thieves and he told me that the local people would take nothing, but that sometimes pirates stole unguarded boats and sailed them to the distant end of the lake to sell. Such a theft was tragedy, for a good sampan cost one hundred and fifty dollars.

We passed a strange-looking steamboat tied up to the shore, not one representing any beginning in the evolution of such craft, but rather a degeneration, a kind of scow with a rickety housing and a dilapidated boiler which periodically was put into condition for a trip down the lake. A thin thread of smoke from its funnel was lacing itself through the leaves of the trees. My new friend regarded it with obvious contempt and, when I asked him if he would like to own it, he said he would not even ride on it, that only the previous year it had sunk in a slight breeze and over a hundred passengers had been drowned. This struck me as a little strange since we were both looking at the vessel, but I was very sympathetic with his evaluation of its seaworthiness.

Near the end of the canal a small but elaborate villa with ornate balconies had been built. From it, the view down the lake must have been beautiful if one disregarded the somewhat dismal surrounding flats. Also, the villa had an appealing, or perhaps protective, aspect of isolation.   A few boys swam and ducked each other near the shore, thereby adding a genre touch to the scene.   Then I heard the strumming of a guitar and, turning around, I saw another sampan containing a number of young men and girls.   They were laughing aloud and enjoying themselves.   This was the new way of life daring to impinge on the old.   As we set our course out into the lake, I had one of those rare and intense sensations of loneliness which I connect with a sudden disappearance of the beautiful.

A clean sweep of air came down upon us as we passed into the blue water of the lake.   Our boatman set up his mast and raised the sail—a square of grass on a skyward stick.   As the faint easterly breeze filled it, the sweeps were pulled inboard and all became quiet save for the creak of straining planks and their swish against the small, crescentic swells.   Before long, a slight rain which had gathered above us like a band of black balloons sprayed down upon the bay.   The storm was local and had sunshine threatening its edges. I wriggled myself back into the darkness under the mat housing. Gradually I began to see about me.   Next to the mast was a small box in which sticks of incense stood up from a sand-filled burner before painted paper gods.   I became aware of a faint fragrance held by the encompassing humidity of the downpour as I leaned back watching the limpid softness of the hill horizons stepping off into the distance.   The wind ceased with the rain and the crew took to their sweeps again.   An hour passed and we approached the diminutive islands of trees which spread out like a horseshoe around the end of the peninsular village.   Then we slid through a gap which had been invisible in the distant verdure and drifted up to the rock-piled jetty with sampans crowded about.   I felt the gentle bump of our bow against the stone.   Thus we arrived at Kao Yao.

5

FIRST DAYS IN KAO YAO

THE END of the street near the boat landing was crowded with people, but before we attracted attention, I took two armfuls of belongings and started up the street, leaving Ho and the cook to arrange for the transport of the remainder of our possessions. The weather had cleared and the people sitting in the three small restaurants opposite the quay were enjoying the noonday sun (Pl. 3, p. 59). The road to our new home meandered just enough so that the vista did not exceed several hundred feet at a time. At the shore end, there were many large, flat stones showing on the surface of the road, but these decreased in number the farther one went until a single line remained indicating the course of a narrow drain. Drab blank walls periodically appeared between the entrances of houses and occasionally there was the open front of a store (Pl. 16, p. 103) or a teahouse. The clay-surfaced buildings were divided between one- and two-story structures, some of the latter being difficult to distinguish from the former. The street itself varied from perhaps twelve to fifteen feet in width and had a noticeable jog or two. At the first of these, near the halfway point, was a well, conspicuously protected by a heavy ring of stone about two feet high (Pl. 25, p. 166). A boy drawing water turned to look at me but I hurried on. From the second jog, distinguished by an open toilet in the street (Pl. 7, p. 67), I could see the entrance to the compound which I had already come to consider as home (Pl. 4, p. 60). Crossing the open market place, I entered the gate, turned left to the alcove which hid a ladder, and climbed to the floor above (Pl. 5, p. 61).

My first reaction was one of disappointment. The money which had been paid for cleaning appeared to have been wasted, but then I smiled in the realization that village standards were different from my own. Furthermore, the open front of the stage provided such a charming view of the pine-covered hills rising directly behind the school that my enthusiasm had returned before Ho and the cook,

58

3. SAMPANS LOADING AT KAO YAO

4. MARKETPLACE ENTRANCE TO SCHOOL COMPOUND

5. STAGE IN SCHOOL COMPOUND, ABOVE DOOR TO MARKETPLACE

accompanied by various porters they had pressed into service, arrived with the rest of our purchases. We devoted the next four hours to making our residence more habitable, much of which effort seemed unnecessary to my companions, although the cook willingly concocted paste so that we could renew the paper on the bamboo lattice which constituted two walls of the north wing of the stage, a section which I had selected to use for writing (Fig. 4, p. 63).

Not until five o'clock did we sit down to a meal which had been cooked over a pot stove placed at the southwest corner of the stage, the area that became our kitchen. I had eaten nothing all day and the food tasted delicious. There were eggs turned black and green from salting, ham sausage fried with slices of bamboo, quick-fried green vegetables, boiled rice, and a soup for dessert. Flies were a nuisance and, later on, a few mosquitoes bit us. By then, the children next door had developed the courage to visit the foreigner, an experience so novel for them that within the hour we had also a score of their friends quietly watching us. About ten o'clock, they were ordered out by a neighbor who insisted on locking the gate of the compound as a protection from thieves. Ho and I finally retired to our cots in the alcove east of the section designated for writing, while the cook made his bed in another of the three rooms behind the stage.

We were up and finished with our breakfast of congee, fried eggs with bits of ham, and salted vegetables before eight. The congee, or rice boiled in enough water in which to serve it, did not appeal to me greatly, but I was too excited over the prospects of beginning work to discuss any substitute for that national dish. As settling into our home had proved, we were still short of necessary furnishings, and Ho was delegated to go back to the city for two more tables and chairs, three additional kerosene lamps, a bucket, a mosquito net which had inadvertently been left behind, and a few other less important things.

Even before he left, our home was again overrun with children toward whom I took a tolerant view, hoping some advantage would result from allowing them to satisfy their curiosity. They crowded around as I sat at my table making an outline of my plans for the week. In the period of field research to which we were limited, much depended on keeping a well-ordered balance in our program. Ideally, it seemed best to divide the day into three periods allocated between

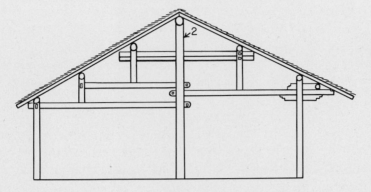

E ← → W   5 feet

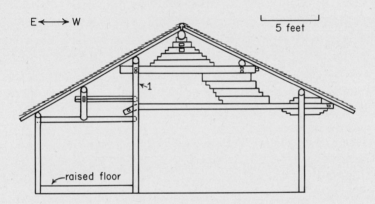

—raised floor

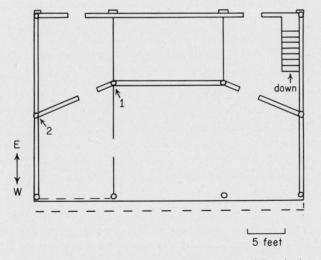

E
↑
↓
W

down

5 feet

Figure 4. Plan of Kao Yao Stage and Roof Bracketing

interviews with informants, participation in the cultural activities of the villagers, and writing up the data. This latter undertaking would range from recording the temperature four times a day to analyzing the results of my ethnographic notes in order to determine where verification or elucidation was needed, as well as to decide on the most profitable directions to pursue.

The children stood without speaking and watched the exotic alphabetic writing flow from the tip of my fountain pen. Perhaps I could have learned to withstand the animated stillness had not those in back shoved those in front with a polite but firm determination to share in the new experience. At last I stood up and walked across the stage to relieve the pressure of human interest, but before I had thought of what next to do, the children began to rush for the ladder. In a minute all were gone save two who likewise fled before I had recovered from an astonishment which, in itself, perhaps blinded me to the otherwise obvious fact that school had started. One shock led to another, for when I returned to my desk, my fountain pen had disappeared. So had the Confucian calm which with good intentions I had indulged the image of myself. I was as incensed as an Irishman whose whiskey has just been snatched.

Fortunately, the cook had gone to bring water and no one saw me before I had regained a reasonable measure of tranquility. Against the loss, I had insured myself by carrying substitute pens, but they were relatively cheap imitations of the fine tool which had served me well for many years. Concluding in the end that worse things might have happened, I returned to my planning. Clearly, a work schedule of from twelve to eighteen hours a day would not leave much time except for eating and sleeping.

When the cook returned, I tried with smiles to explain that some child had carried off my pen. His face took on an expression of incredulousness which at first I attributed to his disbelief but then, by more reasonable deduction, to the fact that he could not understand a word of my Chinese. Our effort to establish communication was interrupted by the arrival of two gentlemen, one a gracious man approaching forty named Pi Ch'un-ming who, I discovered, was the local schoolteacher, and the other, his friend and colleague from another village. The cook soon had us comfortably seated at the table and drinking tea, while he stood nearby playing the role of interpreter, a position of which, despite its mendacity, I was loth to

6. THE VILLAGE SCHOOLTEACHER

deprive him. How we communicated with my modicum of Chinese, I cannot really explain, but in a short time I had been assured that my pen must have been stolen by one of the children of the boat people since such thieving by a member of a village family was unthinkable. I was more impressed by the categorization of the boat people as an entity apart than by the truth of the assertion, and I struggled desperately to learn more, but with little success.

After an hour, necessity required me to excuse myself for a few minutes, and I set off down the street to the place I remembered seeing a toilet. It consisted of a rectangular cesspool approximately three and a half feet square, with a single slab of stone about twelve inches wide placed across it a foot from one end (Pl. 7, p. 67). Immediately I concluded that the narrower opening was for filling the basin and the larger for emptying the valued nightsoil by means of buckets. For various reasons, it was not the most comfortable facility I had ever used, but I had not expected such demands as were made on my intestinal fortitude. This street toilet had originally been set apart by a sun-dried-clay brick wall perhaps four feet high. The latter had crumbled half away on its long side leaving an occupant visible to those who would turn a head in passing. It was quite reasonable to believe that the Kao Yao people, blinded by the commonplace, were not aware that the wall had disintegrated, or at least until my arrival. Novelty, however, makes things immediately visible and begets irresistible curiosity, as I discovered. No one ever had a more inelegant introduction to his village neighbors, and I admit that I found the experience somewhat of a strain.

Having dourly made my way back to my guests, I found them as fully as gracious as before. Despite our formal difficulties in communication, Mr. Pi (Pl. 6, p. 65) managed to convey an invitation from his friend for me to lunch with them at a nearby village. Charmed by such courtesy, I was persuaded to accept and, after recording a noonday temperature of seventy degrees, we walked out of Kao Yao and began to climb the hill that rose behind it. Our progress would have been more consistent had we not been caught in a downpour. The rain itself was an insignificant diversion, but it made the yellow clay underfoot so slippery that I had great difficulty in ascending the path in leather-soled shoes. There was no need for anyone to explain how much more effective were straw sandals or even the common cloth footwear.

7. TOILET WITH BROKEN WALL (VIEW TOWARD MARKETPLACE AND SCHOOL COMPOUND)

8. TOILET ON SIDE STREET

In about a half hour we reached a small hamlet of only four Chinese families, but on the flat in front of the houses were gathered scores of vendors selling articles of food and clothing, as well as other local commodities. We stopped to drink a cup of tea at a

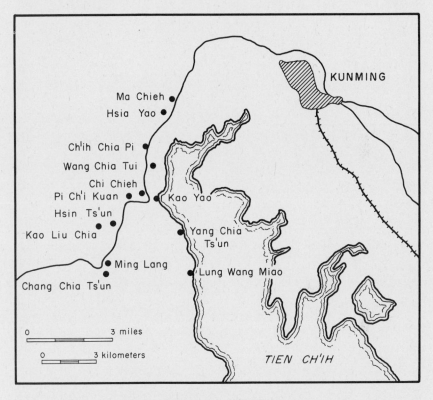

Figure 5. Map of the Kao Yao Area

temporary booth while Pi explained that this place, called Chi Chieh, or Cock Market, was known for the fair set up there every sixth day. Having come only a mile from Kao Yao, we continued our climb for perhaps two-thirds of that distance until we reached P'i Chi Kuan (Fig. 5, above), which village, according to our host, was noted for its restaurant.

To me, the eating place was certainly unforgettable. It consisted of two rooms so small and murky that we seemed to descend on entering the dismal establishment. In each of the rooms was a large square stove with flames glowing above it. One was tended by a man, the other by a woman. We sat down on benches at one of the three small tables in the first room, thereby disturbing a mangy dog lying in the dirt that constituted the uneven floor. With eyes adjusted to the dim light, I could make out diagonally across the room a bed with a cornice lacking the draperies which presumably once hung from it. After a brief discussion, the female cook brought for examination some greenish-colored fish and, our host giving approval, took them away and returned with a pot of wine or, to be more exact, a clear, strong spirit which required considerable familiarity on the part of a drinker to ascertain its attractiveness. At the time, I imagined it might sterilize the rough wood chopsticks that had been cut down an inch by the teeth of a thousand mouths before they were handed on to me. Pi kindly bought me a cigarette, the smoke from which mingled with the innumerable flies around my head.

As might be expected, the meal was excellent. Besides the tasty fish, we had a dish of the smoked ham for which Yünnan was famous, another containing slices of pickled eggs, and one of bland fresh bean curd. Our banquet was not broken up until Pi, who had drunk little or nothing, announced that he would have to return to school to give the children their recess, so after repeated thanks to our host, we retraced our steps to Kao Yao.

I learned from Pi that P'i Chi Kuan, or Jade Cock Pass, where we had dined, was strictly a Chinese village like Chi Chieh and Kao Yao, and that it had a population of about forty families with half as many more on outlying farms. Farming constituted the main activity of the people of the settlement which had been named, along with the adjacent hill, from a large stone faintly resembling a rooster. Representatives of the local families were reported to gather in the village temple on the 19th of the 2nd month to worship their six-armed god known as the "Earth-owner." Chi Chieh, it seemed, had ancient ties with Kao Yao. The latter village was its nearest Chinese neighbor to the east, whereas beyond P'i Chi Kuan to the west lived Pai Tzu (Min Chia) tribespeople. For a long time, Chi Chieh children had gone to Kao Yao for their schooling.

When we reached home, Pi had to return to his students. Exhausted by the excitements of the day and not wishing to strain the hospitality of my friend, I finally excused myself and returned to our stage where the cook seemed happy to see me. Taking advantage of his good humor, I spent an hour trying to adjust my limited knowledge of mandarin to the sounds of the local dialect, and then feeling a strain, decided to walk down the street to see what I could record. I was conscious of some turmoil in my viscera and was also aware of having caught a slight cold.

Actually, within Kao Yao one's movement was restricted by the nature of the low peninsula on which the village had grown. There was the one main street extending easterly from the market place in front of our compound to the rock-protected quay jutting out into the water, a total distance of a little over 400 paces, or approximately 1,200 feet (Fig. 10, p. 110). Along the north side of the street, there were no side alleys at all; the rear of the houses, or their gardens, abutted the flooded rice fields which extended over several hundred acres of flat land and which, from the hills behind, looked almost like a bay of the beautiful lake stretching endlessly into the horizon. Extending south from the street, there were four or five narrow alleys, but they only led past more gates and ended on the border of flooded fields in which I counted a dozen or more thatch-roofed structures which belonged to the best people (Pl. 31, p. 217; Pl. 32, p. 218).

Villagers whom I met on my walk often smiled in recognition, and some tried to engage me in a conversation that I was ill equipped to carry on. At least it was easy to determine the basic costume of the majority for it varied little. The women, almost without exception, wore blue cotton jackets fastened down the right side with the standard cloth buttons and loops and extending below the waist over trousers of similar material ending between the knees and the ankles. Most of the women had either sashes or aprons fastened around the waist, and from the ears of almost all hung jade, or jadelike, earrings. Furthermore, most of the women had fastened blue handkerchiefs over their hair, tucking them under and around the knots at the back of their heads.

Variations did occur. For instance, jackets and trousers frequently bore patches in slightly varying blues. A few women wore white jackets, or white with a wide blue collar section, the latter color extending to the sleeves above the elbows. Some of the aprons were embroidered and, while most sashes were cloth, some were rope or netted material. One old woman wore what looked like a black dust cap; another, in her twenties, was bareheaded, and several had straw hats over their handkerchiefs. The best-dressed woman displayed a sky-blue jacket with dark-blue piping, dark-blue trousers bound tight at the ankles with black cloth, and black embroidered shoes with lavender heel tongues. She also had fastened a jade bar pin across her chignon and an ornament of some red material on its left side. She was carrying a baby on her back in a square of cloth designed for the purpose. Some of the women were barefooted, some wore sandals, and a number had cloth shoes. Of the latter, a few bore decoration including red tongues lapping backward over the heels. Although the proportion of types of footwear was difficult to determine, it was clear that more women wore cloth shoes than did men.

Most men were likewise dressed in blue cotton jackets covering the upper parts of their matching trousers which reached somewhere between knee and ankle (Pl. 9, p. 73; Pl. 10, p. 74; Pl. 15, p. 102; Pl. 19, p. 146). The men's jackets were usually distinguished by being buttoned down the front, although a few were fastened on the right side. About half the males covered their heads with hemispherical black cloth, caps with a button on top, the other half wearing wide-brimmed straws of various styles (Pl. 9, p. 73; Pl. 10, p. 74; Pl. 26, p. 177). Most men used straw sandals (Pl. 9, p. 73), some went barefoot, and a few had black cloth shoes (Pl. 15, p. 102).

There was an occasional variation in the color of the jackets and trousers, about ten per cent being either white or black. Some men's skullcaps had red, rather than black, buttons and one or two were pieced together in motley colors, while several of the straw hats had black or green rain covers; also there were a few felt skullcaps, and one or two European-style felts. I noticed two men wearing long gowns. One of these was a little old man somewhat wizened by his years but with an undiminished twinkle in his eyes. He had three or four inches of pure-white hair on his chin and a thin mustache, also untrimmed, which fluttered down in wisps at the corners of his mouth (Pl. 15, p. 102). I encountered him first by the well, whereupon he stopped short, placed his hands in the attitude of prayer, and bowed with great dignity. Instinctively I duplicated his gesture, placing my palms together with finger tips up. When I had raised myself, he smiled as though we had played a secret game together. We exchanged a few words, and I went on, realizing that I had made a new acquaintance of whom I hoped to see more.

9. A TYPICAL VILLAGER

10. A VILLAGE PORTER

I stopped, perforce, at the toilet on the way home, and then decided to extend my walk behind the village to discover if there was a possibility for relief in isolation. The path from the village led off south for sixty feet from the marketplace, turned the corner of the school compound, and continued a short distance to join a newly improved road running south along the lake and leading to the famous temples of the Western Hill which we had visited on the first of our trips into the country. Stretching northerly from this hill, one could distinguish six more, the third of the range rising directly behind our village, and the fifth, that named P'i Chi which had been pointed out earlier in the day. Just across the improved road was a small, ill-kept temple (Pl. 11, p. 76) which, since there was no priest in attendance, was classed as Taoist by Ho. Water had cut a small gorge back into the hills and, although only a trickle was running, I could see that the heavy rains might quickly create a roaring stream. Climbing upward, I came to a small flat area containing a little forest of pines. Others could be seen growing more sparsely on the hills, along with occasional firs and cedars. From my position, perhaps fifty feet above the school and seventy above the lake, I could look over the roofs of Kao Yao. For the first time, I noticed palms growing in the courtyards, a sharp contrast of color and form to the more common chestnut and mulberry trees. As I turned to retrace my steps, I observed a brown bird that looked like a crested owl sitting on a nearby pine. There were many kinds of birds at Kao Yao, some quite beautiful such as large black ones with blue bands on their wings, others like sparrows which flew fearlessly into our open kitchen for rice.

It was nearly six o'clock, and I returned home to find the cook providing me with a delicious dinner which raised my spirits despite the fact that I broke a tooth in the course of enjoying it. Ho returned from town not long afterward, having acquired all the things that we needed—he was an excellent shopper. After exchanging descriptions of our day's adventures, we went over a program of work. It was late when I had finished writing down the record of my observations and retired full of enthusiasm for learning more.

The cook, reacting to my attitude toward congee, made a steamed corn cake in a cup for my breakfast which was followed by a kind of gelatine concocted with lotus seeds, delicately bland, if not quite taste-

11. THE VILLAGE TEMPLE

less to my unaccustomed tongue. We had just finished eating when I noticed Pi on the school steps and beckoned him to join us, which he did without further encouragement. Whatever Ho's merits as an interpreter, our effective communication improved beyond measure, and I began to express my hopes for making as much of a record of the cultural life of the village as I could in the short period available. Pi, a highly intelligent individual, showed enthusiasm for helping us as soon as he had grasped the procedure. To my delight, we had no sooner asked a few introductory questions about the people of Kao Yao than he went to his room and returned with a list of names of the members of each family of both the village and boat people, together with their sex, marital status, age, years of residence, occupation, and literacy, plus notations on the children who were not attending school when they should have been. It was this last interest which had apparently been responsible for his census made two months before our arrival. It seemed like an act of Buddha to be unexpectedly presented with such important information, and the most essential facts which were derived immediately follow:

	Village People	Boat People	Total Group
Individuals	497	211	708
Families	122	36	158

My first reaction was the realization that I had underestimated the size of the population even eliminating the boat people whom I noticed Pi had set apart. Our informant's work I knew should be checked, but I was quickly impressed by his efforts at accuracy, as well as his unusual objectivity. The first of these characteristics was easily understood as deriving from the traditional Chinese regard for learning enhanced in a teacher, and the second because, as we soon discovered by questioning, Pi himself was one of the few residents not born in the village. As he frankly told us, he had been hired about two years before to teach in the school at a salary of $120 a year plus a few minor emoluments such as a room in which to sleep and an allowance of rice and tea. His real residence, he explained, was in Ming Lang, a village of about fifty families of farmers and carpenters some five miles southwest on the road to Tali (Fig. 3, p. 25). There he had a son of twelve, a daughter three, and a wife who remained at home to work in the fields. Ming Lang was a place notable in local opinion for its pines and its cedars. Also, although

Pi said it was occupied by Chinese like himself, other informants later insisted that the people were all Lolo, and that the schoolteacher himself was. Perhaps it is significant that he spoke both the Lolo and Pai Tzu (Min Chia) languages as well as Chinese. Aware of the sensitivity of my friend, I did not pursue the matter. After all, the most honest men have their foibles and, even if the allegation was true, it perhaps helped to account for Pi's coolly rational statements about the people of Kao Yao who were well known to him even before he began teaching their children. Starting to feel guilty about keeping him from his duties, I apologized. He made light of his absence, and then suggested that we might like to visit his classroom. This invitation we gladly accepted, and thus we can proceed to an account of our visit which actually, as in other efforts to convey a picture of life in the village, consolidates information gained at various times during the period of our residence in Kao Yao.

6

EDUCATION AND PLAY

THE SCHOOL in Kao Yao intruded itself upon our lives during our whole stay in the village. This was inevitable since we lived in the same compound and could hear the children reciting their lessons intermittently from morning until evening. At recess time they played in the yard a few feet below the stage, and we became quite accustomed to each other as the weeks passed by. It was our second morning in Kao Yao that the teacher took us to school with him and introduced us to the children. There were three rows of crudely made flat benches and desks at each of which sat two youngsters with wide-eyed, inquisitive faces. They rose and bowed deeply to us which I felt was a very pretty gesture to the visitor, and then school went on as usual while we devoted ourselves to observation (Pl. 12, p. 80).

The floor of the large room consisted simply of clay somewhat beaten down by years of the tramping of children's feet. Poor illumination was provided through the checker-work of small, paper-covered windows, but more light entered at the wide-open doors. On the front wall, behind the teacher, hung three much worn blackboards, one large and two smaller which could easily be turned about. A series of colored educational posters on a variety of subjects such as the growth of plants, bird life, and human anatomy occupied most of the remaining space, but to the right above the teacher's desk extended eight vertical pennants of alternating green and red paper which bore in large black characters the following mottoes of the school.

1. We should respect the teacher.
2. We should love our schoolmates.
3. We should endure suffering and hardship and swear to avenge our national humiliation.
4. We should save time.
5. We should give attention to cleanliness and make our bodies strong.

12. INTERIOR OF SCHOOL

6. We should have the spirit of cooperation and creativeness.
7. We should continue on from beginning to end when we do something.
8. We should not smoke or gamble.

The children in one row were taking turns reciting their lessons with about the same hesitancy one would find among youngsters in the lower grades of an American school. Every once in a while Pi wrote some characters on the board explaining their meaning. One child would perform well to his obvious satisfaction, and then another would stumble along receiving help and admonition which became sharper with continued failure until I felt pangs of sympathy stabbing me out of the past of my childhood memories. Never mind, my little one, I thought, perhaps one day you can make your master proud he taught you.

While one class carried on lessons orally, the others studied. Some children read in their paper-covered text books, and others wrote characters on small pieces of tin, six by eight inches in size, which corresponded to the slates once used by children of Western cultures. The members of the classes not performing moved about with considerable freedom and engaged each other frequently in quiet questioning. If the amount of movement or talking increased beyond a certain point, the children were told to be quiet, but this Chinese school had obviously more tolerance for noise than the American equivalent where silence was considered golden. One little tot amused me by taking his ink dish out into the yard and filling it with the necessary water from a convenient puddle. He mixed his ink and set to work with his brush making characters on his tin which would hold only two of the size he preferred. Then he would erase them by rubbing over the tin with the side of his hand. Occasionally he brushed a fly from his face leaving a blotch of the ink in its stead, but he went on quite unconcernedly making words, rubbing them off the tin and onto his face, until a little girl sitting nearby began to look at him and then at me with a smile of impish satisfaction.

Just before recess all the children joined in a singing lesson which brought a sudden consciousness of the exotic, for Chinese music rings strangely on Western ears and has almost an eerie quality in the throats of children.

When school was dismissed, we followed Pi to his sleeping quarters adjoining the school. There he had a small portable organ which he had removed from the classroom for a previous evening's practice. I asked him to play for me. He sat down and easily fingered some ancient Chinese melodies which were surprisingly poignant as they issued from the simple instrument. He showed great pleasure at my response and our friendship deepened as we sat in his room almost bare except for a bed and a few pieces of crude furniture. On the wall I noticed a carefully written memorandum framed under glass which, roughly translated, contained the following information written in 1937.

The General Condition of the Boys School of Kao Yao Village

1. History: the Boys School was established in the first year of Hsüan-Tung, the last Emperor of the Ch'ing Dynasty. The founder of the school was Mr. Chiang who was assisted by Mr. Tuan. The first teacher of the School was Mr. Tuan, who was followed by Mr. Tu. The original title of the teacher was the Officer and it has been changed to Manager in 1936.

2. The address of the school: Kao Yao Village, Kunming [District].*

3. The scope of the school:
   a. Villages: Kao Yao and P'i Chi Kuan
   b. Number of families (both villages): 334
   c. Number of people: 1474

4. The school building: three rooms of the temple for the class rooms and one for the bedroom of the teacher.

5. The funds of the school: the school is supported by the shore taxes of the boat men in Kao Yao (about NY$60 per year); the tax on rice of the same village (about NY$120 per year); and the tax on rice of P'i Chi Kuan, the other village (about NY$80 per year) [Total $130 per year].

6. The wealth of the school: there are 10 *mou* † of rice fields in Kao Yao and there are more than 10 *mou* of rice fields in P'i Chi Kuan. The lake shore tax also is part of the wealth of the school.

7. Teacher: Pi Ch'un-ming (36 years of age) [An error, in 1937 he was 39].

8. Number of students: 33 boys, 44 girls.

9. Classes: they are divided into four grades—A, B, C. D.

10. The ways of training the boys in good manners: there is a definite time for giving an instructive speech each week. And

* Brackets distinguish the author's additions.
† A *mou* is roughly equivalent to one-sixth of an acre.

also for teaching the students of all times to have good manners.

11. Course of study: mandarin, arithmetic, social hygiene, drawing, music, physical education, etc.
12. Outside work: students should prepare one or two sheets of writing at home and hand them in to the teacher when they come to school the next morning.
13. Work in hygiene: every student should join in cleaning the school every Wednesday and Saturday. Students also should wash their own clothes on Sunday.

During the weeks which followed we devoted attention intermittently to various aspects of the school life and to the history of education in the village. One day when we were walking down the street, we noticed an almost completely buried slab of stone near the ruins of the old gatehouse, and it was prophesied that we would find a valuable historic record if it were dug up and the characters deciphered. Permission was received from the head man of the village and the excavation easily accomplished. The heading of the monument said, "Inscription concerning the Kao Yao public school of P'u P'ing Li—by order of the Prefect Kuo of Yünnanfu [Kunming] for the purpose of maintaining the free public school and educating talented people—dated the 4th day of the 11th month, 1739." The text was composed principally of the record of a dispute over an encroachment on land set aside for the support of the school and a record of gifts of land to the school in 1731. It is also significant that at the time the monument was set up, a record was made that the school was established "a long time ago." Just how long there is no way of telling although it might be noted that the earliest-dated graves which we could find in the vicinity belonged to the Ming dynasty (1368–1644). The monument which we had exposed we covered again, as no place seemed safer from the ravages of war.

Between the early eighteenth century and the twentieth, we could discover no further record of a village school, and apparently it went out of existence for a time. This is not surprising as education was commonly carried on for the upper classes during the Ch'ing dynasty (1644–1911) by the system of individual family tutors, while families of the other classes grouped together and engaged their own teacher.

In 1907, however, the school was re-established in the temple at P'i Chi Kuan. At this time it was the only school in the *hsiang*. Two years later it was moved to the centrally located P'u Hsien

temple on the hill a few hundred feet behind Kao Yao. By this time
three more schools had started, one in each of the other *pao* of the
hsiang. In 1919, the school was brought into the village itself where
it was located in a temple compound constructed from public funds
in 1908, and there it had been ever since. Finally the priests of the
Hua Ting temple (third from the top among the hill temples) started
a school, which made a total of five in the *hsiang*.

The administration of the school was headed by the school manager who was appointed by the village council whenever the office
became vacant through death or resignation. The school manager
had the responsibility of collecting the school funds, paying the
teacher, and supplying him with his allowance of rice and tea. He
also had to buy chalk for the school, manage the property, and be
responsible for seeing that all children between the ages of six and
twelve attended school. All in all, this was quite complicated, making this public office one of the most important in the community.

As the school sign indicated, one of the principal sources of income came from the shore tax, which was a charge of one copper
($.005) for each person who was taken by boat to or from the vil-
lage. To collect the $30.00 indicated on the sign meant that six thou-
sand passengers arrived or departed from Kao Yao each year, or
about sixteen individuals daily. The boatmen themselves kept count,
one being appointed to watch each day. Also, the boatmen without
passengers checked on those who carried them, as they were responsible as a group for the money.

The school's ten *mou* of rice land in Kao Yao produced more
than ten *piculs* of rice as rental. Half was in red rice, half in white,
which at current prices brought about $47.50 for ten *piculs*.* In P'i
Chi Kuan, the rice fields which produced the school tax were poor
because they lay in the range of flood water which rotted the rice.
Consequently the income was apt to be smaller than the area of land
would indicate. To these items were added the rentals from the six
houses on the school compound, each of which brought about $6.00
a year. There had never been any tuition fees for the students.

Against this income had to be charged the teacher's salary of
$120.00 a year plus rice, and that of the school servant which was
$15.00, as well as certain minor items for chalk, kerosene, and rare
repairs. It was expected that the annual income of the school should
leave some profit for the school manager in order to compensate him

---

* A *picul* was approximately 133 pounds.

for advancing the funds which he had to do, as well as for the trouble of making collections which was not always easy and became one of the principal sources of stress in the village. In our first few days in Kao Yao, while sitting in a teahouse, we saw the school manager, whom we were then aware of as our landlord, trying to garner some of the school income, making the plea that it was a matter of public funds, while the individual spoken to defended his laxity on the ground of being poor. Although the engagement was by no means violent, it served to attract our attention. The previous manager had resigned in 1935 because he could not continue to afford to advance the school funds.

Theoretically the school manager was obliged to report to the department of education if any family, after due persuasion, would not send their children between the ages of six and twelve to school. In such a case the parents could be fined unless the child's labor was essential for the family's support. The family was then encouraged to send the child to night school. Obviously it would be difficult to make compulsory education effective under such conditions, but the manager had the reputation of doing his duty as well as circumstances permitted. Also, there was a government inspector of education in Kunming who visited the school four or five times a year and who could prefer charges against the manager and thus have him removed from his office if he thought the latter had failed in his responsibilities.

The village council also elected a school trustee to assist the school manager. The former officer was always a wealthy member of the community and received no remuneration for his services. In 1938, both offices were held by one man so that it was impossible to observe the relations of one to the other.

Pi, the school teacher, normally went home on Saturday afternoon to see his wife and two children. He taught all year except for a series of two-week vacations in May, September, and January. To his annual salary of $120.00, he was able to add about $20.00 more by underwriting the tax on the sale and killing of animals. Besides his salary he received five *piculs* of rice worth perhaps $25.00 if purchased in the market. According to the rules of the department of education, he should also have received a supply of tea but since, as he said, he had only been able to get twenty or thirty cents worth, he bought it himself.

The school servant earned his $15.00 a year by cleaning the school every morning. He also took care of the teacher's room and helped him to build a fire and cook his meals when he did not go out to eat. Periodically the servant carried school reports to the local office in Ch'ih Chia Pi or sometimes to that of the district government in Ma Chieh (Fig. 5, p. 69). Also, the servant acted as a go-between for the teacher and the school manager. He was sent to the manager's house, for example, to collect the teacher's salary or to tell the former that chalk or kerosene was needed. Actually, the requirements of the position were slight and did not impinge on the servant's regular daytime activities as a farm laborer. Generally he could be seen coming into the compound about seven in the evening and he would soon retire to the bed which was supplied him as part of his compensation.

As noted in the framed memorandum, the school served the two villages of Kao Yao and P'i Chi Kuan, even as was done in the early eighteenth century. Recently, however, most of the P'i Chi Kuan children had found it more convenient to attend school in another village which was nearer to their homes and consequently only about six came to Kao Yao. The school enrollment of seventy-seven had consequently fallen to fifty-two (Pl. 17, p. 125). The following table shows the distribution of students according to age and sex:

Age *	Boys	Girls	Totals
7	–	3	3
8	1	1	2
9	9	8	17
10	11	3	14
11	2	2	4
12	5	1	6
13	1	4	5
14	–	–	–
15	–	1	1
Totals	29	23	52

From statistical summaries of the village population it can be computed with reasonable accuracy that approximately sixty per cent of the children between the ages of six and twelve attended school. Among the boat people, however, of thirty-three children only two were going to school. The figures gave no indication that either sex had any particular advantage over the other in opportunities for edu-

* It must be emphasized that all ages in this volume are given according to the Chinese system wherein a child is referred to as one year of age when born and as a year older the first day of each following year. Therefore, to convert to the Western system, a year and a half must be subtracted in the average case. Cf. Hockett, 1954, pp. 112–113.

cation. This condition had developed only during the preceding few years, however, as a result of a governmental decree that both boys and girls must attend school. Until 1928, there were only one or two girls in the school and, before 1919, none at all as their parents regarded the sending of girls to school as unthinkable.

The official schedule of classes began with a session from seven until eight in the morning except on Mondays when the teacher was usually on his way back from the weekend with his family in Ming Lang. From eight to ten, the children had a free period during which they went home and ate their morning meal. Then they returned to their studies from ten until four in the afternoon, except on Wednesday and Saturday when school closed at three. Also, there was a fifteen minute recess each hour.

Actually, this schedule proved to be only an ideal one, as we soon discovered by being awakened by the children knocking at the gate beneath us at five-thirty in the morning. Since neither the children nor the teacher had watches, considerable irregularity in convening classes inevitably occurred, and if there was a delay, the children played contentedly in the courtyard until the teacher came and blew on his whistle. At least the procedure saved the children from the horrible monotony of forever being what is known as on time. One day we asked Pi how he knew when to call in the students. Without hesitating he answered, "By the sun." We smiled and waited a moment, but we could see that no contradiction of fact crossed his mind. As was not unusual at that season, the rain was pouring down outside.

As stated in the memorandum, there were four classes or grades in the school, each of which sat and carried on recitations together. The following table shows the distribution according to age and grade:

Age	1st	2nd	3rd	4th
7	3	–	–	–
8	2	–	–	–
9	9	4	3	1
10	6	1	2	5
11	–	2	1	1
12	1	1	1	3
13	2	–	–	3
14	–	–	–	–
15	–	–	–	1
Totals	23	8	7	14

A smart student could enter the first grade and in four years be ready to take the examination for the senior school at Ma Chieh, or Horse Market. This village, about five miles to the north, was not in the same *hsiang* as Kao Yao, but in the same sub-district (Fig. 5, p. 69). It comprised more than a hundred Chinese families, many of them Mohammedans, and was noted for its musicians, sedan chairs, and rough mats, as well as for its market for horses and sheep which was held on those animal days of the calendar.* These examinations, which took place in July under the auspices of the *hsiang,* were the real test of the school's capacity for turning out scholars. About three hundred children from various villages had recently taken the examinations and sixty had passed. Four of Pi's students had competed and all had finished among the first twenty, thus surpassing the record of all the other schools. The village people regarded this as bringing considerable prestige to Kao Yao, and the parents of the successful children came personally to thank the teacher.

Many of the children did not move through the school so quickly for various reasons. Some were not promoted because they failed in the monthly written examinations which lasted about an hour. These were undertaken by all grades and the papers marked and returned to the students. Some children dropped out of school for sickness or some other reason. Also, some children, and particularly the girls, returned to school after they had finished, to relearn what they had forgotten.

The school sign devoted a special paragraph to the fact that boys should be trained in good manners, both at a special period each week and generally throughout the course of study. This work formally consisted of reading in a small, thin, paper text called *Common Knowledge* which was a simple compendium of ethics. The students did this themselves, and when they had difficulty, the teacher wrote the characters on the blackboard and explained them. This was the closest approach to anything suggestive of religious education. The curriculum also included mandarin, arithmetic, social hygiene, drawing, music, and physical education. All subjects were taught in all grades. The reading and writing of the local dialect of southwestern mandarin held a place of primary importance in the school studies.

---

* Chinese days are given animal names in a 28-unit series following those of the lunar zodiac. Cf. Bredon and Mitrophanow, 1927: 11–17.

The students of all the grades in their turn learned characters by copying them after the teacher who wrote them on the blackboard. Dictation, common in countries having a phonetically written language, was lacking. For the first grade, composition consisted of filling-in the proper character missing from short sentences which the teacher wrote on the blackboard. The other three grades were given subjects on which they then had to write themes. Also, for the fourth grade, there was special attention given to letter-writing. There was no text, but the teacher presented examples and the children wrote letters to their relatives and friends. For reading, there were texts which the students read aloud, both in unison and in individual recitation periods lasting one or two hours. The children bought their textbooks for a few coppers, and it was the loud reading of them in unison which gave the Chinese school one of its striking contrasts to the American system. Day after day we would hear the rhythmical chanting of the children's voices across the courtyard until it seemed the most natural thing in the world, a kind of vocal symbol that learning was going on. In the school at Kao Yao, there was no attempt to teach the northern or official pronunciation of mandarin.

In teaching arithmetic, Pi put an example on the blackboard and explained it to the students who then worked similar problems in their textbooks. For social hygiene, there was also a textbook containing homely advice which the children read aloud with the teacher. They also learned some of the rudiments of drawing by copying simple pictures which the teacher put up on the blackboards. For this, the student used paper and either brushes or black pencils.

If Pi himself had a favorite subject, it was certainly music, and a day did not pass without one or more sessions on his little organ. He knew more than twenty pieces and he would select one, writing the words on the blackboard with arabic numerals to indicate the notes. Then he would play the tune and the children would sing, but with indifferent success. He had a poor opinion of his own voice and frequently invited one of his former students, a girl, to conduct the vocal work. Also, I think he liked the girl who provided a very modest touch of glamor to further his interest. There was a text available for music, but he preferred his own selection of songs, as did we. Frequently when he would see us eating our late dinner on the stage, he would bring his organ out onto the school porch and give us a concert while we watched the last rays of the sun sink behind the pine-covered hills.

Physical education was scarcely understood in the European sense. Supposedly, the children marched around the schoolyard, but we only saw them form into a line and walk into school. Occasionally they picked the weeds in the small school flower garden, and we asked Pi if this was physical education, but he said it was not. Sometimes the children ran races or jumped over benches but merely as unformalized play. Setting-up exercises or precision drill was certainly an anomaly in the classical ideal of Chinese scholarship, but the government was already making an effort to include it. There were no manual activities such as weaving, but it was said that in the senior schools, various types of handwork were taught.

Discipline was based on certain ideals of behavior which the teacher told the students they must follow. We simply copied them down as Pi happened to think of them and then made them into the list given below:

> The children must get up early in the morning and come to school
> They must be quiet when not reciting
> They must not fight or quarrel
> They must sit up straight in school
> They must hold their writing brushes directly in front of the nose (i.e., in the median line of the body)
> They must pay attention to the teacher at the proper times
> They must not spit in the classroom
> They must remain in their seats except when reciting, and then they must stand erect
> They must keep the buttons of their clothes fastened
> They must not dirty their textbooks

To think that the children vigorously followed these rules would mark one as blind to realities as to believe that American children did not whisper in school. Some of these ideals came as a shock when we recorded them after visiting the school off and on for several weeks. It had not occurred to me, for example, that the teacher expected the children not reciting to always stay in their seats, and observation proved his standard to be very different in this respect from American ones. That the children got up early in the morning, we have already given evidence. Behavior such as being quiet, sitting up straight, and paying attention was hard to measure, but we noticed no great distinction in these matters which would categorize the boys and girls of Kao Yao as different from others of their age. We were very conscious of children spreading ink over their textbooks and everything else, an activity which seemed in direct contradiction to the last of the precepts, but perhaps I had the prejudices of a fussy old pedant.

According to Pi, the commonest infraction of the rules was spitting, which should surprise no one familiar with old China. The teacher unconsciously spat on the floor while having dinner with us. The next most common failing of the children was disturbing the classes by talking. Actually, a certain amount of conversation was permitted, and we observed censure only when the noise interfered with other activities.

Punishments for breach of discipline consisted of whipping the palms of the hands with a light bamboo switch, making the recalcitrant kneel, or keeping the child after school. Whipping was apparently the severest, commonest, and most effective penalty. Pi said he administered the bamboo principally when children were late or for spitting. Every once in a while we heard his voice rise, silence descend on the school, and then the short, swishing sound of the bamboo going through the air. Often we did not hear it all day, and never did we hear a child cry in consequence.

Although kneeling was said to be a less severe punishment than whipping, the greatest stress observed in a case of discipline involved it. At one noon recess the teacher reprimanded a small girl in the courtyard. She cried a little. The teacher told her to kneel, but she failed to respond immediately and he gave her a gentle push with his cloth-soled shoe. All the children stopped their play and watched in fascinated silence. The girl whimpered and Pi went into the schoolroom and came out with his bamboo switch. He hit her over the back of the legs once, but not very hard, which did not make her cry any louder. He was obviously angry over the proceeding and went inside again. The rest of the children soon returned to their play, paying no attention to the girl who continued to kneel for about ten minutes. Then the teacher came out and gave her a short lecture after which she got up and went off looking very sheepish.

Later we asked Pi the cause of the punishment and he told us that she had been fighting with a smaller boy who had gone home crying and then returned with his mother who protested. In such circumstances, he explained, it was almost necessary to punish the other child, even when the guilt was not altogether clear. Pi was a mild-mannered man not given to overmuch discipline, and the children obviously liked him. He had apparently been annoyed only by the child's disobedience. Kneeling was also the punishment for coming to school with dirty clothes, but we observed no instance of it being administered for this cause. When a child talked too much in school, he was made to stand, and if that had no effect, the teacher made the offender hold a stone in his mouth. Pi said he had to administer this punishment about once a month.

The children's play during the summer of our observation was fairly uniform and a description of the activity during a morning recess can be taken as typical. Eight or ten children had returned from breakfast, two of whom were girls. Four or five of the boys had small sling-shots such as one sees in America, and they were flinging pebbles in various directions. The boys were playing with whip tops (Pl. 13, p. 93). One boy climbed on another and proceeded to ride pickaback but had not gone far before a third also tried to mount and all three fell to the ground. One of the boys and one of the girls threatened each other, he with his sling-shot and she with a clump of dirt. She finally threw it irresolutely but there was no trouble, the play being obviously friendly. It is perhaps significant that we never saw any of the children engage in even a halfway serious fight.

Another boy was going around with pieces of blue paper over his eyes. A few minutes later he was holding on to the coat of the smallest boy in the group, evidently pretending that he himself were a blind man. The small boy had on only a coat while the others had trousers to above the knees besides their usual blue jackets. One lad amused himself by trying to climb an upright post in the yard using only his hands and feet in Polynesian fashion. At other times we saw little girls playing ring-around-the-rosy, and often after a downpour the children made mudpies and dammed up the escaping water into lakes and canals. Both boys and girls played a simple form of jackstones, catching the pebbles on the back of the hand. Boys sometimes went swimming on hot days, but girls never.

One popular game among the boys was throwing-at-pictures. The participants had collected the small illustrated cards given away

13. CHILDREN PLAYING WITH TOPS

in packages of cigarettes and used them for the game, two being set up on the ground leaning against each other. The front card was placed almost vertically with its long edge on the ground and with support from a piece of broken tile. Two or more children played, each leaning a card behind the first one. Then they lagged from beside the cards to an imaginary line some distance in front, using more pieces of broken tile of which there was always a supply from the roofs. The one who lagged the farthest had the first opportunity to toss his tile back at the cards, and then the others took turns until someone knocked the cards down. Whoever did, took them all.

One boy who was not playing apparently had a side bet on a throw, since he gave three others a ticket when the player missed. There was some argument with a fourth boy who insisted on being paid. We thought there might be a fight at one point, but finally the loser tried to stuff the questioned card' down inside the collar of the plaintiff's coat to the general amusement of all.

One of the cleverest children was the boy adopted by one of our neighbors. He always played alone and apparently with great personal assurance. One evening I was studying Chinese with the cook, repeating words after him to acquire the local pronunciation. The boy was on the school porch and attracted my attention by calling out a correction with complete nonchalance whenever I made a mistake. He was constructing some kind of toy, so I went down to see it. From a large cardboard cigarette box he had fashioned an automobile with axles of split bamboo and wheels of several thicknesses of the cardboard. In front he had cut two holes for lights and also two windows on each side which he had cleverly fitted with green transparent material. Then he put an old opium lamp inside and lighted it. When I went back to our stage, I was so pleased by the display which he made by pulling the whole contraption with a string up and down the dark porch that I called him over and gave him three peaches. Despite his reputation and the trouble he once caused me, I thereafter always regarded him as one of my favorites in the village.

Pi, apart from his regular classes, also conducted an evening school throughout the year in three terms of four months beginning the first of February, June, and October. The class schedule ran from seven until nine with one fifteen-minute recess. Reading, writing, and the use of the abacus were the subjects taught, the textbooks being supplied free of charge by the board of education. According to Pi, there were about forty pupils between the ages of fifteen and forty-five, all of whom worked during the daytime. During the period of our residence, the class was apparently small as we counted generally only eight or nine in attendance.

The effect of the school on the Kao Yao residents over six years old appeared from an analysis of the data on literacy, and it may be quickly appreciated from a consideration of the following table.

Age and Sex Groups	Village People		Boat People		Sub-total		Totals
	Lit.	Non-lit.	Lit.	Non-lit.	Lit.	Non-lit.	
Males (6–20)	39	19	1	19	40	38	78
Females (6–20)	34	53	1	36	35	89	124
Sub-totals	73	72	2	55	75	127	202
Males (over 20)	59	66	1	60	60	126	186
Females (over 20)	4	159	–	55	4	214	218
Sub-totals	63	225	1	115	64	340	404
Totals	136	297	3	170	139	467	606

The table showed the sharp demarcation between the rate of literacy of the boat people and those of the village. If we take the total population including the one hundred and two children less than six years old not listed on the table we find that 19.64 per cent of the total population was literate and, of these, 71.94 per cent were males. Contrasting the village people with the boat people on the same basis, 27.36 per cent of the former were literate, but only 1.42 per cent of the latter. Life on the water obviously made it difficult, if not almost impossible, for the boat people to send their children to school and the traditional lack of educational opportunities undoubtedly contributed to their lower social and economic position.

Setting the boat people aside as being, for all practical purposes, illiterate, we noted several interesting things about the village group. One was the sharp improvement in the educational condition of women just previous to 1938. For example, whereas 39.08 per cent of the girls between six and twenty years of age were literate, only 2.45 per cent of the women over twenty could be put in the same class. This could be shown in another way by saying that although

one found a reasonable 53.42 per cent of the literate village population between the ages of six and twenty to be male, the literate population over twenty was 93.65 per cent male.

The old Chinese judgments on literacy disregarded the education of women as unimportant. If we did also, we would find that
47.20 per cent of the village males over twenty could have been
classed as literate, and that this figure could be improved for boys
between six and twenty to 67.24 per cent.

The whole problem of literacy had to be considered in the light
of what that concept meant. Although a few individuals in the village could read the average book, the majority only knew a relatively few characters which made the statistics not comparable to
American averages on literacy. The discrepancy seemed to be primarily caused by the radical difference between the structure of the
Chinese and Indo-European written languages, the former being
made up of ideographic characters and the latter of phonetic symbols.
When an American child learns to read and write, he develops a
feeling for the correspondence between written syllables and his
everyday speech which helps him tremendously in deciphering the
printed page, and we often see how a relatively ignorant person will
attempt to write words he may never have seen, the result being
generally decipherable although badly misspelled.

In Chinese, the spoken word gave little or no key to the complexities of the written character and the writer either knew them or
he did not. Furthermore, it had only been recently that the printed
characters had paralleled the spoken words, since the classical form
of writing disregarded the characters used to clarify speech. As one
might suspect, there was a school of Chinese thought which believed
that phonetic writing should be introduced, but the effort seemed
doomed to failure, not only because of the controlling force of custom,
but because the Chinese ideographic system of characters gave to
the whole country, broken up by many mutually unintelligible dia-
lects, a common written language which had a stability through centuries that would have been impossible to achieve with a phonetic
alphabet. Under the system which had so long existed, the Chinese
boys and girls of Kao Yao certainly faced a considerably harder task
in learning to read and write than did their American or European
contemporaries.

7

THE VILLAGE BUILDINGS

WEARY FROM considering the problems of education on which we had been writing most of the afternoon, we set off for a walk down the street. The appearance of the village buildings was becoming more familiar, and it was possible to analyze their construction from an accumulation of images. Apparently in Kunming district to which Kao Yao belonged, stone was readily available, a point of contrast with most of the more populated areas of China. In fact, only two or three miles south along the lake there was a village named Lung Wang Miao (Fig. 5, p. 69), or Dragon King Temple, which was noted for its quarry, as well as for a deposit of coal. Most of the stone was transported across the lake by boat people among the eighty Chinese families who lived there, but some of this building material had undoubtedly been diverted to Kao Yao.

Although no one in the latter place was rich enough to build a whole house of stone, it was conspicuous in foundations. Our school compound probably contained more stone than any other building, three broad steps across the front being fashioned of large blocks (Pl. 6, p. 65; Pl. 13, p. 93). Also, there were various ornamental facings and corners of the same material. Apart from the stone foundations of walls, apparently standard for better structures in the village, the use of stone socles to support wood posts was considered essential. When the post was square, the socle was square; when the post was round, the socle was normally barrel shaped and placed on top of a smooth stone which had its upper surface cut to match the socle (Pl. 5, p. 61; Pl. 13, p. 93). All along the street, blocks of stone were in evidence forming curbs, raised areas on which to stand in front of stores, the lower courses of some walls, the paving of the street, and the covered drain (Pl. 2, p. 28; Pl. 16, p. 103; Pl. 25, p. 166; Pl. 28, p. 186). At the end of the village was the stone-edged jetty and, beyond it, a breakwater in semicircular shape.

Stone obviously played an important role in protecting both wood and sun-dried bricks of houses from erosion by water, as well as the land itself.

When stonework was needed, masons were usually hired from another village, for Kao Yao had only one, and he was not a popular man. Several professionals resided at Ch'ih Chia Pi (Fig. 5, p. 69), or Wall of the Ch'ih Family, a predominantly Lolo settlement of about two hundred families less than two miles away on the road to Kunming. It was a place noted for a ceremony involving swings which took place on the 3rd of the 1st month. Most of the people were farmers, but there were also some carpenters. Stonemasons were also available at Yang Chia Ts'un (Fig. 5, p. 69), or Village of the Yang Family, a mile or two south along the lake, and more at Lung Wang Miao, mentioned as having a quarry.

This localization of professions in different communities characterized the Kunming area, farming being the only activity which was widely shared. Even the commonest Kao Yao buildings composed of sun-dried brick (Pl. 7, p. 67) were usually constructed by outsiders who came from any of three Lolo villages, Ming Lang (Fig. 5, p. 69), Tien Chung (exact location uncertain),or Yü Ch'i (Fig. 2, p. 15), or from either of two Chinese communities, the village of Hsia Yao (Fig. 5, p. 69) or a town called Ho Hsi (Fig. 2, p. 15), or West of the River, of about three thousand families, located four days' walk south of Kunming. Besides having carpenters and builders, Ho Hsi was noted for its production of cloth. Since Lolo and Chinese used identical structures, it did not matter which were employed. Poor rice land or communication facilities were given as reasons for villagers concentrating on the building trade.

The walls in Kao Yao varied from the crudest kind of clay work to elaborately laid bricks, some of which were fired in a kiln. For the most part, rectangular forms of sun-dried clay with a maximum measurement of less than a foot appeared to be the popular material. The courses often varied in the manner of laying, no doubt to add strength while giving a pleasing patterned appearance when not plastered over with a smooth clay facing (Pl. 25, p. 166).

Rarely, as in the front walls of the school or in the porticos of the houses of some wealthy families, long-lasting kiln-fired brick were substituted for the more commonplace material (Pl. 13, p. 93). It is reasonable to believe that some of these bricks were brought

14. WOMAN FLAILING GRAIN

from the previously mentioned village of Hsia Yao, or Kiln of the
Hsia Family, five miles away on the road to Kunming. That community of about two hundred families was also noted for its roof
tiles. At times, however, it was the craftsmen who were imported
rather than their products, two kilns being available for use when
needed below the nearby village of P'i Chi Kuan. Tile covered most
buildings in Kao Yao (Pl. 2, p. 28; Pl. 4, p. 60; Pl. 5, p. 61; Pl. 11,
p. 76; Pl. 24, p. 157; Pl. 25, p. 166), whereas the cheaper structures
were roofed with thatch (Pl. 7, p. 67; Pl. 14, p. 99; Pl. 23, p. 158;
Pl. 28, p. 186; Pl. 33, p. 219). An attempt to survey the roofs that we
can assume included nine-tenths of them, gave us a count of eighty-
four continuous segments that were tile, sixty-five that were thatch.
Such observations might be very misleading, however, unless one un-
derstands that it in no wise indicated the size of the roof units, or how
many rooms each one covered. Also, a rich family was obviously
represented by several tile roofs, whereas a poor one found shelter
under a single segment of thatch.

Our interest in the external appearance of Kao Yao buildings
was soon overshadowed by curiosity as to what was inside them.
Shortly after we started down the street, we decided to call on one
of our nearby neighbors, a plan which was quickly postponed when
we were greeted by vicious dogs that seemed to be hungry for
strangers. A few minutes later, we fortunately met the old man
with whom I had exchanged a Buddhist salutation on the previous
day and he invited us to his home which was one of the best in Kao
Yao. The typical double gate displayed a colored paper picture of
a door god on each side as was usual in the village. His reception
room to which he took us had a floor of hard clay and was well
furnished with chairs and tables with ornamental carvings and red
lacquer tops which he said were purchased in Kunming. The doors
of the room were likewise interlaced with carving, but these also
were not a local product.

We soon discovered that our host was named Tuan Huan-chang
(Pl. 15, p. 102), that he was seventy-eight years old, and that his
family had lived in the village more than a hundred years owning
over ten *mou* of land. He proudly informed us that he had four
sons, three of whom were married and all of whom lived with him,
besides three daughters, two of whom were married and the third
engaged, plus a third generation of five grandsons and two grand-

daughters.* He did not mention either his thirty-two-year-old wife or his slave girl, but that hardly could be expected. When we departed, we invited him to have lunch with us the next day.

Enthused over the prospect of visiting more homes, we continued our walk, stopping at a store on the way (Pl. 16, p. 103). In it were sold cigarettes, wine, straw sandals, firecrackers, biscuits, Buddhist candles, candle lanterns, and some prayer paraphernalia, material which for the most part was intended for pilgrims arriving by sampan from Kunming and proceeding to the temples of the Western Hill. Then we made note of an office where one could leave things to be sent to the city.

Farther along we encountered a pock-marked man feeding a horse and a mule. When we stopped and spoke to him, he also invited us to his home which, although in the same pattern as Tuan's, presented an entirely different aspect. Rooms opened onto a porch around a courtyard as before, but in his combination reception and dining room we sat on straw cushions and were served tea from a pewter pot. While I was drinking, a woman drove a pig so close that it scraped against my back as it stumbled into the next room which sheltered the horse.

Our host, Li Fu, a man of thirty-one, told us that in the house lived his mother, one sister, four sisters-in-law with their children, eight pigs, a cat, a dog, and some chickens, besides the mule and the horse. He did not mention his wife nor, on the other hand, his four brothers with whom he held as common property the house and fifteen *mou* of rice land. I could see two of his huge pigs being fed in the court, the process being watched from the porch by the women and children not otherwise engaged. In discussing the house, he said that it was the largest in Kao Yao, having expanded to more than twenty rooms during the course of generations of which he was certain only of the three previous to his own. When Li Fu told us he made his living as a porter, we immediately made an appointment with him to visit us in order that we might have an uninterrupted account of his activities.

Taking our leave, we continued our walk to the end of the quay where we noticed the occupants of two sampans driving a large flock of ducks to their resting place for the night. We examined

* Two of his married sons had established separate families (*chia*), as we later learned.

15. OLD GENTLEMAN

16. STORE ON MAIN STREET

a beautifully fat water buffalo tethered near the landing, and then turned homeward, encountering a flock of young chickens and one lone goose before reaching the market place where the local militia were practicing. Climbing our stairs, we found Pi talking to the cook and immediately engaged him with questions which were only interrupted while he finished teaching his evening session of school.

Pi did not hesitate to divide the houses of Kao Yao into three groups on the basis of quality and form, and we can refer to them as lower-, middle-, and upper-class residences. This threefold distinction was based primarily on the number and arrangement of the rooms, although it was immediately pointed out that lower-class houses had thatch roofs, whereas the others were covered with tiles.

Lower-class houses consisted of either one or two rooms, in the latter case the kitchen being set apart from the combination dining and bedroom (Fig. 6, p. 105). One house in Kao Yao, although theoretically of this lower class, was so atypical that it must be described. This extraordinary hovel, which was not over eight feet wide and ten feet long, was built of old clay bricks only a half-dozen feet away from one of the public toilets. It had a ridge pole not much over six feet high supporting a thatched gable roof, beneath which the ends were closed up with old woven straw hats. This shelter was occupied by a woman named Li and her six-year-old son. Widowed about the time her child was born, she made her living by working on the highway and picking wild mushrooms to sell. Her small son stayed out of school to help her.

A normative plan of a middle-class house reproduced from Pi's sketch is shown in Figure 6, p. 105. It is distinguished by having rooms with a porch arranged around an open, walled court, and in having accommodations for animals as well as people.

The idealized upper-class house was considerably more elaborate than even that of a middle-class family, although not much more land was necessarily involved. The distinction came in having a residence of two floors with the main living quarters above those of the animals, together with other such niceties as a separate ancestral hall. An upper-class home clearly envisaged an extended family as will be seen in examining Pi's plan (Fig. 6, p. 105). In some instances, we had noticed that two-story houses, instead of having the usual inverted-V-shaped gable roof, were surmounted with one vaguely suggesting in cross-section a Greek omega (Pl. 25, p. 166).

HOUSES

LOWER CLASS

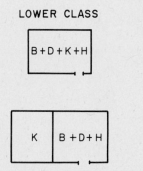

MIDDLE CLASS

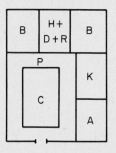

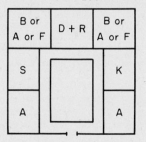

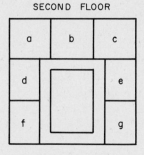

UPPER CLASS

FIRST FLOOR

SECOND FLOOR

A. Animals
B. Bedroom
C. Court
D. Dining room
F. Animal's feed

H. Ancestral hall or shrine
K. Kitchen
P. Porch
S. Study
R. Reception hall

a,c. Old man's bedroom (possibly family head)

b.　　Ancestral hall

d,e. Storage

f,g. Bridal room with continued occupancy

Figure 6. Plan of Houses

At least the ridge was flatly rounded and then the roof dropped off sharply before extending laterally like the more usual ones.

The cost of houses in Kao Yao was said to vary from $200 to $250 for a one-room residence to the $4,000 Li Fu claimed had been spent on his, although the latter figure was hardly comparable since a long period with changing costs was involved. The former university president on whom we had called in Kunming with the hope of renting his house in Kao Yao had reputedly paid $800 the previous year for a plot of land the size of the school compound which it adjoined, and $600 for the three-room house and several small buildings. Sun Lo, another non-participating member of the village was said to have paid over $1,000 for his property several years previously.

In the matter of furnishings, Kao Yao houses were basically the same for all classes, although the quality of some items varied. In the kitchen one found a stove, a vessel in which to cook rice, a vegetable knife with a board on which to cut up the food, an elliptical frying pan with a flat metal spatula to stir its contents, a pair of wood buckets for water, and a carrying pole to convey them to and from the well, plus a wood dipper to transfer water from the buckets when needed (Pl. 25, p. 166). In a family that owned pigs, wood buckets for their feed were also essential and, whether possessing pigs or not, a shallow wood tub in which to wash one's dirty feet was considered a necessity. Glazed earthenware (or stoneware) containers were used in every household (Fig. 7, below). Eared jars served for boiling meat or chicken, as well as for preparing soup. A ladle was associated with the latter, usually one of wood but sometimes of copper or other metal. Large jars provided storage for pickled vegetables.

Figure 7. Glazed Stoneware

The usual dining table was only about a foot high. On it at mealtime one could expect to see bamboo chopsticks and glazed stoneware bowls. Sometimes porcelain dishes appeared, and this was especially true in the case of the teapot. Both rice straw and grass cushions about a foot in diameter and eight inches high, as well as wood stools, were used in the house.

The standard bed was made by extending five strong boards between a pair of wood trestles made like sawhorses approximately a foot and a half high. Theoretically the number of boards should have been odd, but actually some beds did not conform to this ideal. On top of the boards, rice stalks were laid and on top of them a mat, the fineness of which could vary with the price one wanted to pay. Middle-class people were said to lie directly on an added felt blanket, which upper-class individuals likewise used but covered with a sheet. Everyone slept nude, drawing a padded cotton quilt over the body. Upper-class people, however, sometimes interposed a second sheet to complement the lower one. Cylindrical pillows, six inches in diameter and a foot and a half long, stuffed with the husks of grain were standard equipment. Some pillows had square ends and were two feet in length. Upper-class homes frequently had mosquito nets around the beds. Old people, irrespective of sex or class, placed a small vessel for urine conveniently under their beds.

Storage of most materials other than the food and the water previously mentioned was provided for by boxes and baskets (Pl. 16, p. 103; Pl. 28, p. 186). Particularly important was a special type of large, uncarved wood box, commonly of pine stained red. Into one or more was put the family grain, into another, clothing and articles of adornment. The boxes could be piled on top of each other, and most families owned two or three of them. Sometimes boxes made from hides were substituted for storing important papers or money or even for clothes. Shelves or pegs on which to hang things were not seen in the homes, although nails might be used. Instead, a bamboo pole was often suspended horizontally and objects draped over or fastened to it. Baskets served as containers for fresh meat as well as other types of food (Fig. 8, p. 108).

Needless to say, there were objects not necessarily seen in every house. These reflected the special tastes of the occupants as well as their economic position. Articles used in smoking tobacco or those needed for the enjoyment of opium exemplify the former category (Fig. 9, p. 109), while wealthy families in some cases had chairs with tables of matching height, bronze ornaments, scrolls with painting or calligraphy, writing equipment, and quite possibly a clock. Pi guessed that three or four families had a clock, and that possibly a tenth of the men in the village owned a watch. That would amount to about sixteen timepieces among the 122 families in Kao Yao.

Figure 8. Two Baskets and a Scoop

Daily house-cleaning consisted of little if anything more than sweeping the floor. At the year end or, more exactly, beginning with the 27th of the 12th month, the whole house—but ceilings and walls principally—was swept over with a brush made of bamboo twigs unless, by ill chance, the animal corresponding to the year of the birth of anyone in the family was the same as that of the cleaning day—then the sweeping could not be done.

Sometime during the winter, or dry season, cracks in the walls were mended, and the ditches were cleaned or dug deeper wherever such attention was essential to make sure that water would drain off. Once about every five years, the thatching of grass roofs was renewed but only to the degree which was necessary.

It had been our hope to make a plan of Kao Yao so as to check on the actual form of the houses and their relation to courtyards, gardens, and accessory buildings. The initial attempt, however, produced little but the external outlines of the buildings since we were everywhere confronted by walled-in areas which, even when accessible, proved difficult to plot. By good fortune, however, before the end of our stay we found a young man in his twenties who not only knew many of the Kao Yao homes inside and out—a thing natural enough for one born in the village—but had also been given the advantage of middle-school training in Kunming during which time he had been taught the elements of practical drawing for which he showed obvious talent. Happily we engaged him to undertake the project which had been unsuccessfully pursued, and by the last week of our study, he had produced a most admirable plan of the village spread over two sheets of paper approximately forty-two by thirty-one inches in size. Recognizing his gifts, we easily persuaded

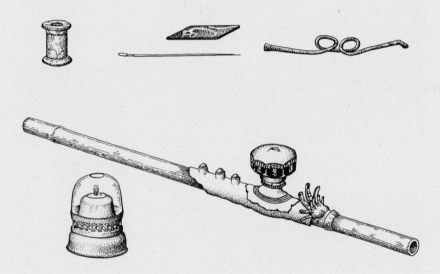

Figure 9. Instruments for Opium Smoking

him to designate additional features and, in another few days, he returned with a completely redrawn edition of his work covered with interesting symbols in various colors satisfying one's curiosity about numerous aspects of Kao Yao ranging from the location of flower gardens and wells to distinguishing true courtyards from simple enclosed plots of ground. Even with its limitations, by using the plan it was quite easy to add to our knowledge (Fig. 10, pp. 110–11).

One of the things the plan provided was a test of the idealized house plans. Curiously, a casual viewing did not seem to confirm them, but after determining which rooms belonged together in household units, it was possible to compute that there actually were 28,

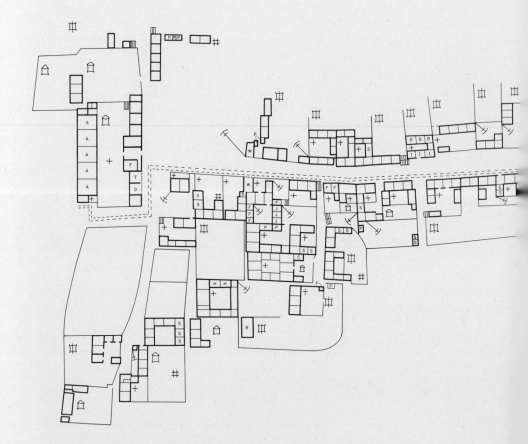

Figure 10. Plan of Kao Yao

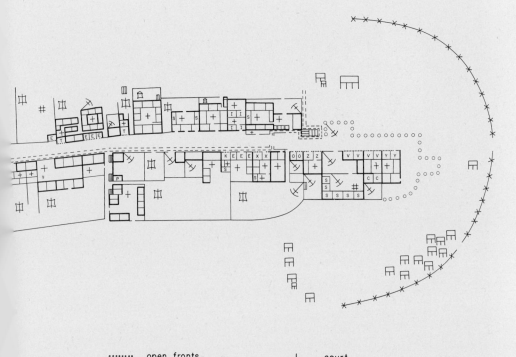

········	open fronts	+	court
⌗	vegetable garden	⊟	toilet
⌂	flower garden	====	drain
#	well	⊟	house over water
⟙	open space	OOOO	jetty
	✕ ✕ ✕	breakwater	

A—School   O—Opium dens
B—Basketmaker   P—Pigsties
C—Coffin shops   R—Rice mill
E—Stores   S—Stables
F—Fuel storages   T—Teahouses
H—Blacksmith   V—Restaurants and teahouses
I—Inns   W—Stores and opium dens
J—Sauce factory   X—Restaurant, inn, and opium den
K—Transport office Y—Restaurant, teahouse, and gambling place
        Z—Teahouse, gambling place, and store

III

or 26.92 per cent, single-room units; 18, or 17.30 per cent, double-room units; 14, or 13.46 per cent, L-shaped units; and 17, or 16.34 per cent, U-shaped units; leaving only 27, or 25.96 per cent, with other ground plans out of the total 104.* Of these latter variants, 7, or 6.73 per cent, consisted of three rooms in a line, while another had ten rooms completely surrounding a court plus two projecting rooms. Most of the variant plans, however, consisted of detached rooms, pairs of single- or double-room units, and bisected L-shaped ones.

It became perfectly obvious that the normal household unit was surrounded by walls and included in 64 instances courtyards. In the remaining 40 units, 23 adjoined open areas without porches, 14 vegetable gardens, and 3 flower gardens. Except for the open areas juxtaposed to the marketplace and a good many of the vegetable gardens that extended to the rice fields north of the village, all these 40 units also were walled. It is significant that courtyards were associated with L- and U-shaped houses for, logically enough, 31 of the 40 units without them proved to be buildings of either single or double rooms, or those with three rooms in a line. Approaching the data in another way, we find that 53 households, or 50.96 per cent of those in Kao Yao, occupied bulidings of one, two, or three rooms in a line, and that these, of which three-fifths lacked the traditional courtyard, comprised on the whole the lower-class dwellings. Even most of the remaining nine units with more-complex ground plans, but also without courtyards, fall into the category of readily explainable exceptions as, for instance, when the houses belonged to rich non-participating village residents or were reserved for the absentee owner, or were part of the school compound.

According to Pi, the private rooms of an upper-class residential unit should have been made progressively smaller as they approached the street, thus allowing for rank in the family, the elders sleeping at the rear near the ancestral hall. This detail, if true in fact, was not confirmed by the plan, although such accuracy in scaling could hardly be expected. What was notable, however, was that nine of the U-shaped units instead of facing the street as expected, were

---

* In this section, the term household unit includes possibly three or four in which no one slept in any of the rooms, as for instance in the school itself, some areas of the school compound, and several fuel storerooms.

turned parallel to it, while three even faced away from it. Also, several U-shaped compounds which did face the street had another residence unit in place of the expected wall. This shift from the theory may possibly have resulted because Kao Yao had so many travelers passing through it.

Other things were discovered from the ground plan of Kao Yao. We could count 380 occupied ground-floor rooms of which some 98 were known to have been used for other than simple occupancy by members of the family. The following list presents the distribution by function and number of rooms. The numbers of units (of juxtaposed rooms) are given in parentheses. The letters in parentheses give the key for locating the rooms on the plan of Kao Yao (Fig. 10, pp. 110–11).

Stables (14)—30 rooms (S)
Pigsties (6)—9 rooms (P)
Fuel storages (6)—9 rooms (F)
Stores (3)—7 rooms (E)
Inns (2)—7 rooms (I)
School (1)—5 rooms (A)
Restaurants and teahouses (2)—4 rooms (V)
Teahouses (3)—3 rooms (T)
Opium dens (2)—3 rooms (O)
Coffin shops (2)—3 rooms (C)
Basketmaker (1)—3 rooms (B)
Sauce factory (1)—3 rooms (J)
Stores and opium dens (2)—2 rooms (W)
Restaurant, inn, and opium den (1)—2 rooms (X)
Restaurant, teahouse, and gambling place (1)—2 rooms (Y)
Teahouse, gambling place, and store (1)—2 rooms (Z)
Blacksmith (1)—2 rooms (H)
Rice mill (1)—1 room (R)
Transport office (1)—1 room (K)

Disregarding the overlapping use of rooms where it existed, we can obtain a slightly different perspective on some of the major business activities of Kao Yao.

Teahouses (7)—11 rooms
Stores (6)—11 rooms
Opium dens (5)—7 rooms
Restaurants (4)—8 rooms
Inns (3)—9 rooms
Gambling places (2)—4 rooms

It should be noted that the institutions listed above were normally also used as residences by their operators. Unfortunately our map maker did not get around to indicating which buildings had two stories but, except for the providers of opium, it is doubtful that second-floor rooms were used for anything but sleeping quarters and ancestral halls, the other activities that have been listed being confined to the first floor.

Finally, near the eastern end of the plan, just below the line where the drain crossed the street, a pair of heavy lines near the curbs indicated the few remnants of a three-story gatehouse which once served as a school. The building burned down about 1932, together with thirty or more rooms at the end of the street.

Before we went to bed, I queried the cook about his killing one of the five-inch lizards that shared our home and sometimes left droppings on my notepaper in passing overhead. He regarded it as poisonous, although the schoolteacher said it was not. The cook insisted that if he had not done away with the lizard it might have killed him by crawling up his nose while he slept. The image thus evoked filled me with merriment, and I retired with as much grace as I could.

8

LEADERS AND LINEAGES

OLD MR. TUAN (Pl. 15, p. 102) who was expected for luncheon on Wednesday did not arrive and, quite apart from the cook's effort in acquiring some rose-scented Szechwan wine to entertain the village elder, I suffered a small pain of the kind that comes with losing face. When I did not show any great appreciation of the drink, the cook demonstrated its quality by pouring a little onto a plate and lighting it with a splinter from the stove. The wine burned in a glow of pure alcohol. Then he picked up some of the blue flame on his fingers and rubbed his hands with it, a pretty trick for which I evinced admiration.

Our friend Pi (Pl. 6, p. 65) had practically moved in with us. At least, he did almost everything but sleep in our establishment. His real desire to identify with our household first impressed me when, while cleaning my teeth over the edge of the stage, I observed him dart into his room and come out with his toothbrush to participate in the amenities of oral hygiene while standing beside me. His companionship was both pleasant and profitable, and we never lost our feeling of amicable rapport even when I told Ho to ask him if he could get along at the dinner table with spitting a little less often on the floor. Later, in consequence, he asked Ho if I liked him, and the latter's immediate reply in the affirmative, together with the candid evidence of my good will, eliminated the insecurity caused by my seemingly exotic request.

Having gained a fairly clear conception of the physical character of Kao Yao, we directed our curiosity to comprehending the political organization. We wanted to know how the village was run. This was a simple subject to approach as almost every adult male informant was willing to contribute a statement of fact or opinion. Pi himself effortlessly provided the formal background of the political system, and furthermore introduced us to his mother's sister's son, a very likable man of thirty who was head of the *hsiang* to which Kao Yao belonged. In due course, we also talked to most of the village officers. In summarizing our information we can first consider the external manifestations of government.

Kao Yao was one of approximately thirty *ts'un,* or villages, included in P'i Chi *hsiang.* Since some of the villages were tiny hamlets, however, they were counted as only thirteen, and the latter were grouped to form eight *pao.* Each two of these *pao* were united to form a *hsiao hsiang.* Theoretically, four of such small *hsiang* were combined into a *hsiang,* then eight *hsiang* into a *ch'ü,* and finally eight of the latter into a *hsien,* or district, but in practice the number was variable (Fig. 11, below).

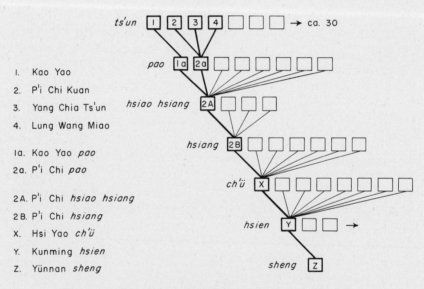

I.   Kao Yao
2.   P'i Chi Kuan
3.   Yang Chia Ts'un
4.   Lung Wang Miao

Ia. Kao Yao *pao*
2a. P'i Chi *pao*

2A. P'i Chi *hsiao hsiang*
2B. P'i Chi *hsiang*
X.   Hsi Yao *ch'ü*
Y.   Kunming *hsien*
Z.   Yünnan *sheng*

Figure 11. Diagram of the Political Affiliations of Kao Yao

Kao Yao itself was a *pao* as well as a village and was associated with a second *pao* to form a *hsiao hsiang.* This second *pao,* incorporating some 266 families, was made up of P'i Chi Kuan, which may be remembered as the scene of the schoolteachers' luncheon; also Yang Chia Ts'un, or Village of the Yang Family, located a little over a mile south along the lake, a place of about ten Chinese farming families noted for its bamboos; and thirdly, Lung Wang Miao, previously mentioned for its quarry, another mile south on the lake (Fig. 5, p. 69). With these four villages, three other *hsiao hsiang* combined to form P'i Chi *hsiang* which spread over an area about eight miles long and included 970 families. P'i Chi *hsiang* was part of a *ch'ü* named Hsi Yao, while the latter was a sub-district of Kun-ming *hsien,* one of the more important districts of the *sheng,* or province, of Yünnan.

Political control on a level above Kao Yao was vested in the *hsiang* council consisting of the heads of the *pao,* the head of the *hsiang* itself, plus the chief of militia, and a secretary. These last three officers, and the council servant, resided in Ch'ih Chia Pi (Fig. 5, p. 69), the largest village of P'i Chi *hsiang* and previously mentioned as one source of stonemasons. Actually, each of these there officers might have been selected from any of the villages in the *hsiang.* Apparently before 1936, village representation was limited to heads of the four *hsiao hsiang,* but afterward the membership was expanded.

Although we were unable to devote much time to a study of the political organization above village level, it became clear that the *hsiang* council functioned as an intermediate control between the district government and the villages, directives of the national and provincial authorities, as well as some measure of public protec-tion, being exchanged for taxes. Pi's cousin, the head of P'i Chi *hsiang,* informed us on the day of his first visit, for example, that he was providing us with police protection at night, a courtesy which I rather forcefully requested he withdraw as I was afraid that the advent of any such officers would intrude upon the effec-tiveness of our work. Ho confided to me at the time that he thought Pi's cousin was a Lolo, since a Chinese would not have sat down so quickly. Some functions of government, however, were not chan-neled through the *hsiang* office as, for instance, the supervision of education which was undertaken in the villages by representatives of the *hsien,* or district, department directly. Furthermore, village taxes seem to have been paid directly to the *hsien* without going through the hands of *hsiang* officials.

To return to the government of Kao Yao itself, the village coun-cil, according to Pi, consisted of the head of each lineage (surname group), plus a few old men by right of age and prestige and, *ex officio,* the schoolteacher himself, although the latter had no vote, being more or less an outsider. The village council met in one of the teahouses (shifting from time to time to spread their trade) following a meeting of the *hsiang* council. In the 12th month there was an annual meeting in Kao Yao to elect the head of the council, and consequently the *pao* (since Kao Yao itself was a *pao*) for a term of one year beginning on the 20th of that month. Theoretically, each lineage had the right to have its head elected *pao* head in turn, but some lineages were passed over on the grounds that their candidates were not suitable for the position by reason of character, age, or the lack of other more subtle qualifications. The representatives of the dominant lineages had a great deal of influence in the choice, and there was reason to believe that in practice less than half of the lineages in Kao Yao were even represented on the council, since most of them consisted of only one family without the required minimum of prestige and power. The obligations of the council included the election of a school manager, a school trustee, and a forest manager, as well as the selection of a schoolteacher, although these offices were not yearly appointments. It may be noted that in case of a disagreement in any matter of business, the council members voted by a showing of hands.

The principal duty of the village head was to collect the land taxes and forward them to Kunming. He also had to enlist men for the armed forces. Quite naturally, he was assisted (or hindered) by his associates on the council, the heads of the leading lineages. Occasionally he called public meetings to discuss such matters as how required public works should be shared or who should be enrolled in the army. It was the effective way of resolving community problems, the news of which, like most other news, was first disseminated through the teahouses. Further, he had charge of the communal property of the village—the quay, the street, the marketplace, the temple, and the school compound—as well as being responsible for keeping the peace. He could supply coffins for the indigent dead, although not food to the starving. It was a position requiring a great deal of tact.

The duties of the school manager have been presented in discussing the school. His replacement usually occurred only when he died or resigned but, as has been said, the incumbent could be ousted on charges of the school inspector. The position was not a sinecure that everyone wanted, and the previous officeholder had resigned in 1935 because he could not afford to advance the necessary funds.

The forest manager was charged with looking after the trees

reserved to supply the wood necessary as timber for building or other village purposes. When someone wished to buy a tree, the price was determined by the manager who then reported it to the council in order to discover if there were any objections. If not, the department of reconstruction in Kunming was informed, and an agent was sent out by them to collect three per cent of the sale money in order that new seed might be supplied. It was the manager's duty to have new trees planted, and he paid someone to do the work from the remainder of the money collected from the sale. Any surplus of funds over five dollars, the manager loaned at an interest of two per cent a month to be paid in cash, or about three per cent if in rice. The manager had also to see that the grass was burned in the village forest and to report to the government in the event that any trees were stolen. For his efforts, he received no financial return, but he was allowed a dollar for each trip to the city that the business required, of which there were usually three or four in a year. If the dollar was insufficient for his expenses, he paid the additional charges himself. In practice, some old man was given the position as it was considered an easy one.

There was also a public courier who lived in the village temple and was its caretaker. For his services he was paid about five hundred catties of rice a year from public funds, and he also was given five cents or more when any villager sacrificed a chicken at the temple. On request, the courier would cry out official news on the Kao Yao street, sometimes beating on a gong to be sure his message would be heard. He also, on occasions, posted official notices outside the school compound and the teahouses. In Ma Chieh (Fig. 5, p. 69), previously mentioned as the place where school examinations were taken, news was regularly posted on the wall by a man who was paid to do so, but there was no such service in Kao Yao which also lacked postal service and newspapers. The courier did not deliver invitations to family feasts, these usually being given to someone who was expected to pass by the home of the people addressed.

There was one club which had some bearing on the government of Kao Yao since it was a district organization of official standing with a branch in each village. The Reform Club had as its purpose the social and moral improvement of the society. Examples of the goals which were presented included such noteworthy acts as dis-

couraging the invitation of guests who came to stay five or six days
(since this wasted money) and stopping the smoking of opium, as
well as the purchase of white cloth presented to mourners at funerals.
People were also to be encouraged to dress uniformly, which really
meant that they should not wear long, full sleeves (wasteful), and
that young women should not cover the tops of their heads to avoid
fixing their hair properly (a weakness of old women).

Twice a year, in the 2nd and 8th months, there was a meeting
of the whole district membership in Ch'ih Chia Pi. This group
elected the heads of the village branches, and each might have one,
two, or none at all. Pi said the village head in Kao Yao was re-
elected year after year as head of the local Reform Club. Membership was limited to sixty in each branch, only men of good reputation being considered by the heads of the branches who had the
power of acceptance or refusal. There were dues of fifty cents a
year in order to pay for sending out notices of meetings and for
purchasing the tea consumed at them. It was possible to have an
extra meeting if some special problem involving bad behavior arose.
In theory, the Reform Club could exert its influence by fines. For
example, a person who smoked two *ch'ien* (about one-quarter ounce)
of opium could be assessed fifty cents.

The Reform Club had over fifty members in Kao Yao, it was
claimed. Educated people and those holding public office were all
said to belong but, on examination, this did not prove to be so. Tu,
the school manager, was reported to be too busy to belong, and the
distinguished Mr. Tuan was not a member. As it turned out, the
Reform Club had little prestige and even less power in Kao Yao.
The only other clubs were Buddhist organizations which will be
dealt with farther on.

Our interest in village government led naturally to a consideration of the family and lineage. As elsewhere in China, one found
the patrilineal lineage system in which primary relationships were
recognized only through the father's line, a unit distinguished by
surname through a recognized series of antecedent generations. In
our first talks with Pi on this subject, he informed us that there
were eleven lineages in the village and he listed them as follows:

1. Li	5. Tuan	9. T'ang
2. Yang	6. Tu	10. Feng
3. Chang	7. Mei	11. Liu
4. T'ao	8. Tai	

His own census proved the gross unreliability of memory in such
matters for, as clearly indicated by the surnames, there were thirty
lineages represented in Kao Yao, not counting himself and several
non-participating families. These we list below in the order of the
number of families indicated in parentheses.

1. Yang (23)	11. Chou (2)	21. Ku (1)
2. Li (22)	12. Hsu (2)	22. Kung (1)
3. Chang (16)	13. Tung (2)	23. Mei (1)
4. Tuan (14)	14. Ch'en (1)	24. Mi (1)
5. Tu (7)	15. Chin (1)	25. Tai (1)
6. Sun (5)	16. Ch'u (1)	26. T'ang (1)
7. Wang (4)	17. Feng (1)	27. Wu (1)
8. Liu (3)	18. Han (1)	28. Yeh (1)
9. T'ao (3)	19. Hu (1)	29. Yen (1)
10. Chao (2)	20. Kao (1)	30. Yü (1)

From our list it is first of all obvious that Kao Yao was not
one of those villages (notably of southeast China) in which a single
lineage comprised, or overwhelmingly dominated, the population.
The numerical superiority of the Yang family by itself was too slight
to give any meaningful advantage over the Li lineage, or for that
matter over those of the Chang's or Tuan's. The village head, we
must note, was a Liu, and both the school manager and the forest
manager were named Tu.

Considering the family unit itself, our first concern was to determine what was meant by the term *chia*. We not only have a list of
the individuals constituting the 122 *chia* of Kao Yao but, more
fortunately, the recorded statement of what the word *chia* meant
to the compiler. The *chia,* family, he defined as a group of individuals who lived in the same house and ate at the same table.
This group might include a man's grandparents, parents, wife or
wives, brothers, sisters, and brothers' wives, together with those
individuals' children. Any patrilineal relative, in fact, could be
part of the group, and also an adopted son-in-law and his mother.
It will be appreciated that in the patrilineal system of Kao Yao,
almost all these members of the *chia* would have the same surname.
The rare exceptions included the mother of an adopted son-in-law
or a child whose family name had been changed in the belief that
his life would be spared, evil fortune having killed his elder brothers.

The size of the families as shown by the Kao Yao list varied
from a single Chang widow to ten individuals in another Chang

family. The latter group consisted of a sixty-one-year-old man, his wife, their three sons aged thirty-five, thirty-two, and fifteen respectively, the two older sons' wives, and three granddaughters. Curiously, each of the three wives was one year younger than her husband. The average membership of all the 122 families in Kao Yao was only 4.07 individuals.

Although it was specifically stated that most families occupied one house alone, the same informant insisted that it was not uncommon for two or even three families to share the same house, the additional families usually paying rent. In some cases however, two families occupying a house might be headed by two brothers who had formed new *chia* whether having divided their common property or not. Thus we see that we must distinguish the *chia,* basically defined as the group who ate together; then secondly, the household, or people who lived in a common dwelling; and thirdly, the economic group composed of all the individuals who shared the benefits of property held in common. Unfortunately the period of research did not provide the necessary time to correlate each *chia* with its household and economic group, and to designate their locations on the village plan, although it must be admitted that the ethnographer would probably not have had the sophistication to accomplish the task completely in 1938.

It should be emphasized at this point that, in the census of the village, individuals were listed as *chia* members whether they were living away from home or not and, among Chinese, absences commonly extended for years. As a consequence of this method, there were a few people in the village who were not considered members of it, the outstanding example being Pi himself whose name would properly appear in a census of Ming Lang where his wife and children resided. The Li widow who occupied the hovel earlier described was apparently not included for some similar reason. Also there were four unlisted *chia* that we shall refer to as non-participating families, all of which presented a combination of status, education, and wealth beyond the level of others in Kao Yao. None of these bore the surname of any of the village lineages. Identicalness in the transliteration of the Chinese characters of course means nothing since the names were actually different, the phonetic equivalents notwithstanding.

The first of these outsiders who was named Yu Yün-lung came

to the village and built a house at the southwest corner about 1918. He was then over forty years old and the head of an army division. He still appeared sometimes in the summer, but none of his family were in residence at the time of our visit. Then there was a man over eighty named Ch'ên Ku-i who was once chief of the district government. Interestingly enough, he stated that he had spent nine months in Washington, D.C., about 1908. He had owned a house in the same area as Yu for about ten years, and recently had become a permanent member of the community. He had two wives, one of whom came from Shanghai. She told us that they were afraid of being bombed. As it turned out, the Japanese did not attack the district until later in the year and then did comparatively little damage even in the capital. The third of the non-participators was named Sun Lo. He had built a house adjacent to Yu's several years before 1938. Our informant, Li Fu, considered it the best in the village and reported that it had cost over a thousand dollars. Sun was said to visit the village occasionally. He was a merchant in Kunming and apparently had also held a high office in the district government at one time. Finally, there was the recently constructed summer house of Tung Chai, the former president of the University of Yünnan. In Pi's opinion, it was the best residence in Kao Yao. It was the one we had been unsuccessful in renting, and we never even got within its walls as the house was constantly closed up.

The study of nuclear, extended, and economic families being not only complicated but involved, a presentation of what more we learned about them may better be put off until we have considered other aspects of the life of the village. Unquestionably, our first week in Kao Yao was full of interruptions and difficulties. My intestines had succumbed to a most commonplace attack of dysentery and, although by a bit of heroics I had arranged the conversion of a storeroom beneath our residence into a toilet, my mental annoyance had merely given up priority to one that was physical.

I awakened early the next morning, and Pi came to breakfast. I restricted myself to a little corn cake and dried ham, leaving all the congee for the others who gobbled it gladly. In an uncertain mood and seeking distraction, I suggested that Pi give me a lesson in Chinese. We went to the schoolroom and he began writing characters on the blackboard a dozen at a time which I copied repeating his pronunciation. We began with the names of obvious parts of the anatomy such as ears, eyes, and nose. As the children arrived, they crowded around me, trying to assist despite great bubbles of laughter. Soon I departed, and the incident would have been lost to memory had not these young friends followed me for several days afterward pointing to various parts of their anatomy and yelling the appropriate word, an exchange which I found very comical. They extended their interests and without solicitation would give me the name for a goose or a well, or any other visible object, finally exhausting their efforts by shouting out the names of the various kinds of excrement that dotted the street. As it proved, there were an extraordinary number. For good or for evil, it rained a part of every day, the downpour doing much to run off the debris. Several times when the wash was a little heavy I noticed how the water swirled around the well. Standing over it when the sun had come out, one could still hear the steady drippings from the street disturb its dark contents. On one occasion I became angry at our cook for not obeying our orders to bring water from the well near the temple which I imagined was being less polluted. The location, if not much farther, afforded not so interesting a walk, and I soon relinquished such efforts for improvement.

On Thursday afternoon, we listened to an argument in a teahouse. The school manager was trying to collect taxes, and excuses were being given. Perhaps the incident was responsible for Pi's characterization of the Kao Yao people a little later as cunning. We encountered old Mr. Tuan again and he showed us an antique brass lock, the subject having undoubtedly been brought to his mind by the presence of an itinerant mender of such objects and of ceramic plates and umbrellas. Compelled by a trait which might be called adhesion to purpose, I forthwith again invited Mr. Tuan to dinner whereupon, after saying he had another invitation and was going to drink wine, he quickly took his leave. Pi was at a loss to explain the old man's persistent refusal to eat with us. My reaction had changed to curiosity from one of pique.

Friday I was up before dawn out of deference to my dysentery. I ate no breakfast. It was market day and the vegetable sellers made a great display of colorful produce beneath our windows. Stimulated by their unexpected activity, I examined my camera and found the film holder bent and the ground glass broken. Quickly making essential repairs, I photographed the fair (Pl. 28, p. 186), the empty

17. TEACHER AND SCHOOL CHILDREN

school, and then the children whom I lined up with their teacher on the steps (Pl. 17, p. 125). Then Li Fu the porter appeared, and we worked with him until evening save for interruptions. Some were pleasant. First came a local policeman who said he had wanted to meet us. He stayed a little while and on leaving told the cook he ought to supply us with better tea. Ho said the remark was meant as a compliment. Then the chief of police of the *hsiang* appeared, stating that he had received orders from the ministry of internal affairs to give us protection. We thanked him and declined.

Li Fu was obviously impressed and his cooperation was most amiable. He sympathized with my physical disability and offered to bring me opium with the necessary equipment which, he assured me, if used would not only allay my suffering but cure the disease with which I was afflicted. My temptation to accept his suggestion was contravened by my awareness of the sensitivity which Pi had shown when I had first asked him if there were any opium users in the village. Pi had admitted there were perhaps two or three and the subject was dropped. The market disbanded about four, the cook bringing back two small chickens for which he had paid a dollar and the porter stayed to share one.

That evening, the school manager came to call and when he too offered me his opium pipe, attributing to the drug the same virtues as Li Fu had, I accepted his advice. Perhaps the first three pills which he rolled for me had less physical effect than those that followed, since the art of consuming opium must be learned but the social impact was undelayed. My status in the community immediately changed. Opium smoking being a cause of national shame, the people in Kao Yao had been embarrassed by the presence of a questioning foreigner. Hence they felt grateful toward one with whom their weaknesses were willingly shared.

9

PROPERTY, MANNERS, AND CRIME

OUR FIRST Saturday in Kao Yao was a most memorable one. Before I had finished my third pipe the previous evening, there had been intimations that it would be. One of our neighbors named Mei came to ask our protection from the police. He was fearful of being arrested as the receiver of stolen goods. Our visitor was an unkempt, ill-appearing creature whose wrinkled face made him look older than his sixty-five years. On several occasions, we had heard him quarreling with his wife, a woman of thirty-two. From their den had come the first faint fumes with a sweetish smell vaguely suggesting chocolate that I had learned to recognize as opium. The discovery had pleased me and, toylike, I had turned it in my mind, musing on it as an obsolete bauble of the romantic East. This association had prejudiced me in favor of this unhappy man.

Ho explained that it was thought that Mei had my pen. One of the members of the village council had told him to his face that he was a receiver of stolen goods. I told our visitor I had made no accusations, but that I could not be responsible for what the police might do. Pi vehemently warned the man that he had better find the purloined article, repeating the obvious threat as fear and misery increased on the listener's face. When our neighbor had departed, Pi said that on the morning the pen had disappeared, after calling the children to school he had looked up at the stage and recognized the lingering boy and girl. The boy had further distinguished himself by staying away from school that day. Later, under Pi's questioning, the girl had confessed that her companion—the one whose ingenuity would win my peaches—had absconded with the pen.

There had been so many excitements grasping at my interest that the loss had become shadowed by new demands. The recovery of my property, however, promised a demonstration of social interaction as well as the pen itself, and therefore it was anticipated with pleasure. It was no complete surprise when soon after breakfast

0128 VILLAGE LIFE IN OLD CHINA

we were waited upon by the head of the village and the school manager, as well as the local policeman. They presented me with my
missing pen, stating that they hoped I would not have a bad opinion
of China. I assured them I would not and that the same thing
would have happened in America if I had been so careless as to
leave such temptations before children. We agreed that it would
be happier for everyone if the matter was forgotten, and a dollar
was presented to each of the three visitors who graciously received
the gift. Ho had nudged me with the information that this was
the appropriate thing to do. That day we wrote down a great
many notes.

The question of property was on my mind, and the Kao Yao
view of the matter should be presented. Private, communal, and
joint types of property were recognized, informants emphasizing
that private property was the most important. As far as could be
discovered, there was no idea of incorporeal property such as titles,
songs, dances, recipes, or privileges. For convenience, the kinds of
property owned have been classified into obvious categories and
listed below.

Land	Well
Residential	Grave
Farm	Animals
Market place,	Human beings
Street, Path, Quay	Money
Grave	Food
Trees	Clothing
Structures	Ornaments
Residential	Household
Business	furnishings
Animal	Tools
Storage	Weapons
School	Boats
Temple	Miscellaneous

Kao Yao individuals could and did own examples of the above
items except for the marketplace, street, quay, school, and temple,
although older adult males clearly had an advantage over younger
men, women, and children in obtaining them. Children and women,
unless widowed, owned little indeed in their private capacities. It
was denied, incidentally, that the wives or children of a man could

be considered his property, although female children could be sold.

Communal property—besides the marketplace, street, quay, school, and temple with their appurtenances—included farm and residential land as well as the structures on it, and also trees. To these, wells, some guns and, at least temporarily, grain and money, could be added.

In theory, anything that could be held by individuals might be owned jointly. Personal clothing and ornaments were hardly ever so considered, however. One common circumstance of joint ownership was that of brothers who had inherited property from their father. It was specifically stated that property, real or personal, was not held by the *chia*, but rather by the male head of the family. What we interpret this partial contradiction to mean is that the *chia* did not necessarily function as the economic family, the latter possibly coinciding with the nuclear, joint, or extended family. The economic family, although apparently not designated by a single term, was an entity in itself. In theory, the property accumulated and used by the economic family was owned by its head, the eldest male in the patrilineal line. Such ownership often consisted of merely the right to make certain decisions, but even these were in many cases permanently delegated. Therefore the members of an economic family felt that the ownership of most things was in some measure shared.

The fact that a man could not disinherit his sons (or his daughters if they were his only children) probably implemented that feeling. Again, although the food eaten by the family was stated to belong to its head, wives probably seldom consulted their husbands in expressing their control over it as cooks. As elsewhere in the world, Kao Yao wives in some cases dominated their husbands to such a degree that the position of the latter as head of the family was nominal at best. The teahouse gossips were constantly attesting to that.* It must also not be forgotten that a wife more realistically became the head of an economic family when she was widowed with young children and, as the sons grew, it was often hard to displace her, although the eldest son did become head of the *chia* on his marriage, the equivalent of reaching maturity. Actually, of the 122 Kao Yao families, there were twenty-two with women listed as the heads, there being no married male in such families.

* For an exceptional description of the position of women in the Chinese family, see Johnston, 1910: 197, 201.

Old men could divest themselves of their nominal authority as head of a *chia,* passing it on to a son, and such action was no great rarity in Kao Yao. Indeed, there were eleven cases, or one out of each eleven families. In the table below is the age of the son who had succeeded and the age of his father, as well as that of his mother if living.

Age of Head	Age of Father	Age of Mother
29	53	39 (2nd)
24	51	52
29	50	–
25	77	32 (2nd)
40	70	–
28	50	56
26	78	68
38	62	54
27	53	58
37	60	60
24	61	47

Although probably some of the fathers who relinquished the headship were poor or decrepit, some were certainly neither, and they really only delegated their authority, retaining covert control as well as respect. Informants concluded that in general the individual with the greatest personal ability usually was the ultimate decision maker, and that in about half the families, that person was a woman. This real position of power, however, like the economic family itself, was not distinguished by name.

The lineage could also possess property, but in Kao Yao it seems to have been limited to farmland, grain, money, and trees. When trees belonging to a lineage were sold, sometimes the money was distributed among the families—economic, we presume.

In general, ownership was said to carry the right of enjoyment, destruction, alienation, and transmission after death. Usually property could be given, loaned, and rented, but there were limitations on these rights apart from those already mentioned. The Kao Yao council could not have sold the village street. Pi said no one could stop a person from using the village-owned wells. The power to alienate public land was vested in a level of authority at least as high as the district government. The village rarely acquired land by gift. Most of it came by reversion when there was no one in a legal position to inherit it (small lineages easily became extinct). The council periodically purchased land, and often in other villages, when it could be acquired cheaply. Thus Kao Yao owned land in P'i Chi Kuan and in Wang Chia Tui (Fig. 5, p. 69), or the Dirt Pile of the Wang Family, a hamlet of about twenty Chinese families located about a mile and a half to the north between the road and the lake. Its name undoubtedly came from the fact that the place was surrounded by water. Conversely, the village of Yang Chia Ts'un and Ch'ih Chia Pi owned farm land in Kao Yao.

It was also stated that lineage land could not be alienated although perhaps, in reality, this meant that none was known to have been. Lineage rights in land were acquired by the extinction of a landowning family of the lineage. Such property was said to be always rented and the income used for the lineage as a whole—possibly by the purchase of pigs which were then butchered and divided among the families.

Individuals owning land, whether their economic unit consisted of only themselves or of an extended family, could do what they wished with their land. Land was not often sold, and few individuals except of the age groups over twenty controlled any. It was stated that when a man built a house on vacant land, he had to leave a path to it and that this path became public property. One of the more extraordinary bits in our notes points out that, despite the fact there were neither records nor markers of land parcels, there were no quarrels over boundaries. This seemed miraculous, if true.

Giving was a formalized activity in Kao Yao on certain occasions, notably when families exchanged presents at the ceremony of betrothal. Guests at a wedding also brought gifts, and presents were given to a friend on his birthday,* or to any individual as a token for a service. Money was the commonest gift. Contributions were not made to the poor, however, and there were said to be no secular beggars. Requests of money were sometimes made to a temple when an individual was childless, but no bequests for public works were known to have been made within the memory of informants.

Borrowing and lending was commonly practiced in Kao Yao. Village and lineages, as well as individuals, lent money at an interest

* Maurice Freedman has written me, "Surely, birthdays are celebrated only among old people?" Apart from babies (of which he was presumably not thinking), there seems to be evidence that edibles, such as cakes, were sometimes given on a birthday to a friend who was not old.

of two to three per cent a month. Security was demanded for a loan. A borrower could approach a likely lender of cash at any time in the lender's home or even on the street. Negotiations started, the amount, security, interest, and date of return of the principal was discussed; and if agreed upon, a contract was written and signed by the parties involved plus one witness. The interest was brought to the lender one year from the date of contract, and normally at least one year's interest had to be paid. If the interest was not paid, the lender could collect his security and the borrower was helpless to intervene. If the lender was willing, however, the borrower might work for him in lieu of the interest, but a lender could not force a borrower to do so; there was no pledging of service for debt. Also, if the principal was not returned on the date agreed upon, the lender could not foreclose on his security as long as the interest payments were continued.

Property often was rented in Kao Yao—land of all kinds, water buffalo (Pl. 18, p. 133; Pl. 24, p. 159) and transport animals (the female for breeding), houses and furnishings, utensils for feasts, and various other things. Small tools, it may be said, were often borrowed without payment—as where not. Farm land was probably the most important item rented. Contracts were written after argument over the price, and the rent paid when the produce was harvested. An attempt was made to estimate the average rental for several kinds of fields. The results are given in the list below. All prices are computed on the basis of one *mou* for one year with repayment in produce grown.

Mou of rice land (best)—3 *piculs* *
Mou of rice land (average)—2 *piculs* 4 *chin*
Mou of rice land (poor)—1 *picul* 8 *chin*
Mou of maize land (best)—1 *picul*
Mou of maize land (average)—8 *chin*
Mou of maize land (poor)—6 *chin*
Mou of seed land (one kind)—1 *picul*

When field rents were paid, the tenant remained to dinner with his landlord.

The renting of homes and business structures was also commonplace. Prices are listed at top of page 134.

---

* In theory, 1 *picul* equaled 133 lbs., 1 *chin* (catty) equaled 1⅓ lbs., 1 *mou* equaled ⅙ acre.

18. WATER BUFFALO ON MAIN STREET

Upper-class house—$1.00 per month per room
Middle-class house—.40 or .50 per month per room
Lower-class house—.20 or .30 per month per room

The two one-room business establishments in the school compound each rented for $6.00 per year. The rent for the restaurant at the end of the street adjoining the quay was $15.00 a year. Our rent was $10.00 per month (for the equivalent of six rooms), but that was a special, short-term arrangement. Ordinarily one gave security for the equivalent of half a month's rent, but the actual rent was not paid until the end of each month when it was done without ceremony. The security became a permanent advance returnable when occupancy of the building was given up. The owner of rented structures had no right of entry, and in case of fire, he suffered the loss.

The destruction of property was not an emphasized trait of Kao Yao culture although some objects were buried with the dead. In discussing the subject, Pi said that the only things really destroyed were firecrackers. Even this was done sparingly except for ceremonial outbursts; we did not record hearing any during our stay.

Inheritance was patrilineal, property passing from a man to his sons. There was no real will and none was ordinarily necessary as a father could not disinherit his children. Rarely, however, a man might leave a document of instructions to his sons, but this was actually an admonition on the proper rules of conduct following the death of a parent. The inherited estate was theoretically managed by the eldest son if he was unmarried and old enough to care for it. Except for what was known as the "eldest son's rice field," the property was said usually to be equally divided among the sons if, or when, they were married. A son also inherited from his mother; that is, jewelry and money.

If there were only daughters in the family, the eldest was often married to a young man who was willing to come to her father's house to live and be adopted into his wife's lineage, taking her father's surname in place of his own. He would then inherit as would a son born into the family. Only one case of son-in-law adoption was clearly recorded in the village, a young man of twenty-seven who had taken the family name of his wife, twenty-one. The parents also had a six-year-old son. Like instances among older couples would probably not have shown up in the census, however, unless the parents were living.

Should this expedient of adoption not be achieved, the daughter would inherit. In the case of a man with a wife but no children, the wife inherited the property, but what remained at her death reverted to her husband's lineage. When a child was left an estate by a father, the mother took charge. In the case of an orphan, neighboring members of the lineage would be expected to look after the property and at no monetary recompense. How the theory worked out in practice is uncertain. Once Pi was asked if a man could disinherit his son by giving away his property before he died. He answered simply that there was no such case in the village.

It was said that an ordinary article found on the street could rightfully be taken home and kept. There was only one trumpet in the village and everyone knew whose it was. Pi insisted that it could still pass into the permanent possession of another under the conditions described above. It is presumed that the trumpet would have had to be lost and not temporarily put down. Land, however, could not be acquired by squatting on it.

One type of property that demands special attention was human beings. In Kao Yao, the slaves were all girls. Boy slaves such as were reputedly used in the tin mines of Yünnan, or for any other purpose, were unknown. It was said that even the neighbors of a family who sold a boy would protest. It was added, as by free association, that a boy slave would not be economical as it would be necessary to give him a wife.

Girls were sold to, and acquired from, slave traders, a profession to which no Kao Yao person belonged. K'un Yang, or Brilliance of K'un (exact location uncertain), south of Kunming, was noted for its slave trade. The selling of daughters by Kao Yao parents was said to be rare, but one case had occurred the previous year. Poverty was the usual cause of the sales, but occasionally a man was not above selling his brother's orphaned child. Girls when purchased by Kao Yao families were seldom under ten years of age since if they were any younger they would not be of much use. Usually only the wealthiest families owned them. Slave girls were obtained primarily as house servants, helping with the cooking, acting as nursemaids, undertaking domestic errands, and so on. A widower left with small children might buy a twelve- or thirteen-year-old girl to care for them. If she was nice looking, he might pay her relatives forty to fifty dollars, but if she was ugly, not more than ten. The girl might be used to satisfy the sexual desires of her master, but such utilization was not socially approved. Still, it was believed no one had the right to interfere.

The treatment of a slave girl depended on the character of the members of the family into which she was brought. Her master could not rightfully kill her, but he could beat her to the point of severe injury without interference and, of course, he could sell her. Although discipline and control of a slave girl was nominally in the hands of the family head, any member could order her around. Women were often meaner to her than men. In most cases, however, it was argued that slave girls in Kao Yao were reasonably treated and not readily distinguishable from a member of the family by observation alone. In a rare case, such a girl might remain permanently in a household. It had been known in Kao Yao for a man and his wife who were without children to marry off their slave girl to a boy who was then adopted into the family, the girl thus becoming their daughter-in-law. Such cases were rare enough to dream about; in most, once a slave girl was married, she was quit of the family forever.

When a slave girl was punished too often, she might run away. There was an instance of this in Kao Yao the year of our visit. The child was apprehended, returned to her owner, and beaten. There was no asylum for her to seek. A magistrate would have been indifferent to her appeal, and the police would have brought her back to her master, the fact that all slavery had been abolished by national law notwithstanding. Least of all was there any chance of her purchasing her own freedom. The most she could be said ever to own were her clothes.

It was possible for an owner to rent out a slave among relations of some intimacy. A girl might even be loaned to a close friend, but there was said to be always a monetary gift involved (nothing of a sexual nature was implied by the record). At the age of twenty, a slave girl could expect to be sold as a wife to some poor man who found it expedient to buy one. There was a moral obligation on the part of her owner to arrange the transaction. Thus she gained her nominal freedom, and her master from sixty to a hundred dollars. Incidentally, no instance had ever occurred of a person simply buying a slave girl in order to free her. When I proposed such an action as a possibility, my coterie promptly insisted that no one in Kao Yao would sell in such irregular circumstances. Besides, what would a poor girl in old China do without any family at all?

Slaves were admittedly held in contempt by free members of the society. Our map maker said that if a slave was married to someone in another village, her position in freedom would be much better than otherwise, as would seem obvious. There were only two or three slave girls in Kao Yao according to informants, but they seemed to have overlooked one or more cases. This was easy to do since slave girls did not really exist in the social sense, as was indicated by their not being included in the schoolteacher's census. In Pi's personal opinion, slavery was contrary to the principles of humanity. By some chance, he added immediately after this pronouncement that to have more than one wife was all right, but then quickly stated for the record that he was content with only one, and there I have put it.

Some things may be reported about the manners of Kao Yao people, and they will be linked into the chain of daily events. In theory, everyone got up at sunrise, and certainly most people did if one means the period between the first rays of dawn and a full view of the sun over the lake. There was little indication that much body washing took place at that time, and much reason to believe that little did. It was specifically stated, for example, that women usually went to the hot springs located about ten miles west of Kao Yao once in several years for a bath, but that they took no bath in the meantime beyond the regular washing of the feet. In the heat of the 2nd and 3rd months before the rainy season, men went into the lake in order to cool off, but they did not bathe otherwise. The school-teacher periodically took a sponge bath using a wash basin, and some other fastidious residents may have done so, but for the majority, it was the hands and feet that were believed to get dirty and the hands and feet that got washed.

Breakfast was eaten around eight o'clock, usually after a session of work. There was no regular time for going to the toilet, and both men and women used the public ones (Pl. 7, p. 67; Pl. 8, p. 68), except for some upper-class females who had buckets in their bed-rooms. When a toilet was occupied, one waited until it was free.

People meeting on the street made the gesture of yielding the way when being polite. This became more obvious when parties were traveling on the roads. Bowing without using the hands was commonplace between acquaintances. The head was bent only slightly, the body even less. To do so with hands clasped over the chest indicated a more formal occasion, as when paying respect, asking help, inviting people for entertainment, or thanking them for some service. Pi said that the right hand should cover the left, and we observed a Buddha in one of the temples with his hands so clasped. Ho thought it made no difference, and I observed most people covered with the left, including Pi himself. A woman in bowing held her right thumb in her left hand in front of her chest. Kowtowing was reserved for one's ancestors and the gods, and not used in paying respect to parents.

Other gestures had commonly recognized meanings. Rapidly moving one's hand from side to side in front of the body while talking emphasized a negative. The hand was held vertically in the dorsal-ventral plane. To wave one's hand from side to side, palm toward someone in the distance meant "Do not come." It also could indicate a negative answer. Shaking the head in Western fashion was recognized as an alternative. A nod of the head meant "Yes." To wave the hand as a Westerner might indicate "Good-by" in Kao Yao was to convey the notion "Come here."

If someone called to a person to ask where he was going and could not hear the answer, the person questioned, were he going to grind rice, would make a circle clockwise with his hand pointing downward and then throw his hand over the opposite shoulder. Were he going to cut rice, he would hold out one fist and move the other as though cutting with a sickle. Were he going to transplant rice he would put out one fist after another. If he were going to cut wood, he would extend an arm and then chop toward it with the edge of his hand, and then would put his right hand on his forehead and nod several times as a finishing gesture.

To call a person to join in a trip to the hills to pick mushrooms, one made an oval with the thumbs and first fingers, then raised the hands and moved them in the direction of the hills. If one put one's fists against one's forehead with the fingernails out, it was a signal to bring the water buffalo. To call a person to have a smoke, one placed his fingers to the mouth as though holding a cigarette; if to sleep, one bent his head sidewise, resting it in the palm of a hand; if to drink tea, a clenched hand was raised to the mouth several times; and finally, if to eat, an imaginary bowl was held to the mouth in one hand and the motions of using chopsticks indicated by the other. In utilizing any of these gestures, it was expected that the individuals involved were too far apart to hear. Furthermore, shouting was considered impolite except in the hills, and then only from an elder to a younger person. Whistling also was not permissible except in the hills.

The theoretical dinner hour in Kao Yao was six o'clock. When guests were invited, the seat of honor was given to the person of superior status. Two people of different status would try to avoid sitting together. As a rule men ate with men and women with women, but should the hostess appear at the men's table, it was expected that the guest would stand and say some words of appreciation while the host remained seated politely repeating *"Pu tung, pu tung,"* or "Don't be disturbed." The host invited his guests to drink and eat by setting an example. When wine was being served, talk was without restraint, but polite people tried to refrain when the rice had been brought in. This was not done until the guests refused to drink any more wine. As each new dish appeared, the host invited his guests to partake of the food. There was no rule which restricted one to eat from the nearest dish, one being allowed to reach where he pleased.

If one sneezed or exuded food onto the table, it was bad manners, but to sneeze without spitting was permissible. Also, one could expectorate saliva, but to eliminate anything else from the mouth, one had to leave the room. Committing a flatus was a breach of good behavior about which one could do nothing but sit in embarrassed silence. Belching, hiccoughing, and yawning were permissible, there being nothing impolite about being sleepy even at a party. Picking one's teeth was acceptable if done with a toothpick, but scratching was bad form as it indicated one had an excess of vermin.

When one was finished eating, a man might put his chopsticks on top of his bowl pointing toward the middle of the table. Then the host might ask him to have more food or say "Don't wait for us; be free to do as you please." The man might then smoke. When everyone had finished eating, the chopsticks were put down on the table to the left of one's bowl. The guests indicated their gratitude verbally. On departing, the host asked, "Are you about to go? Are you in a hurry? Stay longer so that we can enjoy ourselves." Then he conducted them outside the door and they bowed to each other.

People could show disrespect by gestures. Turning a shoulder toward a person indicated contempt which could be emphasized by moving away. Winking was considered insulting and might be done almost involuntarily without allowing the person disliked to be certain of the intent. It was considered offensive for anyone to speak of bean curd soup in front of lay readers of holy books because they normally ate it when performing. In short, it was considered as innuendo to speak of anything characteristic of one's profession.

For a man to discuss, or even mention, sexual matters in front of a woman was insulting. Obscenity was commonplace but only effectively opprobrious when in the classic Chinese form of referring sexually to the mother of the person spoken to. Actually, bashfulness about sex was noticeable. An effort was made to hide the body except for the hands and feet, the only exception in practice being such exposure as was necessary in nursing a child and, in this case, one's class did not matter. A tear in a woman's costume was considered immodest unless she was so poor as to be literally dressed in rags. Even for a man to have his coat open was bad form as, for that matter, was any independent variation in dress.

There was no special time for rest during the day, but men often went to a teahouse after dinner. At nine o'clock, in theory, everyone went to bed, people sleeping on their backs or sides, and sometimes rolling around.

According to informants there was little actual crime in the village and less punishment. Li Pu said there was not much danger of anyone stealing his horses or mules, although he admitted that if they were allowed to wander off someone might do so. Mei, our neighbor, claimed that his store had been robbed of over a thousand dollars about 1932 by eight men armed with pistols and swords who had come at two in the morning, broken down his door, and threatened his life. He said that other people in the village had been awakened by the robbers, but that they had done nothing to stop them. Other people said the case was not as simple as had been stated and that perhaps Mei was involved in illegitimate undertakings himself. In any event, even Mei said that his store had been the only one robbed since he had come to Kao Yao from the eastern gate of Kunming in 1926, and that for the four last years he had no longer been afraid as ten men in the village had been deputized as unpaid police and given pistols, as had seven or eight other men in P'i Chi Kuan (Fig. 5, p. 69).

This was a surprise to us and we turned to Pi, the schoolteacher, whose knowledge of the local government seemed authoritative. He said that there was no one with police authority stationed in Kao Yao, but that there was such a man with an office in the Chi Chieh temple. This police chief had five assistants who might be called policemen, although their powers were very limited and they did not carry guns. They seldom appeared in Kao Yao, however, except on market days when, if someone became intoxicated and started a fight, they might report the culprit or take him to Chi Chieh to be fined by the police chief. Apart from this protection, if such it may be called, a watchman was employed in Kao Yao during every 1st month when there was traditional fear that thieves might be abroad. That period was the darkest and coldest of the year, and the villagers went early to bed. The watchman made his rounds at seven, nine, and twelve in the evening, and again at three in the morning, striking a small gong periodically to give comfort to those in their beds. As has been said, no robber had been seen in many a year. It should be mentioned, however, that there were small structures put up in some fields so that a member of the farmer's family could be sheltered while watching over the ripening crops to prevent their being pilfered.

Pursuing information about the police chief in Chi Chieh, Pi stated he had the authority to mete out minor punishments, levy fines, or sentence an offender to jail for any period up to a month. Significantly, half the money which accrued from the police chief's judgments was kept by himself, the other half being forwarded to the district government.

Although no cases involving Kao Yao residents were recorded, we went as far as to try to determine what punishments would be meted out for various acts. For murder, an alleged criminal had to be brought before the court in Kunming and, if convicted, the sentence was execution or a term of years in prison. Trial in the capital was also required for the charge of either attempted murder or accidental homicide. A case was known of an old woman being killed by an automobile on the highway. The driver was fined $300. Robbery was said to bring punishments by prison terms of various lengths depending on whether injury was involved. Arson was a capital offense. A celebrated case involved the burning of many houses in P'i Chi Kuan. The person accused of the crime was sentenced to ten years in prison by the court in Kunming. Accidental causing of a fire, however, was not a punishable act.

Simple theft was an offense that could be settled by the victim beating the guilty party if caught in the act. On the other hand, if the thief escaped, the injured person could go to the police for redress. If the thief was caught, he was forced to return the stolen goods, or the equivalent if he had it, and then was subject to imprisonment and fine. A burglar who was discovered could not be physically abused, however, or at least if he were, the police would have nothing to do with the case. Burglary, it was said, was the most common crime. Trespass, even in a home, was no legal offense, and all that an owner could do without grounds for charging the intruder with theft, burglary, or damage was to throw him out.

Damage unintentionally committed, for example, by animals had to be compensated for by their owners, the value involved in most cases being determined by the village head, although the forest manager would assay any destruction in the village forest. A man was responsible only for the acts of himself, his wife, his children, and his animals, although formerly the whole lineage was involved. Contrariwise, if a child injured himself while on the property of others than his family, the owners could not be held accountable. Insane persons were exempted from liability for their acts, but in serious cases, the family head might find himself in trouble for not watching over the person. Assault was dealt with by the local police chief.

The following crimes, although not likely to have occurred in Kao Yao, were recognized by the schoolteacher. Treason, he said, would be punished by execution. Counterfeiting also was a capital crime, and he knew of a counterfeiter who had been sentenced to death in Kunming. Forgery was unknown to this informant, but was recognized as a commonplace cause for imprisonment, all cases of it being handled by the district court. Embezzlement Pi divided into classes on the basis of whether public money was involved. For embezzlement of public funds in an amount of over $500, a convicted person could be executed, but for any amount less, a prison sentence was meted out. In private affairs, the main effort was to retrieve the loss, and a prison sentence followed conviction.

Malfeasance in office was regarded as so difficult to prove in Yünnan that nothing could be done about it. Although a person might be discharged from public service for receiving a bribe, he was more apt to be given a demerit on his record. To offer a bribe was not believed to be a punishable offense. Perjury in the sense of a false verbal statement was believed not to be a crime, but a false affidavit made the signer subject to imprisonment and, until some time before the end of the nineteenth century, the offender was punished by the cutting off of a hand. In the case of breach of contract, an appeal might be made to the local police chief, and if he could not settle the matter, another could be made to the Kunming court, but that involved lawyers and a lawsuit.

Sorcery was not recognized as existing, and the practice of shamanism was said to be no crime. A Buddhist monk who failed to observe his vows might be driven out of the community, but a priest was said to be no different before the law than any other man. Slander was dealt with by the local police and a person might be punished by having the palm of the hands beaten with a stick. Drunkenness in itself was not punishable but, on the other hand, it did not relieve one for responsibility for concomitant offenses. Asked what would happen if a drunken man appeared in the street without any clothing, Pi said that people might spit on him. For lying, a person was scolded.

In the matter of offenses between the sexes, it was stated that no one in Kao Yao would interfere in a case of incest, even though it was known to be illegal. Any protest would have to come from within the family, and the members would certainly try to hide the offense. A rapist was fined. Adultery, in theory, could also be punished by a fine levied at the police office at Chi Chieh. Fornication and seduction brought not only fines but the man involved could also be forced to marry the woman. The guilty parties were not subject to corporal punishment, however. Sodomy was said not to be a crime, and at the same time it was asserted that the practice did not exist. Polygyny was stated to be permissible, and apparently Pi did not know of any Chinese law against it. Cases were certainly not unusual. Desertion on the part of a husband was not an egregious act, but if a wife fled from her spouse and was caught, she might be fined as well as divorced. Actually, cases of women leaving their husbands were claimed not to be uncommon, and two men in Kao Yao were known to have deserted their wives.

In the opinions given above, it was not certain how many referred to customary law and how many to those of record, also the question of actual enforcement could not be substantiated in many cases. Traditionally, the power of money on the courts of old China was notorious, but perhaps life was relatively little affected in a small village such as Kao Yao. Status, except in the case of slaves, was said not to affect the outcome of cases, but perhaps in our brief survey of crime and punishment we did not get far from ideals.

The afternoon of the day my pen was returned, old Mr. Tuan came to call. He said that the reason he had not previously accepted our several invitations had been because the pen had not be returned and, while the village was thus disgraced, he was ashamed to visit us. It struck me as a very clever little speech, but there was nothing to make me believe it was not an essentially true one. Tuan was immediately invited to dinner and he as quickly accepted. Before we could persuade him to sit down, he bounced around the room on his bare feet examining everything, periodically giving a little laugh, but not unclasping his right hand held over his chest with his left one. He went into the study and even hopped in and out of our bedroom, the only one of our visitors who had dared to do so. Finally, he settled into a chair, half-rising several times when offered a light for the cigarette which had been given him. When wine was brought to the table, his content seemed complete.

What impressed me most was the softness of his voice and the expressiveness with which he used his hands. When he reached over and ran his fingers along the edge of the table, I observed that his nails extended half an inch beyond the flesh, and that he used them frequently to scratch his head through his thinning hair. He was dressed in black cotton trousers and jacket (Pl. 5, p. 61). The latter had spherical buttons of clouded glass and the sleeves were rolled up revealing a slightly dirty, white flannel undercoat with a blue pin stripe.

We got along excellently as I expected. At dinner, I learned something about manners from the cook who would not bring us our rice while Tuan was still drinking, although the rest of our dinner was about gone. Tuan said that he had a bronze vase that he wanted to show me, but was afraid that someone might think that he was trying to sell it, a logical inference since we were already accumulating a sample of typical village possessions. By the time old Tuan had left, I knew that he would be a frequent guest. Before he departed, he offered us the use of two rooms rent free in his house which he said would be more suitable accommodations than our stage. The schoolteacher, who also had dined with us, remained to work until a few minutes before midnight.

10

PRODUCTION AND ENJOYMENT OF FOOD

IT WAS eight o'clock before I was awakened. A louse was jumping between the sheets but I could not catch it. I washed my feet
and dressed before eating eight or ten twisted doughnuts the cook
had made. These, with a cup of tea, constituted an excellent breakfast. The opium had begun to affect my viscera and I felt better.
The village artist, Li Wan-nien (Pl. 19, p. 146), who the previous
week had brought some of his wood carvings to sell, was already
sitting at the edge of the stage working on a wood stand for an ink
dish. At an unmentioned interval in the memorable previous day we
had engaged him full time and, as was proper, he literally sat at my
feet to demonstrate the integrity with which he pursued his work.
This had some disadvantage at first since he groaned and yawned
intermittently, suffering from an infected sore on his cheekbone out
of which pus oozed down his neck. He said it had resulted from his
being hit in the face with a fragment of rock. Furthermore, when
he chanced to see a stern look on my face, he was worried and then,
when I smiled, he would bring his carving for appreciation, interludes which soon merely wasted our time. Therefore, when one of
the village farmers arrived with an oversized pair of straw sandals
that I had commissioned, he was quickly persuaded to take us to his
fields (Pl. 20, p. 147). He became somewhat disconcerted, however, when I insisted on participating in the work, although my interest in the agricultural production of Kao Yao did not surprise
him, for nothing was more realistically important in the life of the
villagers.

The rice was already rising high in the paddies which were dotted
with people bent over in the act of pulling the weeds. The mud
seemed peculiarly soft as it pressed between my toes when, with
trousers rolled above the knees, we waded into the six inches of
water that covered the field. Naively, I expected no more difficulty
than a sore back to complicate the experience. To my chagrin, I

19. A VILLAGE ARTIST

20. FARMER AT EDGE OF RICE FIELD

soon discovered that I could not distinguish the weeds from the grain and was pulling as much of the one as the other. The farmer showed no surprise, but patiently taught me to differentiate with my finger tips the slightly more prickly stems that were choking the rice. In our few weeks, time was allowed to collect information about only the more important or unusual food plants, and even the data we could record about them were limited, but we asked a great many questions, the answers to which have been reduced to the following few paragraphs.

For the villagers of Kao Yao, rice was the most important crop, and after it, three other grains—wheat, maize, and sorghum, these being followed by the peas and beans of which there were no less than nine varieties raised. We probably cannot begin better than by listing the varieties of Kao Yao agricultural produce, although for some we could not find a commonplace English name.

Grains
  Rice (2 varieties)
  Wheat (2 varieties)
  Maize (2 varieties)
  Sorghum (Kaoliang)
  Barley
  Rye
Pulses
  Beans (8 varieties)
  Peas
Tubers
  Yams
  Taro
  Turnips
  Potatoes (sweet)
  Potatoes (white)
  Water chestnuts
  Radishes
Cabbages, etc.
  Cabbages
  Green vegetable
  Bitter vegetable

Onions
Scallions
Lettuce
Misc. vegetables
  Eggplant (2 varieties)
  Red peppers (2 varieties)
  Green peppers
  Cucumbers
  Caladium (sagittaria)
  Cedrela odorata
Melons and gourds
  Bitter melon
  Fragrant melon
  Hairy melon
Fruit
  Persimmon
  Peach
  Plum
  Apple
  Pear
  Mulberry

Rice seed beds were prepared in the 3rd month by men. Both sexes then engaged in fertilizing them. When the seed beds, usually located near the lake, were in shape, both men and women, but usually the latter, spread the seed of which there were two varieties, the red and the white, both treated the same way. From the middle to the end of the 4th month the seedlings, which had grown to six or seven inches in height, were transplanted to the fields, usually by the men who had already plowed them using water buffalo or bovine cattle for power. After the transplanting, the rice fields were hoed (Fig. 12, right, below). From the 7th through the 9th month when the harvest took place, both sexes shared in the weeding which was

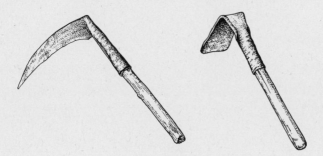

Figure 12. Sickle and Hoe

undertaken with the hands. It was said that from 100 to 120 days were necessary to ripen the grain. The red rice matured about two weeks ahead of the white, although some of the latter, known as flood rice, might take even two weeks longer to mature. At whatever time the grain was yellow and ready, the water, about six inches deep, was drained from the paddies, and everyone of an age to work started cutting the grain with their sickles (Fig. 12, left, above), tying the harvest into sheaves with pieces of rice straw. The sheaves were then piled against each other in stacks of ten for two or three days to dry in the sun which bleached their color. Then they were carried to the village on the backs of the farmers, or by means of shoulder poles, and piled in the courtyards. That rain was infrequent at that time of year was fortunate, for if the harvested rice became wet, it had to be separated into small bundles and dried once again.

In the 10th month, after an interval in which both wheat and various beans were planted, the rice grains were separated from the stalks by beating them against a stone. The rice grains were then collected in basketry trays by the women, one pouring them onto a rough mat, while another stretched it by jerks, thus winnowing the chaff. The rice was finally put into bags which the men took away and sold, or dumped into their rice chests. Any public place, as well as private courtyards or enclosed areas could be utilized in the final stages of harvesting.

Water for the paddy fields was a problem in the men's charge. There was always enough, but often too much, which ruined the fields near the water, many of the Kao Yao holdings being too close to the lake for excess water to run off in years of much rain such as 1938. On the other hand, in drier ones machines had to be regularly used to draw the necessary water up into the same low-lying fields since those behind, slightly higher, absorbed the supply from the hills. Ordinarily, water was allotted to each family on a particular day.

After the rice had been cut and the fields had dried, the ground was harrowed and wheat planted in the furrows. Then the seed was covered by drawing a rakelike implement over the ground to level it. Weeding was undertaken in the following 2nd and 3rd months, and late in the latter or at the beginning of the 4th, the wheat was harvested. Any person might plant or harvest wheat, but most of the work usually was undertaken by men. The reaped grain was washed and, when it had dried, ground into flour, sometimes by hand but more often by taking it to the water-powered mill at Hsin Ts'un (Fig. 5, p. 69), or New Village, one of seven small communities a little over two miles to the west which altogether provided homes for about three hundred Pai Tzu (Min Chia) farming families and were known by the collective name of Kao Liu Chia, or the Kao (lineage) of the Six Villages, a seventh having apparently been founded later. Spring wheat was also grown, it being treated the same way in every respect. Wheat could be planted in either dry or wet fields. There was the advantage in the latter that the crop could readily be supplied with water but, of course, the wet fields were needed for rice when spring wheat was being grown.

Maize was also an important crop occupying perhaps ten per cent of the Kao Yao agricultural land. Any dry field was used since the corn did not need too much water and it was planted between the 3rd and 4th months, which was the rainy season anyway. Shallow holes were dug about eight inches apart and three kernels of seed put into each which were then covered with fine manure and then dirt. In a week, the shoots showed. The crop was harvested from early in the 7th month to the 15th of the 8th. The ears were picked one by one, then the stalks were cut down for cattle fodder. This field work was commonly done by men. The ears were carried home in baskets. At home the husks were usually peeled back and braided into strings of fifty to sixty ears which were then hung over poles in any room of the house, bedrooms and ancestral halls not excluded. White and yellow maize were distinguished, the significant difference being one of size.

Sorghum or kaoliang, which the naive sometimes mistake for maize, was taller and had its fruit on top (Pl. 21, p. 152). It was planted in dry fields at the same time as maize and ripened in the 8th month when it was cut at the root. Then the panicles were removed and piled on a threshing floor to be beaten with flails. The grains were then sieved, dried, and ground to get rid of the husks. Less than ten per cent of the land was planted with sorghum. Both men and women participated in growing it.

Various kinds of beans were planted in the 10th month at the same time as wheat and had the same growing span. One might find them in any dry field, and beans were also conspicuous in single rows along the dikes of the paddies. Beans, like wheat, required little care and the two crops were often rotated in the rice fields. A few other garden products may be mentioned (Pl. 22, p. 153). Taro was frequently planted in the dry fields during the 1st or 2nd month. A whole taro was put about one foot into the ground and the area was weeded when the need arose. The crop was harvested in the 8th month. Both white and sweet potatoes were included in the list of crops. Two varieties of eggplant, a spherical one and an elongated one, were planted in the 2nd month. Dried seeds were sprinkled over smoothed ground and then covered with pine needles. The next morning the seeds were watered and in a few days shoots appeared. When the shoots had grown three or four inches high after perhaps twenty days, they were transplanted to suitable places. The eggplants began to ripen in the 5th month and continued to do so until the 8th. Cucumbers, like eggplants, were commonly grown. Seeds, having been saved and dried, were planted in the 3rd month in a dry field by workers of either sex, and the crop harvested progressively between the 6th month and the end of the 8th. The bitter melon, a little longer than a cucumber, and also fragrant melons, were planted in a dry field by men or women during the 2nd and 3rd months. Almost every family grew some of these. Both took three

21. HOEING IN FIELD OF SORGHUM AND TOBACCO

22. HOEING DRY FIELD

months to mature but supplied food for the table during three months more. Before considering fruit, it may be noted that tomatoes were neither grown nor eaten by the villagers.

Fruit trees were not numerous in Kao Yao. They were planted by individuals of either sex, most often at the edge of a dry field, but sometimes close to the wall of a compound. Their possession was not correlated with any particular social class in the village although, of course, one first had to own land to possess a tree. Most common were persimmons, it being estimated that there were thirty of these trees owned by village families. There were two varieties, one of which was said to reach a height of thirty-five feet.* To have a persimmon tree, one planted another tree (species unidentified) in the 11th or 12th month, and a cutting from some persimmon tree was grafted onto it during the 2nd month by someone experienced in that technique. Persimmon trees required four to five years to mature, blossomed in the 2nd or 3rd month, and produced fruit for about thirty days beginning in the 9th month.

There were also a few peach trees of two varieties owned by Kao Yao families. A whole pit was planted in the good soil of a dry field in the 12th month, and then in the 2nd month the tree was transplanted to the edge of the field. Two to three years of growth were necessary before any fruit were available. The tree blossomed in the 2nd month and then produced peaches in the 4th for a period of four months. The trees grew to ten or eleven feet high.

There were four or five plum trees of several varieties in the village, some growing, it was said, to twenty to thirty feet tall. A plum pit was dried and planted more than a foot deep during the 11th or 12th month. Seven or eight years, however, were claimed to be required to bring the tree to fruition, but years go by quickly in a village. Plum trees were said to bloom in the snow (1st month?), with the fruit ripening in the 5th month and continuing for two more.

Apple trees were valuable but rare in Kao Yao. Li Fu, who had one of the few, informed us that they were always grown from a cutting which had to be oriented as was the parent tree. An apple tree, he related, has a face as does a man and, if it cannot see in the

---

* These estimates on the height of fruit trees are in Chinese feet, or *ch'ih,* so one may add up to sixteen per cent if one thinks it worth while. It would probably be more realistic, however, to recognize such measurements as rough estimates, those for plum, apple, and pear trees being almost certainly exaggerated. Clearly, I should have examined them myself.

right direction, it will die. Transplanting was undertaken after the 5th month and five years were required to obtain the fruit of which there was only a single variety. Blossoms appeared in the 2nd and 3rd months, apples in the 6th, continuing to ripen for three more months. The trees grew forty to fifty feet high which certainly gave them a good view of the village.

Pear trees were as rare as apple trees, although many varieties were known. Some unused bit of land was required at the edge of a field or on the slope of a hill in which to first plant a thorn tree. This was usually done in the 6th month. Then one had to wait until the 2nd month to graft on a cutting from a pear tree. Fruit appeared in three years, the tree blossoming in the 3rd month and producing pears in the 7th. Pear trees, it was said, would continue to have fruit for five months were it not all picked in the 8th. Trees grew to be thirty-five to forty feet tall.

Before concluding our comments on fruit trees, a word must be added about the mulberries of which a few grew beside the dry fields in Kao Yao, although there was no raising of silkworms from their leaves. Actually, there were two varieties, one wild and the other cultivated, the largest about thirty feet tall. Mulberry shoots were dug up and planted during the 11th or 12th month. At least ten years were required for the tree to mature. It blossomed in the 3rd month, with its fruit ripening in the 4th and remaining available about thirty days during which time it provided stomach-aches for the children.

Two other products should be mentioned among those grown. Either of two varieties of hemp, one domestic and the other wild, occasionally were planted between the vegetables in the dry fields during the 2nd or 3rd month, and then harvested in the 7th or 8th, or shortly before the rice, by cutting the stalks at the bottom and stripping them while green. The hemp was put over bamboo poles to dry in the sun, the outer layers being twisted into rope and the stalks serving as fuel, torches, and wicks of simple lamps. More important was the planting of tobacco between the 4th and 5th months on a patch of dry land. The tobacco also was cut before the rice, but usually in the early part of the 8th month. It was planted, cared for, and harvested by men.

We can summarize the round of the agricultural year by recalling that taro, eggplant, and melons were planted from the last half of the 1st month into the beginning of the 3rd (Fig. 13, below). In the latter month life became busier, for it was necessary to prepare the beds and plant rice seed, as well as the maize and sorghum. The 4th month, with the reaping of the winter wheat, the plowing

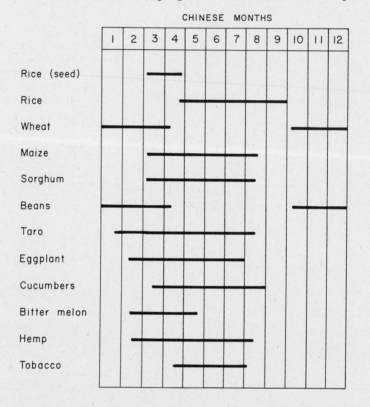

Figure 13. Chart of the Growing Period of Grains and Vegetables

of the wet fields, and particularly the transplanting of the rice seedlings, was the busiest time of the year. Then followed a lull, with the weeding of the rice increasing the labor demands as one approached its cutting in the 9th month. Also, the fields had to be watered if the weather was dry. Harvesting the rice, with the second plowing of the fields in preparation for sowing the wheat, together with the planting of beans, all in the 10th month, constituted the second busiest segment of the agricultural year. Then there was a release from intense activity as the people looked forward to the New Year's festivities. Actually, no one worked beyond the usual limits of farmers and, although the 6th to the 8th month was recognized as the period of food shortages, no one starved.

The gathering of foods was significant in Kao Yao, and especially of mushrooms and tree fungi, some eight varieties of which were found. Also, bamboo shoots, pine nuts, the tender sprouts of ferns, the wild quince, plum berries, as well as various lake weeds and other unidentified plants were collected. Snails were found along the lake shore as well as one kind of frog. To this list we should add the eggs of all domesticated fowl—chickens, ducks, pigeons, and geese, which might be expected to be of more importance than they actually were. Also, bees were kept for honey.

Domestic animals were important in the production of food, and especially pigs, which were allowed to breed freely and basically kept to be slaughtered for meat (Pl. 23, p. 158). Nine rooms in the village were designated as sties and thirty as stalls for cattle. Water buffalo (Pl. 18, p. 133; Pl. 24, p. 159) and oxen proved significant as the pullers of plows, and they were also used to draw carts. Even horses, mules, and donkeys may be added to the list of contributing animals for, even if utilized entirely for transport, their manure was carefully collected to be spread on the fields. For this service, pigs were again primary, grass being spread in their sties to absorb the manure. Indeed, fertilizer was so valued that dog's excrement was collected. All these animals were kept in the house, only chickens being allowed to run loose. They were fed and watered regularly in the morning, and cattle were washed and rubbed once a year in the 2nd or 3rd month. All the large animals were groomed about twice every month. There were no goats or sheep in the village. Fertile chickens' eggs were usually hatched, twenty being put under one hen, ducks' eggs being sometimes included. The latter might also be incubated by being buried in hot rice which was heated each day for twenty in succession.

While on the subject of animals it will be convenient to interpolate a few words about pets. In that role, especially among children, dogs were without peer, although adults regarded them primarily as caretakers. Li Fu said his watchdog would bark and then bite a stranger coming into the house, but would not disturb anyone on the street. Various kinds of dogs, acquired by purchase from families that had puppies, lived in Kao Yao. Li Fu also had a cat to reduce the rat population, but it would also kill baby chickens if

23. BUTCHERING A PIG

24. WATER BUFFALO TETHERED NEAR UPPER-CLASS HOUSE

left alone with them. Besides dogs and cats, birds (the thrush, parrot, pigeon, pheasant, and quail, besides domestic fowl, being specifically mentioned), monkeys, squirrels, white rabbits, fish, crickets, and snakes were kept as pets, an unidentified song bird being acclaimed as the favorite. Pi said that the people loved and protected their pets, but that was perhaps an idealistic comment. Birds, as well as dogs and monkeys, were taken for walks, but on the other hand, someone was always teasing the monkey that was chained to a house post on the main street. Even Pi was observed throwing tiles at it, but possibly attention was considered to be the equivalent of affection. Dogs were likewise frequently complimented. The rat was admittedly abused, individual ones not infrequently being tortured in the course of execution. The hemp snake ranked next in disregard, although the same species was sometimes tamed when caught young. Pets were considered as being principally associated with adults because children would not take care of them.

Some of the Kao Yao men periodically engaged in hunting, using old-fashioned muskets to stalk deer, fox, hare, and wild dogs in the hills. The hunters went in groups of twos or threes, traveling to a distance of ten miles. When the hunt was successful, the meat was divided as well as the money that could be gained from selling the skins. Bent-tree spring snares could be used to catch deer and rabbits, as well as pheasants, and the latter were shot with guns, young pheasants being utilized as decoys. Pitfalls covered with branches and a thin layer of dirt might be set for any kind of animal, such as wild boar and various species of the deer family. Leopards were known to have been taken in a pitfall with a dog used as bait. Foxes and wild dogs were sometimes killed with poison. Nets were spread for pigeons and sparrows, the latter being killed as a nuisance.

The question of what was available to eat and how one prepared it was as interesting a subject in Kao Yao as it has always been everywhere. One of the first questions we asked Pi was how many meals the villagers ate in a day. He immediately said two, one in the morning and another in the evening. Two days afterward it was noted that some people ate a light lunch at noon. Twenty-four hours later, Li Fu, the porter, confirmed Pi's statement, but amended it to the degree of saying that between the 3rd and 5th months and the 7th and 9th months, his family, for example, ate three meals a day because the women were working in the fields. They took their

lunch, while he and the children ate at home.   He also said that when
he was traveling with his animals at any time of year he always ate
three meals. Before our study had ended, it became clear that although two meals a day was the normal pattern for most people in
Kao Yao, at least some of the time any individual would eat three
meals if he thought he could afford it, and quite a few did.

Unquestionably, rice was the commonest and best loved food in
Kao Yao. This fact was checked with special care as I did not find
that food indispensable each and every meal. The people valued
wheat flour (noodles) next. One encountered statements such as,
"The people will not be able to fill themselves regardless of how
much they eat of other things." The collective guess was that rice
contributed seven-tenths of the diet, wheat or any other grain two-
tenths, and vegetables plus meat or other foods the rest.

Very little meat or fowl actually was eaten in Kao Yao. The
flesh of the ox, cow, or pig was relished if the opportunity to serve
it was afforded, however. A well-to-do family, such as Li Fu's,
sometimes butchered a pig, but usually they felt the necessity of selling the animals. The blood of all animals eaten was also utilized as
food. The meat of horses, mules, donkeys, dogs, monkeys, and
water buffalo was not acceptable fare in Kao Yao, although it was
pointed out that Mohammedans (of which there were none living in
the village) ate the last. It might be added that there were no goats
or sheep in Kao Yao; also, no milk was drunk, but this may have
been because of its cost since milk was common enough in Kunming.
On New Year's and certain other feast days, a fowl might be killed,
but chickens were kept primarily for their eggs as has been previously
stated (p. 157).

Breakfast was regularly congee which, in season, was made with
an admixture of cornmeal. Luncheon consisted of rice. For supper, in the 3rd, 4th, and 5th months the people's basic food was rice
and wheat mixed together; in the 7th, 8th, and 9th months rice and
maize mixed together; between the two periods the richer people ate
rice and the poorer ate wheat, the latter being much cheaper. To any
of these meals, other things and particularly vegetables plus mushrooms and bamboo shoots could be added, but it was claimed that all
meals of the day were of the same quantity and importance. It was
agreed that everyone ate to the point of satisfaction if the means to
do so were available.

We can now turn directly to the treatment of the food. Rice was most commonly cooked by boiling it in water for four or five minutes and then simmering it perhaps half an hour longer. Congee, on the other hand, was prepared by continuously boiling the rice in an excess of water for an hour. Sometimes an intermediate method was adopted, in which case the rice was boiled a half hour, after which most of the water was removed and the rice simmered until dry, or a second half hour. Another important method of treating rice was to steam it until soft, perhaps half an hour; then it was taken from the stove, water added and drained off, the rice finally being steamed again for an hour. This procedure made the rice very soft so that it could be made into such things as noodles and dumplings which were used in soups. Raw rice, we might add, could be kept about two years in the household chests.

No record of the use of wheat was made except that when ground into flour, it was often made into noodles. Cracked wheat presumably was mixed with the rice. Wheat flour, it was said, kept less than a month, or at least tasted bad after that time. Ears of maize were boiled or roasted when eaten fresh, whereas the dried corn was ground and made into steamed bread, to me most delicious, or mixed with the rice. From the point of view of human consumption, maize was considered an auxiliary food in contrast to rice or wheat. There was no prestige in eating maize. The boiled meal was fed to the pigs. Interestingly, maize was one of the few foods mentioned as being cooked in other places than the kitchen such as the fields or open hills. Maize could normally be kept for a year, but by then the worms began to get into it.

Taro, which was common in Kao Yao kitchens, usually was used in soup after the skin was removed. It was also fried, however, after being boiled. It was always stored close to the ground where it could be kept for a year without serious decay. Most vegetables were quick-fried or boiled in soup, but eggplant received special attention. It was most commonly boiled, then skinned and served with a salty sauce. Sometimes it was fried and then boiled; also, it was salted. Finally, eggplant was not infrequently candied by cutting it into squares after skinning, then boiling it, and putting it into fresh water with sugar. This latter preparation was often eaten between meals. Eggplant was not eaten raw, and it would keep for fifteen days at the most. Cucumbers, however, were eaten raw, especially at odd times, but for meals they were often quick-fried and then boiled. Cucumbers also were salted down as otherwise they would keep only four or five days.

Bitter melons would survive only the same short period. They were thoroughly washed to reduce the bitter taste and then cut up without being skinned and fried in lard, after which water was added and the melon boiled. Bitter melon was impossible to eat raw. Cooked, it was considered excellent to neutralize the effects of eating too much fried food in hot weather. Fragrant melons were boiled or fried; the skins being taken off only when hard. These melons were also preserved either by putting pieces in honey for at least twenty to thirty days, or by boiling them in sugar all day until dry, and then bottling them. The first variety would keep for many years, the melon removed only when it was to be eaten, and the second for more than a year. Candied melon was made by practically every family in Kao Yao, and was frequently given to the children, especially when they cried. But everyone ate some. In the raw state, if hard, fragrant melon would keep for three or four months in baskets, but if soft, only a few days.

A good deal more fruit was eaten in Kao Yao than was grown, for it was cheap in the market when in season. Everyone over twelve months old ate fresh and dried persimmons. Fresh ones would last a month, but even if they decayed, they were eaten. The persimmons were very hot like a pepper, and had to be soaked in water for two or three days before the skin was cut off and the fruit consumed. Obviously, the persimmons were picked in their astringent condition and not allowed to ripen. To dry the fruit, it was peeled and pressed under a stone, then placed in the sun for at least twenty days. The dried persimmons were put into baskets and at night, if it was not raining, exposed to the dew which was said to make the fruit sweet. Fresh persimmons would last for a month and dried ones about six, or at least until the New Year's period when they were given as a delicacy to the children.

Before eating peaches, some individuals peeled them, while some were content to rub them on their clothes. They were always eaten ripe and raw, none being pickled. Peaches might be enjoyed anytime except after meals as it was thought they would cause sickness if eaten then. The fresh peaches, of course, rotted quickly if kept more than a few days.

Plums were eaten raw and unskinned despite the fact that they were very sour. They were also eaten after being dipped into wine, but this practice was a prerogative of men. Sometimes they were left in the spirits, and the drink was then referred to as plum wine. Plums were mentioned as being eaten anywhere, not only at home but on the street or in the teahouses. At night, one ate them when tired, for they were said to give one new energy. Plums were stored in baskets in an upstairs room if available, as were peaches and pears, since dryness was desirable. Plums pickled in wine would keep about a year and those which were salted even longer.

Everyone in Kao Yao ate apples, usually before meals. Even the fragrance was appreciated when simply held in the hand. Apples were never cooked, but sometimes small slices were put into wine. Apples stored in baskets would keep up to five months if carefully treated. Moving broke the skins and caused decay.

Pears were only eaten raw and without peeling or cleaning. There was no pickling of pears. They were eaten anytime except after meals when, like peaches, they were believed to cause stomach-ache. They could be kept from the time they were picked in the 8th month until the 1st if placed in baskets and covered with pine needles.

Mulberries were eaten raw from the tree but only by boys and girls, who rarely carried them home. Adults would not eat them as they said they caused stomach-ache. This the children risked and apparently digested the fruit well enough, which was attributed by Pi to their playing so hard.

Most foods of which the preparation has not hitherto been mentioned were either quick-fried, fried for a longer period, or boiled. This statement would cover the cooking of rare delicacies such as fowl and meat and the more commoner fish and fungi. Village people, it should be said, did not fish with the exception of children who occasionally did so for fun, using hooks. Fish were readily available, however, as one group of the Kao Yao boat people made their living by fishing. Soup was often served with meals and sometimes poured onto the rice by the individual eater. All cooks used salt and various sauces in their dishes, but it should be noted that salt was not used in preparing rice. Some spices were planted in the dry fields and more were purchased in town.

Plain water was commonly drunk in Kao Yao and perhaps, measure for measure, more of it than tea. Unboiled, it was drunk cold, but when it had been boiled, taken hot. Children under five drank unboiled water and no tea. Women also drank unboiled cold water, but few men did so. Old women generally drank unboiled cold water with a little sugar mixed into it after supper, and this mixture was also given to women who had just borne a child. Some poor families drank only unboiled cold water, while for many middle class ones, boiled water was the common drink.

The main source of water in Kao Yao were the three public wells. One informant said there were four, but then changed his mind, reducing his count by one; another informant said two, but demonstrably forgot one. There were also private wells, but of the number of these the guess was always low. Five are shown on the plan of the village and it is conceivable that one or two were overlooked since, whereas the public wells were said never to go dry, private ones apparently did and a dry well can be easily passed by.

The most obvious well was the one several times mentioned as being half way along the main street (Pl. 25, p. 166). It was dug about the end of the nineteenth century. According to our authority, T'ao Hua, the village had been more prosperous before the event, but this well spoiled the beneficial aspect of Kao Yao, it being likened to a boil on a man's face. The description seemed most apt, and I had a feeling that at least part of the change might be explained on the simple grounds of sanitation, but I merely asked why the well was not replaced with one more fortunately located. It was made clear that the situation could not be remedied because the people were too lazy to walk farther. Besides, to abandon the old well would be a matter which would have to be taken up with, and approved by, the district government.

The second well was located at the northeasterly corner of the marketplace, an almost natural drainage pool. Often there was so much water on the surface around it that it was difficult to approach. The water drawn out in wood buckets was dark in color, but more than ten families used it. Pi said the people simply did not care if the street water ran into the wells. Another informant named Li said that he did not like the water in other villages because it tasted different, as one might easily conceive to be true.

The third well was above the road near the village temple. When we went on our round of wells, a woman was washing rice there, using a large wood spoon. This well, like the others, was rock-

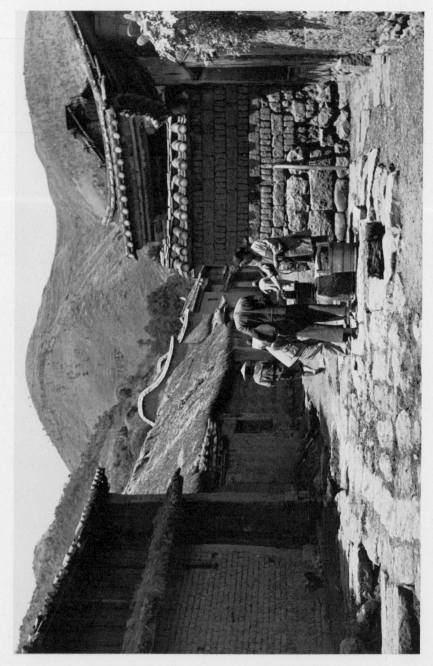

25. WELL ON MAIN STREET

bound, and the water looked clean. Unquestionably, it was farther away than the other two wells for most of the Kao Yao families. Anyone could use the water in any of these three public wells. Most of the private wells were apparently the property of the wealthier families, who not only boiled their water but usually drank tea.

Tea, the national drink of China for a thousand years, was never as universally used in the country as Westerners have often imagined. This was simply because many people could not afford it. Periodically, however, everyone in Kao Yao over five or six years of age drank tea, males more often than females, and the members of upper-class families to the exclusion of water. Pi said that tea itself was not sold in the stores of Kao Yao, and that one had to buy it in town. This would be understandable on the basis of the small quantities used even of the cheaper types, considering that tea suffers when not stored properly. On the other hand, our neighbor Mei, who operated what was really an opium den under the guise of a store, listed tea among the several articles he purveyed.

Tea, wherever acquired, was brewed by putting the leaves into a pot and pouring boiling water on top of them. The same leaves were used all day, water being added as needed. After supper the old leaves were replaced with fresh ones. Tea was not drunk at meals. If available in the house, tea was always served to a guest on his arrival. Drinking from the spouts of individual-size porcelain teapots, a common custom in Yünnan, was a practice usually observed in the homes of tea drinkers in Kao Yao, but not in the restaurants or teahouses. Three grades of tea were said to be drunk, the cheapest costing one-third the price of the best which was perfumed by the addition of flowers. The medium grade was simply a half-and-half mixture of the other two. Only upper-class people were likely to drink the best.

Wine, contrary to tea, was enjoyed at the beginning of meals, especially supper. Usually the rice bowl, filled to two-thirds of its capacity served as a cup. Mr. Tuan and the school manager were singled out to exemplify men who drank each time that they sat down to eat. Many individuals were so fond of drinking that they sacrificed other things, even food, in order to buy wine. A few people drank between meals, but that was unusual. In the schoolteacher's opinion, it was not rare in Kao Yao for people to drink to excess and, when they did so, they talked too much, sometimes quarreling and fighting, sometimes crying. The second week of our stay, a man who lived across the marketplace became drunk, cried, and asserted that he was going to kill his wife because she had questioned him when he rubbed his baby's face. He said that the baby was his son and consequently nothing was wrong with his rubbing its face.

Pi said that the previous month a man was intoxicated, fell down, and rolled on the ground. Giving the name of a widow with whom he was in love, he kept repeating, "I will sleep with you, I will sleep with you." Our friend Mr. Tuan was himself very fond of his drink and the effect could be noticeable. At such times, one of his repeated remarks whimsically expressed in the teahouse was, "Alas, my wife is making love to the temple priest because I am old and he is young." Our records indicate that at the time the lady was forty-five years his junior.

Teahouses in Kao Yao did not sell wine. The owners said that it was too much trouble to provide both wine and tea in the same establishment. There was nothing objectionable, however, in a customer's buying a measure of wine at a neighboring store and bringing it back to the teahouse to drink with roast beans which the latter place provided. He might even borrow a bottle in which to carry the wine providing the wine merchant had one available. A drinker who anticipated his intentions usually brought his own container, however.

The three principal types of wine purchaseable in Kao Yao were made, respectively, from rice, maize, and wheat. The first had the highest alcoholic content and the other two were of medium strength. They were all said to come from An Ning (Fig. 3, p. 25), or Peace and Tranquility, a district seat of three or four thousand Chinese families about thirteen miles west on the road to Tali. An Ning, one of the principal stations of the porters, was noted for its hot springs and large onions, but charcoal and mats, as well as the wine, were brought from there. In Kao Yao, one could also purchase what was called white wine, a very weak alcoholic drink made from glutenous rice.

Tobacco was smoked by many men in Kao Yao, but only by old women. Although young boys were said not to smoke, we saw one doing so in a teahouse. Li Fu, our companion, immediately said the case was exceptional. No one chewed tobacco or used snuff, the

latter practice having been said to have disappeared, except among
Mohammedans, about the time of the first world war. Manufactured cigarettes and cigars were sold in the stores as well as two
kinds of tobacco, one the local product and the other a fine, mustard-
colored variety used in water pipes which was said to come from a
place about forty miles to the south. As a general impression, long
bamboo pipes with small metal bowls and bamboo water pipes, were
most common, but there were other varieties in use including all-
metal water pipes such as were so common in southeast China, but
only a few were owned in Kao Yao. Pipelike holders for small
cigars were commonplace, and once a man was noticed smoking a
cigarette in the Hindu fashion with the fingers covering the mouth
so that little air was inhaled that did not pass through the tobacco.

The bowls of the Chinese pipes were so small that they had to be
continually stoked with tobacco, a burning incense stick being kept
in the hand to ignite it, which action leads us to make a few comments on fire.

Fires were made with flint and steel up to about 1928, but since
then matches had been used. The more frugal families, however,
when in need of fire, borrowed a piece of burning wood, carrying it
in hemp stalks which were in flame before they reached home. Anyone would give a person fire. When a stove was not in use, during
either day or night, red embers were preserved in the ashes.

In Kao Yao, fire was used for cooking, light, heat, and ceremonial purposes. Most cooking was done in elliptical iron pans fixed
into a large square of stone and mortar with a chimney rising from
the rear and, beneath the pan, a fuel box filled from the front. For
ordinary purposes, twigs and grasses gathered in the hills served for
fuel, but when entertaining, roots or heavier wood were essential as
there was not time for continually feeding the stove. Charcoal was
not regularly used for cooking except by restaurants, and although
coal was mined in nearby hills and shipped to Kunming, none was
burned in Kao Yao. Besides the typical kitchen stoves, small pot
stoves of stoneware were frequently seen, as well as some of actual
stone. Pot stoves served principally for the boiling of water. Rarely,
one saw gasoline cans converted into pot stoves.

For lighting, small glass kerosene lamps with vertical flat wicks
were most commonly used, although there were some simple dish
and spout lamps as well. Some people had flashlights which cer-

tainly were no novelty, being of provincial manufacture. No one had a gasoline light, an import that was much too expensive. Heating was provided for one-third of the year by burning charcoal in braziers of iron or stone. Red candles, it should be noted, were used for ceremonial purposes, but not for light. Most white candles for use in lanterns were imported and cost three cents for the six-inch size. Then there was the little kerosene lamp that used a cylindrical wick and supplied the flame needed to smoke opium.

The second day we knew Pi, he told us that there were two opium dens in Kao Yao, but that they were too dirty for me to visit, and that he would bring me the apparatus if I wanted to smoke. The same day Li Fu admitted that there were about ten residents who smoked, then raised it to fifteen or sixteen when pressed to be exact, adding that only the old and the sick used opium. Pi, Ho, and the cook said they had never tried to smoke, but the cook later proved himself adept at rolling the pills. By the end of our visit, I had the feeling that they were the only adult males left in the village who had not, but that was an exaggerated notion. Smoking among women was rarer, as money and time were scarcer commodities among them. As has been indicated before, the opium dens of Kao Yao were exceeded in number only by teahouses and stores, but even Pi concurred somewhat proudly in the assertion that Yünnan opium was the cheapest and best in the world. Then he rather shamefacedly added that a real addict would sell his wife's pants just to buy it. When I smiled, he not only gave me the name of the man, but told of another who took the rice from the water into which his dutiful wife had just put it, and sold it for money to buy opium. This much must be said of the evils of overindulgence.

11

BUSINESS AND COSTS

M Y HAND had become adept at cooking an opium pill, the thin silver needle rolling across my fingers with a deft push and pull of my thumb while the brown juice on the needle's end bubbled like burning rubber a few inches above the candle-sized flame (Fig. 9, p. 109). Usually the first coating of the pin went well and, after dipping it into the opium for the second, I had little concern that I could not cook that one too. It was the final coating that usually gave me trouble, probably because I was tired and impatient. It annoyed me so often to see my efforts carbonized in a momentary burst of flame. I smiled, nevertheless, when I thought of what a fortune it would have cost to learn the art of cooking opium in New York, and continued my practice.

Cooking the opium was not the only difficulty. Intrinsically, it was simple to roll the resultant globule on the small stone, but to form a neat little cone was not achieved the first time. Neither was the reheating of the pill and jabbing it into the pipe bowl done perfectly at every attempt. The real problem was to free the pin deftly so that the cone stuck to the pipe and was not withdrawn with the pin. All these complications were merely mechanical, however, compared with the smoking itself. At first, I frequently caused the pill hole to plug up, but I finally learned how to draw with regular and strong inhalations, keeping the bowl of the lamp at the right distance over the flame.

My gratification not only came from the beneficial effect of the opium on my viscera, but from the esthetic satisfaction of handling the equipment. The pipe stem, about twenty inches long, was bamboo browned with age and there were green jade fittings at the ends. Even the simple silver pin and the small square wafer of mottled black marble gave pleasure to the fingers, while the glow of the lamp on the dark stage captivated the eyes. This lamp was a charming thing in itself, and its owner had told me with pride that its silver base had been made in Su-chou, the city famous for its beautiful women, while the globular glass cover with a hole in the top came from Canton.

Two or three pipefuls of opium never made me dream wildly, and I woke full of anticipation to continue my work, first showing appreciation of the cook's rice noodles boiled with smoked ham and served with steamed dumplings containing indescribable stuffing. Having come to a reasonable understanding of agricultural production in Kao Yao, it remained to discover other essential factors in the economic life of the village. As had been made clear in reference to surrounding communities, each seemed to have its specialty and, with this notion in mind, it was simple to recognize the principal business in Kao Yao. It was transportation, and our friend Li Fu, a leader in the profession of porters, provided information. The first day that we discussed the matter Li said there were more than ten families in Kao Yao who depended for their livelihood on using pack animals for transporting goods. A few days later, he doubled the number, apparently as the result of further reflection, but it brought out the problem of which families could be truly considered as porters since all undertook more or less farming as well, and some apparently only functioned in the transport business when commissions were plentiful. In any event, it is significant that over ten per cent of Kao Yao families belonging to various lineages shared in the business.

The richest porter possessed four or five animals and could drive all of them himself. Li owned a male horse which he preferred as being stronger and more energetic than a mare, and a female mule which he regarded as more tractable than a male. The animals of his choice were consequently more expensive than those of the opposite sex; also, mules cost more than horses because, in general, they were healthier. Mules walked slower, however, and had to be watched so that they did not throw their loads. One porter in Kao Yao worked with four donkeys, but they could carry only small burdens. No preference for the color of transport animals was evinced.

When a horse or a mule was to be purchased, it was considered better to buy an animal raised in the village, since such a one was certainly adapted to the local climate. Li Fu said that if a horse or a mule were moved from a hot region to a cool one, the animal would be difficult to feed, although the alternative did not create as much of a problem. Horse raising was encouraged in the district. Proud breeders could compete for prizes at a fair held just south of Kunming at a place called Yang Ma Shan, or Horse Raising Hill (exact location uncertain). For the winner, there was a new Western-type saddle, plus money and a ribbon, and for his closest competitors, several lesser awards, but it is doubtful that anyone from Kao Yao ever won them.

Actually, in Kao Yao, horses were allowed to interbreed freely. For mules, the female horse was taken to the donkey in the 2nd or 3rd month of the year, a stud fee being paid for the service. Male donkeys were kept for that purpose only, and were said to be capable of performing ten times in a day. There were no fertility rites for animals but, when pregnant, they were not worked and were better fed. The offspring were kept in a stable with the mother for a month, and then released to run around. The animals were given grass and beans twice a day when at home, and three times when working. Beans were brought from Kunming as the none-too-plentiful local product, much appreciated for human consumption in the village, was more expensive. Occasionally animal feed had to be packed to supply the necessary food on a trip. Horses were sometimes castrated by an itinerant specialist, as were also cattle and pigs.

Both horses and mules had to be three or four years old to be packed. Both could travel over twenty-five miles a day with a full load of from 120 to 130 catties. Both had a working life of about ten years. The pack saddles were all of one type bought in Kunming. They consisted of a wood frame with a second separate one which supported the load and fitted over the first. The saddle was fastened on top of a blanket on the back of the animal. Head harness was of two types, of which one had a bit. Pack animals were allowed to go their own familiar way, the driver leading them if it were uncertain. By crying "O-oo," he could attract their attention to the right road, but no call was used to stop them. Horses were sometimes ridden with a native saddle (higher in front than in the rear), a Western-type saddle, a blanket alone, or nothing at all, the reins being pulled in the direction one wanted to go. Water buffalo, it might be noted, were never used as pack animals, but they were often ridden bareback to and from the fields by boys who took care of them. Pack animals were reputably not given to fighting each other and, if one got away, assistance would be given in recovering it, most porters being capable of recognizing the beast's owner.

To obtain work, the porters looked for commissions, although sometimes customers sought out the porters. Most of the through transportation was arranged by cooperation with the original carrier. Li Fu, for example, received goods from certain of the boat people, and presumably favored them with produce moving into Kao Yao from the opposite direction. Kunming-bound items which we noted during our visit included salt, slate, stone, bricks (both baked and unbaked), tiles, rice, water buffalo hides, boards for the construction of boats, boards for coffins, wood fuel, and charcoal; moving west-

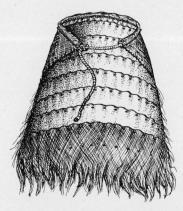

Figure 14. Fiber Cape

ward, we saw imported goods including kerosene, as well as tobacco, cigarettes, cakes, cloth, and presumably many other kinds of articles in unidentified packages. Li Fu claimed that rice and charcoal were the most common goods carried. In any event he preferred to carry rice as it was transported in small bundles. In contrast, wood beams were onerous to move as anyone might appreciate. In the rain, damageable goods, as well as the porters themselves, were protected with palm-fiber covers, of which the Li Fu family made its own (Fig. 14, above; Pl. 26, p. 177). The material was acquired by stripping small pieces of sheathing from the trunk of a palm tree and placing them under stones for an evening to flatten them. Afterward, the strips were sewn together. A typical cover had an over-all size of thirty inches square. The dense ends of four pieces were folded over a length of rope and sewn in place by stitches one inch apart. Three more strips were sewn onto the first four one inch below the rope, and then six more rows, each three inches below the previous one, thereby utilizing twenty-five strips altogether. The four pieces of the top row fell the full length of the cover on the outside, and each row below was shorter. The last, or eighth, row of three strips was turned with the inner surface of the fiber facing in. The cover was fastened in place by slipping the long end of the rope over which the fiber had been sewn through a small loop in the other end and tying it. It may be added that among the knots and lashings known in Kao Yao were the slip knot, the square knot, the clove and the timber hitch, and the sheet bend.

Carriage on materials transported was charged for by weight and by distance, most of the porters in Kao Yao working between their home village and Kunming, Ma Chieh, or An Ning (Fig. 3, p. 25). Four or five families made a business of storing goods in Kao Yao, and others did the same in Ma Chieh and An Ning, while in Kunming there were regular warehouses. Most of the long-distance transport was handled by outsiders, although Li Fu, for example, welcomed the chance for a long journey. Normally, however, he carried things back and forth between Kao Yao and An Ning, a round trip that he could complete in a day. Consequently, it was only two or three times a year that he had the opportunity to spend the night away from home. Once he conveyed stone to a village called Ssu Hsu (exact location uncertain) which he estimated was a distance of 160 miles from Kao Yao. On such trips he never took his family. For local journeys, such as to Ma Chieh and An Ning, the porters used the same highways that served for the antiquated buses plying to and from Kunming, but on their wider travels, they often followed old stone-paved roads or paths that meandered endlessly over the hills. There were no direct taxes for using these unmarked roads and even the bridges were free. At Kao Yao, however, there was a charge for transferring most types of goods from boats to animals, or vice versa.

In traveling, people greeted each other with the question, "Where are you going?" and offered the other party the right of way. On entering an inn, the owner was immediately asked, "Have you a room for us, *lao pan?*" using the honorary title for a proprietor or anyone in a position to provide a service. If the answer was affirmative, the traveler unloaded his animal, then watered and fed it. While it ate, he usually prepared food for himself. If the man was alone, he occupied a room by himself, but it might be shared by others if in his party. In the morning, after readying his animal and eating his breakfast, he settled his account without comment.

On distant journeys, a train of pack animals might be joined and their owners camp in a tent shaped like an inverted V. Food was cooked over an open fire. Two or three watchdogs were usually taken along, and the porters often carried weapons of one kind or another. Formerly, travelers frequently bowed or kowtowed before any God of the Earth, or roadside shrine, praying for protection, but such deference to religious tradition had largely disappeared in our time.

Before turning to other productive enterprises, a word should be said about the carrying of loads by human beings (Pl. 26, p. 177). Most heavy burdens within Kao Yao were transported on the back with the help of a packboard and tumpline. The packboard was the width of the shoulders and about six inches wide with an oval cut out to fit around the back of the neck and a hole bored at each end. The tumpline was made of water buffalo hide except for the short central section of twisted palm fiber which rested against the forehead. The ends of the line were passed through the holes of the packboard and then around the load which almost invariably rested on the distinctive type of palm-fiber mat used as a raincoat when need be (Fig. 14, p. 174). A Kao Yao adult could carry from 60 or 70 to 120 catties, and there was not much difference in the ability of the sexes. A staff might be used for assistance. Baskets and buckets were often utilized for transporting agricultural and other materials, one of a pair being used at each end of a shoulder pole.

Except for porters and soldiers, few villagers ever made journeys of more than one or two days. Religious festivals and theatrical performances were the particular attractions of which three were specifically mentioned as reasons for traveling. On the 15th of the 1st month some people went to Ma Chieh (Fig. 5, p. 69) to see a drama called Meeting for the Emperor in a temple alleged to have belonged to a Han dynasty (206 B.C. to A.D. 219) ruler. Then, on the 19th of the 2nd month, a few individuals might go to Kuan Tu (Fig. 3, p. 25) south of Kunming to see a wood image of the God of the Earth seated on a white water buffalo which walked back and forth while firecrackers were exploded. Also, a few women went to wor-

26. FIVE PORTERS ENTERING THE VILLAGE

ship a famous Kuan Yin fifteen or twenty miles west of Kao Yao on the 19th of the 6th month. A few journeys were undertaken to buy rice or cattle, or just to make visits. The Kao Yao travelers inevitably walked. If in a group, there was no rule about position or keeping in step, but older people were allowed to precede so that there would not be any danger of their falling too far behind.

One day we saw a litter with two bearers moving up the street and, on another afternoon, a woman in a yellow sedan chair. The latter was a rectangular box with a pole extending fore and aft at each side through slots. At the ends of the poles were cross pieces like a packboard which rested on the shoulders of the two carriers. For such vehicles, four men might be employed. Both yellow and green sedan chairs were used by wealthy travelers. Green ones were festooned with red cloth and flowers for marriages or, for funerals, draped with white cloth. No sedan chairs of any color, however, were owned by residents of Kao Yao. In the district, one also occasionally came upon solid-wheeled carts pulled by either water buffalo or oxen. These vehicles were said to have a capacity of about five hundred catties. Small two-wheeled carts, or occasionally four-wheeled ones, were brought into service when much dirt was to be moved in Kao Yao.

We have seen that the economy of Kao Yao was based primarily on agricultural production and secondarily on the specialized business of transporting merchandise, a natural development considering Kao Yao's location on the opposite side of the lake from the capital. There was still a third distinctive economic feature, although related to the last in that it undoubtedly was stimulated by the same factors and also involved travelers. We refer to the teahouses, stores, opium dens, restaurants, inns, and gambling houses, which certainly would not have proliferated to such an extent in an average village. Although these institutions served the residents of Kao Yao, they catered in considerable degree to travelers who on certain days passed through the village on picnic pilgrimages to the famous temples in the hills behind Kao Yao or came intermittently to set out on peregrinations to the west. The amount of this business should not be presented in exaggerated form; indeed, except for weekend holidays, such people were seldom noticeable in the village.

Apart from these service institutions, there were a number of local industries, but we have no evidence that any of them sold much of their production outside of Kao Yao. There were two coffin shops which together might be considered to have had the potential capacity of constructing fifty coffins a year, but it is certain they did not produce them for, although coffin-making was the primary criterion of the shops, they also engaged in many aspects of the carpentry trade, making tables, tools, boxes, and various other village necessities (Pl. 27, p. 180). For some of this work, the lumber came from either the village forest or private woods owned by the local residents. The trees were cut down with an ax and then the logs sawn into planks which were dried. Should a tree be cut in a graveyard, a chicken was sacrificed. Also, when trees were to be cut in a private forest, the owners and neighbors were invited to a dinner so there would be common knowledge as to what and whose wood was being cut. The woodworking in Kao Yao, however, did not include the fashioning of buckets, ladles, pack saddles, or boats. Carpenters, as such, were distinguished from coffin-makers just as in Western culture they can be set apart from skilled cabinetmakers. The single basket-maker probably did not supply all of the local demands, nor did the blacksmith with his assistant. The latter obtained his stock of iron from Kunming and, after heating it in his forge with a draught supplied by a simple hand bellows, he beat it into the shape of heads for various common farm implements. He also spent a considerable amount of time making nails, but horseshoes were beyond the range of his activity. There was also a barber in Kao Yao. The sauce-maker was so inconspicuously located near the end of an alley that we did not even discover him until the end of our stay, and consequently our data on his production was so incomplete that I am not even certain what kind of sauce it was that he made.

In all the Kao Yao activities, one had little feeling of bustle or turmoil. To work was considered a matter of necessity, since food, clothing, and a place adequately cared for in which to live were recognized as necessities. The motive of achieving economic independence in order to obtain a wife did not influence a young Kao Yao man to work hard, but it probably did affect his parents who arranged their children's marriages. Pi offered the comment that the richer a man was, the more he would work to increase his wealth. Clearly the prestige and status derived from having money was an incentive. Perhaps in a sense it at least symbolized the possibility of enjoying

27. A COFFIN SHOP

leisure which was almost universally considered better than working. Still, to be lazy caused a certain amount of ridicule. The few people who loafed or malingered were looked down upon, while there was recognizable approbation for effort, especially as it related to professional pride. There was some sense of competitiveness in accomplishment, but the conception of labor as a duty was considered a newly introduced notion. Perseverance was said to be relatively lacking before the end of the empire, but since that time people were believed to be learning to coordinate their efforts. To sum up, it would seem that although leisure was idealized, to be idle was actually bad.

As has been pointed out in connection with the agricultural round of seasons, work became intensified at the times of transplanting and harvesting rice. On the other hand, as always there were rest periods taken three or four times a day during which people sat down for about twenty minutes, the men usually smoking, but not engaging in games. There was no alleviation of dullness by playing music in the fields, as did Korean farmers, for example. Occasionally while transplanting, the younger people might sing, but their elders considered such behavior undignified. For those who enjoyed it, the smoking of opium could be a palliative. Involuntary unemployment, incidentally, was unknown in Kao Yao; for every man, some job was available.

Distinctive categories of despised and honorable labor—commonplace concepts in the civilizations of the East—did not seem to be recognized in Kao Yao. Although the traditional hierarchy of descending rank from scholar to farmer to merchant was generally acknowledged, no one conceded that it was bad to be a barber, although in traditional Chinese culture such a trade was considered shameful. Needless to say to the sophisticated, no one was demeaned by the daily activity of carrying night soil from the men's toilets to the fields.

The sexual division of labor in Kao Yao can be appreciated most expeditiously by presenting the lists of activities compiled in the village.

Men and Women

Planted the rice seed (but women usually)
Harvested rice
Planted maize, wheat, and other vegetables

Hoed corn
Carried night soil to fields (from men's toilets)
Fed animals (and children)
Bought food in market (women usually)
Built fires (by whoever cooks)
Brought in fuel
Cared for stores
Made sun-dried bricks
Hauled house building materials
Thatched roofs

Men

Plowed the fields
Controlled water supply to fields (by machines and dams)
Planted, cared for, and harvested tobacco
Butchered pigs
Killed fowl (women did this sometimes)
Cooked (when women were in the fields, and on other special occasions)
Cooked all restaurant food (except rice)
Took care of large animals (except conducting them to and from the fields
    and pasture which was done by boys or girls)
Made wood shoes (in rainy season)
Repaired buildings
Did all stone work
Carried on all the professions (but women could operate stores and tea-
    houses)
Did all business involving property
Held all political offices
Acted as pallbearers
Dug graves
Read holy books to others
Played musical instruments

Women

Transplanted rice
Weeded rice (but men assisted)
Did most of the cooking
Did all of the sewing; clothes, etc. (i.e., in the village)
Made palm fiber raincoats
Made straw sandals (but not good ones or often)
Took care of children (with daughter's help, but rarely men's)
Cut children's hair
Cleaned houses
Emptied own night jars into men's toilets

It was conceded that in Kao Yao women kept busy more of the time than men, although the differentiation was more apparent than real if one judged by the men's sitting around in the teahouses, since women were by custom forbidden to enter them.

There were a few obvious distinctions in the activities of the young, as well as in those of the aged. Three formal age grades were recognized: childhood from 1 to 20, adulthood from 20 to 40, and old age over 40. Babyhood was not distinguished as an arbitrary period. Most children had some play time, and most spent many hours in school. As they grew older, the boys were often apprenticed to the professional workers in the village or to others in Kunming. Those children who remained at home, and especially the daughters and elder sons, grew up working in the fields and tending to the household chores. In 1938, many of the young men were drawn into the army.

For most of the aged, advanced years brought an increasing measure of leisure, although this was undoubtedly greater for men. In general, old people watched over the house and the young children in it, while the more active adults labored elsewhere. They also fed the animals and brought grass and firewood from the hills which could be collected at no cost. It always amazed me to see what a sizable load the ageing Mr. Tuan would bring down on a nice day. Soon afterward he would change his clothes and set off for a teahouse where he was sure of finding old cronies.

Labor in Kao Yao impressed one as being more individualistic than cooperative, although there were definite occasions for the latter. Groups of workers concentrated in the fields of a single family, one after another, in both the transplanting of rice and its harvesting. The head of the family, in whosoever's field they had gathered, directed the operation. In the rare case when a public building was to be constructed, the village head invited people to help and they generally did. He was also responsible for cooperative work on the roads and other public facilities. One more example was the case of collectively planting trees on village land in the hills (but not the Kao Yao forest). In due time, the timber was cut, sold, and the money divided among the participators. Needless to say, the inhabitants of Kao Yao also cooperated in the preparation for certain festivities, but such activities were not looked upon as real labor.

Labor relations were not complex in Kao Yao. If a man was needed to work in the fields, the head of some poor family was directly approached to see if he was willing to be employed. Should he be agreeable, he would be offered $20.00 to $30.00 for a year, besides being supplied with food, shelter, clothing, and tobacco. Such a man helped with the ordinary farm work including irrigation and care of the cattle. He ate with the family by whom he was employed, wore the same kind of clothing, and was treated for the time as a member of the household. These agricultural laborers were looked upon simply as individuals with not very active minds; otherwise they would have learned trades if they had no farms. Farm laborers could leave their employers at any time, in which case their wages were prorated. In Kao Yao, there were neither forced labor nor unions.

An effort was made to find out how much labor could be expected from a farmer. First of all, Tu Wen-ch'ing told us that the term *kung,* equivalent in area to one-third of a *mou,* or to one-eighteenth of an acre, or about forty-eight square feet, traditionally represented the area of rice field which one man could plant with seedlings in a day. By and large, it was his opinion that a man who really worked hard could take care of four or five *mou* of rice fields during a year, and Pi concurred with this opinion. On the other hand, Li Fu once told us that a worker could take care of two *mou* of rice land. He was perhaps reasoning from his own statement that the fifteen *mou* of rice land belonging to him and his brothers was cared for by the five or six women in their households with friends helping when need be.

Finally, in our survey of workers, we should mention the itinerants, although most of them will be discussed under the category of entertainers. A man who sharpened scissors and razors appeared once or twice a year and was apparently well patronized. He was not offered knives, as these the owners needed to sharpen frequently and therefore had learned to accomplish the task themselves. Hardly more often came a mender of umbrellas, dishes, and locks. I was tempted to buy an old lock for fifty cents from one such itinerant I encountered, but my friend Tuan bluntly informed me it was no good and that I could buy a new one in the city for sixty. I explained that I did not want a new one for myself but as an interesting specimen for a museum, whereupon he promised to acquire suitable examples in the village, which was much more to my liking (Fig. 15, below).

A consideration of itinerant peddlers brings our attention to the village market, or fair, which convened in Kao Yao every sixth morning, as it did in P'i Chi Kuan three days later (Pl. 28, p. 186). The vendors came from various villages, and some from Kunming. Two were residents of Kao Yao, of whom one sold cooked noodles and the other kerosene. These participants made the rounds of the market with the group. Since we saw the market people and their customers gather, intermingle, and disperse beneath our windows on five different occasions, we became quite familiar with the fair and can present the fleeting picture presented during the third meeting we observed.

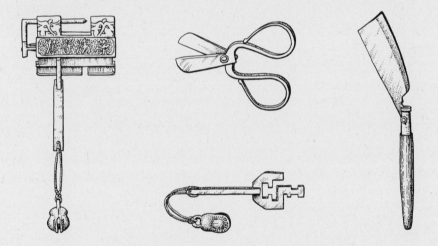

Figure 15. Lock, Key, Scissors, and Razor

The weather was tranquil and the temperature varied from sixty-eight degrees in the morning to a pleasant seventy-six at four in the afternoon by which time the vendors had vanished from the scene. Diagonally across the square near the public well were two or three lines of bundled tree branches about four feet long. Paralleling this supply of firewood, was a double row of large baskets containing vegetables—some white, some green—and near them, rich purple eggplants, both the long type and the round. Two upper-class women with dainty parasols walked down the lane between the vege-

28. VIEW OF THE MARKETPLACE

tables, intermingling with the crowd of villagers in commonplace dress. Leaving room for a third passage, a row of a half-dozen tables had been lined up, several shaded by canvas awnings stretched over bamboo poles connecting the tops of vertical bamboo crosses, the lateral ends of which were tied to the corners of the canvas. On one of the tables rested dishes of noodles interspersed with bowls of beans, both yellow and brown, all placed in front of long benches which tempted the visitors to seat themselves. One man was cooking food in an oval copper dish over a fire made in an old gasoline tin with the top cut out. Nearby, on his stand, a handful of bright red chopsticks projected from a crude, green-glazed jar. Beneath our windows were the grain sellers, their large, tightly woven bags neatly rolled into collars at the tops. On both sides of the street where it bordered the marketplace were sellers of city goods—beads, clothing, paper materials, and cakes. Almost in the center of the square under a large umbrella sat a man with a huge stoneware jar which may have contained kerosene or vegetable oil.

In between the vendors moved crowds of people, both males and females of all ages. They stared more than they talked, although here and there buyers and sellers challenged each other over prices. On the whole, the gathering was orderly, and many of the visitors showed peaceable smiles. Meanwhile, down the street went porters with loads of all kinds, occasionally one crying out so as not to do damage with his burden of boards. Several times a whole train of pack horses stumbled through the mob. As the sun became warmer, several of the market people erected awnings by putting a vertical pole into the center of a square of canvas stretched at the corners by crossed sticks of bamboo. Intermittently a dog nosed his way through the throng. There was a woman with magenta trousers—faded ones, the color of a morning glory. A food vendor had a pipe more than a yard long which he rested on the ground, leaning its thin stem against his stand, the jade mouthpiece sticking up like a snake's head. Some of the market people had large paper parasols, and there were a number of old, black, European-style umbrellas held by the visitors to keep off the sun. The tobacco merchant heaped up his supply for water pipes in neat yellow mounds, weighing the finely cut leaves on the small brass tray of a hand balance when a sale was being made. The grain sellers dipped up their wares, pouring them into square, wood measuring boxes resting in circular basket trays. Then they smoothed the grain very flat with a hand, brushing the excess into the tray and later returning it to the bag from which it originally came. A butcher sliced off bits from his slab of meat. Straw hats and straw mats were everywhere. Striking to the eyes were great blocks of salt. There was a girl with the back of her trousers pink, the front blue—also a blue patch on the pink. The market was well under way by ten in the morning and by two the crowd had already thinned out.

On the fourth visit of the market during our stay, we requested a woman to list all the commodities sold with their approximate prices, a task which a foreigner could not effectively undertake. Even with a Chinese compilation, it must be appreciated that prices fluctuated rapidly in Kao Yao, not only because of the bargaining abilities between buyer and seller, but because there were standard differences between vendors which only sometimes reflected the quality of their wares and, finally, because costs were being affected by the beginning of wartime inflation. The comment must be added that it is certain that some items which were sold in the market were not recorded.

Merchandise Priced in the Kao Yao Market (*August, 1938*)

Rice (cheapest)—$3.80 per *tou* (equals $4.22 per *picul*)*
Cabbages—.10 to .15 per head
Eggplants—.10 to .15 for ten
Onions—.05 per bundle
Green peppers—.02 per catty
Potatoes—.25 per catty
Ginger—.05 per catty
Bitter melons—.10 to .15 for ten
Peaches—.01 each (sizes averaged)
Plums—.02 per bowl
Pears—.01 each (sizes averaged)
Fish (ca. 4 inches long)—.06 per lump of six or seven
Pork (salted)—.32 per catty
Pork (fresh)—.20 per catty
Rice noodles—.02 or .03 per bowl
Glutenous rice custard—.01 per piece
Bean curd (sliced)—.30 per catty
Bean curd (1½ inch squares)—.04 for ten pieces
Bean noodles—.15 per catty

* A *tou* of rice equaled ca. 0.9 *picul;* a *picul* equaled ca. 133 lbs.; a catty ca. 1.33 lbs.

Potato chips (local)—.20 per catty
Vegetable oil (cooking)—.20 per catty
Cakes (local)—.01 per piece
Salt—.18 per catty
Wine—.08 per catty
Tobacco (local)—.02 per bundle leaves
Tobacco (water pipe)—.15 for four ounces
Matches—.02 per box
Soap—.03 per cake
Towel—.10 or .15 each
Tooth powder—.03 per package
Tree branches (fuel)—.40 to .50 per bundle
Sandals (coarse)—.02 per pair
Stockings—.18 per pair
Belt—.18 to .25 each
Thread (various colors)—1.50 per bundle
Thread (silk)—.09 per tenth ounce
Needle case (wood)—.03 each
Comb (fine-tooth)—.10 each
Comb (coarse)—.05 each
Hairpin—.05 each
Hairnet—.04 each
Copper earrings—.05 per pair
Copper ring—.02 each
Flashlight—1.00 each
Batteries—.20 for two
Incense sticks—.03 for bundle of ninety-six
Silver paper for dead—.36 to .40 per 100 sheets
Paper garments for dead—.01 per set

Items Not Priced

Pork (fresh)
Mushrooms
Toothbrushes
Cloth
Embroidered cloth
Lace
Needle case (lead)
Scissors
Patent medicine
Cord
Lamps
Locks and chains
Pottery
Hoes
Various farm implements

It may be interesting to compare the prices listed above with those accumulated from various other informants during the course of our study.

Prices from Various Informants

Rice (white)—$5.00 per *picul*
Rice (red)—4.50 per *picul*
Persimmons (fresh)—.05 for ten
Persimmons (dried)—.40 per catty
Peaches—.03 for ten
Plums—.10 for five or six catties
Apples (large)—.10 each
Apples (small)—.04 or .05 each
Pears—.03 for ten
Pork (fresh)—ca. .20 per catty
Chickens—.50 to 1.00 each
Duck—.50 each
Vegetable oil (cooking and lamps)—.30 per catty
Salt—.17 to .22 per catty
Honey—.27 or .28 per catty
Tea (perfumed)—1.20 per catty
Tea (ordinary)—.40 per catty
Tea (mixed)—.80 per catty
Wine (cheapest)—0.8 per catty (1⅛ pints?)
Tobacco (local)—.18 per catty
Opium (liquid)—2.50 per ounce (Chinese)
Grass (dried)—.10 per basket
Twigs (fuel)—.20 to .25 per basket (large)
Wood (fuel)—.01½ per piece (2 ft. L by 3 in. D.)
Wood (fuel)—.20 per 50 catties
Kerosene—.60 per catty
Candles (6-inch)—.03 each
Flashlights—1.20 each
Batteries—1.20 to 1.80 for two
Horse—50.00 to 60.00
Mule—70.00 to 80.00
Water buffalo or ox (best)—100.00
Water buffalo or ox (2nd grade)—70.00 to 80.00
Water buffalo or ox (3rd grade)—30.00 to 50.00
Slippers (coarse rice straw)—.02 per pair
Slippers (inside of rice straw)—.05 per pair
Slippers (wheat straw)—.20 per pair
Silver coin ornament—.80 each
Silver bracelets (plain)—3.00 to 4.00 per pair (minimum)

Silver bracelets (incised)—3.30 to 4.40 per pair (minimum)
Silver earrings—.70 to .80 per pair (minimum)
Silver rings—.70 to .80 per pair (minimum)
Silver hair ring—.30 each
Jade bracelet—6.00 each (minimum)
Jade earrings—1.00 per pair (minimum)
Jade ring—1.00 each (minimum)
Houses—200.00 per room (minimum)
Gate pictures (paper)—.02 per pair
Brass lock—.60 each
Carving knife (artist's)—.30 each
Guitar-like musical instrument—1.50
Five-foot gut string for above—.05 each
Coffin (standard)—10.00 to 1000.00
Coffin (plain box)—1.00 to 2.00
Grave plot (good)—50.00
Grave plot (poorest)—5.00
White cloth (for funerals)—.15 per person
Paper lanterns (decorated)—ca. 1.00 each
Costumes (Flower Lamp Feast)—50.00 for set
Slave girls (trader buys)—10.00 to 40.00
Slave girls (sold for marriage)—60.00 to 100.00
Betrothal presents to bride's family—30.00 minimum
Betrothal presents to bridegroom's family—8.00 minimum

Before commenting on these lists, we will add one more which represents—with one significant exception—the items sold in one little store with their prices. The information was recorded during the second day of our residence in Kao Yao, a period when it seemed wise for both the owner and us to politely overlook his business in opium although its odor was obvious.

Merchandise Prices in Mei's Store

Rice (1st grade)—$.60 per tenth *picul*
Rice (2nd grade)—.55 per tenth *picul*
Rice (3rd grade)—.50 per tenth *picul*
Tea (1st grade)—1.00 per catty
Tea (2nd grade)—.80 per catty
Tea (3rd grade)—.50 per catty
Charcoal—.15 per catty
Cigarettes (1st grade)—.15 for ten
Cigarettes (2nd grade)—.10 for ten
Cigarettes (3rd grade)—.08 for ten

Beyond the simple fact of what things cost, our lists give little indication that commodities were cheaper at the marketplace than in the stores. Rice was slightly lower, but one cannot be certain of the grades. Vegetable oil was so much cheaper that the comparable figure is suspect, but again possibly different qualities were involved. Peaches and pears were much higher in the market than the price given by informants, but the latter costs may reflect seasonal peaks of the commodity. On the whole, the lists seem to complement each other, and most of the comparable items tend simply to confirm the prices given by different informants.

There were relatively few salaried groups in Kao Yao and we learned the amounts paid to just three.

Schoolteacher—$120 per year plus rice worth ca. $25.00, plus room
Carpenter—$.50 to .60 per day
Farm laborer (male)—20.00 to 30.00 per year plus food, shelter, clothing, and tobacco; or .10 per day, plus two meals for short term labor
Farm labor (female)—.05 per day plus one meal for short term labor

We also knew that the temple caretaker who doubled as courier was paid 500 catties of rice per year with a value of perhaps $25.00 and that the school servant earned $15.00 per year, but that was for part-time employment. From the Kao Yao professionals engaged in various services, the following charges were recorded.

Barber (haircut)—$.10
Barber (headshave)—.05
Porter (with one loaded animal)—.60 to Kunming or An Ning
Porter (with one loaded animal)—.30 to Ma Chieh
Porter (with two loaded animals)—2.60 for one day's maximum distance
Stud donkey owner—.50 per service
Doctor (bonesettter)—10.00 to 20.00 per bone set
Woodcutter—.20 to .24 per day (50 or 60 catties at .004 per catty)
Innkeeper (room without bedding)—.05 per night
Innkeeper (room with bedding)—.10 per night
Innkeeper (stable for animal)—.05 or .06 per night
Landlord (upper class house)—1.00 per month per room
Landlord (middle class house)—.40 to .50 per month per room
Landlord (lower class house)—.20 to .30 per month per room
Money lender—2 to 3 per cent per month
Calligrapher (coffin inscription in liquid gilt)—.30 to .40
Calligrapher (coffin inscription in gold leaf)—3.00 to 4.00
Drama teacher—.50 per night

Boatman (to Kunming)—1.00 for 500 to 600 catties
  (including loading and unloading)
Boatman (to Kunming)—.50 to .80 for a party with some baggage
Boatman (to Kunming)—.08 for individual passenger (wait for a load)

There were also a number of outside professionals called to Kao Yao on particular occasions.

Musicians (for wedding)—.70 to .80 per day
Chair bearers (two with chair for wedding)—5.00 to 6.00 per day
Chair bearers (two with chair for funeral)—2.00 per day (chair empty)
Priest (reader)—1.50 per day
Lay readers—.50 to .60 per day
Chanter—.16 plus half measure of rice
Shaman (without assistants)—2.00 or less per session
Shaman (to ward off rain or fire)—3.00
Shaman (teacher)—30.00 to 40.00 per pupil

Finally, we have a small series of itinerants making set charges who visited Kao Yao one or more times a year.

Razor and scissor sharpener—.05 per implement
Castrator—2.00 per ox
Castrator—.20 to .50 per pig
Castrator—.05 per cock
Blind singer—.10 per song (ca. half hour)
Peep show (more than 10 pictures)—.02 per viewing

We can conclude the presentation of our limited data on economics by turning to taxes. The primary tax in Kao Yao was on land which was assessed in three classes and nine grades according to the following schedule. The distinctions were based both on quality and use of the land. The amount in each case is the annual tax per *mou* (about ⅙ acre).

1st class 1st grade—$1.20
1st class 2nd grade— .80
1st class 3rd grade— .40
2nd class 1st grade— .24
2nd class 2nd grade— .13
2nd class 3rd grade— .07
3rd class 1st grade— .06
3rd class 2nd grade— .03
3rd class 3rd grade— .025

These taxes, largely on rice land, were payable in the 9th month to the village head who forwarded his collections to the district government. There was also a tax of four per cent on the price of all land sold. Sales taxes were also extended to horse and mules, the rate being five per cent. This tax, as well as that on the killing of food animals, was collected by some individual who had to underwrite the amount set by the government which in 1938 was $13.60 for both types. Pi, the schoolteacher, was collector of the two animal taxes and stated that he earned about $20.00 a year from so doing. The rate for killing animals was as follows.

Water buffalo and cattle—$2.25
Pigs—1.70
Goats and sheep—.50

Poultry, horses, mules, and donkeys were exempt from this slaughter tax.

There was a transport tax on goods (except rice, oil, charcoal, and tobacco) passing east or west through P'i Chi Kuan, less than two miles west of Kao Yao, but even a porter such as Li Fu did not know the amount as it was presumably paid in Kunming or some western town before the goods were sent out. All the porters saw was a receipt proving the tax had been paid. Three customs stations were said to have existed between Kao Yao and Ch'u Hsiung (exact location uncertain), a city about sixty miles west. Finally, we should not forget the school tax of one copper, or $.005 for each passenger coming or going from Kao Yao by boat, an assessment which was expected to produce about $30.00.

Old Yünnan money was the common currency of Kao Yao, and the one in which people usually thought of financial transactions. New Yünnan money of twice the value and the national money (used in our computations) of ten times the value were also acceptable. The schoolteacher quickly gave the units of Old Yünnan money as .20, .25, .50, 1.00, 5.00, 10.00, 50.00, and 100.00 notes; when it came to New Yünnan money, he knew silver coins of .10, .20, .50, and 1.00 value plus notes of 1.00, 5.00, and 25.00, of which he had seen the 25.00. He then added that he had heard of 10.00, 50,00, and 100.00 notes. Of national money, he knew as no longer used the square-holed brass cash with a value of one-fortieth the national cent, then the three copper coins of .0025, .005, and .015 value, the

.05 nickel, and the notes of .10, .20, and 1.00. He had not seen the .25 or .50 notes, but had heard of others in value of 2.00, 5.00, and 25.00. Needless to say, there were no banks in Kao Yao and people seldom saved cash, regarding it as complicated and undependable. Any considerable excess money was most often invested in buildings or land. Smaller savings were loaned at interest. Sometimes grain was purchased to be sold when prices were high. The people, however, seemed to guard themselves unconsciously from anyone attempting to corner the supply.

Higgling at sale was so commonplace that it appeared almost mandatory. Certainly for one not to higgle was queer. One could argue about the price of anything, even matches, without being offensive. Any deal between friends was an exception, however. The seller set his price; the buyer could accept or refuse and, if the amount had to be debated because of the value involved, a middleman was appointed. An ordinary business transaction, such as occurred in the market, was considered irrevocable, but an article acquired from a friend was inevitably returned on demand if there was any real feeling in the relationship. Otherwise, there would be an unpleasant loss of face.

The barter of commodities was rare in Kao Yao, seeds being the only objects regularly exchanged, different amounts of different kinds being considered equivalents. Labor, it may be noted, was usually paid for in grain.

Gifts, except those made at the Middle Autumn Feast especially between families whose children were betrothed to each other, in theory did not have to be reciprocated and often they were not.

12

KAO YAO FAMILIES, THEIR HISTORY
AND STATUS

LIFE IN Kao Yao had its petty annoyances. Soon after our arrival, it had been arranged that Pi would act as an informant at least four hours each day. With his teaching demands, this meant that we usually had to get in an hour soon after daybreak, one or more before supper, and the rest of the time during the evening. Frequently our schedule ran late. On this particular morning, the cook had been delayed with our breakfast because he had found a squirrel in his bed and insisted on keeping the animal on a leash. This took a long time to arrange as the squirrel objected and the cook was justifiably afraid of being bitten. Apart from this interlude, I was a little disturbed by Ho, who found his task of interpreting more and more exhausting and would disappear to his room and practice calligraphy at the first opportunity. It was not that I did not understand his attitude. The process of recording ethnographic data was much more of a strain than anyone can realize who has not undertaken it intensively for weeks on end. The emotional interaction that builds up in developing each new contact, the unease that comes from probing for previously unexpressed ideas, often of a personal and confidential nature if not actually unintended disclosures, can only be supportable and exciting in long doses to the avaricious and insatiable professional. Actually, Pi had more interest in the culture of Kao Yao than did Ho. The latter had his virtues, however. He was even tempered and careful in his endeavors, even when pushed long and hard by a frenzied ethnographer who liked him. Also, he had an exceptional gift as a buyer, and many of the additions to our enlarging museum collection would never have been purchased without his joyful enthusiasm for obtaining a bargain. He went after a desirable specimen like a confident terrier pursuing a rat.

It was ten-thirty before I had finished putting in order the notes recorded from Pi. Ho looked a little dismal as he laid down his brush when I said that we must look for another informant. It was part of the daily ritual, for the average individual we beguiled into telling us about Kao Yao would survive only a few hours of inter- rogation. Some could not leave their regular work for longer, and from many the rich vein of their special knowledge was quickly exhausted. Competing against time, there was no means of process- ing crude ore.

We had not gotten halfway down the street when I saw my colleague, Li An-che, marching toward me. In the shorts and pith helmet which were part of his costume, I could hardly recognize my friend, the Yenching scholar. Kao Yao had absorbed me for nine- teen days and our dream of a meeting in Yünnan had begun to appear so unlikely that I had forced it out of my mind. He introduced me to his wife, a short, heavy-set woman who had been born in Shantung and educated in Japan (Pl. 29, p. 198). They had passed through the Japanese lines on their way from Shansi to Shanghai, and then followed the same route as had I to Kunming where they readily found the location of the exotic American. They were bound north- ward by the arduous overland route to Chengtu, there to join the staff of West China Union University.

It was obvious from the increasing tempo of the war that field work could not go on undisrupted much longer in Kao Yao, for the village fathers were already holding off the military authorities from using every available space to quarter their troops on the grounds that it would disturb "their scholar." Somehow I had been touched by that excuse even though it was obvious that the welfare of their own families, and particularly that of their children, was primarily in their minds.

Returning to the stage, we lunched on the fat boiled duck which the cook had acquired for only fifty cents when the market had disbanded a few days before. This was a double satisfaction to me since the cook had kept the duck tied in the corner of the kitchen where it made enough noise to waken me at sunrise. The Lis decided that they could be quite comfortable in the remaining unoc- cupied room of our stage, and Mrs. Li went back to Kunming for the afternoon to make the necessary disposition of their few belong- ings, while Ho happily accompanied her.

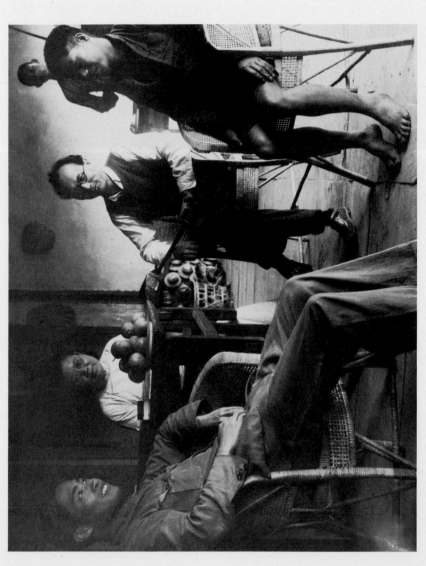

29. INVESTIGATORS AND INFORMANT (LEFT TO RIGHT: HO, MRS. LI, INFORMANT; COOK IN REAR)

Once quietly settled down after lunch, I rapidly reviewed the cultural data which had been recorded in Kao Yao. My friend was amazed since it seemed almost incredible from his sophisticated eastern-Chinese viewpoint that certain of the customs existing in Kao Yao could have survived. I estimated that there would possibly be two more weeks of work and, when I told him of the weakness of having to depend on an inexperienced twenty-year-old boy as an interpreter, he almost gleefully offered to take his place for the last few days. Neither of us considered what had been or could be accomplished as a rounded-out field study; it was for me merely a fascinating introduction to old China. Later it would be necessary to return and complete what had been started.

In the first two days, Li read all my notes and we checked on the points about which he was doubtful. To the delight of both Ho and myself, amplifications there were, but corrections were negligible. Even Ho was proud that we had demonstrated that we knew the village much better than Li did. From then on, not only Ho was exhausted, but Li and, most of all, myself. Li was shocked at my smoking opium, but before we were through I convinced him of its value in more ways than one.

Li's special concern was social organization, and I had originally counted on his bearing the brunt of that phase of our studies. In Kao Yao, however, he apparently recognized the hopelessness of trying to do much, and he quite punctiliously kept to his role of interpreter. Generous as always, he clearly wanted me to have whatever credit there might be for my mad venture. In a deep sense, he was also exhausted and, faced with the appalling difficulties of a war that promised no ending, I could see that he was wise. For two weeks we had the joy of our friendship, while the distinction of our house had been greatly increased. Even the cook became much happier in newly reflected prestige. There was a reasonable suspicion that he had thought me slightly insane, and he consequently derived security from the tacit implication that I was probably harmless, being so well regarded by an estimable colleague.

One of the subjects on which Ho and I had not been successful in unearthing information was the history of Kao Yao. I had been under the erroneous impression that Chinese villages were replete in family documents from which one could reconstruct with some degree of certainty their origin and development. This was not true of Kao Yao. Even Li could not discover the meaning of its name which might have been a better argument for its antiquity if various informants had agreed on the characters, it being alternately written as Kao Ch'iao, or High Bridge, and Kao Yao, or Lofty Highness. It seems that at one time there had been a bridge behind the village, but it was eliminated when the highway was built. On the other hand, Li's final opinion was that the name originally meant "The Hill of the Emperor Yao" and there we let the problem remain as one of no great consequence.

According to certain of our informants, Kao Yao had been in existence since the beginning of time, but this seems unlikely. A search through some of the provincial records revealed the notable fact that Yang Shên (1488–1529), a famous Han-lin scholar, while living in one of the nearby temples after his banishment by the Emperor, wrote a poem in which he mentioned the smoke rising above the houses of Kao Yao, thus proving its existence a hundred years before the Puritans landed in Massachusetts Bay. The earliest-dated graves we could find were erected at the beginning of the Ming dynasty (1368–1644).

Pi said no one cared about anything that had happened over three generations previously. There was neither any story of an original ancestor nor any well-known traditional history, although it was stated that Kao Yao had always been a port. He did give us some information about the course of affairs in his time. He said that in 1921 there were a thousand bandits in Ming Lang, his home village, and those surrounding it. People had to contribute money to them or be raided. The Kao Yao residents were afraid every night of what might happen, but the nearest village to be attacked was Ch'ih Chia Pi, a little over a mile away. Finally, the government took action and in two years the bandits had disappeared. One reaction, however, was the establishment of local protective organizations. In 1924, all these village associations were summoned to make a final roundup of the bandits. Their leader, Yang Hung-shang, was captured with nineteen of his men, and beheaded at Lung T'an, or Dragon's Pool, a town of more than two thousand families, mostly Pai Tzu (Min Chia) people, about fifteen miles northward from Kao Yao. Apart from charcoal, Lung T'an was noted for the loose reputation of its women, a charge which no doubt merely reflected the extraordinary virtue of the Chinese. There were several villages of similar repute, one of which I shall mention out of attachment for its name. It was a Lolo community of about a hundred and fifty families seven to ten miles north called Mo Yü, or Ink Black Rain.

In 1925, a highway was built between Kunming and An Ning, and the villagers participated in the work, being paid five cents a day. Pi was then teaching at Ming Lang, and as head of the *hsiang*—at that time a position with much less responsibility than it later acquired—supervisor of the road laborers. In 1926, there was a civil war between an ex-governor's brother named Tang and the current governor. Tang's forces were beaten and they retreated. In 1928, another challenge to the governor arose on the part of his former associates, Hu and Chang. Heavy fighting occurred at P'i Chi Kuan and many men died. Chang was captured and Hu fled.

In 1936, the new road to the Western Hill with its temples was built. Also, the local militia was organized out of the village protective associations. Every able-bodied male citizen between the ages of sixteen and forty was supposed to belong. About sixty were recruited. A man was nominated to be the leader and, after approval by the district government, he was given some training. He then instructed his village corps. In theory, the militia had to drill in the early morning before going to work and again in the evening, also on Sundays and every day in January. The training course lasted three months, and when it was finished, one class was replaced with another. Sometimes in the late afternoon we saw a small group marching back and forth in the marketplace practicing with farm tools as weapons. The militia was expected to guard the roads when an occasion called for it, such as after a robbery or during the New Year's holiday season.

In 1937, P'i Chi Kuan was partly destroyed by fire, and Pi came to Kao Yao. Then the hill at Chi Chieh (Fig. 5, p. 69) was leveled off to make an adequate space for the market. In 1938, the district construction bureau was trying to build a new village at Chi Chieh to replace the loss at P'i Chi Kuan. A kiln for tiles was built there for that purpose. So much we learned that might be called history.

One could make some inferences about Kao Yao, such as that the Yangs or the Lis were the founders. We cannot forget that one of the closest settlements was called Yang Chia Ts'un, or Village of the Yang Family. Even if we included the Changs and the Tuans among the possible founders, such suggestions would rank only as guesses, for the eclipse of first families is as notorious in China as in other great nations.

As has been stated earlier, the lineages were patrilineal. Although of great importance in Kao Yao, the system appeared weaker than in China generally, quite possibly as the result of migration and a long association with intelligent tribespeople who remained the numerically superior group in the province. Of the 122 *chia* in Kao Yao, eighty consisted of nuclear families and the remaining forty-two were extended. Twenty of the nuclear families were broken and of these only the woman remained in nineteen which fact suggests the relative difficulty there was for a woman in Kao Yao to remarry. Among the forty-two extended families, thirty included one or both parents, there being twenty-one cases of mothers only, and three of just fathers. It was also notable that an analysis of the village *chia* indicated the great rarity of joint families, or those with married brothers who had not separated, only one case being found. Also, there was but one *chia* that included four generations of the family.

Residence was patrilocal apart from the exceptional cases where

Population by Age Group and Sex

Age Group	Females	Males	Totals
0–5	36	28	64
6–10	35	20	55
11–15	31	25	56
16–20	21	13	34
21–25	20	19	39
26–30	23	23	46
31–35	23	15	38
36–40	20	13	33
41–45	23	13	36
46–50	16	13	29
51–55	17	9	26
56–60	11	8	19
61–65	2	6	8
66–70	3	1	4
71–75	3	3	6
76–80	1	2	3
81–85	1	–	1
	286	211	497

a son-in-law was adopted into the family of his wife. The majority of wives were said to come from outside the village but within a radius of fifteen miles. The composition of Kao Yao by sex and age is given in the table on page 202.

The extraordinary aspect of these data is the excess of females over males. This might be explained in the age groups between thirty-one and fifty-five as the result of men leaving Kao Yao to work elsewhere had not Pi made explicit that individuals away from home, even for extended periods, had been counted. Unfortunately, we never raised the question in Kao Yao since the computation was not derived from the census until later (but see page 265).

The kinship terms recorded in Kao Yao have been listed in Appendix C. Kinship terms were used in addressing relatives who were not intimates, and also in the following cases.

> By younger children to elder
> By children to parents
> By grandchildren to grandparents
> By siblings' (brothers and sisters) children to parents' siblings
> By cousins to one another (except male paternal parallel cousins if elder)
> By parents-in-law, step-children, and step-siblings
> By any more distant relatives

All male cousins had reciprocal kinship terms. Any of a parent's siblings might call a sibling's child by the correct relationship term as a matter of endearment. Residence did not affect the matter except that the more removed the parent's siblings, the more apt they were to use the terms showing affection.

The proper names of individuals were used in the following cases.

> By elder children to younger
> By parents to children
> By grandparents (paternal or maternal) to grandchildren
> By one cousin (father's brother's child) to another if the latter were younger
> By parent's siblings to sibling's child

Teknonymy, or the custom of addressing an individual as the parent of his child, was used by either spouse to the other, providing they had offspring and were not looking at each other. Should they be looking at each other, no term of address was used, a clear case of avoidance. If the couple had no children, one spouse might address the other as so-and-so's brother or sister. Teknonymy was used when speaking about a spouse to an intimate, but the kinship term would be substituted with any other person. Also among non-intimates, such terms as *inside manager* might be used in referring to a wife, or *manager* to a husband. Furthermore, teknonymy might supersede the use of either proper names or kinship terms if the speaker were older or belonged to the same generation, but not if of a younger generation. The use of teknonymy was considered respectful because it recognized a person's advanced status in having children, but to elders, the kinship term was proper, since to use the name of a child of the person addressed in such a case would be an improper assumption of equal rank (generation) with the individual spoken to. In teknonymy, the sex of the child whose name was used did not matter, and should the second child be the first son, the parents were still referred to as the mother or father of the daughter.

It was said that grandchildren were loved more tenderly by paternal grandparents than the latter loved their own children. Paternal grandparents might take the role of disciplinarians but were not as strict as fathers. Grandchildren were notorious for telling tales on their mother and father to their paternal grand-parents. Should a grandparent be blind, it was most natural for a grandchild to guide him around.

In theory, paternal uncles were supposed to be disciplinarians of a child, but in practice the mother interfered with that function. The paternal uncle was the most respected relative apart from a mother or father and, in fact, he was considered the equivalent of a father. Male paternal parallel cousins, if older, were sometimes responsible for a child's discipline. The relationship was usually an intimate one, ranking next to that of a brother or sister. Any other type of cousins treated each other as guests with no responsibility for each other's behavior. Joking relationships between them were possible, as they were not between male paternal parallel cousins, paternal uncles and sibling's child, or grandparents and grandchildren.

Contacts were not limited to the patrilineal relatives, especially in cases where a mother's family lived in Kao Yao. Even in the more frequent instances of the maternal kindred's residing in other places, visits were made back and forth for periods of up to a month.

A father's sister's home, a mother's sister's home, and that of the maternal grandparents were the houses to which people usually went.

Cutting across the lineage system was the viewing of families by class. The notion of three classes, seized upon by Western social scientists, apparently was an old one in Kao Yao as in China itself, three being an ancient symbolic number. At least no informant found it strange to mention three classes or to discuss them as though they actually existed. Classes, however, were abstract conceptions projected upon the populace with frequent examples of the normative fallacy of judging the individual on the basis of generalities. Actually there were differences of opinion, not only as to the class to which some families belonged, but as to what were the criteria of judgment. Such disagreements and uncertainties in no wise invalidated the genuineness of classes in Kao Yao; we can affirm that there was a clear consciousness of class, but there was no class organization. On the whole, relationships between people of different classes were friendly, and there was certainly no indication of class conflict. Special disabilities or prerogatives for any one class were denied, the whole attitude conveying a sense of that democracy so often attributed to the village people of China who made up the overwhelming majority of the population.

Wealth was stated to be the primary criterion of class and, when pressed, some informants said it was the only meaningful one. Categorizing families in terms of their wealth soon demonstrated, however, that this criterion was in considerable measure merely the symbol of more obvious empirical data. Usually, dress proved the most visible distinction, but house type was of considerable importance, as has already been indicated. Other factors such as education, public position, and length of residence could not be ruled out, but most of these were said to be merely the concomitants of wealth and less commonly met the eye than the clothing that a person wore.

In reviewing the dress of the Kao Yao residents with an eye to status distinctions, we found that a lower class man typically wore a hip length cloth coat which buttoned down the front and covered a cloth belt, tied with a slipped square knot, which held up ankle length trousers untied at the bottoms. Some belts were wide and had pockets in them, but these were more popular in years past, and already were becoming rare. On the feet, about half the people wore straw sandals and half went barefoot, while a few used cloth slippers on the street, especially in winter, and more did so at home. The head, unless bare, was covered with a felt skull cap or a straw rain hat, but a black cloth skull cap with a button on top might be worn (Fig. 16, left, below; Fig. 17, below).

Figure 16. Silk and Felt Hats

Underwear of a type clearly distinguishable from the outer dress had not been adopted by any class in Kao Yao. The regular costume could be worn in several layers, however (Pl. 10, p. 74), and a few lower class men had unpadded vests to wear over their coats, but these were rare. The short palm fiber cape also was a typical adjunct to the costume, and it was used as a protection both from cold and from rain (Fig. 14, p. 174).

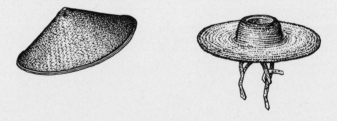

Figure 17. Straw Hats

The lower class woman's costume was somewhat more complex than the men's, and certainly more decorative. She wore a waist length undercoat which buttoned from the center of the neck to below the armpit and down the right side, covering it with a second coat of the same pattern. Over this was a sleeveless vest, either padded or unpadded. It may be interpolated that the only difference between summer and winter dress was the amount of clothing worn plus the use of cotton padding. The women's trousers were like the men's, but they were sometimes embroidered. Trousers were held in position by a belt as were the men's, but women, if they chose, also wore outside ones of cloth. They wore the same footwear, or went without any, as did men, but their cloth shoes had pointed toes and embroidery. The commonest headdress of any class of woman was a blue handkerchief tucked in and around the chignon at the back of her head. Younger women added an apron over the rest of their costume, the design being either a simple piece of cloth suspended from a belt around the waist or one with a flap that turned up and fastened at the neck button of the coat.

The costume of middle class men and women varied from that of the lower class principally in the quality of materials used. Whereas the ordinary native cloth sold in the village market satisfied the lower class, cotton yard goods of a better grade were purchased and sewn into clothing by the middle class women. This material was usually purchased in Kunming because it was cheaper there than in Kao Yao. Some middle class men had the buttons on the right side of their coats, the older, more conservative style. The proportions of people wearing sandals, going barefoot, or using shoes were about the same in the middle and lower classes, but middle class men more often wore black cloth skull caps with buttons (Fig. 16, left, p. 206).

Middle class men occasionally wore locally manufactured vests made from the skin of an animal of the deer family, whereas a lower class man would not do so. Also, middle class women employed a better quality of embroidery on their garments. There were four women of this group in Kao Yao who wrapped the bottoms of their trousers with three-inch-wide ankle bands, a clear case of cultural survival indicating conservatism.

Upper class men, in addition to the coat worn by the lower and middle classes, wore long gowns buttoning down the right side. The trousers were of the standard design, but of finer quality and material. Materials were significant as upper class people used silks and wool as well as fine cottons that could be purchased only in the city. On the feet, one of two grades of cloth shoes were usually worn (Fig. 18, p. 208; Pl. 15, p. 102; Pl. 19, p. 146), and a few men had pairs of leather shoes of Western type. Western-style stockings, bought in Kunming, were even more common.

In rainy weather an upper class man would quickly take to straw slippers for the simple reason that no other form of footwear would prevent one from slipping on the clay so characteristic of the region (Fig. 18, below). It is reasonably certain, however, that the better grade of rice straw sandals made from the inside of the straw would be purchased even though they cost two and one-half times as much. They lasted no longer but were easier on the feet. Wheat straw sandals, by far the most expensive and pleasantest to wear, broke easily if they became wet.

Figure 18. Cloth Shoes and Woven Sandal

The common hat of the upper class man was either a black silk skull cap with a button on top (Fig. 16, left, p. 206) or a Western-type felt (Pl. 25, p. 166). Tuan told us that the latter first appeared about 1911, and that they were still so expensive only a rich man could buy one, which he usually did when he married. We might have asked him whether he obtained his at the time he acquired his young wife, but we did not. Only old men of the upper class were said to wear the high-brimmed felt hats which could be pulled into rakish angles or have the brim pulled down for warmth (Fig. 16, p. 206). These hats were known to have been used for several generations, although but one was in use in Kao Yao in our time. It had been purchased in Kunming where it had been sent for finishing from Ming Lang, a place noted for the manufacture of these felt hats as has been stated before. Upper class men sometimes wore vests of animal skin as did men of the middle class. In addition, some had overcoats of Western style. Some wore their fingernails long.

Upper class women's costume was about the same as that of their middle class contemporaries except that the quality of the materials was better. They also had knitted sweaters, and none went barefoot since none worked in the fields, in itself a significant upper class distinction. Also, long, Western-style city stockings were worn, whereas formerly in the time of bound feet, no stockings were worn.

The binding of feet deserves special comment. It was stated to have been practiced from time immemorial, a period which in this case we can date as the T'ang dynasty (618–906), until 1930 when, with the reorganization of the local government, it ceased entirely. Footbinding had been legislated against with the advent of the Chinese Republic in 1912, but eighteen years were required to free Kao Yao women gradually from this torture. It is notable that formerly all women in Kao Yao, primarily a farming village, had their feet bound, regardless of their class or occupation. In short, all women over twenty-eight years of age at the time of our visit had experienced footbinding, and only those under eight had been sure to escape. The most significant factor, however, to realize with respect to these statements is that the degree to which feet were constricted did vary with class and occupation. For the fortunate poor, and those who would labor in the fields, this luxury, designed to make the gait graceful, could not be afforded in its really restrictive form.

A girl's feet were bound when she began to walk, a strip of cloth about four inches wide and five feet long being used. The toes were forced down toward the heel under constant and painful pressure, the binding being replaced each day without ceremony by the mother until the child was about five. At that age, the process had become mechanical and painless, and the child thereafter undertook the binding which continued for the rest of her life. One woman who sold me a pair of her shoes said that she no longer could wear them as her feet had enlarged since she had stopped binding them (Fig. 18, left, p. 208). The few barefooted women we had a chance to examine showed little mutilation, but these were the poorest of the poor.

The data presented on distinctions of class in clothing, both with respect to materials and styles applied in most cases to children as well as adults. A few variations, however, may be handed down to posterity. Babies had no trousers and their coats were fastened by means of string ties rather than buttons. Young children wore trousers with no seats in them, which saved washing. Babies normally wore open-topped hats, really two crescent-shaped pieces of cloth, more or less embroidered, fastened together at the ends. Girls continued to wear these hats, often elaborately embroidered, until they were married, whereas boys had a variety of headgear. Black skull caps were standard, but all kinds of modern variations were beginning to appear, especially copies of those worn by the armed forces.

Of special meaning were babies' hats, not open at the top, but with flaps at the back and little buttons or ears representing tigers' ears on the top which were meant to ward off evil spirits. Often recognizable features of a tiger were embroidered on the hat. Both sexes might wear such protective headdresses and girls did so until aged five. Class distinctions showed themselves in the quality of embroidery as well as the material used (Pl. 30, p. 211). Upper class babies were given such hats embellished with ornaments of silver which, with the bright colors of the silk and ornate decoration made them unquestionably the most ostentatious article of Kao Yao dress and no doubt quite startling to ethereal spirits.

In theory, everyone supposedly wore some kind of hat or, at least, such was said to be the case by informants. To me, observable hatlessness pointed up the contrasts between ideal and manifest behavior, for both men and women were not infrequently seen without them, and children more often than not. The disregard of custom among the young, it must be admitted, was probably influenced by a government regulation that students had to remove their hats when in school. In Kao Yao it was easier to leave them at home.

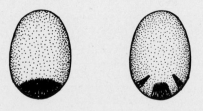

Figure 19. Shapes of Boys' Tonsures

From the hatless, it was easy to verify the assertion that almost all males, regardless of age, had their heads shaved once every one, two, or three months. A few boys and men had their hair merely clipped short, and a few boys had distinctive tonsures such as are shown here (Fig. 19, above). A few men had Western-style haircuts, a preference which did not seem to be a matter of class. A mustache and whiskers distinguished all men over fifty, providing they had the necessary facial hair, but they were not worn by younger men, thus constituting a prerogative of age, not class.

30. CHILD IN FESTIVE HAT

Female hairdress was also not a class matter, but one which separated the unmarried from the married. Girls wore one or two plaited pigtails extending down their backs, while married women combed their hair straight back, twisting and coiling it (not plaiting it) at the rear of the head where it was held in place by means of a bar pin. A red string was fastened on the right side (if the wearer was not in mourning) and a hair net put over the coil. Young married women might vary this classical procedure by making a U-shaped part around the frontal bone almost following the suture. The front hair was brought forward and then down at the left side. Brazen courage was demonstrated by a few older, unmarried girls who had bobbed their black hair, whereas among younger girls, bobbing had become commonplace. Fingernails were cut with scissors and discarded anyplace, but some old men let their nails grow as long as they would, an inclination not followed by women.

Articles of personal adornment in some degree also reflected one's class. This was less true of silver, however, than of jade or gold. Thin silver ornaments (pressed figures) were sewn onto babies' hats, as has been noted. Other types were fastened to some outside belts worn by young women and they were likewise used on aprons, as were silver buttons, irrespective of class or marital status. Silver earrings for pierced ears and bracelets, one or more on either wrist, were cherished by women of any class, but they were likely to be discarded by the old. A silver bar pin for the hair was a standard ornament for all ages and classes of married women, while even the latter limitation did not apply to silver finger rings. Young men about eighteen years of age also wore them just to show off. A woman decorated the third or fourth finger of either hand, but a man wore a ring only on his left. Men between the ages of sixteen and thirty were not above wearing a single bracelet on the left wrist, but that was unusual. Both sexes, if relatively young, might attach a silver ornament to the side of a straw hat. Silver buttons were used on coats, gowns, or shoes, the latter usually by girls, but only by upper-class people, and then rarely. Silver necklaces were not part of Kao Yao culture except for a special silver neck ring put on children, especially boys, who parents feared might die.

Jade was more greatly valued than silver, and all but tiny pieces were restricted to the upper class. Needless to say, gem jade is not being referred to. Jade ornaments were put on babies' hats. Small pendant earrings of real jade were worn by married women irrespective of class. Old women used them only when visiting, while unmarried girls had to be satisfied with an imitation stone. Bracelets were available in either genuine jade or copies, but they were worn only by young women. Genuine jade finger rings were prized by all ages and classes of women, and some upper class men wore them also. One or two might be worn by the rich every day; by the poor, only when visiting. It impressed me that there were no buttons of jade. Genuine jade, incidentally, was purchased in Kunming where it was supplied from Tali (Fig. 2, p. 15), one of the largest cities in western Yünnan. There was no jade working known to take place in any of the villages in the Kao Yao area.

Gold finger rings were worn by two or three people, and the mountings of jade earrings were frequently gold-plated silver. Copper bracelets were worn by either sex at any age, but this was done to ward off illness, the men wearing them on the left wrist, the women on the right.

Young women of all classes used a face cream in the morning after washing. It could be purchased either in the city or at the Kao Yao market. No native oils served such a purpose. Powder was said to have been appreciated by women until the middle nineteen-thirties, but then it went out of fashion and, even in Kunming, little was purchased. No one applied rouge.

Upper class men in Kao Yao might carry a fan, but to do so was unusual. Lower and middle class people sometimes wore baskets on their backs when going to market. Men of all classes carried tobacco boxes and matches in their coats or vests which had pockets on both sides. Pipes sometimes had a little chain which could be fastened to a coat button. Often pipes were carried in the hand or put into a pocket. It was said they were not stuck under the coat at the back of the neck, but a man was seen carrying his pipe in that fashion one day at the market. Money might be placed loose in the pockets, but was more often first put into purses of various qualities and kinds. They were used by all classes. People also had money-belts, either cloth ones made in P'i Chi Kuan or stronger ones of skin obtained in Kunming. Formerly knives were suspended from the belt to be used as weapons, but this was known to be illegal since the establishment of the Republic, and considered unnecessary since the coming of the police.

As a final comment on class, it may be said that Pi estimated that thirty per cent of the people of Kao Yao, including slaves, constituted the lower class, fifty per cent the middle class, and twenty per cent the upper. My guess would be fifty, twenty-five, and twenty-five per cent for the same categories. There were also some classless people in the Kao Yao sense. The four non-participating families were quite reasonably excluded, although they might be regarded as a peripheral super-class. Then there was a Miao family living down one of the south alleys. This husband and wife came to Kao Yao about 1930 from somewhere along the Golden Sand River in Szechwan, a journey of about twenty days. Since these were the only non-Chinese in the strict sense, they were still considered essentially as visitors in the community although not as foreigners, for they represented one of the classical six components of the Celestial Empire.

13

THE BOAT PEOPLE

ALTHOUGH WE tried not to be diverted from devoting full attention to the village culture of Kao Yao, it was not possible to ignore the contiguous boat people, mention of whom intermittently came up during the course of our studies (Pl. 3, p. 59; Pl. 31, p. 217; Pl. 33, p. 219). Also on several occasions we made use of their sampans and it seemed valuable to accumulate whatever information we could when we did so. No one in the village would have denied that the people did not belong to Kao Yao. Mutual respect and admiration were stated to be shown by both boat and village people in remarks about each other, which in itself was one link in the long chain of evidence that made both groups recognize that they had become disparate societies. The fact that once the separation had not existed was attested by the distribution of lineages among the boat people when compared with those of the village. These are given with the number of families in parentheses.

1. Yang (17)   5. Chin (1)
2. Li (8)   6. Tu (1)
3. T'ao (4)   7. Tuan (1)
4. Chang (3)   8. Wang (1)

Comparison with village lineages (p. 121) shows the populous Yang and Li lineages to predominate in the same order while all but the single Chin family belong to the nine lineages with the most families in Kao Yao. This correlation would seem to remove any doubt of a divergent origin, were there any reason to suspect one in the first place. It was the boat people's lack of land, their residence on the water, economic activities, illiteracy, and relative poverty which had combined to set them apart socially, although remaining a juxtaposed and familiar group.

There were thirty-six boat families comprising 211 individuals which meant an average of 5.86, a figure considerably higher than the 4.07 of the villagers. The difference in the distribution by age and sex given below, when compared with that for the villages (p. 202), shows that there was no such excess of females over males as was the case among the people living on shore.

Boat Population by Age Group and Sex

Age Group	Females	Males	Totals
0–5	17	21	38
6–10	20	9	29
11–15	12	6	18
16–20	5	5	10
21–25	6	7	13
26–30	7	10	17
31–35	6	5	11
36–40	12	13	25
41–45	5	10	15
46–50	4	5	9
51–55	3	2	5
56–60	4	3	7
61–65	3	2	5
66–70	–	–	–
71–75	4	2	6
76–80	1	2	3
	109	102	211

The boat people themselves were thought of as being divided into two groups. About two-thirds of the families engaged in the transport business, ferrying passengers and commodities chiefly between Kao Yao and the port of Kunming, while the other third made a business of fishing. This latter group was richer and owned some land on the south side of Kao Yao below the P'u Hsien temple (Pl. 32, p. 218). There they built houses at the edge of the water, while a few had houses on islands (Pl. 31, p. 217). None of these, however, was viewed as a part of the village of Kao Yao. One boat family, however, did have a house in the village, a fact which did not contravene the occupants' established social identity.

The fishing was undertaken with large dipnets supported by the bent ends of a pair of long bamboo poles fastened together where they crossed in the center like an X (Pl. 33, p. 219). In certain cases, the poles were maneuvered in the manner of scissors. Also, basket traps were used, the essence of a vegetable oil being put inside to attract the fish. Despite this activity, the diet of the boat people

31. SAMPANS AND BOAT PEOPLE'S HOUSES

32. RICE FIELDS ADJOINING VILLAGE

33. FISHERMAN WITH NETS

was stated to vary but slightly from that of the people on shore, although it was claimed that the boat people ate food of a poorer quality.

Boat people were said to dress the same as the lower class villagers, and the only distinction we noted was that sometimes young girls wore red trousers which we did not see in the streets of Kao Yao. The men frequently wore black skull hats and the women had the usual hairdress and jewelry. The clothing did seem ragged more frequently, while bare feet and trousers rolled up to the calves were natural results of life on a small boat.

Superficially, the boats looked much the same, and it was also stated that they varied little. Those that we saw were an estimated thirty feet long and divided by bulkheads into three sections of approximately equal length but not of area as the vessels were pointed at both ends. The bottoms were flat. The boat we examined in detail had seven boards, one above another, composing the sides which flared outward especially amidships where an additional vertical washboard was added to compensate for the loss of height above the water. The depth of the hull in the center of the boat was about twenty inches, the beam six feet.

The forward bulkhead was more heavily constructed than the one aft and had a groove cut on the bow side into which was inserted the mast. On the stern side it also supported a pole which held up the bamboo mat covering of the forward part of the amidships section. In the bow section of the boat was a secondary bulkhead setting off the after third of the area which contained two fore-and-aft planks on the port side, while forward of the bulkhead were two narrow crosspieces with the appearance of seats. The amidships section was divided by two ribs four inches high and two inches wide extending across the floorboards and up the sides. The stern section contained no ribs but had two seatlike thwarts and lengthwise seats along the sides.

The cover of the forward two-thirds of the amidships section consisted of a semicylindrical framework of bamboo wickerwork covered by straw mats, the whole supported by a fore-and-aft ridge pole between two vertical bamboo poles five feet high with a pair of semicircular bamboo poles passing over the ends and wired to holes in the vertical washboards. In some boats these bamboos were doubled

at the stern end where there was no mast to provide firm support.
Between these semicircular bamboos, an additional pole extended at
each side of the ridge pole and parallel to it.

Masts, which were easily removed, varied from fifteen to twenty
feet tall and were four to five inches in diameter near the base where
they were roughly squared. A mast was supported by a line from
the top which was made fast in the stern. The sail consisted of
pieces of matting sewed together and bent to six or seven bamboo
yards at equal intervals from the top to within about three feet of
the bottom. The sail was raised by means of a line which passed
through a hole in the top of the mast. On the bow side of the sail
along with the bamboo yards was a vertical line of paired tie strings
which were fastened around the mast as the sail was raised. These
were somewhat on the port side of the sail, thus keeping the sail to
starboard with a fair wind.

The usual method of propulsion was by use of sweeps, however,
sails providing merely auxiliary power when the wind was favorable.
The sweeps comprised three pieces of wood, a long loom with a
blade about eight inches wide and two and a half feet in length
fastened to one end by means of two iron straps while, at the other,
a short perpendicular handle with a hole in one end was fitted over
the peg end of the loom. The sweep was also attached to a foot-long
wood pin by two or three loops of heavy line which passed through
a hole in the top of the pin and then over the top of the sweep, circling
back under it to the inside of the pin which itself fitted into a slot
made by nailing a piece of wood against the side planking of the boat
close to the gunwale.

The principal sweep was located on the port side near the stern.
The individual who was rowing stood with his left foot on a seatlike
thwart, and his right on the lengthwise seat along the starboard side,
thus balancing his weight. The rowing was done by allowing the
blade of the sweep to dip vertically into the water, then giving a
sharp push on the loom and quickly throwing the perpendicular
handle forward, and consequently the top of the blade, so that the
sweep could be drawn back into position for the next jerklike push.
A second sweep had its pin locked to the starboard side of the boat
just aft of the housing. It was handled from the center of the boat.
A third sweep, also on the starboard side, had its pin fastened at

about the middle of the bow section, the rower facing forward on two fore-and-aft planks on the port side. On the boat we examined in some detail, the husband handled the stern sweep, his pregnant wife the one amidships, and their daughter, about eleven, the bow sweep, leaving a five-year-old son to tend the stove.

No navigational aids such as a compass or chart were carried on the boat. When traveling at night, the horizon pattern of the hills served to determine directions. None of the boats had rudders, but each one carried an anchor. Most of the boatmen and their sons could swim, but not any of the women, since such behavior would have been regarded as immodest.

The amidships section of the boat in some respects corresponded in miniature to a two-room house on land. The forward two-thirds under the mat cover was the bedroom and the after third constituted the kitchen. In the forward starboard corner of the latter area a diminutive cylindrical clay stove had been built on a large, concave metal pan which in turn rested on a notched square wood frame placed on the bottom of the boat. The cooking took place primarily in a second concave metal pan which rested on top of the clay stove. In the case under observation, potatoes were being boiled in the pan while on top was a wood rice bucket in which not only rice was being steamed, but also some green vegetables on top of a cloth covering the rice. Capping all of this food was a bamboo hat. Fuel for the fire was supplied through an opening in the side of the stove, in this instance a single tree branch several inches in diameter, the larger unburned end of which was supported a foot outside the stove by resting it in the crotch of a pair of charcoal tongs. When the meal had been cooked, the piece of wood was removed, the burning end was dipped into the lake, and then the stick was returned to the small pile of kindling behind the stove.

Near the stove were a basket of vegetables and a dozen green glazed bowls including four of the size characteristically used for serving rice, smaller ones containing various relishes, plus another reserved for matches. There were also larger bowls which apparently took the place of plates and a shallow one of brass. A green glazed jug and teapot completed the complement of ceramic wares. Hanging onto the nearby semicircular support of the mat housing was a container cut from a section of bamboo from which chopsticks and a spoon were protruding. That was the kitchen and, when the mem-

bers of the family were ready to eat, they seated themselves on
narrow boards resting on bricks or blocks of wood at the sides of
the boat.

The bedroom, or area under the cover over the forward two-
thirds of the amidships section, contained mats to be unrolled before
sleeping, and a bundle or two of clothes which required a second
look to distinguish them from rags. Most important, at the starboard side of the bulkhead supporting the mast was fastened an altar
consisting of a wood box about a foot wide and half again as much
high. The edges of the box projected two inches and on the sides
were pasted paper decorated with paintings of gods. Inside the box
altar were fastened more papers with the names of various deities
including the Dragon God, the Fish God, the Pig God, the Water
Buffalo God, the Tiger God, and the God of the Fields. In front of
the altar was an incense holder and a dish with several small pieces
of charcoal. On suitable occasions deference was shown to these
protectors, but usually they did not encroach on the conscious environment of the boat dwellers. Just forward of the bulkhead was
an openwork basket imprisoning a chicken.

One notable thing about the boat people in contrast to those of
the village was that, of the total thirty-six *chia,* only fourteen were
nuclear. The remaining twenty-two were extended, and all but five
of them included one or both parents, although it is significant that
of eleven with one parent, only two of these were fathers. The
implication in the last statement is that males had the choice of
whether or not to give up their position as head of the *chia* whereas
widows automatically lost it on the marriage of their eldest son.
There were eight cases of men relinquishing nominal authority and
their ages relative to those of their sons, as well as the existence of
a wife, seem worth recording.

Head's Age	Father's Age	Mother's Age
41	61	61
50	78	–
41	62	62
27	53	50
41	75	74
23	57	55
21	77	76
38	72	–

Except for two instances, in the Chinese view, those retiring were very old men.

It is also significant that among the twenty-two extended families, only three included two or more married brothers and their wives. These three joint families accounted for only one of the three *chia* containing four generations.

The limited size of the Kao Yao boats seemed to cause no restriction in the number of children a woman might bear under her mat shelter and raise to a marriageable age. In one family there were seven. Also, we found a mother with twin twelve-year-old sons, the one case of multiple births discovered during our study. The chance that the boat people's children would attend school or otherwise learn to read was minimal. Of the total thirty-three, only two were attending classes, as has already been recorded (p. 86). Apart from the practical difficulties obvious for a floating population, the Chinese familial system militated against any separation between mother and child that could not be eliminated by either in a matter of minutes. For the young, there was little individual freedom, and therefore the boat people remained illiterate.

Although the age of marriage was not specifically given, it is significant that there were no married females among the boat people under the age of twenty, and no unmarried females who were older. Also, we found that of forty-six wives, half were one to three years younger than their husbands, whereas the range was from eleven years younger to five years older as the following table will indicate.

Age of Wife	No. of Cases	Age of Wife	No. of Cases
+5	1	−4	0
+4	0	−5	2
+3	2	−6	1
+2	2	−7	2
+1	3	−8	1
same	6	−9	1
−1	8	−10	1
−2	8	−11	1
−3	7		

No significant shift in pattern was shown by consideration of the age of the husband. The youngest, aged nineteen, had a wife two years older, and the eldest, aged seventy-seven, had a wife one year younger. It was a man of only forty-three who had a spouse eleven years his junior.

Among the thirty-six boat families, there were two cases of son-in-law adoption, plus a third in which the young man was listed as a daughter's fiancé. He had already assumed the name of his prospective bride's family although the marriage had not yet taken place. He was twenty and she seventeen (perhaps fifteen and a half by Western computation), so apparently they were waiting until she was older. In any event, an instance of the adoption of a boy was shown without the theoretical conjunction of marriage even when the latter was unmistakably intended, for the family was father-less with five daughters and no sons. It may be presumed that the idea of marriage was usually associated with a boat of one's own and, except for the economic problem involved, there was still space on the lake of Kun for population expansion.

Death also was expensive. Not only was there the cost of the coffin, as cheap as it might be, but the necessity of buying a plot of land in which to bury it. A piece in a good location cost about fifty dollars and even the poorest at least five. Fundamentally, funeral ceremonies were the same as those in the village. The coffin was taken onto the boat as into a house, and then there was the usual procession to the grave. Elaborate entertainment or delays in the disposal of the corpse were less likely than in the village, however, if only for economic reasons.

14

PLEASURE

LEARNING ABOUT life in Kao Yao was often so exciting that it was difficult to sleep and, awakened by the bang of the gate below one Monday morning, it seemed as though I was as tired as I had been the night before when the teahouse woman had gone out into the darkness to beat the fleas out of her bed mat. The dull thumping had continued intermittently until I had gradually become aware of little friends in my own bed, even more than were there. Yawning, I heard the door to the schoolteacher's room open and close. I looked at my watch but had to use a flashlight to see that it was only a quarter to five. I smiled with self-satisfaction that I knew what was going on in the village. Pi had been playing mah-jongg all night with his friends in P'i Chi Kuan. He was a good man, I reflected, and deserved all his small pleasures. I looked for some fleas but had not found any when I became conscious that Ho was occupied in a similar search. The sun had appeared and we dressed, our interest drawn to other diversions.

That evening we asked Pi to conduct us on a round of the opium dens and of the teahouses where gambling centered. Although we were courteously received, it was obvious that our presence was not always timely. We surprised several soldiers smoking opium and, despite the assurances that the foreigner smoked too, they seemed to be afraid that their heads would be cut off in one way or another. Neither was a stranger's presence the most provocative influence in making a man risk his money, and I felt guilty of dampening the excitement that accompanies quick profits and losses. Besides, with the settings fresh in my eyes, it was more effective to ask questions at home where Pi could talk frankly and without interruption.

Gambling was apparently deeply rooted in Kao Yao, yet interest was seasonal for the majority, and intense for merely a few. The games were of three kinds: cards, mah-jongg, and dice. The heaviest stakes wagered were risked on a pair of bone dice shaken

226

between two bowls and dropped onto a dish by the banker. Anyone betting on an even number to win put his money at the banker's right hand; on an odd number, at his left. The total points on the upper faces of the dice determined the result. The stakes ranged from fifty cents to ten dollars, too much for any but adult men to pay. An individual could obviously win a lot in an evening. Pi affirmed that most of the Kao Yao gamblers were very good losers and would sell their animals or rice fields if they had to without any unpleasantness.

Another game was played with three dice bumped out of any empty rice bowl. Anyone could throw first, the participators betting with or against him. If the numbers face up on all three dice were the same, or four, five, and six, the thrower won; if the numbers were one, two, and three, he lost; otherwise the rolling continued until at least the faces of two dice were alike when, if that of the third dice were higher than those paired, the thrower won; if lower, he lost. On this game, the stakes were usually smaller, and boys were sometimes seen playing. This pastime, like mah-jongg and cards, could be enjoyed by people at home.

Three other well-known gambling games were strictly seasonal and only played with itinerant professionals who came to the village in the 12th, 1st, and 2nd months, the time of year in which the people had a traditional proclivity for gambling, especially for small stakes. One of the itinerants had a paper with four different words written on it which he spread out on the ground. Those tempted to risk a coin would put it on the word of their choosing. Then the gambler would spin a hexagonal top with a word on each of its six sides, four of which corresponded to those on the paper. If one of the latter was up when the top fell over, the gambler doubled the money of those who had placed coins on the words, and collected the wagers on the other three for himself. If one of the two words having no corresponding term on the paper came up after the spin, the gambler collected all wagers. One might wonder why people bet money at such odds, but the element of simple amusement is shown by the fact that they did.

Another itinerant gambler appeared with a wood-rimmed sieve about eight inches in diameter and six inches deep with a thick piece of mosquito netting for a bottom. This, he set up on the ground in a slanting position, using a stone or a piece of brick under the edge.

Those induced to gamble lagged copper coins from a distance of ten feet. If the copper stayed in the sieve, the gambler paid double, but this was unlikely since, even if the toss was accurate, the mosquito netting usually bounced the coin out, and thus into the pocket of the gambler.

A third itinerant laid out a paper on which were written the names of the five famous heroes of China's best-known novel, *The Romance of the Three Kingdoms*. People made their wagers by placing two copper coins on the hero of their choice. Coppers, so-mentioned, were worth half a cent, so the risk did not have to be great. Then the gambler chose one card from a pack of over a hundred on each of which the name of one of the five heroes was written. After showing it to all the participants, he gave each person who bet on that hero a small package of cigarettes but picked up all of the money. To have the odds greatly in his favor, either the cigarettes must have been cheaper than those sold in Kao Yao or his fingers were tricky; so we must assume the former, as it would be shameful to accuse an unknown man of dishonesty. None of these three games introduced by itinerant gamblers was played without professional inducement or in any other season. Pi said the itinerants made enough money in the New Year's period to live for the remainder of the year, but I saw them, or their confreres, operating on the streets of Kunming in June.

There were entertainments which did not involve gambling, and also were particularly enjoyed during the year-end holiday season. Of these chess was outstanding. Not only grown men played, but children as well. A man with a peep show in which one might eye lovely ladies from Su-chou, famous scenes of the province, or even the horrors of war at two cents a viewing usually came during the New Year's season. Also a man with a monkey riding a dog entertained the Kao Yao populace on two or three occasions each year. The owner carried a gong and a drum and, when a crowd had gathered, he would have the monkey, dressed up in a red coat and hat and wearing a sword, demonstrate his repertory of tricks after which the performer took up a collection from the onlookers. There was also a magician who visited Kao Yao as often as ten times a year. He performed in the marketplace, took up a collection, and was gone within an hour. Begging priests with a wood drum came through

Kao Yao at odd intervals, but their public activities could not properly be classed as entertainment.

Despite these special diversions, the most common social pleasure in Kao Yao appeared to be derived from conversation and gossip. For males, this activity centered in the teahouses. Those who worked took their rest there, and those who did not, spent most of the day in them. There was no other place to go. Only after supper did families sometimes visit each other's homes. The teahouses functioned as men's clubs, in a sense, and a villager could sit in one without spending a copper if he wished. Most Kao Yao residents liked to talk, but there were occasional reticent ones like the artist who had become a daytime member of our household. The chief topic of conversation was stated to be prognostications about the weather, a subject which was reasonable enough among farmers. This was followed, as should be expected, by conversations about the condition of the rice fields. These questions satisfied, a man might boast of the quality of his crops. Should he do this too often, however, someone would be sure to make the aside that the braggart must be a man with two plows.

Some men talked of the merits of their children. Others told of their troubles and pointed out their poverty, statements acceptable as demonstrating humility when coming from the poor, but a rich man would refrain from such talk. Occasionally there was a discussion of general news, especially that pertaining to nearby villages, but also of such tragedies as destructive floods and the impinging war. Only educated men told stories, and these were very rare in the teahouses or homes in Kao Yao. Sooner or later the people settled down to gossip about each other. No subject was taboo in the teahouse, but nothing shameful was discussed in front of the person shamed, and enemies avoided each other. A favorite subject was any indication of a woman's ill treatment of her husband's family, or any friendship established by a woman with someone of the opposite sex. Puns were frequently utilized, being simple to make in Chinese. The sound of the character (*tan*) for eggs and for testicles happened to be the same, for example. Pornography was said not to be absent from the teahouse, but rare.

Humor deserves a few paragraphs, for the Kao Yao people were fond of it, especially of the kind that involved teasing or was slightly sadistic, although much of the joking was simply horseplay. If a man had many children, people inevitably made facetious remarks about his sexual ability. They also frequently teased a man about being fond of a woman, most often when he was not. People would laugh at an engaged girl and boy who approached by mistake. Even if an old married couple walked on the road together, people would laugh, as a husband and wife did not associate publicly in Kao Yao. Also, if a girl were married very young and had a child right away, everyone would laugh if she carried it on the street, simply because she was small.

People would laugh at either a man or a woman who appeared in a new coat, unless it was New Year's or some other feast day. They would laugh no less blatantly at a person in very old dirty or ripped clothes, irrespective of the sexes involved on either side. A man or woman who split his trousers in public, which could readily happen while working, would surely produce guffaws from onlookers. Even if a person became sick and vomited, or had a mishap and hurt himself, people would laugh, at least, until they discovered the injury to be serious. We were once hindered in trying to save a man's life by the onlooker's hilarity which I judged to be in essence a sympathetic nervous reaction quickly contagious. If a man or woman making noodles dirtied his face with flour or dough, people would laugh, we presume because the person looked funny, a stimulus which undoubtedly functioned as a causative factor in some similar cases.

Very good friends, including certain permissible relatives, indulged in horseplay when visiting. A woman might put stones in a man's pockets, a flower in his hat, or pull his chair away when he expected to sit down. He might reciprocate by putting his hat on a woman's head. Such joking relationships were notably non-tactile. When Li Fu was asked what women did for entertainment, he said they sewed. He admitted that they did ask their friends to the house for tea on rare occasions, but even then, he insisted, they sewed. Within the family, women might do a great deal of talking among themselves, but perhaps their greatest pleasure came when the work of the day was done.

Although sports, apart from mere childplay, were seemingly nonexistent in Kao Yao, there was some appreciation of art. Li Wannien who sat on the huge floor plate running along the edge of the stage was evidence of that. He was born in Kao Yao in approximately 1895 and had been brought up as a stone cutter, the profession of his father who was also born in the village and the son of a carpenter. Li stated that he could already produce ornamental objects in bamboo and other woods at the age of ten, a skill which had been fostered by his father who had likewise demonstrated artistic talent. In due course, the son had been married to a woman a year older than himself and together they had produced four daughters, one of whom was married. Although basically a stone cutter, Li apparently functioned equally as well as a carpenter, a profession he was engaged in when we had the privilege to become his patron.

In time, he was persuaded to work on the sheltered school porch so that he would not embarrass other informants who might make confidential disclosures. There he was quite content, for we had only to look up to discover him diligently engaged, usually with one to ten people respectfully watching him, itself visible evidence of interest in esthetic activities. Li told us that he had done ornamental carving on tables and chairs as well as the larger decorative elements in houses, such as lattice work for windows and doors. He had also carved small figures on the ends of such implements as fly whisks and pipes (Fig. 20, p. 232). Fine work took many days and had to be carefully conceived, although one of our casual informants said Li could carve anything of which one could make a picture. He added that our artist was not considered friendly by his fellow villagers, and consequently not liked. This attitude was probably explainable by Li's self-sufficient silence, but it impressed me that the man who was probably the most gifted and sensitive native of Kao Yao, the only carver in the village, was looked upon with so little affection. His work was appreciated, however, and for him, perhaps that was enough.

We tried to acquire some of his best sculptures and were fortunate since he repaid our personal interest with his own greatest treasures. One specimen of his skill was a fly whisk cut from the odoriferous wood of a tree found on the Western Hill, the ornamented section being carved from the root after it had been dried fifteen days, and the handle from the trunk. This wood always turned a beautiful brown in about two years. The hair on the whisk had been taken from the manes of black and brown horses. At the end of the twenty-inch handle he had created a representation of Kuan Yin, the

Buddhist Goddess of Mercy, with a child in her arms and the latter bearing an old knife-shaped piece of money which indicated that the child would be rich when it was grown (Fig. 21, below). When asked how he came to choose the design, he answered that it fitted the form of the root. The specimen, made in 1936, had required two weeks of his spare time for carving and ten per cent more for the horsehair work. Only a few families had such ornate implements because of their cost, most people using fans or straw whisks to chase the flies and mosquitoes which plagued the residents of Kao Yao from the 2nd to the 8th month. Our artist had made only five others, each with a dragon, a tiger, a lion, a dog, or birds.

Figure 20. Pipe in Form of Human Figure

Figure 21 Carved End of Fly Whisk

Another of his creations, acquired from a relative, formed the end of an opium pipe, the wood being carved into a clasped hand supporting the bowl. The starkness of the conception and the reality of its expression transferred to the user an unmistakable emotional impact (Fig. 22, p. 233).

The finest example of his work in our opinion was an ink dish sculptured in 1932 from marble which his father had brought back from Tali fu. This piece which required twenty days to make was about seven inches long and five inches wide. The same tools and methods were used as in his woodcarving. Set into the face of the dish were recesses for water and for ink, the former taking the shape of a fan. Lotus flowers surrounded the area for water, and at the corners of the two sections, plum flowers had been cut in low relief. Bordering the face was a continuous band of fret work, so characteristic of old China. Whatever may be said in praise of the face of this restrained and finely executed utilitarian object, unexpected pleasure came to whoever turned it over. The back of the inch-thick ink dish was skillfully cut out leaving a water buffalo in high relief at the base, its head turned backward and upward to view drifting

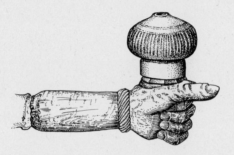

Figure 22. Opium Pipe in Form of Human Hand

clouds indicated by scrolls. In the center at the top was a moon with the character engraved, and beneath it, clouds stringing downward. The sculpture on the obverse face of the ink dish represented a depiction of a stanza of a poem which tells of a rhinoceros but, as the artist had never seen any such animal, he wisely substituted a water buffalo which seemed an infinitely more appropriate expression of esthetic feeling in Kao Yao (Fig. 23, p. 234; Fig. 24, p. 235).

Li Wan-nien came every morning with his basket of tools containing nine handleless steel chisels, a large sharpening stone about eight by fourteen inches and a small one only two by six for the finishing touches, together with an H3 pencil. When he was expecting to begin a new carving and had to cut a piece of wood from a rough block, he would also bring his bucksaw (Fig. 25, p. 236), a small ax, and an ordinary wood chisel with a one-inch blade set into a handle. His sculpturing chisels varied from five and three-quarters to six and a half inches in length, a difference in weight being significant. One had a pyramidal point, another a conical, while the others had shorter or longer beveled blades sometimes curved, but usually straight, and either perpendicular or diagonal to the axis of the tool.

After preparing the block, the artist first outlined on the wood with pencil the design that he had in mind. Then, holding the wood eight or ten inches from his face—the artist owned glasses and was apparently nearsighted—he grasped one of his little chisels in the palm of his right hand, at the same time pressing his thumb against its side near the butt and allowing the blade to extend about one half inch below the proximal end of his little finger. Nearly always the

Figure 23. Stone Ink Dish

tool appeared in a vertical position, but sometimes it approached the horizontal. Rarely, when using his smallest chisel, Li held it between his thumb and the tips of his four fingers. The cutting was done by either pressing in the corner of the blade and flicking off a chip or by cutting V-shaped grooves and chiseling out the intervening sections. In some cases he seemed to be actually pushing his heavier tool. Often he rested the edge of his hand (near the point of the blade) on the wood being cut.

Li had to sharpen his tools periodically. This he did by first pouring water on the large slatelike stone and then rubbing back and forth the cutting edge of a tool held between the thumb and fingers of his right hand while exerting pressure near the blade with the middle finger of his left. Content, he finished with a light honing on the small stone. The only carvings that Li did not mention ever making were those on musical instruments but, if he did not do them, he certainly could have.

Figure 24. Bottom of Stone Ink Dish

From the quantitative view, most of the extant carving in Kao Yao, principally exhibited in the appendages or furnishings of houses, had been done by wood carvers from other villages, although no particular community, understandably enough, was noted for artists. Li also did incising, especially on bamboo, but he admitted that he was not trained to cut metal.

Very rarely were any pictures painted in Kao Yao, although scrolls depicting various gods were purchased in Kunming to be hung· in ancestral halls on suitable occasions. The outstanding exception was brought daily to our attention since it consisted of a wood panel four and a half feet wide and six and a quarter high bearing a polychrome painting of the God of Heaven and his attendant minister (Pl. 34, p. 237). This backdrop of our dining room which faced the open court was flanked on each side by two panels which had never been painted and had become slightly warped, while underneath the unfinished triptych were five smaller rectangular panels. The borders of all eight panels were painted a deep blue with an edging of dull red, the bottom panels being filled in with the same color.

Figure 25. Plane and Saw

The center panel had a central figure four and a half feet high, with a subservient one at the lower left a little over half that size. The central figure, or God of Heaven wore an ornamental hat painted black and white with two dots of red as well as a green border. Two lateral attachments representing clouds were painted in two shades of brown, while a feather in red projected from the top of the hat. The main figure wore a drooping black mustache and trisected whiskers, two sections of which fell from the ears and the third from beneath the chin. These were independent of a tiny beard beneath his lower lip. Rarely noticeable were a pair of long green pendant earrings. Over a somewhat corpulent body, the main figure wore a red robe decorated with gold embroidery and trimmed at the collar and cuffs with dark blue set off at the edges with a lighter shade of the same color. At the edges of the sleeves, a white undergarment showed. An upper belt was also painted in two shades of blue with white buckles and ornaments, while a lower belt was green with its white buckles and ornaments edged with tan. The shoes were black with white soles. In his right hand, the God of Heaven

34. PAINTED SCREEN ON STAGE

held a green ceremonial *ju i,* the well-known Chinese symbol, which bore details in blue, tan, and gold, while his left hand relaxed on his belt.

The subservient figure of the attendant was dressed in a somewhat similar headdress of the same colors. The rest of his costume was almost identical in design with that of the God of Heaven except that the mass of the material was green and, for contrast, the lower of his two belts was red. The attendant had no whiskers, and in his hands he held a red plate on which was a small tripod wine cup in black, tan, and white. The background of the whole panel was deep blue, and children had somewhat defaced it with characters and drawings done in chalk, but not sufficiently to destroy its ornamental and beneficent effect on our meals. This painting of conventional type was probably completed shortly after our building was erected in 1908, but we learned nothing of the artist who was brought in to do it.

It may be mentioned in connection with painting that plaster or wood walls in Kao Yao were sometimes colored in tints of red, green, blue, or in black, as well as the tans and white that most commonly met the eye. Also we must say a few words about calligraphy. One blank wall on the main street bore the character for happiness (*fu*) several feet high as an exhortative ornament. Pairs of narrow vertical strips of paper embellished with classical quotations, or less frequently with an utterance of Sun Yat Sen, the father of the Chinese Republic, adorned the side posts of almost every outer door or gate in Kao Yao. A free translation of one pair follows.

"Between heaven and earth, study is the most precious thing."
"Within the family, respect to parents and kindness to brothers come first."

These had a greater charm, at least, than the utilitarian notices put up by the government with respect to health and the war. Calligraphy was also in view when new scrolls were prepared for the ancestors at New Year's although, again, the expression was usually more dutiful than esthetic.

Embroidery in various colored silks was a minor art in Kao Yao where it was said to be practiced by every woman in the village. It was also used almost exclusively by women on shoes, hats, aprons, and pocketbooks, although male babies as often had embroidery on their hats, and men used embroidered pocketbooks. Until about 1930 when their sleeves became narrower, women also embroidered the edges of their clothes. This custom had not disappeared among the Lolo, but the designs which the latter used were always distinctive. Handkerchiefs or table coverings were not embroidered. Paper patterns, readily purchased, were sometimes utilized (Fig. 26, below). The designs favored were primarily those of flowers, although swastikas, portraits of babies, and birds were mentioned. In our collection from Kao Yao, we find confirmation of this statement.

Figure 26. Embroidery Patterns

It may be pointed out in concluding our remarks on embroidery that the interest in common flower motives had some reflection in the flower gardens of which eight were found in the rear of houses belonging for the most part to the wealthier families. This latter fact probably did not indicate a class appreciation of flowers as much as it did the availability of leisure and land to express such an interest. Poor people often grew flowers in a less profuse manner. It did not seem unusual for the woman who had the small teahouse in our compound to have red and white flowers in a black vase on her counter.

Music seemed to be more ceremonial than popular in Kao Yao, a situation which the schoolteacher was doing his best to correct. One of our first informants claimed there was no music at all, but he must have been either generalizing or not thinking about special occasions. We can interpolate the statement, however, that there was agreement in Kao Yao that there was no dancing of any kind. One fact that clearly militated against the development of music was the attitude that any woman who played an instrument would be regarded as a prostitute, a prejudice apparently associated with the long Chinese tradition of professional female entertainers being well trained as musicians and singers. A blind singer with another man to lead him, was a regular visitor to the village in the New Year's season. He walked the street playing a violin and anyone who wanted to be entertained would invite him to his home where the blind man would sing a song which lasted about a half hour for a fee of ten cents. Also, an occasional itinerant who came from Kunming two or three times a year to tell stories in the teahouses sometimes sang songs.

Pi said the only singing by residents of Kao Yao was in his school, but then noted as an exception that the village militia sometimes sang when they marched. Certainly individual singing was rare, Pi claiming that mothers only hummed to their children and did not sing lullabys. Although individuals of all ages and sexes might whistle, they did not do so at home, for the head of the house would claim they were hurting his ears. Pi added that he was the only person he knew of in the village who kept time with his hands or his feet when music was played; the others only listened.

When we came to review the annual round of ceremonies, however, we discovered there was music in Kao Yao, although most of it was performed by non-residents. Instrumental music was a concomitant of weddings and funerals, besides providing an accompaniment for reading or reciting the texts of holy books. It was even more important at the Flower Lantern Feast which took place on the 15th of the 1st month, and for which practicing went on during the whole New Year's season. This aspect of music we can leave until we take up the annual festivals, merely reviewing at this time the instruments known to have been used in the village.

Among those that may be classed as ideophones, there were sev-

eral gongs, cymbals, bells, rattles, and clappers (Fig. 27, below). A
large brass gong a foot and a half in diameter hung in the village
temple. It was used while holy books were being read by striking
it with a stick that had a strip of cloth wrapped around the end.
Also, when necessary, it was used to call the people of Kao Yao together. A similar gong, but only eight inches in diameter was carried by the watchman and struck by him periodically on his rounds
of the village during the 1st month. It was also used during the

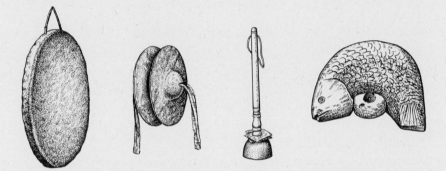

Figure 27. Musical Instruments of Percussion Type

Flower Lantern Feast. It was this size of gong with which the professional castrator of pigs announced his presence in Kao Yao.

Concave brass cymbals with flat edges and handles of the same
metal were known in the village and distinguished according to size.
The largest pair was about a foot in diameter, the intermediate about
eight inches, and the smallest six. Any of the three might be used
when holy books were being read, or at funerals. The largest also
served at the Flower Lantern Feast and the smallest for weddings.

Bells of several kinds made up part of the religious paraphernalia of priests who used them when reading their holy books. One
type was the common hand bell of brass with a clapper. A second
kind was similar in that it had a handle. The bell itself, in the shape
of half an egg, was struck by an unwrapped stick, however. Finally,
there was a similarly shaped bell without a handle which rested
mouth up in a cloth holder. All three types of bell were used only
by priests who, after striking them, always kowtowed. Finally, there

was a bell-rattle which could produce nine different tones from nine flat pieces of brass fastened into a square of threes in a flat frame with a handle. The pieces of metal could be struck with a curved-end bamboo stick by any person reading a holy book.

Wood clappers, so characteristic of theatrical orchestras, were heard at the Flower Lantern Feast and also at other performances on the Kao Yao stage. Drums, in various forms of hollowed-out wood, were placed on a table and beaten with a single wood stick by holy book readers. Peripatetic begging priests who came to the village also wore such an instrument on a cord around the neck. We obtained one of these in the shape of a fish nine and a half inches wide and five and a half inches thick for our museum collection (Fig. 27, p. 241).

The membranophones known in Kao Yao were all drums which fall into three categories by shape—the cylindrical, the tubular, and the spherical. Cylindrical drums, with a diameter greater than the depth, were distinguished in three sizes. The largest, about a foot and a half in diameter was used by a priest when reading at a table. A smaller one, about eight inches in diameter, a priest carried when walking and reciting. A similar drum only six inches in diameter was used by a child as a toy. All these spherical drums were beaten with a single plain stick.

A tube of bamboo two and a half feet long and four inches in diameter having a snake skin drumhead at one end was used in Kao Yao by itinerant storytellers who beat on it with a pair of specially made bamboo sticks that also were used as clappers. A drum of similar length but eight inches in diameter and made from different materials was beaten with one plain bamboo stick at the Flower Lantern Feast.

The spherical drum, used only at theatrical dramas such as were sometimes given on the Kao Yao stage, had a heavy wood frame and a skin cover on one side. It was beaten with slender wands the size of chopsticks held in each hand. A specimen purchased in Kunming was ten inches in diameter, but the hole in the center was no more than two inches. The skin was held to the frame by a double row of tacks around the side which was two inches wide, and it had a half-inch iron band around the lower edge to keep the wood from cracking. The wood, near the hole, was a half inch thicker than at the edge toward which it sloped off under the cover.

Of the three cordophones known in Kao Yao, all were used in theatrical performances and for personal amusement, while two were played at the Flower Lantern Feast. The latter consisted of a violin-like instrument, or *hu-ch'in* (Fig. 28, below), with a bow, two strings, and a skin cover on its sound box, and a mandolin-type instrument, or *p'i-p'a,* with a wood cover on its sound box which was said to have only three gut strings vibrated by the fingers or a pick. The third cordophone, or *hsien tzu,* was more like a guitar with three gut strings stretched down a long neck and across a sound box covered with snake skin. It was the instrument also played by blind fortunetellers.

One day a young man of twenty-nine named Chang Ts'eng came to the school porch to use some of the carver's tools in making one

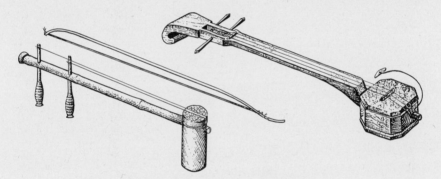

Figure 28. Musical String Instruments

of these guitar-like instruments, and we took the opportunity of learning what we could of the process which dragged out over a period of four days (Fig. 28, above). Chang told us he was a farmer but not working as he was in poor health, a condition which augured no good for his wife, who was a year younger than himself, or for their two-year-old son. He was a native of Kao Yao and in the course of his life had made five other specimens. In answer to our queries, he said that only two or three other men in the village could make such musical instruments although there were five or six men who played reasonably well and did so on any occasion they felt moved.

Chang cut the basic parts from wood of the flat-leaved cypress, but the three pegs from a branch of the round cypress simply because he had no more of the other. The bridge, he cut from bamboo, and for the top of the sound box, he used the skin of a hemp snake he had killed in the courtyard of his house only six weeks before. The snake, non-poisonous and rare, was about seven feet long, and he did not know what had attracted it to his home. The skin was fastened in place with some water buffalo glue he had purchased in Kunming. The pick, he contrived from a piece of water buffalo horn while the gut strings he cut from pieces five feet long which he had purchased in the local market for one cent each. The instrument was twenty-five inches over-all and, except for the pegs, cut from a single piece of wood. The octagonal sound box was hollowed-out and had apertures cut through the base. Others would have probably been cut into the sides had there been time.

Chang said that he was not aware of any respect being shown for his ability to make such an instrument but that his fellow villagers admired anyone who played well. When not in use, such a guitar was hung up on a wood wall and, if it did not become broken, it was said to be better the older it became. Chang was pleased to provide us with dinner music which I only regret we could not have recorded.

Of aerophones, the most elaborate and continuously used was the foot organ owned by the school and played with charm by the teacher. One of the interludes in Kao Yao for which a special nostalgia remains were those times when, after going home to wash before dinner, our friend Pi would bring out the organ onto his porch in the dusk and play an ancient Chinese melody which I can only recall by the title of *Pitiful Girl.** A more classical instrument was the horn with six stops and a trumpet-shaped end which was used at weddings, funerals, and when reading holy books (Fig. 29, p. 245). Then there was a bamboo flute, probably a *ti,* which was blown through a lateral hole and was said to have six stops (presumably not counting one covered with skin). It was blown in theatrical performances, when holy books were read, and sometimes for amusement. A similar bamboo flute, also with six stops, was held in a position straight out from the mouth and played only for pleasure.

* Unless my memory fools me, I have recently recognized this song as one sung by Miss Li Li Hua under the name of *Sorrowful Wife* or, in Chinese, *P'i-p'a Yüan* and recorded on a Capitol Record (T10087).

Figure 29. Musical Wind Instruments

Odd types of aerophones included harmonicas which had been acquired by children. Even girls dared to play on these. Then there was a Western-style trumpet on which the local policeman was said to be practicing, and his police whistle should also be mentioned since the schoolteacher likewise used one to call in his children. Finally, we might conclude by recording that the children themselves had a fancy for making temporary whistles from tree leaves, but they did not know whistles of tubular bark.

15

KNOWLEDGE

THE INTELLIGIBLE universe of the average Kao Yao villager, insofar as we could estimate it, was realistic and positive. Even in the area of religion, the people indicated intolerance toward the more tenuous aspects of any faith. Both with priests and with shamans, they were more impressed by perceptible performances than by anything said. Their meaningful world consisted of a few acres of flat land, a background of hills, and the bordering lake. The greater part of their lives was lived out within a mile of the marketplace, and their intellectual activities were largely restricted to things that pertained to that limited locale.

More familiar than the lake, which they kept away from except on rare trips to Kunming, were the seven hills ranging behind Kao Yao and forming a barricade to the west. Almost everyone knew their names beginning with the one farthest away about five miles to the south. It was called Hsi Shan, or Western Hill, and was famous for its temples on the nearer slopes. Next to it and closer was T'ai Hua Shan, named from the T'ai Hua Temple, although perhaps Shih Pai Fang Shan, or Stone Column Hill, was an older designation. Directly behind Kao Yao was Kung Chung Shan, or Public Hill, also called Lao Tsai, or Hill of Old Tsai. Slightly to the north of it was Hsi T'ou Wa, or Concavity for Washing One's Head. Then came P'i Chi Shan, sometimes referred to as Ta Ying P'an Shan, or Great Barracks Hill, because of the watchtower on its top. Sixth in line to the north was Shih I Tzu Shan, or Stone Chair Hill, which some people called Pai Hu Tsa Shan, or White Beard Hill. Finally, drifting into the distant clouds lay Mei Jên Shan, or Beautiful Person.

The residents of Kao Yao had no ready explanation as to what caused the hills or the famous caves that were in them. The latter were not the dens of the dragons that lived in the mountains, however, as it was insisted that a dragon's den could not be seen. Some of the people believed that dragons were responsible for the springs, the rivers, and consequently the lake which they spoke of as a sea, having a considerably exaggerated notion of its size relative to other large bodies of water. Storms of one kind or another were thought of as being caused by dragons which were either fighting or creating a general commotion on their way to heaven. Thunder and lightning were the manifestations of the gods, and if someone was struck by a bolt, his misfortune was regarded as a punishment. The body of such a person was considered to be too heavy to move, and the intercession of a type of shaman known as *hsi po* was necessary in order to bury the corpse. Rainbows were regarded as the means by which water was sucked up into the sky. Slight earthquakes, noticeable to the people, made the water in the lake move with a distinct sound at no special season once every three or four years.

The children of Kao Yao under the guidance of Pi were being taught that rain, snow, and storms were natural phenomena, as some of the more intelligent adults already knew. Pi stated that the sun was formerly considered a deity, but that he was explaining to his students about the rotation of the earth and its place in the cosmos. His cosmos had a diminutive structure, however, as he himself could not comprehend the solstices or equinoxes and, what was stranger, he had not heard of the oceans. In Kao Yao there were no maps.

People recognized the morning star and the seven stars of the Dipper which was important in Chinese mythology; also a Plow Head star which at the time people were expected to plow disappeared, as it descended for that purpose itself. Comets were looked upon as gods and the moon was worshipped at the Middle Autumn Feast. It was said that in the moon there was a rabbit pounding medicine under the tree which produces Chinese cinnamon. With the rabbit was a monkey making medicine too, which gave the scene a novel Yünnanese touch. On the rare occasions when an eclipse of either the moon or the sun occurred, the people of Kao Yao beat on gongs or metal containers to save the heavenly body from calamity, but what calamity was uncertain, a dog not being immediately accused of swallowing the moon as in some parts of China.

The classical calendar divided the year into four seasons, but it may be noted that these ran somewhat ahead of the West. In 1938, for example the 1st of the 1st month fell on January 31. The 1st, 2nd, and 3rd months of the year—corresponding roughly to winter

in the West—were considered by the Chinese as spring. In Kao
Yao, a realistic view divided the year into two equal seasons on the
basis of temperature, a cool one which began with the 8th month and
ran through the 1st, and a warm period which lasted the other half
of the year. Snow might fall once, twice, or not at all during the
10th, 11th, 12th, or 1st months, and years were known when it lay
on the ground for a week. At the same time came the strongest
winds which blew from the north. By the 1st month, and during
the 2nd, the prevailing winds were from the west. Cyclones did not
occur. The period comprising the 4th through the 7th months was
looked upon as the rainy season.

Few Kao Yao villagers had any knowledge or use for the national
calendar. They did give attention to the almanac, however, and we
present the contents as given for the first few days of the previous
year so that one may taste of its flavor.

1st: Suitable for paving roads.
2nd: Suitable for making sacrifices; to pray; to visit relatives; to
leave one's family; to seek a partner in marriage; to wed; to
move to another house; to cut cloth; to set up posts; to make
wine; to open a shop; to write a contract; to feed animals;
to buy animals; to bury the dead.
3rd: Suitable for making sacrifices; to pray; to visit relatives; to go
to one's post (i.e., civil or military); to seek a partner in
marriage; to arrange a betrothal; to marry; to move; to re-
pair a house; to fish; to plant trees.
4th: Suitable for making sacrifices; to take a bath; to see a doctor;
to clean house.
5th: Suitable to cut hair; to fish.
6th: Suitable for nothing.
7th: Suitable for making sacrifices; to pray.
8th: Suitable for visiting friends; to dig a well.
9th: Suitable for making sacrifices.
10th: Suitable to visit relatives; to seek a partner in marriage; to put
the bed on the floor.

Each month consisted of twenty-nine to thirty days and was
named in sequence as the month of the rat, ox, tiger, rabbit, dragon,
snake, horse, sheep, monkey, cock, dog, and pig, or more commonly
by number as the 1st month through the 12th. In this classical Chi-

nese calendar, there was an intercalary month every two and a half
years (two 7th months in 1938), and a cycle consisted of sixty years,
but such permutations were simply accepted by the villagers without
any attempt to understand them. Feasts or anniversaries were celebrated only in the first month of a double one.

The Western seven-day week made its impact on Kao Yao since
the school operated in terms of it, and because holiday visitors from
Kunming passed through the village on their way to the Western
Hill in noticeable numbers on Saturday and Sunday. More inti-
mately, the week was also recognized in Kao Yao in the sense of the
seven days beginning and ending with each market day. Any day
was spoken of as so-and-so many days before or after the market
convened. The perceptive reader will compute that there were five
of these weeks in each thirty-one days plus a lien on the end or beginning of two others.

Except for the few individuals with access to watches or clocks,
the day and the night were each divided into five theoretical points
of reference with regard to the position of the sun or moon. Sunrise,
noon, and sunset, with the halfway mark between each two, served
for the day while at night the calendrical statement of the position of
the moon was made for each of the five points. An example would
be, "On the 20th of every month, the rising moon indicates the 2nd
watch." Two of the twelve classical Chinese divisions of each twenty-
four-hour period were ignored. The complexities of such a system
were less disturbing when one realized that the people were only
guessing anyway, as much of the time neither the sun nor moon was
visible.

Mensuration, at best, was often a rather poor and inconsistent
attempt to approximate values. The villagers could count and, when
in difficulty, used the fingers, folding over a thumb to begin. They
had the benefit of the decimal system, and the abacus was popular,
for the older people, at least, had difficulty in adding without it.
This became obvious even among merchants in the marketplace
whenever we purchased a series of things at one time. There were
a few adults in Kao Yao, however, who could do simple calculations
with arabic numerals given the use of ink and a brush.

From Pi, we recorded the following tables, to which corrections
and additions have been contributed in brackets.

Lineal Measures

[10 *li*	= 1 *fên*]
10 *fên*	= 1 *ts'un*
10 *ts'un*	= 1 *ch'ih*
10 *ch'ih*	= 1 *chang*
[10 *chang*	= 1 *yin*]

Also

5 *ch'ih*	= 1 *pu*
240 [360] *pu*	= 1 *li*

The first unit of lineal measurement was omitted probably because it was too small for any practical use in Kao Yao, whereas the *yin* unit was rare in China generally. The 240, instead of 360, apparently was a mistake. As may be guessed, the two *li* units are two different characters.

Area Measures

6,000 sq. *ch'ih*	= 60 sq. *chang*
60 sq. *chang*	= 180 [240] sq. *pu*
180 [240] sq. *pu*	= 1 sq. *mou*

Also

10 [100] sq. *li*	= 1 sq. *fên*
10 sq. *fên*	= 1 sq. *mou*
100 sq. *mou*	= 1 sq. *ch'ing*
[540 sq. *mou*	= 1 sq. *li*]

The statement of 6,000 sq. *ch'ih* equaling sixty sq. *chang,* instead of 100 sq. *ch'ih* equaling one square *chang,* is interesting in showing emphasis on the culturally important number sixty. The substitution of 180 for 240 apparently was a mistake, and perhaps related to the previous one of the same kind. A square *li* was probably too large a unit for meaningful use in Kao Yao.

Volume Measures

[10 *shao*	= 1 *ho*]
10 *ho*	= 1 *sheng*
10 *sheng*	= 1 *tou*
[5 *tou*	= 1 *hu*]
10 *tou*	= 1 *tan*
[10 *tan*	= 1 *shih*]

Weight Measures

10 *li*	= 1 *fên*	
10 *fên*	= 1 *ch'ien*	
10 *ch'ien*	= 1 *liang*	(tael)
16 *liang*	= 1 *chin*	(catty)
[100 *chin*	= 1 *tan*	(picul)]

Also

1 sheng of rice = 9 *chin*

The units of equivalents left out were mostly too small or too large to be of very common use in Kao Yao, although it is curious that the *tan,* or *picul,* was not listed. For transferring key units of the above tables into their theoretical English equivalents, we can provide the following aids.

1 *ts'un*	= 1.26 inches (may vary from 1.11 to 1.48 inches)
1 *li*	= 2,275 feet
1 sq. *mou*	= 806 sq. yards (ca. one-sixth acre)
1 *tou*	= .9 to 2.00 U. S. gallons (1.13 to 2.50 English gallons)
1 *sheng*	= ca. 1 quart (dry)
1 *chin* (catty)	= 1.33 pounds
1 *tan* (picul)	= 133⅓ pounds

These figures are grossly unreliable, however, as the equivalents change more in different districts of China than either foreigners or Chinese have generally realized. For the actual measuring, various implements were used. There was a one-foot (*ch'ih*) rule of wood, or rarely of brass, and another of five-foot (*pu*) length. The latter could be used to measure a *li,* but longer distances were usually determined by steps. Area was computed by multiplication. For volume, wood boxes with sloping sides were available in units of one *ho,* one *sheng,* and five *sheng.* Small spoons and dippers also were commonplace means of measurement, but these were not standardized. Weights were calculated by sliding balances in the form of steelyards of which two sizes were generally available. Also, we found perfect balances with weights to put on the pans.

How much the residents of Kao Yao knew about the details of their environment was uncertain, but we tried to learn what we could. Liu, the head man of the village, listed the following trees that grew naturally on Kao Yao land.

Green Pine	Chestnut
Red Pine	Willow
Fir	Palm
Round Cypress	Mulberry
Flat Cypress	The *tz'u t'ung* tree

Pi gave us the names of the wild animals which he said were frequently seen in the vicinity, but we could not recognize all of them. They are put in the order he remembered them.

Rabbit	Gray fox
An elklike cervus	Wild boar
Leopard	Wild pig (short-tailed)
Wild dog	Foxlike animal (with thicker
Jackal	tail) which eats bees
Black bear	Porcupine
White fox	

Then the following birds.

Pheasant (3 varieties)	Sparrow
Thrush	Egret heron
Turtle dove	Goose
Crow	Wood pigeon
Jay	Swallow

Of birds, Pi did not name many; we saw others which, if unidentified, did not fall within the scope of his list which probably represents the birds more significant in some way to the villagers.

Finally, we have a list of seven fish commonly taken from the lake which have been identified with certainty in most cases by a Chinese specialist.

1. Golden Carp: *Carassius auratus* L.
2. Carp (ordinary): *Cyprinus carpio* L.
3. Chub or Silver Carp: *Hypophthalmichthys molitrix* (Cuvier)
4. (No common name): *Mylopharyngodon aethiols* (Basilewsky)
5. Grass Carp: *Ctenopharyngedon idellus* (Cuvier and Valenciennes)
6. (No common name): *Cirrhina molitorella* (Cuvier and Valenciennes)
7. Bighead, Black Silver Carp, or Spotted Silver Carp: *Hypophthalmichthys nobilis* (Richardson)

We attempted no listing of the insects in Kao Yao but the number seemed marvelous. Flies were most common during our stay, and then a small moth the size of the type that eats clothes but not that one. Mosquitoes were troublesome in the evening after the flies went to bed, and the fleas, lice, and bedbugs after we had done so. Our cook amused himself with a large beetle which he kept in an empty matchbox. My personal preference was for moths, a favorite being a pure white one with black rings around the body.

The people of Kao Yao were also aware of themselves and their neighbors. Less than two miles away in plain view was the village of Ch'ih Chia Pi, the largest in the *ch'ü* to which Kao Yao belonged, and it was composed almost entirely of Lolo. No feeling of superiority was evinced, yet it was clear that the Chinese believed their history gave them a place of power and distinction. It was pointed out that if a village was Chinese, it was entirely Chinese, but that there was often a minority group of Chinese in villages of other people. To us, this seemed a historical phenomenon, since most of the Chinese were relatively latecomers to Yünnan. As everyone knew, the Lolo ate similar food and lived in the same type of houses, but their dress was distinctive. The fact that the women put their hair in knots on the top of their heads was specially mentioned. Between the Chinese and Lolo there was said to be no intermarriage, but we did not check on this point with Pi who had Lolo relatives. Our friend Li Fu claimed there were no other people except Chinese and Lolo in the immediate vicinity which was an interesting oversight of odd families such as the Miao household in his home village, or perhaps an understandable failure to distinguish linguistic differences in non-Chinese speakers the way Pi could. About all phases of linguistics, the Kao Yao villagers, along with most people in the world, were extremely naive. They learned to speak from their parents and an increasing number were learning to read and write in the school. Still, few people in Kao Yao wrote letters. If a man did, he would leave his epistle at one of the stores for someone to take into the city. There was also a postal station at Ma Chieh, however, five miles away (Fig. 5, p. 69).

We attempted to discover how an individual regarded the human body and discovered that a tall person of either sex was thought of as having the best figure. Although no one in the village was really fat, the pleasant plumpness that took its place was considered a sign of happiness. To be extremely thin certainly was not highly regarded. Ill people were thin. The residents of Kao Yao had either black or brown eyes, and there was a belief that the latter were less apt to become sore. Complexions varied somewhat, and a lighter color was considered preferable to a dark. The noses of boys and girls were pinched to make the bridges higher, a form which was considered particularly attractive. A projecting chin on an individual was looked upon as an ill omen, as this characteristic was interpreted as the earth overshadowing heaven. Some people were said to possess too large a tongue which interfered with their speech. The governor of the province had ears of unusual size, and therefrom it was deduced that large ears were auspicious, no reference to the Buddha being made.

The Kao Yao people all had straight hair, mostly black, but in some cases quite brown. Shades ranging toward the red were frequently seen among the people of the province. The hair of older individuals sometimes turned white. Head hair was not usually preserved or kept out of the hands of others, but a few people when their hair fell out saved it for the making of wigs or fur felt. Body hair was regarded as natural. Nothing was done to encourage hair growth. Finger- and toenails were cut with scissors when they became long enough to be a nuisance. Pi said it was troublesome and dirty to wear one's fingernails long but guessed that there were five or six men in Kao Yao who did so as a symbol of their social position. One could not be a laborer with long nails. A large belly was said to be the sign of a wealthy person, and again the similarity to representations of the Buddha was ignored. Women were reported to hold the related notion that the deeper the navel, the more fortunate the person.

Pi had correct general conceptions of the functions of the major internal organs such as the brain, heart, lungs, liver, kidneys, and intestines, and he said that almost all Kao Yao men were aware of such facts, but that most women were not. He specially pointed out that whereas formerly the heart had been considered the organ of thought, everyone was currently aware that thinking was a function of the brain, whereas the heart pumped the blood through the veins. The circulatory system, of course, was only comprehended by the educated men, said Pi, who was apparently basing his judgment of the villagers on what he knew to have been taught, thereby recalling to us the charts of human anatomy which had been hung on the schoolroom wall.

Concerning blood, however, there were some special notions which, despite their wide distribution, were not scientifically correct. Outstanding was the idea that consanguinal relationships were primarily based on blood, in that manner creating a vital, physiological connection between members of such groups. There was no identification of blood with the soul, however. Blood was also thought of as the binding element in the bilateral social unit which included certain of the maternal kin as well as the paternal. Injuries to anyone in this common blood group involved feelings of revenge and, conversely, a responsibility for the acts of other members.

An extension of this fundamental idea about blood was the establishment of special relationships between two or more individuals of the same sex irrespective of any family connection. Pi rather astutely distinguished two types of blood brothers, a first which was made up of scholarly or peaceable individuals, and a second composed of idle ruffians. The latter sometimes developed into gangs and were said to be dangerous in Kunming. Seeing a well-dressed man in the street, one of the members might give him a push and, if the person took offense, the gang would then beat him up. An individual in a blood brotherhood group often influenced the others to follow him in some special activity which might range from banditry to joining the army. Some of the blood brotherhoods were based on professional relationships, being found among carpenters, masons, gamblers, and so on. Among such associates, it was natural to make intimate friends.

A man who was close to another broached the subject of their becoming blood brothers. Once agreed, they performed the necessary ceremony in front of the ancestral tablet in either man's home. First of all, incense was offered to the ancestors, the participants kowtowing; afterward a boiled chicken with rice and some water. The sacrifice made, the two men feasted on the food, drinking the chicken's blood as a token of their permanent alliance and intention of mutually sharing the enjoyments and sufferings of life. It was the ideal even to die together. Women also could have such relationships. Blood brothers addressed each other by their honorable names bestowed by a scholar, providing they had them, or by the kinship term for a sibling. It was customary for them to exchange gifts on New Year's Day and ordinary occasions but not at the ceremony when the relationship was formalized. Asked if a woman was ever shared sexually by blood brothers, Psi said such behavior was not expected. We had made note of the common gossip that he shared a mistress with a close friend.

The custom of choosing a blood brother, an act most frequently entertained by young men about eighteen years old, was declining in Kao Yao. By the end of the Ching dynasty (1911), it had become usual to establish as many of such relationships as were possible for purposes of protection since, as has been pointed out, many of the brotherhoods, if not actually dangerous, were potentially so. With the organizing of the militia and police, the menace of these groups had passed, and with it the need for extending blood brotherhood ties beyond the range of intimate and personal friendships.

Before leaving the subject of blood it may be noted that the final brush stroke of the last character (chu, or efficacious) which was inscribed on a wood tablet made between the death and burial of an individual for deposit in the ancestral hall, was written in blood if the deceased's family were rich. One of the leading citizens of Kao Yao was requested to make the brush stroke, he puncturing his left thumb at the base of the nail to obtain the necessary pigment. Such service was rewarded by a piece of white cloth and perhaps fifteen cents or more in cash. Bloodletting was also performed to cure illness, which brings us to the problems of health.

It was stated that in Kao Yao people became ill because of the heat, or of the cold, or from not eating well, or by being injured by evil spirits. Bodily harm might result even from an irreligious attitude. There was no notion of the evil eye, however. Contagious diseases were thought to be contracted from a sick person's perspiration.

Ideas about preserving one's health included the notions that one should not eat cold rice balls or unripe fruit or go to sleep immediately after eating, which was thought to be an easy way to catch a cold. On the contrary, to be healthy one should go to bed early and get up early, take physical exercise, and have due regard for the gods. If one went climbing behind the village, one should worship the God of the Hill in order to avoid accidents. Other methods of frightening off the evil spirits that caused disease and death included the wearing of copper bracelets, silver neckrings, or images of tigers on the hat, all of which means have been previously mentioned. A piece of yellow cloth was also recommended as a preventive of sickness when worn as part of one's headdress.

In the years just previous to 1938 some new theories had been thrust upon the village. Representatives of the health department in Kunming and various students had visited Kao Yao giving propaganda lectures on sanitation and publicizing a statute making the people responsible for the cleanliness of the community. The washing of clothing, disposal of garbage, and keeping the streets free of manure were among the various duties specifically mentioned. Demonstrations were given of street sweeping and, more important, certain vaccines were made compulsory for school children and free to anyone else in the village, and epochal change apparently resulting from foreign support of Chinese effort to resist the Japanese. The children were also given special lectures on the prevention of disease and told to spread the information in their homes.

The specific results of these campaigns were mentioned as twofold. In the 3rd month of 1937, a woman was jailed for forty-eight hours for allowing her pigs to run in the streets. Since then, there had been a noticeable drop in the pig population of Kao Yao. Secondly, families in which individuals had a contagious disease were forced by social pressure to send the sick person to the government hospital in Kunming for treatment. The only malady which was recognized by the populace as contagious, however, was one called the "water talking" disease, a name resulting from the feverish patient constantly demanding a drink. As early as 1935, all the lepers, of whom there were many in the villages, were removed to an area of isolation outside the east gate of Kunming.

Pi listed the illnesses commonly found in the village in the following order.

Stomach-ache
Goitre
Sore eyes
Malaria
Gas in any part of body
Diarrhoea (dysentery)
Typhoid (less frequent)

He might have added smallpox, but we made no special effort to extend the list which could have been expanded endlessly.

Apart from recourse to the doctors and Chinese medicine shops in Kunming, the people in the case of accidents could turn to a village doctor in Ch'ih Chia Pi, a mile or two away. Such unlicensed men were essentially bonesetters, family-trained from generation to generation, and often highly skilled in their special techniques. They worked with their hands plus a penknife and some medicines, the best of them reputedly capable of successful operations on a fractured skull. In dealing with a case, the doctor examined the patient and settled on the price, half to be paid in advance, the remainder only after the patient was well. Some people had recourse to male or female shamans at the same time. Perhaps we should also mention the itinerant snakecharmer who came once a year in the New Year's season and who, having excited the villagers by allowing his serpents to slither up one of his sleeves and down the other, sold them an ointment for boils concocted with snake excrement.

Certainly most cases of illness among the people of Kao Yao were treated by members of the family or lineage who knew the traditional cures. For example, paper ash was used to stop the bleeding from small areas. Ligatures were known for cut veins, but there was no cauterization or sewing up of wounds. Lard was applied to burns, and bruises, and strains were massaged with burning wine. Massage was also resorted to for relief from the pain of stomachache.

Apart from the snakecharmer's ointment, a local plant including roots and leaves was pounded up and plastered over boils. To cure coughing, the leaves of the loquat were picked and dried over the fire, then covered with honey and boiled. Every half hour the patient drank a small cup of water in which two or three of these prepared leaves had been soaked. The leaves themselves were not swallowed. The peppermint plant, dried and boiled with honey, left a liquid which also was drunk as a cough medicine but more usually taken as an internal cure for dry and cracked skin. Scrofulous sores were treated with an ointment compounded of lard, gunpowder, and the mashed roots of a plant called *ta lan tu,* which was difficult to find and had a dangerous odor. Before application, the ointment was warmed over a fire. Infections that could be seen were said to be literally sucked out by placing the wound in a small incision in the stomach of a goat.

This technique was reported as equally effective in the case of snake-bite, although it was quicker to apply the snake's tail if that could be cut off. For ear trouble, a person might burn a little of the skin of a hemp snake and put the ash in his ear. No incidence of the success of these treatments was obtained.

For any type of soreness in the eyes, leaves of the mulberry tree were boiled in water and the vapor allowed to enter the eyes. Also when cool enough, the liquid was used as an eyewash. As a parting gift, the head man of the village brought me three varieties of beans—one red named *ch'ih hsiao tou,* another green called *lu hsiao tou,* and a third black with the designation *hei hsiao tou.* These beans were never used as food. A teaspoonful of the black beans when boiled in a small cup of water for more than an hour provided a brew which when sipped would not only cure sore eyes but enable one to see clearly. Even better, if a teaspoonful of each of the three varieties of beans were boiled together in two cups of water for over an hour, the person sipping the concoction could be cured of smallpox. Not to limit the benefits conferred on myself, it was recorded that the beans could be planted in a dry field in rows about one foot apart. Three or four beans of one should be put into a hole two inches deep in the 4th month. This would provide a crop of more beans in the 7th month, a procedure which if adequately expanded might supply medicine for all of America.

To cure a cold—the back of the neck, the Adam's apple, and the bridge of the nose was massaged by pulling. Constipation was eliminated by drinking the liquid in which the roots and leaves of a plant called *hei ma yeh* were boiled. For other disorders of the intestines, a wild melon which grew in the hills was boiled and the liquid drunk. This melon called *shui tung kua p'i* was not good to eat but the plant could be used for fuel. Women's sickness, such as the head-aches and stomache-aches occurring before and after childbirth were helped by the boiled infusions of a dried vine, called *t'eng,* or a pulse named *pai chia tou.* Three cupfuls were drunk at one time, and it is notable that almost all medicines were taken in three doses of some kind.

Typhoid fever, recognized by red spots on the skin following a stomach-ache and fever, was treated by drinking water—three tea-cupfuls at a time—in which a species of tamarix had been boiled. This brew was said also to be good for one suffering from smallpox.

Malaria was treated by soaking the root of an unidentified plant in wine over night and then feeding the raw root to the patient. If this did not produce results, medicine was obtained from Kunming. For any dental work, the residents of Kao Yao also went there. A disease called *ni ch'iu sha,* or eel cholera, was characterized by fever, headache, stomach-ache, and two swollen muscles on each side of the chest "as though eels were inside," was treated by rubbing the muscles forcibly with the fists and pressing the swellings at their upper ends with the fingernails to prevent them from going over the shoulder. This process turns the area crimson, but if the "eels" succeeded in reaching the back, the patient died. Mental disorders which were not of long standing, were attributed to mental exhaustion or sometimes to the effects of extreme poverty. Most cases among women were said to result from anger caused by their husbands.

No special training was required for diagnosing the common illnesses or for concocting the local medicines, and almost everyone was presumed to know how to use them. When local treatments failed, then the people turned to some professional practitioner. Nursing, which consisted of supplying an ill person's wants, including rubbing the body, could be supplied by anyone in the family, but if the illness of a husband continued, a wife was excluded from the group who attended him for fear she might stimulate him to his disadvantage. Visits and gifts of food to the ill by friends and family were customary in Kao Yao, but such people did not bring flowers.

It was reported that a severe epidemic of typhoid killed from one to two hundred villagers about the time when the highway was built to An Ning in 1925, and again, when more road work was undertaken in 1936, scores of people in the area succumbed to some unidentified contagious disease. Although vital statistics were not available, four adults in Kao Yao were said to have died between the 7th months of 1937 and 1938, and one among the boat people. In the same period, eight babies were born in the village, five of whom had failed to survive, convulsions usually preceding the death.

16

BIRTH, CHILDHOOD, AND SEXUAL RELATIONS

THE ARRIVAL of a new human being into the community through the most natural course of events created little excitement in Kao Yao. People said the birth of a baby was too commonplace. No religious rites were observed and, quite typically, an informant who promulgated the idea of reincarnation when discussing the soul denied it when he talked of an actual child. Except as being the direct consequence of sexual intercourse, the people had little knowledge of the development of the foetus and no curiosity about it except as it bore on the matter of paternity. Ten months or three hundred days was regarded as the period of gestation or, more exactly, the time that should elapse between the date of the mother's last menstrual period and the birth of her child. Posthumous children, born within that period, were considered legitimate.

An upper-class Kao Yao woman normally had her accouchement lying on her back on some straw in a side room of the first floor of the house, but for others there was little or no choice of location. When possible, the woman's mother was in attendance, as well as two or three other experienced women, but there were no professional midwives in Kao Yao. All men, including the husband, were excluded from the room, but no one paid any attention to children of either sex less than ten years of age as long as they did not get in the way.

When a birth proved difficult, nothing was done to facilitate mothers until there was fear for the woman's life. In that extremity, it was possible that someone might go to the city in search of a doctor. Should a child be stillborn, it was buried in a mat on the side of the hill without ceremony. If the mother herself failed to survive the ordeal, she was treated in the same manner as if death had resulted from some other cause, and no explanations were sought as to why the disaster had happened.

Following a successful birth, one of the older attending women cut the umbilical cord with an ordinary pair of scissors. Instead of tying the end, she used a paper clot, wrapping it in cloth. When the cord dropped off at the navel, it was simply thrown away. The placenta, once discharged, was carried out in a dustpan by one of the attending women and casually buried in the vegetable garden or on the hill. Breech presentations or premature births were accepted with a matter-of-fact attitude, although the women were aware that, in the latter case, feeding the infant might be difficult. A deformed child received the same treatment as others. There was no general explanation of such cases, but Pi said a harelip was the result of a mother eating too many rabbits, an obvious association with the congenitally divided lip of the animal which the English word hare in itself indicates. Bearing twins was quite acceptable and if they were boys truly meritorious. Our census, however, did not show that any woman in the village had borne twins, although we have noted one case among the boat people.

When a child had arrived in the world safely, the parents were expected to send a messenger with a bottle of wine as a gift to the mother's family. It might be hoped in return that they would receive presents of pork, eggs, red cloth, a baby's cap, and perhaps other food as well, but the contribution in large measure depended on what the donors could afford. If it were the case of a first child, however, even the poorest grandparents would contrive to send some gifts, although they might not continue to do on the occasion of following births, as well-to-do people always did.

For thirty days after the birth of a child, a Kao Yao husband was not supposed to talk to his wife or even to see her. Sexual inter-course was strictly taboo. In other ways the father continued in his normal routine of life, perhaps temporarily adding a few chores such as cooking. If the child was his first and a son, he was adequately compensated for the difficulties of life, but even if the first child was only a girl, he and his wife had gained the status of adults by pro-ducing it, and they would henceforward be addressed as the parents of the child.

The mother herself was allowed more rest than usual during the month after giving birth, and her diet was improved in certain ways. Besides rice, she was provided with eggs, pork, and brown sugar to eat, and chicken was added if the family could afford it, but vegetables were banned. Also during the thirty days, she was supposed to avoid drafts and not climb any stairs and she received only female guests. All these benefits and restrictions were understandably emphasized in the case of a first child.

As for the infant itself, soon after it was born it was washed in warm water and, when dried, given to the mother to nurse. The nipple was put into the baby's mouth if it had any difficulty finding it. If, by ill chance, the mother was dry, some friend was expected to act as a wet nurse without pay. One or two days after the birth, a small hat like a skullcap was put on the baby, together with a jacket which tied at the side. To this costume was added a cloth diaper with cotton or paper inside. No cradle was supplied for the infant who was expected to sleep with its mother, a blanket being wrapped and tied around the child's legs to prevent it from kicking all over. In theory, the mother never rolled on the baby and, in reality, to do so was rare.

Except for being washed daily in warm water, the infant received no special treatment during the first thirty days. It was fed whenever it cried, and if it sucked its thumb, the mother did not mind. No pacifier was used. Often the mother played with the baby a great deal, kissing it, humming to it, or telling it all kinds of wonderful things the way a fond parent will. Although the father might also play with the baby, he was not expected to provide any of its care which was the responsibility of the mother who in some measure was compensated by having to do less of her usual strenuous manual labor.

At the end of the thirty-day period, but only following the birth of the first-born infant, a feast had to be given to the friends of the family whether the baby was a boy or not. Invitations were written on red paper and sent out to the guests. The celebrations had the functions of reuniting the husband and wife as well as providing the child with its first given name consisting of one or two characters. If the baby's paternal grandfather was alive and at home, he selected the name, simply announcing it without ceremony. Should he not be available, the father of the child would choose what his offspring should be called as well as, indirectly through teknonymy, his wife and himself. The selections were various, none being barred except that the name of another person living in the area of personal contact was not knowingly chosen. Words connected with the seasons might be selected such as Spring Flower, or with the year name linked on. Others seemed to have no obvious basis for their choice, such as Duck, Water, or Wood for females, and Two Locks or Has Seven for males. One girl was called Small Ball, referring to her shape, and one boy, Dog Excrement. An only son was sometimes given a bad name to make him seem less valuable to evil spirits that might cause his death. Girls' names had a tendency to involve flowers or pleasant odors, while those of boys often had one character meaning either *valuable* or *rich*. The name given to a child at its thirty-day feast was ordinarily used only until a school name was conferred, but in some cases it remained the intimate designation of adults.

In cases when a family was left with an only son, its brothers having died, the child was sometimes supplied with a silver neck ring or an earring for the left ear as has been previously mentioned. This proceeding was initiated by the parents asking a coin or two from a hundred nuclear families—friends, neighbors, and relatives— the donations symbolically meaning that the contributing families were protecting the boy. The money was used to purchase a neck ring or earring. Then on an auspicious day determined from the almanac after the child had passed its first New Year's Day, the relatives and friends were invited to the bedecking ceremony at which the neck ring, or single earring, was put on the only son by his mother's brother or, in lieu of that relative, by his mother's father. If none of these kindred were available, the mother ornamented the child herself, fastening the neck ring or puncturing the left ear lobe with a sewing needle and putting in the earring, which was of an ordinary kind, herself. The hundred-family neck ring, as it was called, was worn without removal by the boy until thirty days before his marriage, if he survived, at which time it was removed and converted into jewelry that was presented to his betrothed on the day before the wedding ceremony. A lone earring was also given, it being presumed that the bride could obtain another to match it. Although it was positively stated that a girl was not given a silver neck ring, the school manager's granddaughter was observed wearing one, a typical example of the contradiction between ideal and manifest behavior. We may presume that the girl's parents were particularly fond of her as they had no sons.

Although reference has been made several times to the adoption of sons who were actually sons-in-law, it should be noted that boys were also adopted without any consideration of marriage. Such undertakings were always initiated through a go-between who sought out a family with several sons, the child to be negotiated for being usually of an age from five or six to more than ten. The ideal source was the father's brother's family, but a wife's sister's son, or a father's sister's son was also favored. If the go-between proved successful, a verbal agreement was made. Then the initiating family gave presents of cloth, some catties of wine, together with rice and meat to the boy's parents, after which the boy moved into his new home. From then on, the child, who received his new parents' surname, was entitled to all the rights that would have been incurred had he been born into the family. Furthermore, it was common opinion that adopted sons were treated as well as natural ones, if not better. An adopted son not only used the proper terms of address to members of his new family, but he also continued to do so to his former one. Obtaining a son-in-law, however, was the preferred form of adoption. Pi claimed there were more than ten cases of adoption in Kao Yao, whereas there was usually only one case to be found among the population of several villages. He accounted for the local situation, which was not indicated in his census, as the result of the abnormally high mortality among male children in Kao Yao.

On a child's first birthday (it would have been two years old the previous New Year's day when referring to its age), friends and relatives were invited to a feast at which the infant, whether boy or girl, was given one hard-boiled, undecorated chicken's egg as a plaything. No explanation of the gift was generally recognized, it being simply described as customary.

About a year after birth, a child was suddenly stopped from nursing. The mother put either tobacco juice or chicken excrement on the nipples of her breasts, additions to the expected meal which prevented the child from enjoying it. As a substitute for her milk, the mother put congee into her infant's mouth using a finger to simulate the nipple. There was apt to be considerable protest toward this arbitrary shift in the diet, and it was recognized that a baby often had a hard time in making the necessary adjustments.

As the infant grew, it was taught to behave as a good Kao Yao child should. When it dirtied its clothes in urethral or anal activities, the mother pointed to the mess and lectured her offspring, perhaps slapping its hands if the action seemed appropriate. Infantile masturbation was also punished by slapping if the visual stimulus on the mother made her uncomfortably conscious of what was going on. Gradually the child was made aware that quarreling, fighting, stealing, lying, and disobedience were bad, the inculcation coming largely from reiterated scoldings and lectures, sometimes reinforced by a switching on the back of the legs. For good behavior, a child might also be rewarded with presents of money from its parents, and brushes and books from its teacher. Inevitably, the effort and result varied from family to family but, by and large, one received the impression that in Kao Yao the children had the nether hand and their parents were in charge. The ideal image of the good child was readily described. He was humble, industrious, thrifty, honest, and obedient to his parents. My impression was that such children were not unusual in Kao Yao, however much they may have unconsciously hated their parents for making them so. When boys or girls did not quite live up to the expectations of their fathers and mothers, it was commonplace to claim that the grandparents had spoiled them. Children were also undoubtedly influenced by their contemporaries, both siblings and friends. The former were significant in the preschool years when toddlers were not infrequently conveyed on the backs of sisters only a few years their elder. School, quite inevitably, opened up a whole new world of relationships, and one's entrance into it was marked by the conferment of a new given name.

Each child on his first arrival at school was asked his family name. In the case of a boy, it was then ascertained whether he had an elder brother, and if so, what was the brother's name. If the new student was a girl or an eldest son, some two-character name was substituted for the one acquired at the age of thirty days. The teacher made up the names and Pi told us that in all the years of his teaching he had not given the same one twice. The example he rolled off his tongue was Handsome Scholar, and it did not seem necessary to strain him further. From a list of his students, the following boys' names have been selected at random: Lofty Star, Glorifying Ancestors, Fine Forest, and Cloud Opener. Among the girls we found: Young Fragrance, Pretty Fêng-bird, Bamboo Fairy, and Beautiful Lily. In the case of a younger brother, only a last name was chosen, the middle character of the elder sibling's name being retained to identify them as brothers.

While on the subject of names, our discussion of them may as well be concluded. Actually, an individual might have three names plus a nickname in the course of his life, not counting being referred to as the parent of his first child. A new given name was acquired for a third time not infrequently by a young man, or rarely by a woman, who had finished school. This was done simply by requesting a scholar to bestow a name, a favor which he would perform by selecting two suitable characters from a poem. For this service, usually solicited just before or after a marriage, the scholar would be presented with a gift, very often some cigarettes or tobacco. A scholar, it may be added, in the local sense was a person who had been graduated from middle school. There were two men of that status who belonged to the Kao Yao community. If a man had a name given by a scholar, it was the preferential one to use, but a woman was normally addressed as the mother of her child when she had one (see p. 203). It also should be pointed out that secondary wives were expected to address the first wife as elder sister, although in one known case in which the second wife was the dominant person in the family, she did not do so. Also, if a man or woman was old, the person was never addressed by name. If one generation older, a man would be called Old Uncle, a woman, Old Aunt; if two generations older, the terms would be Old Grandfather or Old Grandmother.

When written after marriage, a woman's family name was added to that of her husband and followed by the character *shih* which indicated that the woman was married. On formal announcements such as those for marriage, the birth of a son, or death, a woman's given names were also included. Finally we may add that the rich, non-participating families in the community gave names to their houses. That of Ch'en Ku-i, for example, was called "Very Satisfying Garden."

Anyone up to the age of forty could be given a nickname, but nicknames were rare in the village. Some unusual personal characteristic seemed to invoke them. One woman was called Fat, another Big Goitre, and a man with a tick in his eye, Monkey, since a similarity was seen in the movement of simian eyes. Such names could be used in direct address, the person being said not to care as he could reciprocate. About this, one may suspect rationalization.

To return to the problems of growing up, the play activities of school children were not so much different from those of preschool age, but there was less time for personal amusement. Boys did have stones, clay, broken tiles, sticks, sling-shots, wood tops, and kites for toys, while girls had cloth-faced dolls. Girls also helped the boys fly kites of various shapes in the Chinese spring when the weather was nice and the wind was strong. Tops were spun in the autumn when the ground was dry. With the approach of the new year, both boys and girls played with drums, cymbals, and paper lanterns in anticipation of the coming festivities.

Most activities of children were imitative of those of their parents and soon blended into work. While girls helped their mothers with the younger children, boys cooked rice and cleaned up the house, but they were not allowed to wash the dishes for fear that they might break them. In the summer they pretended to transplant rice in the school garden. They also pretended they were carpenters and masons, but the favorite game was to be a soldier and fight the Japanese. With youthful tolerance, some boys periodically faced the necessity of playing the role of invaders and gleefully chased the Chinese. Both boys and girls pretended they were priests reading holy books, freely punctuating their efforts by ringing bells.

Girls not only helped their own mothers with the younger children, but they pretended to feed babies of their own. Boys selected partners among them and said, "I must go out to work now; you must cook dinner." An interest in the opposite sex continued after puberty. Male masturbation was considered normal, but it was also said to be bad. The realistic attitude actually was one of disinterested toleration. By the time a girl had been menstruating two years, restrictions in her contacts with males were increased. If she was observed talking to a man very often, or even looking at one repeatedly, her mother would tell her that such behavior was shameful and that she might better be dead. Before she was sixteen (fourteen and a half by Western reckoning), no one paid much attention, however. Serious irregular sexual involvements among adolescents were claimed to be so rare that the situation seemed almost unbelievable, at least to one who had an ethnographer's reluctance to accept negative statements on such more or less taboo subjects. Strong elements of control did lie in the fact that practically every child was betrothed before puberty so that each carried a concrete sense of obligation toward a real person with whom he would ultimately live, and secondly in the strength of the view held by all villagers that premarital intercourse with its threat to the family system was evil. Nevertheless it did occasionally occur. Although a girl of susceptible age was not allowed to wander about alone, especially in the evening, she still might find an occasion to talk to a boy in the fields and then meet him in the hills the next day. To accept such an invitation, however, was the equivalent of agreeing to a sexual relationship. There were risks involved apart from the familial, for if a boy was seen taking a girl off into the woods, anyone might pursue them and beat them with sticks, even causing serious injury without fear of retribution. One informant admitted to having participated in meting out this informal kind of justice. In such circumstances, invitations to indulge in sexual liaisons were rare, and acceptances understandably rarer. Still, a few boys and girls did give and accept them.

When a couple was known to be intimate, but not intercepted in the act, the parents of an injured and innocent fiancé might bring the matter to the attention of the village head man who in turn would refer it to the council. The family of the girl might then be fined, but the engagement not necessarily broken. It is not certain whether such a case existed only in theory or was also exemplified in fact. In an analogous complaint against a boy, it was said that nothing could be done unless his mistress conceived a child, in which case he could be given corporal punishment and his family fined by the village authorities.

Apparently the occasional weak strand in the rope of morality was the seduction of one future spouse by the other which was possible if both grew up in the village. If caught, the couple would only be scolded and the date of their marriage advanced. No one would raise a question of the behavior being anything but a family affair. An informant hazarded the guess that only two per cent of the girls in Kao Yao were not virgins at the time of their marriage, and added that he had known only three or four men who had engaged in premarital coitus. Class status was not correlated with illicit sexual relations, and no one had ever heard of an elopement.

Information about sexual attitudes and behavior was not easily obtained in Kao Yao because the values fostered by the Ch'ing dynasty (1644–1911) for several hundred years had been puritanical, whereas in the earlier tradition sexual activity had not been so much repressed as confined. In Kao Yao, many people voiced a reaction of disgust toward physical intimacy, holding that sexual intercourse was a secret matter about which no one should talk. Others were more enlightened.

The basic explanation of the sex impulse was the Chinese traditional one. Man possessed the positive *yang* principle, and woman the negative *yin;* naturally they united. The semen impregnated the ovum and a child was developed in ten months. Too much intercourse resulted in females; either restraint or great strength produced males. In a teahouse we heard a man being laughingly accused of having been sexually overactive because he had fathered a daughter. In support of the theory, it was pointed out that the schoolteacher who did not get home more than once a week had two sons. The classic Chinese notion that the ideal time for sexual intercourse was midnight was stated as fact, with the gratuitous assertion that no couple would indulge themselves during the daytime, even in an illicit affair with a widow which we suggested as perhaps not being covered by the rule.

No specific time of the month was recognized as favorable for conception, but intercourse was prohibited during periods of menstruation, sickness, and for thirty days after a birth. It was the sexual act that was considered dangerous, not menstruation. The woman was not isolated and the man slept in his usual place beside her. On the other hand, if a man was confined with an illness, his wife would avoid even standing in front of him for fear he might become sexually aroused and consequently weakened. This notion was extended in the belief that to see any couple in copulation would bring very bad fortune, quite possibly death to a person in the observer's family.

The anticipation of first intercourse was reported not to be frightening, but a man was speaking. Admittedly, he was apt to be disconcerted, if not actually annoyed, on his bridal night by the privileged intrusion of his friends. A husband was forced by custom to go to the bridal chamber and bring his young wife to the reception hall while he served strong wine to a special group of male guests who came in after the formal ceremony was over. All were older than himself and none in relationships where there should have been avoidance. No bridegroom was expected to enjoy doing this, as his friends tried to make certain. Time and again he put a wine cup on a tray, presented it to his bride to fill, and passed it to a guest. The guest put the cup on the table and said, "We have come here today to drink to your marriage; we hope to come a year from now to drink to a son." Then the bridegroom repeated in essence the first half of the sentence, and the bride responded with the second. After the response, the guest drank the wine. This ritual was repeated for everyone.

If the groom was an educated man, which in Kao Yao implied with six years of schooling, he would be asked to sing a song while the bride clapped in time before each guest drank. Then he might be requested to hold a small cake in his mouth while the bride ate the extruding half. Other ridiculous behavior could be enforced while embarrassing things, if judged by Kao Yao standards, were said such as, "Oh, you are so happy tonight," as well as similar gentle allusions to the young couple's anticipated intimacy. At midnight the guests departed and the wife went to her bridal chamber alone to be followed by the groom. Actually, the tradition of ribaldry on a marriage night, ancient in China, was less exacting in Kao Yao than in many parts of the country where tickling and other forms of tactile disturbance were practiced.

Usually a bride and groom cohabited the night of their marriage, although this consummation would be deferred if the bride happened to be menstruating. Defloration was not considered dangerous but, since no sex education was given, the husband could be quite brutal. There was considerable concern on the part of the family as to whether the new member was a virgin and the initial intromission was expected to produce blood stains. If the husband received the impression that his wife was not a virgin, it was assumed that he would hate her, but he had no recourse but to accept the situation. Such cases were apparently negligible.

Although at one moment an informant would deny any preliminary sex play, a different approach proved that spouses did hug each other, rub noses, bite cheeks, and kiss in the most erotic fashion within the dark confines of their bed. Caresses were not limited to the face. People slept nude and sometimes in each other's arms.

In coitus, the man ordinarily took the initiative, but a woman might influence her husband to act. Ideally, the couple were expected to sleep first, or at least not indulge themselves before ten in the evening. The position considered normal was for the woman to lie on her back and the man to make his approach by kneeling over her. The female orgasm was not necessarily recognized by husbands, and frigidity consequently not understood. Impotence was known to result when a man intending intercourse was frightened by the sound of someone in the vicinity. It was claimed that men enjoyed sexual intercourse more than did their wives, which has little meaning (since no women gave opinions) unless coupled with the masculine admission that the female orgasm was of no fundamental significance. Whatever the night offered, the next day the husband and wife gave the appearance of avoiding one another. There was one notable exception; they might fight. That was bad manners in Kao Yao, but not sexually reprehensible.

In a case where a man acquired two or more wives, each had a bedroom. The Kao Yao husband, as in classical Chinese tradition, was expected to visit each woman in turn, agreements being made as to the number of nights with one wife before moving on to the next. Any disruption of an established procedure caused trouble. Pi said all co-wives quarreled anyway—but he was not in a position to know. It is probable that most co-wives did, but also that there were some who did not.

Economic cooperation between co-wives was clearly under the leadership of the woman with the strongest personality and her authority was backed up by the husband, for whom peace in the household was of the greatest importance not only for immediate personal reasons but because of his reputation in the village as one who was master of his home. Even if in fact he was not, it was essential to save face by appearing to be. In some ways the situation of having three wives was claimed to be easier than having two, since usually only one would refuse to cooperate with the leader and then the contender would be blocked in her struggle by two women.

It should be interpolated that in the polygynous households of Kao Yao, informants agreed that all children in the home were treated essentially in the same way by their aggregate of mothers, and that they did not create distinctions among themselves because of difference in parentage. The equality of plural wives and the lack of concubinage was perhaps the outstanding distinction of Kao Yao society in representing villages in the local area of Yünnan as distinct from the classical culture of China.

In some households, polygynous or otherwise, adultery occurred. Where wives were involved, the extramarital relationships were most often incestuous in the sense of involving some male in the household apart from the husband. Of the rare cases, intercourse between a father and his son's wife was suspected to be the most common because in some families a married son was so young. A husband's brother, however, might also succumb to desire. When the adultery of a woman was discovered within the family, it was kept very secret, not only from shame but because incest was regarded as so bad that even neighbors might interfere. Punishment was in the hands of the lineage head who could order the culprits hung up and beaten.

Since some husbands were frequently away, it was possible for them to find their wives in possession of a child they believed they had not sired. Opinion held that such a man would keep his own counsel rather than risk public shame; that he would support the child but not love it very much.

A woman who found herself pregnant by a man other than her husband might attempt to abort the child, especially if it had resulted from an incestuous union or if she was a widow. No instances could be found in Kao Yao, but it was discovered that the wife of a Lolo policeman in one of the nearby villages was known to help females who were in difficulties providing them with an unidentified drug. Irrespective of the motive for undertaking it, abortion was looked upon as an evil, and one instance was known in the district of a woman being caught in the act. She was taken to the temple, strung up by her wrists a foot off the floor, and beaten.

The unfaithfulness of a husband was another matter. If the behavior became publicly known, it caused gossip but nothing more, except at home where the wife might make things unpleasant. A husband often was not sexually attracted to his wife, for their relationship was seldom established by mutual choice. From childhood, a man was trained to disregard that fact, but sometimes, after carrying out his social, economic, and sexual responsibilities, he felt entitled to a little romance.

Kao Yao men did not hesitate to express their image of the ideal woman. The desirable beauty would have no scars or distorted parts, while her body would be strong and well built. The lighter her skin, and the rosier and smaller the mouth, the better. A high-bridged, narrow, pointed nose was preferred. Eyes would be neither too big nor too small. Her whole face would be tender. The breasts and hips of the ideal woman would be large enough to protrude noticeably, her legs straight and thick enough to be fleshy, and her feet medium sized and soft. She would be of a height so that a man's nose touched her eyes, while the man should be at least five Chinese feet tall. The value of a woman depended, not only on her appearance, but on her virtuous qualities. It may be inserted that the ideal physical man differed little except for an obvious distinction in buttocks and breasts, together with the expectation that a man's skin would be darker.

These considerations about a woman were said to affect an amorous man, whether a husband seeking a mistress or a widower seeking a wife. If there were many women who Kao Yao men thought satisfied all these requirements, it would be only one more proof that love can be blind. In any event, in his search for the woman, a man had difficulties. Prostitution was unknown in Kao Yao or in any of the neighboring villages. Among some of the not too distant communities, however, which were populated by neither Chinese nor Lolo, the women were said to be less moral. The opportunities thus suggested had little meaning for errant husbands in Kao Yao who traditionally kept their eyes on the widows closer to home. In making erotic overtures, innuendo was used, but not love magic, aphrodisiacs, or songs. A man might wink at a woman when some degree of intimacy had been established. Winking did not indicate that the individuals had reached the point of having sexual intercourse, but it did have sexual connotations. Illicit sexual contacts were said to be conducted in the same manner as those between husband and wife. Only one case of sexually aberrant behavior was discovered, but this was attributed to a man in another village who made his wife lie naked on the floor in the daytime while he danced wearing a red turban before he threw himself on top of her, his purpose being to represent himself as a donkey in the interest of fertility. Cases of rape were not unknown. The year before our study a man over fifty attacked a young girl in one of the boats.

He was arrested and fined sixteen dollars. Nocturnal emissions were said to be the result of simply dreaming about women.

In concluding the information pertaining to sexual matters, it must be noted that the moral tone of villages in the district was known to vary from place to place, and that the people of Kao Yao had the reputation of preserving a relatively high standard. Whether this meant more than that the villagers were Chinese, and were being judged by their own standards, is uncertain.

17

MARRIAGE: SINGULAR AND PLURAL

FOR THE people of Kao Yao, marriage and sons were a social and spiritual necessity, not merely customary and desirable. The results, although appearing the same, were fundamentally different in that the Chinese considered the family to be the pre-eminent unit of society in contrast to Americans who traditionally place the primary emphasis on the individual, or Russians who, under socialism, give priority to the state. In Kao Yao, the idea of a boy and girl falling in love and forming a new family was as indecent as would be the idea of a girl in the United States being forced to marry a man she had never seen. Attitudes about the individual, the family, and the state are, first of all, ideals about which people may be more or less conscious, and more or less consistent in carrying into practice. In Kao Yao, the people were definitely conscious of their ideals of marriage and remarkably consistent in carrying them out.

As soon as a son was born, the family began to think about his betrothal, which could be contracted as soon as the child had passed its first New Year's Day. Marriage contracts were seldom confirmed before a boy was five, however, and most betrothals occurred at the age of ten or eleven, by which time it was expected that such matters would be settled. The mother and father discussed the problem, reviewing all the families in neighboring villages with unmarried daughters fitting the prescribed rules of preference. The ideal choice was for the son to become betrothed to his mother's brother's daughter because, it was said, she had his mother's name, or if such a one was unavailable, the daughter of his mother's sister. In fact, a betrothal was almost compulsory in Kao Yao if a boy had a maternal cousin no more than three years younger, and it could be arranged if the girl was older. Naturally, however, a girl of the desirable age and relationship did not always exist. Another thing which might happen was for a boy to inherit his elder brother's widow.

A betrothal to a daughter of a father's sister was also desirable, and a man might marry any of his mother's relatives except her sister. On the other hand, a marriage to a father's brother's daughter was unthinkable incest, as both individuals involved would have the same surname and belong to the same lineage. However, there were marriages occasionally between families of the same surname if the females did not belong to the same lineage.

The mother and father also considered the wealth and prestige of the family of a potential daughter-in-law. As a rule, equality was expected between the families in such matters, but there were exceptions. In any event, the qualifications of family were primary and those of the individuals secondary. Sooner or later a decision had to be made, and then the parents invited a woman friend of the family to dinner with the intention of asking her to act as a go-between or matchmaker. Professional go-betweens did not exist in Kao Yao, and only rarely was the office performed by a man. The name of the girl selected was given to the go-between and she, after supper, made a call on the girl's family, presenting the proposal to them for their consideration. If they did not accept it, the go-between left but might return the next evening to renew the negotiations. If still rejected, she could return a third evening, but if the family remained adamant in its decision, the refusal was recognized as final. The go-between reported the result to the parents of the boy, and if it was negative, they faced the necessity of suggesting another girl.

On the other hand, the go-between's proposal might have been received with some favor by the girl's parents, who then said that they wished to talk over the matter. In that case, the go-between drank her tea and asked on what day she might return for an answer. The time settled upon was from two or three days to a week afterward. The go-between returned after supper on the evening of the appointed day. If the betrothal were finally agreed upon, the go-between conveyed the information to the boy's family whereupon the almanac was consulted to see which days were noted as auspicious for formally confirming a betrothal. The date had to be at least one week away, and preferably two. It was invariably accepted by the girl's parents.

The next step in the procedure toward marriage was the exchange of gifts between the contracting families. Someone in the boy's family killed a pig, or bought pork, and sent it with sugar, eggs, wine, cloth, bracelets, earrings, and similar things to the parents of the girl. The least that could properly be given had a value equivalent to thirty dollars. These gifts were presented at any time of day by the go-between. The girl's family accepted the presents and sent others to the boy's parents in return, perhaps cakes which happened to be in the house, as well as clothing, and particularly a hat and shoes, for the prospective bridegroom. These were of a size to fit him at the time of his engagement, not a bridal costume. The value of the reciprocal presents was said to be at least eight dollars. No engagement ring or other symbol of their relationship was worn by either of the betrothed. As might be expected, the kind and quality of the gifts exchanged depended primarily upon the wealth of the families involved, and constituted one of the few distinctions between the marriage of people of one class and those of another. Ideally, no money was ever included with the betrothal gifts but, if a boy had rich parents and the girl was poor, her family might be given sixty dollars some time during the first six months of the engagement. There was one case in Kao Yao of an exceptionally brilliant but poor boy who was betrothed to a daughter of an upper-class family. The latter paid the cost of his advanced schooling, and he was currently a teacher in a nearby village. A boy's family also gave the go-between a present of a pig's head or some meat but not until after the marriage. Should the go-between happen to die in the meantime, the obligation was automatically canceled.

During the period of the engagement, a betrothed couple did not meet; indeed, if they approached one another on the street, they would turn back or, if they could not readily escape passing, they would turn their heads away in embarrassment. The parents, however, might exchange visits on New Year's and feast days, as their relationship through marriage was considered already established. There was no written announcement of the betrothal, but the news spread quickly nonetheless.

Once a betrothal had been contracted, it was seldom broken off. One of the children might die, however, and the death simply canceled all obligations. Occasionally one of the families broke an engagement. If the girl's parents did so, however, they had to return an equal value for the betrothal gifts which had been accepted.

Since the end of the Ch'ing dynasty (1911), children had occasionally refused to marry their selected partners on learning of physical defects. Blindness, deafness, facial disfigurement by fire, or goitre were becoming sufficient causes for refusal, whereas formerly there had been no escape as long as a person had the physical capacity to move around. Any instance of breaking a betrothal contract had to be approved by the go-between, however, as she was considered responsible for the engagement in the first place. If a rupture was attempted without her consent, she could protest to the district government and the case would be judged on its merits.

Parents could not inaugurate a betrothal contract for a daughter except in the special case when a son-in-law was to be adopted. Thus a family ordinarily had to continue to support a daughter if she was not wanted as a wife. Once we saw a child of about fifteen years of age walking around with the pigtails which were the distinguishing sign of single girls, and I asked when she would be married, hoping to be invited to the wedding. We were told that she never would be as she was not engaged and was already too old for a betrothal to be arranged. A boy was expected to be at least fourteen years old to marry, or so the matter was regarded until the government increased the age a little in 1937. For a girl, the ideal was the same. In any event, no marriage was formalized before the age of puberty. An analysis of the census of village families showed nine marriages in which one or both of the spouses were under twenty-one. Eight were girls and three boys, as the following table shows.

Husband's Age	Wife's Age	Husband's Age	Wife's Age
21	20	28	20
14	14	30	19
15	14	35	18
21	19	20	25
22	20		

It may be added that there were twenty unmarried boys and the same number of unmarried girls in the village between the ages of fourteen and twenty inclusively. Also, there was only one girl over twenty who had never been married. She was twenty-three and feeble-minded. Furthermore, in order to determine the relative ages of husbands and wives, we have examined the one hundred and fifteen cases of marriage in the village in which both spouses were living, including two cases of plural wives (but several marriages were not counted as the partners could not be allocated with certainty). The eldest and youngest wife, of course, can also be quickly computed.

Relative Age of Wife	Number of Cases	Eldest Husband	Youngest Husband
+10	1	45	–
+ 6	1	50	–
+ 5	2	53	20
+ 4	1	28	–
+ 3	1	43	–
+ 2	2	57	28
+ 1	12	51	21
same	22	60	14
− 1	13	61	15
− 2	11	52	21
− 3	4	33	26
− 4	7	60	27
− 5	4	65	38
− 6	6	58	27
− 7	2	46	31
− 8	6	62	30
− 9	3	60	30
−10	6	78	35
−11	1	30	–
−13	1	50	–
−14	2	61	53
−15	1	48	–
−17	1	35	–
−27	1	57	–
−30	2	75	51
−33	1	65	–
−45	1	77	–

Following often years after the betrothal agreement and ceremonial exchange of gifts, finally came the wedding. The boy's family determined the date after consulting the almanac again for a lucky day. Most marriages in Kao Yao took place in the 10th month. The go-between called on the girl's family and announced the date which had to be accepted. It made no difference whether or not the bride had elder sisters who were unmarried or not yet betrothed. A boy, however, would not be married if he had an elder brother still single. One month before the marriage day, each of

the families involved independently sent out invitations on red paper
to all their friends and relatives inviting them to attend their wedding feasts. Sometimes people received invitations for both celebrations, in which case the husband might attend the feast at the home
of the boy's family and send his wife and children to the girl's
parents. He would not attend both, however.

Guests from other villages might begin to arrive before supper
on the day preceding the wedding and remain several days, friendly
neighbors helping to supply sleeping accommodations. On reaching
the house, they were met by the parents and greetings exchanged by
bowing with clasped hands. Then the guests presented gifts to their
hosts, a man to the father of the bride or bridegroom, a woman to
the mother. The presents consisted of rice, clothing, jewelry, scrolls,
money, or almost anything which the parents could use. Pi said
he usually took a dollar or sometimes a scroll. The newcomer
remarked, "This is a little something," or words to that effect, and
the parents replied, "Thank you, thank you." After being shown
a place to sit down and served tea and cigarettes, the guest was free
to converse with those present. At mealtimes, guests were provided
with food.

Just previous to the wedding ceremony, the bride had to be
conveyed to her new home. To do this, certain equipment and
attendants were necessary—two ordinary green sedan chairs, each
with four bearers, three musicians, red cloth for decoration of the
bride's chair, and a ceremonial headdress for the bride. Since these
things were not available in Kao Yao, they were hired from one of
the villages about five miles away which specialized in such services.
Each chair with four bearers cost perhaps five or six dollars, but
this included decoration and the bride's headdress. The three musicians—never more—were paid about seventy or eighty cents apiece.
The arrangements and expense had to be taken care of by the boy's
family even when they were poor and the bride's rich. On the day
of the wedding, the go-between and the bridegroom entered the sedan
chairs after breakfast and set out for the bride's house. In front of
the procession walked two musicians, one behind the other, playing
on horns with six stops. They were followed by a third musician
with a drum and cymbals. Then came the go-between in a sedan
chair borne by four men and, behind her, the groom in a second chair
decorated with red cloth. Riding a horse at the end of the proces-

sion was the best man, chosen by the bridegroom among his friends or relatives. As the procession marched along, the musicians played a special tune called *The General's Song,* but no other. They went by the direct route to the bride's house, with children tagging behind and their elders stopping to watch.

When the procession arrived at its destination, the bride's brother (or if she had none, a paternal cousin) came out bowing to the bridegroom who descended from his chair and followed his host into the house. The bridegroom took the rear seat in the reception hall

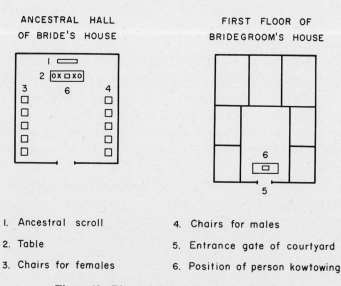

ANCESTRAL HALL
OF BRIDE'S HOUSE

FIRST FLOOR OF
BRIDEGROOM'S HOUSE

1. Ancestral scroll
2. Table
3. Chairs for females
4. Chairs for males
5. Entrance gate of courtyard
6. Position of person kowtowing

Figure 30. Plans of Arrangements for Wedding

and talked to his welcomer a little while before following him to the ancestral hall above (if they were in an upper class house). Against the back wall and in front of the scroll of the God of Heaven and Earth (ancestral tablet) stood a table on which were two red candles with two vases of flowers between them and, in the center, an incense burner. The side walls might be hung with one or more paintings beneath which were rows of chairs (Fig. 30, above). The one who welcomed the bridegroom invited the latter to burn some incense before the tablet, whereupon the bridegroom kowtowed three times with three sticks of incense between his clasped hands, afterward placing the incense in the burner. When he had finished, the bride's brother called some of the older male and female relatives of the bride who entered the ancestral hall and sat down in the chairs along the side walls. The men sat to the right of the door and the women to the left. Once again the bridegroom kowtowed three times to the ancestral tablet of his bride's family, after which all the relatives rose and bowed once in unison. After this ceremony, the bride's brother took the groom downstairs to eat.

Soon afterward, the go-between called for the bridegroom to leave on his homeward journey, even though the young man had not finished eating. The bride's brother then went for his sister, who was supposed to act as if unwilling to depart from her home, regardless of the real state of her feelings. Consequently her brother carried her pickaback to the sedan chair previously occupied by the groom who had transferred to the best man's horse, leaving the latter to walk behind. The bride's dowry was also added to the cortege. It consisted of such personal belongings, as a mirror, wash basin, mats, bedding, boxes of clothing, eating utensils, a stove for warming the room, and things of that sort. The least that she was certain of having were the special boxes which served for storing clothes and personal ornaments. The procession set off as before, except that the bride's chair preceded that of the go-between, and the party returned directly to the home of the bridegroom.

When they arrived, boys of the groom's family shot off firecrackers outside the gate. Just inside the entryway stood a table on which were red candles, vases of flowers, and an incense burner, arranged as were those in the ancestral hall of the girl's family (Fig. 30, p. 282). The bridegroom dismounted from his horse, walked through the gateway, and going around the table, kowtowed three times before it, facing the entrance. On the table, incense was burning. Then he went into the house.

In the meantime, the bride sat in her sedan chair. After the groom had come in, his sister and sister-in-law (or two women of the family) went out to the bride and put on her head the ceremonial red headdress with red flowers that had been rented from the owners of the sedan chairs. Then she was brought into the house without stopping at the table placed inside the gate and taken to the bridal chamber which, in an upper-class house, was an end room of one of the second-floor wings. There she sat down on the bed behind the bridal mosquito net which she closed. This netting, red in color, was a ceremonial requirement whether or not there were insects. The women who had accompanied her to the room then brought her something to drink and eat. When she had thus refreshed herself, she was led down to the courtyard where the groom awaited her in front of the table before the gate. Then they both kowtowed three times before the burning incense. With his bride standing before the table, the groom invited his older relatives to join them and the latter lined up, men on the right side and women on the left. Then the bride and groom kowtowed three times as before, after which the relatives bowed once. This concluded the formal ceremony of the marriage and the new wife returned to the bridal bedroom where she remained behind the bed netting to await her husband's pleasure.

On the day following the marriage there was a ceremony called Returning to the Bride's Family. If the family of the bride was wealthy and could afford to entertain their guests in the meantime, the ceremony might 'be briefly postponed in order to select a lucky day by consulting the almanac. The ceremony started when the bride's brother arrived and invited the newlyweds for a visit. The latter returned with him either on foot or on horseback (never in a sedan chair) and were entertained at a feast. Then they went home again. After this ceremony, the bride was considered to be an ordinary member of the groom's family and as such took up her normal household duties.

When a month had passed, there was a second such ceremonial visit to the bride's parents. This was called After a Month Celebration. On this occasion the husband might remain for two days, perhaps leaving his wife to stay several more so that she could have a rest. It was a peculiarity of this second ceremonial visit that the young couple were not allowed to share the same room, it being believed that should they have sexual intercourse, the girl's family would gradually become poorer and poorer.

The ceremonies connected with marriage which have just been described were typical of all classes of people in Kao Yao. The number of guests and the length of their stay did vary considerably, however, since to entertain them was expensive. Likewise, the gifts that were exchanged and the dowry that was brought by the bride could be of little or great value. Also, the accommodations provided depended upon the category of house. In a poor family the performance was crowded into the one or two rooms available but the pattern of behavior was the same. A marriage was neither licensed nor registered, the feast providing public validation of the union.

A variation in the typical procedure occurred when a young man was adopted into a family as a son-in-law. This could take place when a couple had only daughters. The ceremony differed only in that the betrothal was inaugurated by the girl's family—a thing which was never done otherwise—and in that the girl was brought by the bridegroom from either her father's sister's, or her mother's sister's, home to which she had gone for the express purpose of being conveyed back to her father's home. In short, for ceremonial purposes, the girl behaved as though she had been expelled from her own family in order to be married into it again as the wife of the newly adopted son. Young girls were not adopted into families to become future daughters-in-law, however.

A second marriage of a man or woman after the decease of a spouse involved a minimum of ceremony. The ideal existed that a woman should wait three years, but actually she might remarry in three months, although an interval of six months was more usual and, of course, it was possible that she might never marry again. The same restriction in time applied to widowers. When the wife of a young man died, it was probable that he would marry her sister, if she had one who was not betrothed. Instances of this were not common for obvious reasons. Marriage by capture was another rare way of obtaining a bride. About 1935, three years previous to our visit, a widow on her way to market was seized and transported to the home of a widower who wanted her. The woman reasonably accepted the situation as she probably expected to be married off without being consulted anyway. The man who thus married her —and there was no ceremony involved—then went to her former husband's parents and arranged to pay an amount estimated at seventy to eighty dollars.

Besides monogamy, plural marriages had an acceptable place in the life of Kao Yao as has been pointed out. One distinguishing thing about them was the fact that at least one of the parties involved, namely the man, was acting from individual choice and not simply as a pawn in the family system. The actual number of cases was few, and the schoolteacher could only think of three in the village. The census seemed to confirm his estimate in listing three families with plural marriages, but in one of them there were three wives. The principal thing which militated against plural marriage was the fact that to marry was expensive. Furthermore, it could lead to domestic complications which the man did not enjoy. In theory, the fundamental reason for taking an additional wife was the religiously determined necessity to have a son, and if a man seemed to have no chance of doing so with one wife, he was entitled to try with another. In such cases, the man might well be twenty years older than his new consort, while the latter would certainly be young enough to bear children. Our neighbor named Mei was a man of sixty-five and his second wife, thirty-two. She had borne no sons, and five from his first wife had died of typhoid. He often bemoaned his situation and gave thought to doing something about it. He told us that he knew of a woman he could marry, but that the cost would amount to fifty dollars which he did not have. The woman he had in mind belonged to a poor family and furthermore was over thirty years of age, a drawback since children were desired. Apparently he was also a little afraid of his wife, although he denied being so. Often we could hear them yelling at each other, and she seemed to give as much abuse as she received. They had a bad reputation in the village.

Sometimes polygyny was the result of a man taking his deceased elder brother's wife. This was a normal procedure if the younger brother was unmarried and an older brother died, but occurred otherwise only when both parties were agreeable. It was considered a desirable solution, but no compulsion was supposed to be exerted to bring it about. One of the practices common to China was concubinage, which differed from plural marriage primarily in that concubines did not have the same family status or privileges as wives, although they were socially accepted and their children suffered no legal limitation of rights. Concubines apparently had no place in the culture of Kao Yao, and if a man wanted to live openly with two women, he had to be married to both. A man, as has already been made clear, might clandestinely enjoy a mistress, but that was an entirely different matter. A woman, on the other hand, could have only one husband at a time, although as with a man, it followed that illicit relationships were possible.

A marriage could be dissolved by a divorce obtained through the government courts, but our informants knew of no one from Kao Yao who had ever been divorced. In the nearby village of P'i Chi Kuan, however, a man won a divorce because his wife went back to her parents' home and refused to return. Also, a woman in Ming Lang divorced her husband because he was dumb. When both parties wished a divorce, mutual incompatibility was said to be sufficient grounds. If there was one child, it remained with the father; if there were two, one remained with each parent—a boy with his father, a girl with her mother. A divorced woman always left her husband's home and went to live with any of her agnatic relatives who would accept her. The divorced husband and wife furthermore avoided one another, and if they chanced to meet, they would act as though they had not seen each other. A divorced person could at any time marry without ceremony another individual who had been divorced, but when a divorced man married other than a divorced woman, the procedure followed the customary pattern. This did not occur in the case of the woman, for an unmarried boy would never be betrothed to a divorcée.

18

DEATH AND FUNERALS

DARKNESS was falling over the village. We had finished a late dinner and were still sitting around the table when the second wife of our friend T'ao came excitedly to the door. A man had attempted suicide by eating opium and the foreigner was urgently requested to help. Taking an emetic with us, we walked down the street guided through the blackness by the weak rays of a flashlight. Presently we came upon a crowd of people and wormed our way into the house behind them. The sick man lay on his back on the small, stone-flagged court between the front and rear buildings. Men, women, and children were packed so closely about him that it took several minutes to reach the prostrate form lying as though in a cataleptic trance. His face had a ghastly appearance as if induced by terrific pain, and yellow foam clung to the corners of his mouth like tidal scum on a beach. An old woman was trying to insert a twist of hair down his throat without success. By persuasion we managed to clear just enough room to kneel beside the body and ask for hot water. The man's pulse was imperceptible and I wondered why this poor fellow who seemed under thirty had wanted to die. It took some time to force the emetic into him and, as we worked inside a pocket of human beings, I could look up and see reflected in the light of a candle a score of Chinese eyes twinkling like faint stars. The people who were close remained quiet, while those behind talked loudly and tried to penetrate the inner circle. Children squeezed between legs and crushed about us until I could feel their breath on my face. It occurred to me that perhaps it would be no great loss if one man who wanted to die should have his wish, but when I had begun to wonder if his case was hopeless, he suddenly commenced to contract and relax his muscles. The people reacted with excitement, and the news spread quickly from those in front to those in back. Then there was a new wave of pushing and the man was raised to his feet.

There being nothing further we could do, we stepped aside to watch the outcome.

The drugged man was hauled into the murky darkness of the front room where someone suspended a looped rope from the ceiling in order to form a crude swing in which they sat the patient. Then the people wound him around and around, twirling him from one to the other until the supporting rope was twisted all the way to the top whereupon with a shout they let him go and he spun in a circle as the rope unwound itself. The people who tried to prevent his being flung against the walls used sudden and not altogether successful gestures that brought about a general outbreak of laughter. After several repetitions of this treatment, it seemed certain that they would either kill the patient or cure him, and we walked home through the dispersing crowd. As we passed, one woman who was worrying over the possibility of the man's dying reassured another by saying, "Do not fear, the foreigner is in the village." I appreciated her confidence but did not share it, and consequently was relieved to learn a little later that the man had vomited and was apparently out of danger.

Suicides were said to be uncommon and no other attempts had been made recently in Kao Yao. At Ming Lang, however, a man had strangled himself after a family quarrel. He had struck his wife and the latter's relatives objected, claiming the husband was at fault. Having thus lost face, he tied a rope about the size of a clothesline to a beam and around his neck while he stood on a chair. Then he jumped off.

In theory, drowning was the preferential manner of doing away with oneself, regardless of sex, age, or the reason which drove one to self-destruction. Eating opium was considered too painful. Besides family quarrels, suicide was said sometimes to result from suffering the agony of starvation or from the shame of losing one's wealth.

Very rarely did a murder disturb the peaceful life of the community. Two people could start quarreling in the fields with one killing the other by a blow from the implement with which he was working. Traditionally, violence was also attributed to trouble over money, especially gambling debts. Families did not attempt direct revenge but appealed for redress to the government.

There was a sharp and notable difference in the attitude toward taking life on the basis of age. To kill an elderly person was an idea the suggestion of which created a feeling of horror. This undoubtedly resulted from the respect inculcated for people who had the tenacity to grow old. On the other hand, an unmarried mother was said to be very liable to strangle an unwanted baby with her hands regardless of its sex. In such cases, a father or brother—or a fiancé of the girl if she had one—attempted to catch the man responsible for her predicament, hang him up, beat him, and force him to pay perhaps thirty or forty dollars if he could obtain so much money. Whatever was collected was used for public works such as paving the road. No informant knew, or would admit of knowing, any actual case of infanticide, but neither could we discover any unmarried mothers.

The best way to die, according to the people of Kao Yao, was at home in bed surrounded by one's sons and family. When illness came, the approach of death was indicated by a weak pulse, a pale or yellow face, and by the fact that the nose turned up. We did not see anyone's nose turn up, but Pi said that it was natural and that he could tell that way, so we pass on the information. No effort to restore life was made after this happened, but prayers might be said beforehand for the restoration of the ill person's health. Whenever a person was dying, he was asked whether he had made his will, also whether he owed any money or others owed him. A woman could indicate the disposition of her property by word of mouth. The relatives and friends gathered around and cried, but no preparations for the funeral took place before the actual death, nor was the dying person dressed in special clothes for his departure from the world of the living.

A son ordinarily determined whether death had taken place by holding a finger to the nostrils to feel if there was any lingering breath and by noting if the body had become cold. When life had gone, someone was sent to announce the death to relatives and friends. Members of the family bought incense and candles, and killed a pig in order to feed the arriving guests. Then someone, perhaps a paternal cousin, went to buy a coffin if the dead person had not previously acquired one for himself. This was done immediately after the person died unless it was past midnight, in which case there was a delay until the next morning.

In Kao Yao there were two coffin shops which indicated the importance of the industry. The principal one faced the boat landing between the two restaurants at the end of the village street (Pl. 27, p. 180). There the carpenter and his helper, naked to the waist, were busy all day long and on into the evening, hewing and sawing the large planks from which the coffins were made. The best coffin wood was the China fir (*Cunninghamia lanceolata*) which was said to come from K'ai Hua (exact location uncertain), a distant town also noted for its opium, but wood of that quality seldom if ever found a market in Kao Yao for such a coffin would cost from a hundred to a thousand dollars. The wealthier village people used the good cypress of Mi Ts'ao or An Ch'a (exact locations uncertain), but even then the price could run up to a hundred dollars. Poorer people had to be content with ordinary cypress cut in the hills near the village.

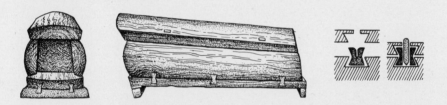

Figure 31. Coffin and Locking Mechanism

We watched the carpenter at work. First he would hew the planks with an ax having determined their proper size with a square and a crude marking line which rolled into six inches of the end of a water buffalo horn. The line marker had a rough, homemade spool at the end wound with string which could be pulled out of the small end of the horn after passing through a mass of rags with ink poured over them inside the horn. At the end of the line was a square-holed cash to prevent its being wound up too far. When the line had been extended over the proper distance, the carpenter would snap it in the middle, as we do with a chalk line. Then he would cut the planks with his saw and smooth them off with a typical Chinese cross-handled plane (Fig. 25, p. 236). After that, he would cut grooves in the pieces with chisels and bore the holes for the peculiar locking wedge and pegs which would fasten the cover permanently in place (Fig. 31, above). For the better coffins, a single piece of wood formed the sides, but cheaper ones had narrower pieces glued to-

gether. Finally, artificial lines to represent the grain of more attractive wood were painted on with a solution of brown sugar, then
covered with candle wax and rubbed to a high gloss with the rim
edge of a fragment of a heavy pot. The whole procedure of making a
coffin might take the carpenter two weeks.

It was customary for well-to-do men or women in the village to
buy their own coffins if they reached the age of sixty, but not otherwise. Those who did so kept their coffins in a storage room of their
house, or sometimes at a neighboring temple where the head priest
was asked to watch over it. This service he would grant at no direct
cost to the owner.

One day it occurred to me that it would be interesting to have in
America a specimen of the local type of Chinese coffin so we consulted the coffinmaker, suggesting that he construct an accurate quar-
ter-scale model, a proposition to which he was agreeable. No sooner
had we begun to discuss the project, however, than a crowd of people
from the nearby restaurants joined us, quite excited over our novel
proposal, but the educational benefits having been pointed out, everyone seemed to accept the matter in the best of humor. The coffinmaker asked twenty dollars for the undertaking and we finally agreed
upon eight, three dollars being paid in advance. Six days later he
brought me the finished coffin but I could see at a glance that it did
not have the characteristic shape which was rigidly established by
custom for the area. This fact discouraged him but, on having it
pointed out what a great misconception would result in America, he
agreed to make another. Two days later we went to the shop to see
how the work was progressing and discovered that his measurements
were again disharmonious. In our struggle to explain the quarter
fraction to him, the simple expedient of doubling and redoubling the
string of his line marker was discovered, a technique which he
grasped immediately and so set to work with confidence. By the
end of the week, he delivered a perfect miniature coffin claimed to be
exactly one-quarter of the regular size which custom dictated as having a length of 5.2 Chinese feet. On walking up the street to bring
it to me, the coffinmaker had gathered a considerable retinue of the
curious who seemed to be fascinated by the small object, and in the
following days we gradually became accustomed to having visits
from the people in nearby villages who, as they were about to leave,
politely asked if it was permissible to see the foreigner's small coffin

(Fig. 31, p. 291). As a result, I always sensed a pleasant feeling of a special relationship between the carpenter and myself for having unwittingly created something of a sensation in Kao Yao.

When a coffin had been purchased after a death, some flowers might be painted in gold on the ends of the side pieces and, likewise, circular medallions with a design like a swastika could be added to the center of the bottom and top pieces. A vertical column contained the deceased person's name and age. The decoration and writing might be done in gold by a specialist in Kao Yao, providing, of course, one could afford the price. Gold leaf cost three or four dollars, liquid gilt only thirty or forty cents. If both were too expensive, some member of the family could do the necessary work in ink.

Four friends or relatives of the deceased's family went to the shop and brought home the coffin, supporting it with carrying poles inserted in loops of rope fastened around each end. They placed it directly on the floor of the reception hall. Should the death not have taken place inside the home, however, the coffin was not brought inside the gate, but left outside on the street. The explanation for this was that a death which occurred outside the home was ignoble and the family would not accept it. When presented with the hypothetical case of having to bring the coffin and body inside, people said that an aperture would be made in the wall rather than using the gate as a means of entry. This suggested that the people feared at least some forms of death believed to result from a spirit which they did not wish to find any such easy means of entering the house as was afforded by the gate.

After the coffin had arrived, perfumed resin and oil—unless the people were too poor to afford it—were poured into the bottom as a preservative and then covered with cotton. Fine coffins reputedly lasted several hundred years in the ground. The relatives did not wash the corpse, but they dressed the deceased in his best clothes and, if the family was wealthy, jewelry as well. Then they placed the body on its back in the coffin with hands down by the sides. Before the cover was put on, a piece of silver jewelry and a dried date were placed in the mouth of the dead, but there was no Charon-like story as explanation—it was said merely to be custom. When the coffin was closed, the religious ceremony began.

The services preceding burial varied in elaborateness proportionate to the wealth or social class of the family involved and, accordingly, might last one, two, or three days. The principal distinction between the services was the inclusion of a priest who only performed in the two- and three-day funerals of the middle and upper classes. We shall describe the ceremony for a wealthy man as an example.

The coffin containing the corpse rested on the floor at the back of the reception hall with the head toward the door. Parallel to the coffin along the side walls were rows of seats for lay readers. At the head of the coffin stood a small table. On it was a wood grain measure filled with rice to support two red candles and between them sticks of incense. Nearby stood a lamp with vegetable oil and plates containing fruit and various other foods that were available. These were the offerings to the dead. In front of this first table was a second containing the musical instruments to be used during the chanting of the funeral service—a pair of brass cymbals, a bell rattle, a drum made of hollowed-out wood, another about one and a half feet in diameter with a skin drumhead, and lastly two wind instruments, one a plain flute with six stops (*ti*) and the other a clarinet-shaped flute likewise with six stops. Between the musical instruments and the door was placed a large table on top of which was a small one with a chair for the priest to sit on while performing the services. On the priest's table were candles, an incense holder, paper images of the gods, and the holy books from which he would read. The general arrangement of furniture in the ancestral hall during a two- or three-day service for the dead can be understood from the diagram of Fig. 32, p. 295.

The religious ceremony began after the coffin had been closed, generally the day following the death as time was required to arrange for the coming of the priest and the lay readers of the Buddhist Club who conducted the funeral. The Buddhist Club was a *hsien* organization with perhaps fifty members of whom only two or three lived in Kao Yao. Any man able to read the Buddhist holy books could join the association, which had come into being about 1913 in order to regulate the fees being charged by lay readers for services which were essential for proper burial of even poor people. Formerly prices had ranged from thirty cents to a dollar a day, but the rates had finally been standardized at from fifty to sixty cents. The club also gave approval to the fee of one dollar and a half which was paid to priests for each day's chanting. The members met once a year at a time decided by the chairman in the temple of his village.

RECEPTION HALL ARRANGED FOR FUNERAL

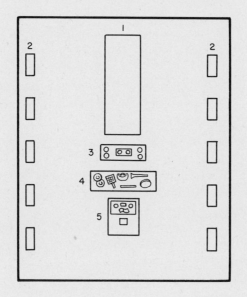

I. Coffin

2. Seats for lay readers

3. Table with offerings

4. Table with musical instruments

5. Table on which is a table and chair

Figure 32. Plan of Reception Hall Arranged for Funeral

Annual dues of fifty cents were collected to cover the cost of sending notices of the meeting to the various members in the several villages and to buy the tea which was served at the gathering.

Since six lay readers were considered the minimum required, some had to be obtained from outside Kao Yao. The family selected any member of the club to make the arrangements and he asked the others, serving as a go-between in the matter of payment and sometimes profiting thereby as he might be presented with a sum in excess of the fixed price. After paying the other members of the group sixty cents, he kept the balance for himself. Actually, the larger the payment the family made, the more virtuous they were considered to be.

The priest was engaged from a nearby temple frequented by the family. Before starting the ceremony, he washed his hands and face with water which had been placed in an ordinary vessel and dried himself on a new towel. The recitation of the scriptures took place preceding and following the morning and the evening meals, the services usually extending up to a half hour in length except for the evening performance which might last three or four hours since most people came to show respect to the deceased at that time.

The members of the family moaned and cried during the whole period, sons and daughters taking what rest they could at night while lying at the sides of the coffin. Many guests arrived the morning after the death and ate breakfast with the family. Food had to be supplied during their stay. Each guest honored the dead by kowtowing three times and, as he knelt, the son of the deceased also kowtowed at his parent's right shoulder. If there were two sons, the second kowtowed at the left shoulder. Meanwhile, the chanting continued with intermittent clanging of gongs, playing of wind instruments, and rhythmical beating on the drums.

At the end of the first day of the religious service the coffin was raised on two benches, one placed at the head and one at the feet. In a lower-class funeral, burial then followed. Middle- and upper-class services continued for one or two more days when the priest offered the prayer which preceded the removal of the coffin. This was considered the most important function of the priest who in exceptional cases might be invited only for the last day of a two- or three-day ceremony. The priest, however, never attended a single-day ceremony.

On the morning of the interment, some laborer of the village dug a grave about three and a half feet deep in the family graveyard. The direction in which he aligned the grave depended upon the year. For his work, he was not paid because digging a grave was held to be one of the most honorable acts a man could perform, although not one which a man of prestige would ordinarily undertake.

Before the funeral procession started, a son—or someone acting for him—knelt before the coffin and presented a tray which contained a roll of white cloth and at least sixteen cents. The elder brother— or some other relative—then stepped forward and hammered twice with an ax on one of the wood pegs which locked the coffin cover in place. This peg at the head of the coffin had purposefully been left unfastened for this ceremony. It was finally driven home by any person who wished to assist. The relative who performed the ceremonial hammering received the offering of white cloth and money which he took home for his own use.

Eight of the younger male relatives of the deceased carried the coffin to the grave. A pole was inserted under a loop of rope passed around each end of the coffin, then another pole under the ends of each of the first two, while the ends of the second set of poles were apportioned among the shoulders of each of the eight pallbearers. As the coffin was raised, the son kowtowed three times while the priest read his holy book and clanged on his cymbals. Then everyone started off to the graveyard, a journey which always took place in the morning and was not delayed because of either snow or rain.

In front of the procession went the priest and lay readers and three or more musicians, one with cymbals and the others playing on flutes. Since there were no professional performers in Kao Yao, the musicians were hired from Chang Chia Ts'un (Fig. 5, p. 69), a village previously mentioned as being about five miles to the southwest on the road to Tali. Then came the male relatives followed by the son and, after him, the female relatives. The son wore a white robe with a white hood similar to those sometimes used by monks but these funeral garments were not properly sewn. A daughter had a white cloth fastened around her forehead and knotted behind. It suggested a hood but did not cover the eyes or top of the head. White was the color of mourning, and formerly it was the custom to supply white cloth so that all the male relatives might drape themselves in robelike costumes and all the female relatives and friends could wear white headdresses. Since 1931, however, it had been one of the ideals of the Reform Club in Kao Yao to suppress this practice because of its extravagance. We were told that seventy-five dollars was once spent in Kao Yao to supply five hundred guests with white mourning cloth, but this may have been a slight exaggeration to impress us. After being used for the funeral, the white cloth served as material for the soles of shoes or as rags for various purposes.

Also in front of the coffin two men carried a green sedan chair decorated with white cloth. Two bearers were sufficient since the chair was empty except for the soul of the deceased. The conveyance and carriers were hired for two dollars for the occasion and generally came, like the musicians, from the village of Chang Chia Ts'un. If an enlarged photograph of the deceased, or a charcoal drawing from a photograph, was available, it was transported in front of the coffin in a bamboo, silk-covered shrine constructed to look like a building. Inside it, incense was lighted to burn before the picture. This innovation had grown increasingly popular in recent years.

As the procession moved along, the son from time to time kow-towed to the remains of his deceased parent. After passing the limits of the village, the coffin was put down and the son led the chanters in a procession around it, first in one direction a few times and then in the other, until the chant was completed. Again the son kow-towed three times and the coffin was started on its journey once more, passing over his still-bowed head. This was simply part of the ritual, the reason for which our friends in the village could not give.

The sedan chair was then dismissed from the cortege, but the remainder of funeral party continued to the family plot in the cemetery where the bearers rested the coffin beside the open grave. There the son once more kowtowed three times to his parent and repeated the act before all his relatives and friends in appreciation of their respect and assistance. While the group mourned, the coffin was lowered into the shallow grave and people gathered clay to sprinkle over the coffin. There was a disagreement recorded as to who sprinkled the clay (the graveyard soil was almost all clay). One informant reported that it was done by the brothers-in-law and daughters-in-law, another by the sons and daughters. We suspect the former was the ideal pattern but that in actual practice anyone could do it. After the ceremonial covering, the grave was filled in by the relatives who then went home. The next day they returned bringing clods of grass to build up a dome-shaped mound over the place of interment, and later a stone monument might be added by dutiful descendants.

Such a funeral, it must be understood, only occurred for a man or woman of the middle or upper class who had a son. When a woman died, only her direct descendants mourned, her husband making no formal sign of his loss. Otherwise the procedure was the same as for a man. For the poor, or lower-class people, the form was the same without the elaborateness. There would be only the one-day religious service involving six lay readers, but without the priest; also, a poorer coffin and no gravestone.

A much more significant difference than that which resulted from wealth occurred, however, in the disposal of a person without descendants. Such an individual was of no importance after he had ceased living and he was not buried in the family plot in the graveyard. He was put into a plain wood coffin costing only a dollar or two and buried as soon as the grave had been dug any place where a little land for the purpose could be obtained. Some lay readers might be employed for the funeral, however. The cause of a person's death, however, did not influence the way of disposing of the body. Bodies were never left in caves or dumped into the lake; they were always put into the ground although the people were sometimes careless in the manner they did it. Small babies that died were simply wrapped in a mat and buried anywhere. On the road a short distance outside the village, we once came upon the body of a baby which apparently some dogs had dug up from a too shallow grave. My companions showed no surprise, but they passed by on the far side of the road. The village people in Kao Yao never practiced cremation, but the priests in the nearby temple did.

The unavailability of land for burial was a problem of first rank for the ordinary individual, and no matter how poor a person was, he or she tried to obtain land for a final resting place. It was much less important if one died without a coffin for, in that case, even if one had no family, one's neighbors or the village council could be expected to supply a coffin, although of the cheapest material, and see that it was put into the deceased's few feet of ground. When the plots of well-to-do families became filled, they chose another part of their land. One stone noticed had the center column of characters engraved with the name of the deceased, "Grandfather and Grandmother Li," while on the right column was the date of erection "Middle Spring, 1932," and on the left, "Built by Nephew's son Sheng and granddaughter's husband Chung." In other plots were stones of the past century and fresh mounds of earth with none. Having no gravestone was said to be a characteristic which distinguished a lower-class family, while middle-class parents had simple stones, and the upper class more elaborate ones.

The period of mourning to be observed by a wife and direct descendants of a man extended for three years. The mourners wore a white cloth girdle regardless of their sex and sons might wear black caps with white buttons on top. When the relatives built the mound covering the grave on the day following the burial, there was a ceremony at which some grass, such as was used for thatching the roof of a house, was planted in a receptacle on top of the grave. The person who planted the grass, then sacrificed a chicken which was cooked and eaten by all those who helped to build the mound. As the grass grew, so it was believed would the prosperity of the descendants of the deceased. The grass controlled their well-being. For anyone to interfere with it would cause serious trouble. The Chinese have a proverb saying, "A single grass blade removed will cause a lawsuit which three years cannot settle." The grass on the grave we observed seemed to be in very poor condition and left the suspicion that the people of Kao Yao did not go looking for trouble on this score. Mourners had no particular purification rites after attending the ceremonies of interment.

The principal occasion for visiting a grave during the year was the Planting Trees Festival which occurred in the 3rd month. If one did not have the opportunity to do so then, one might go at the time of the Receiving Ancestors Festival on the 15th day of the 7th month, or later at the Winter Arriving Festival in the 11th month. Actually, few people went to the graves on these latter feast days although the thought of doing so resulted from the fact that the ceremonies involved paying respect to the ancestors. If a person was away at the time of the Planting Trees Festival and did not have an opportunity to visit the graves, it was quite sufficient to make the sacrifices wherever he happened to be, and then on his return he might visit the graves any day. There were no other special customs during the mourning period except that blue gate pictures of the gods were substituted for red.

Poor people terminated their period of three-year mourning by making offerings of food and incense at the grave. It was not necessary to sacrifice a chicken at this time, although a pious gesture if one could afford it. Rich people might make such a sacrifice and ordinarily hired lay readers to chant during the evening in the ancestral hall. Poor village people could not always uphold the ideal of a three-year mourning period. A widow, for example, as has been noted, might marry three months after the death of her husband.

19

THE SHAMAN PERFORMS

ONE NIGHT we chanced to hear that a *tuan kung* or shaman, was about to perform in the village in order to save the life of a sick child. At our request, one of our informants who was a close friend of the people involved asked permission for us to attend the ceremony, and word was sent that we might do so. We went out into the darkness, the cook leading the way with a flashlight across the marketplace to a nearby house. While the cook held three growling dogs in a shaft of light, we edged to the door. The head of the family greeted us politely, ushering us into the common hall.

Near the center of the room a fire was burning in a five-gallon kerosene can on top of which rested a shallow bowl about two feet in diameter. From the corners of the can, glowing charcoal threw off enough light to illuminate the shaman standing behind it. He was rhythmically moving his arms and hands while chanting softly. Beyond him against the wall was a large clay stove piled up on each side with farm and household equipment. On the stove rested a large square bowl along the edges of which were stuck clusters of incense, and in the center lay a pile of eggs. At one place where the incense sticks were the thickest, ten- and twenty-cent notes had been stuffed among them.

Near the bowl lay a sheet of paper about one foot wide and two feet long. On it had been placed a green wine jug, a shallow dish with the same glaze, and various small pieces of paper. At the shaman's right a low square table stood next to a partition of woven bamboo strips plastered with paper, long dirty, which hid the room beyond. As we became accustomed to the darkness, we could see that the common hall in which we were standing really consisted of two rooms, and that the second, which the shaman faced, also had a clay stove at the far end. At the rear, a ladder reached to the upper floor and, along the sides, there were stalls for horses, two of which put their heads into the hall, apparently attracted by the performance which was taking place.

We moved back into the blackness of the second room in order to face the shaman and then sat down. At first I sensed nothing around me except the chewing horses, but gradually I discovered the edges of the room to be crowded everywhere with farm and household equipment. I could see members of the family grouped around me. Nearest on my right was an old woman with teeth protruding at such odd angles that at first glance I thought some were missing. She sat smoking a metal water pipe pressed against her body with the stump of her left arm. With her one hand she intermittently pressed the silky yellow tobacco into the pipe bowl, applied the slow match, and puffed two or three times. Behind me was another old woman who rested quietly. A large dog had come in and lay against my side while a small puppy climbed over him. The latter's fur was white and soft like lamb's wool. On my left, a woman held a baby of about two, while a child or three or four sat in front of her. On the opposite side were standing two men. Their faces, like those of all in the room, showed in the dim light a rapt attention to the actions of the shaman.

In the dish on the fire a chicken boiled in bubbling oil. The shaman asked for salt which was brought to him in a green dish. He spilled several spoonfuls on top of the chicken, accentuating his actions by flourishes of the hand. Then from time to time he deftly stirred the mixture with his finger tips. The mincing movements of the shaman immediately suggested the intensified effeminacy of a homosexual. He wore white trousers of ordinary cut of more than usual fullness so that they hung over his black shoes. His jacket had a strange sky-blue color in the firelight, vaguely reminding one of a ballet costume. His head was completely shaven and showed several lines of scarification down the center. The fire had made his face florid and his eyes bulged neurotically like immense, black-spotted pearls. A narcissistic leer on his face at times approached a smile that somehow intimated the loneliness of an exceptional mind.

His fingers did not seem to suffer from stirring the boiling oil as the chicken cooked. Picking up some bits of paper from the table, he carried them to the stove and put them among his other paraphernalia. Then taking several in his hand, he set a match to them and held them in the air. In the sudden flame I could see that they had characters written on them. Just as the flame began to grow hot, he dropped them into the boiling oil in which the chicken was cooking. Returning to the stove, he poured wine from the bottle into the green dish and, with several flourishes, dashed it over the burning papers. As he did so, the wine burst into a sheet of blue and yellow flame which cast a green light over everyone's face. Several times he repeated the burning of the papers and the pouring of the wine which, with attendant gestures and facial expressions, increased the hypnotic spell he was casting over his silent audience.

At last our host who was sitting near the shaman took one of his children on his lap and pulled up her jacket, thereby exposing her stomach. As he did so, the shaman dropped his hand into the burning wine and twisted it flaming into the air. Just as the fire had about disappeared, he rubbed his hand vigorously over the child's stomach. She was shrieking loudly by that time, apparently in an agony of fear brought about by the shaman's maniacal expression and threatening performance with the flaming hand. The shaman made several applications to the apparent delight of the father who was beaming with pleasure whereas the child had fallen into a state of moaning exhaustion.

After one child had been treated for stomach trouble, a slightly older son had the same application of the burning hand on his face to cure a sore eye. By this time a considerable part of the tension had disappeared. The father and mother were smiling at each other and at everyone present, besides trying to quiet both children with affectionate embraces. The small boy had not liked the attention he received from the shaman any better than had his sister and could not be completely comforted, although he stopped yelling. The shaman continued to gesture, with even more obvious pride and satisfaction. I sat and watched, half-consciously cuddling the white puppy.

The father, apparently by special request in the manner of a theatrical encore, held up his smiling face and received an application of flame. The shaman used the balls of this thumbs to rub the veins of the man's forehead for ten seconds. When he had finished, he crunched up the sheet of colored paper which had been placed under his paraphernalia on the stove and wiped off the stomach and faces on which he had previously applied his flaming hand.

The bowl in which the chicken was boiling still burned slightly.

The shaman lifted it on to one hand, protected only by a piece of paper. He poured another dish of wine into it and, as the fire shot toward the ceiling, he carried it into the room partitioned off by the papered bamboo screen. There he poured more wine on the flames, thus freeing the sleeping quarters from the evil of sickness. Finally, on returning to the common hall, he took a mouthful of the wine and spat it into the bowl, making one last flash of smoke and fire. This done, with an assistant he carried the bowl outside the house. While he was gone, someone explained that the shaman was returning the spirits to the gods. I also think he ate the chicken. When he came back, the ceremony was recognized as being over, and he received the attentions of the guests in the manner of an artist who had just finished a great performance. We walked home in the darkness, the cook leading the way with the flashlight.

The shaman's performance interested me greatly and we had hardly started to discuss the matter before it seemed essential to attend another exhibition of the art. That feeling increased on my learning that what we had seen by no means represented the full potentialities of the shaman's abilities. Unfortunately, there was little probability of his being called to Kao Yao again during our residence. Wearily my mind moved from one thought to another in searching for a means to acquire further experience and, since nothing better resulted, I settled on the simple expedient of suggesting that I myself was sick. My friends laughed, but I insisted, tongue in cheek, that after weeks of long hours devoted to my studies I was on the verge of a complete collapse and, if there was a doctor who could save me, I would be foolish not to ask for his services. The plan appealed to my colleagues' sense of humor and, since it was the most direct means to satisfy the curiosity of us all, they approached the shaman. He was flattered to accept the commission and agreed to send for additional assistants immediately so that the ceremony might be performed the following evening at our house.

The next night we lingered around the dinner table for some time, discussing local customs with the several guests. It had been dark for so long that I had about given up the shaman when it was announced about nine o'clock that he had just arrived at the gate with three helpers and a string of horses bearing their equipment. The shaman and his cortege seemed very pleased with the facilities for the performance offered by our home, a fact which might be expected since it had been constructed as a stage (Fig. 4, p. 63; Pl. 5, p. 61). We put our dinner table back against the mural of the God of Wealth. The shaman sat in the corner pleasantly smoking a bamboo water pipe while his assistants made the necessary preparations. He was dressed as we had seen him before—in black shoes, full white trousers, and a baby-blue jacket, which had the sheen of fine silk.

One of the assistants began to put on make-up, covering his face first with white paint and then adding red to his cheeks and lips, the effect being novel as he had only one eye. His costume consisted of elaborate shoes, a green skirt, and a red jacket with a black vest on top of it. All these garments were covered with rich embroidery. Finally he put on a headdress of elaborate theatrical type which he took out of a large tin box specially constructed to safeguard it. Having thus attired himself as a female character, he picked up a tambourine-like drum with an iron frame about one foot in diameter and a short wood handle. He proceeded to tighten the drumhead by holding a burning paper close to it in order that the heat might contract the skin. Over his left wrist he hung a cloth loop supporting an eight-inch brass gong. Then he took the drum in his left hand. In his right hand he held both a beater for the gong and a switchlike drumstick, and beat on the gong and the drum with them at the same time to hear if the sounds were satisfactory. The second assistant of the shaman was at the same time putting himself in readiness for the performance by painting his face, which he distinguished by adding a large black mustache indicating a male character. His costume was similar to the other but he wore an elaborate headdress with numerous furry white balls on the end of long pins.

While two assistants dressed themselves, a third set the table with a metal bowl holding a small pile of eggs in the center surrounded by incense sticks and two red candles. At one side of our mural of the God of Wealth, he hung a specially painted scroll with the God of the Earth on the left and Lord Kuan on the right, the latter's two attendants standing below. The old woman with only one hand who had sat next to me on my first encounter with the shaman was folding paper money for the dead and placing it on the table.

The performance really began when the old woman took a white chicken in her hand and kowtowed three times with it in front of the scroll of the gods while the first assistant sang, accompanying himself by beating on his drum and gong. Then the second assistant took the chicken and passed a burning paper clockwise around its neck a few times, after which he allowed the chicken to eat from a bowl of rice placed upon the floor, he himself at the same time picking up a small handful of the grain and allowing it to fall back into the dish from above the chicken's head. At the same time he recited a prayer. He sprinkled a few drops of water on the chicken's head, then drank some. At last, borrowing a pocket knife from our cook, he punctured the chicken's comb and dipped into the blood with the plain wood end of an incense stick. Then with the blood he touched various parts of the face and body of the gods on the scroll, while the other assistants and the shaman himself created a din with drums and gongs. When the second assistant had finished, the performance of touching the scroll with blood was repeated by the shaman who followed it with a song and a drink of what seemed to be water. Then the second assistant lighted the incense in the burner and bowed before it with the chicken. Picking up the two red candles from the incense burner, he crossed one over the other in front of various parts of the scroll of the gods, singing a song while he did so. Then he sprinkled a few drops of water on the candles.

At this point he casually interrupted the ritual by pouring himself a cup of tea from a pot which our cook had provided for the performers. Having quickly satisfied himself, he bowed twice with the candles before the scroll and put them back in the incense burner.

The shaman and the first assistant began to dance around the stage, accompanying themselves with gongs and drums. Meanwhile, the second assistant sat down and proceeded to make a hat brim out of a straw cover from a rice steamer. This he wanted to use in the theatrical section of the evening's performance. He had taken off his elaborate headdress, which was apparently too heavy for the dancing, and had wrapped his head with a black scarf which he spent considerable time in adjusting. The shaman soon sat down to leave the first assistant to dance alone, but the latter was presently joined by the second assistant and, singing together and pounding on their instruments, they created a terrific noise. The shaman paid no attention, occupying himself with tying a piece of red cloth to the end of a bamboo stick to be used in a later dance. While the dance continued, the husband of the old woman with one hand took the white chicken out of its basket and carried it to the edge of the stage where he stuck it in the throat causing it to kick violently. At this point the two performers in the center of the stage began to dance more actively and the old man let the blood of the chicken drop into a bowl, the one, as I could see by its color, from which I had eaten my dinner.

That the next part of the proceedings required no overburden of seriousness, the shaman indicated when he stopped the second assistant and tucked up his skirts so he could dance more energetically, an act which caused some laughter from the onlookers. Most of the people in the village had gathered in the courtyard to see the show and our neighbors and friends crowded the stage. A row of children sat along the front, constantly startling me by almost falling over the edge into the audience below.

The dramatic performance lasted about two hours and was acted principally by the first and second assistants while the shaman rested quietly by, smiling pleasantly or smoking his bamboo water pipe. I sat next to him in the entrance of our study exhausting myself in the process of recording what was going on. It was difficult to hear anything and still harder for the interpreter to make sense out of the banalities in the local dialect which were bringing great laughter from the courtyard. Some of the scenes buffooned love-making or flirtation between the sexes. One contained an imitation of birds. The action so excited the son of our neighbor, a simple-minded child of about eight, that he removed the jacket which was his sole garment, and playfully wrapped it around his waist. The performers frequently interrupted their activity to suck a mouthful of tea or take a puff on a cigarette. One dancer left a lighted cigarette on the table, and, after an enthusiastic start to a dance, remembered it and returned to put it out so that it would not waste away.

At one point the performers stopped and gave a recitation-like announcement that the dancing was undertaken in honor of the gods and then named the gods individually. Next, the second assistant called for the support of everything which brings fortune. Following this appeal, the second assistant took a candle and stood it up in the middle of the floor, laying down a red cloth beside it to represent an ancient time-telling device. The shaman joined the activity in this instance, kneeling with his drum close to the floor, while the second assistant knelt before the gods, chanting and beating the drum. They were asking the time and calling the watches of the night. At last they came to daybreak, the fifth watch, and the second assistant called out, "Daybreak and work must be done."

Actually, it was after midnight and the crowd in the courtyard had begun to thin out. I was exhausted and hoped that we would soon come to more serious matters, but the show went on and on. Periodically the assistants would kneel on the floor and begin to worship the gods, rocking from side to side, with the shaman encouraging them from the sideline. The noise of the drums and gongs was so loud that the simple boy held his hands over his ears, and a baby that had fallen asleep awoke with a start and almost toppled over the edge of the stage, which caused a temporary uproar among the women of the audience.

The first assistant pretended to be a female shaman revealing to the second assistant, in the role of a husband, all manner of things about his family affairs. The husband insisted on knowing the worst, and the would-be shaman said that his wife was unfaithful and that he was a tortoise, which is a Chinese term for cuckold. The husband was furious and begged the shaman for assistance in obtaining the help of the gods. The shaman sat in a chair pretending to be possessed and soon began asking for a series of things completely impossible to obtain, such as the hair of a toad. Whether this was done to make light of female shamans, or just for the sake of humor, was not clear. Finally, the show stopped at quarter to one and the preparations for the more serious part of the service began.

The brief interval of quiet provided a sharp contrast to the hours of clanging gongs. The shaman placed a black scarf over his head and, pulling it flat across his forehead, twisted the sides into a cord and tied them behind his ears in buccaneer fashion. Then he warmed his drum.

In the meantime, assistants placed a table about one foot high in the center of the floor putting on it the candles, incense, and eggs which had remained in front of the scroll of the gods. Behind the incense and other things, the third assistant arranged ten of our empty rice bowls in two rows of five, covering them with a piece of red cloth. He also unwrapped a cloth container—which held among other things some papers and a book—and took from it an old razor which he wrapped in a very soft kind of red paper and put in the incense burner with the eggs.

The shaman came to me and asked for a gift of money, a special part of the ritual. Usually he was given about sixty cents but, in ignorance, I offered only a twenty-cent bill, which he accepted without further question. No one, it was said, would refuse to make the extra contribution at that time as it was the crucial moment before the shaman called on the spirits. The shaman, just as he was about to start the ceremony, slipped something into his mouth. I could not discover what it was, but our cook, something of an authority on such matters, insisted it was chicken livers.

Suddenly the shaman walked over to the gods and, facing them, began to drum fast, his second and third assistants accompanying him. Then he began to yell, a long melancholy howl, and the assistants left him to carry on alone. He turned toward the audience and the table between them with smoke rising from the incense. Continuing to drum with an even beat, he sang, but his voice became almost inaudible against the heavier sound as he placed his lips close to the drumhead as though singing into it. He began to shake his head as if possessed by spirits—a strange, ethereal expression appearing on his face. This continued for what seemed a long time and until even the spectators felt the strain. Suddenly he began to chant. Then he stopped, exhausted, before the table with the incense.

The third assistant approached and unwrapped the shaman's black head scarf and washed his forehead with a rag, and then walked away. The shaman picked up the red cloth covering the ten dishes and laid it over his left shoulder, tying the ends under his right arm. Then he made a sign with his right hand by placing the end of his thumb against the tip of his third finger. According to the schoolteacher, this sign was used only by shamans and served as a supplication for protection from the spirits. He recognized the gesture as Buddhistic, however, when the fact was pointed out to him.

In the meantime, the third assistant had collected some burning embers of charcoal in our washbasin. He spat some wine into it which immediately burst into flame, while the shaman played with an iron rattle with rings on a circular frame. Then he brought the washbasin and the razor to the shaman who took the latter between his teeth, still facing the table with his back to the gods. The shaman held his head over the basin while water was sprinkled on the coals and steam rose against his shaven head. Suddenly the shaman raised his arm and made two vertical cuts high on his frontal bone. From the distance of a few feet I could plainly see the blood running down his forehead. The shaman leaned over the first of the ten bowls while his blood dripped into it. As each bowl was thoroughly spattered, he moved on to the next until all ten had been coated from his bleeding head.

At this point in the ceremony, I was startled by being called on to kowtow three times before the gods in front of the entire audience, a duty which I performed with all the dignity I could command, not wishing to lose any of the benefits which I suddenly remembered were being sought on my account. The shaman had collapsed into a chair while his assistants bound up his head again. He began to drum softly and rose shaking his head slightly. He walked to the scroll of the gods and bowed before it once. This ended the ceremony.

It was ten minutes after one, and I thanked the shaman for his services. Baring his forehead, he showed me that his cuts did not bleed. Then he asked for an additional two dollars, besides the ten (a high price) which I had previously paid him, but accepted his lack of success very pleasantly. After presenting me with the scroll of the gods, he explained that I must hang it up and worship it regularly by burning incense and kowtowing. By so doing not only was my health assured, but I could expect both a son and a raise in rank the following year. On the other hand, he added by way of warning that should I fail in the proper observances, I would suffer from sore eyes.

The threat disturbed our cook very much and the next day he helped me to arrange a proper altar. Since we lacked a suitable incense burner and I was somewhat amused by the solicitation of our creator of celestial food, it was suggested that when such an article was needed in America, it was always provided as a gift from the cook. On hearing this he went off rather glumly and was gone most of the day. Late in the afternoon I was surprised when he returned with a very satisfactory incense burner, which we used from that day forward with considerable pride.

Our continuing study of shamanism showed that there were several categories and kinds of such individuals. First of all there were regular shamans called *tuan kung*, of which two schools were recognized. These schools were differentiated on the basis of

whether the shaman made a knife stick into his head or merely cut
gashes with it. The latter group had the reputation of comprising
a higher class since, according to Buddhistic teaching, the more
damage inflicted on the body, the lower the class. Besides the *tuan
kung,* there were novices known as *kuan jen,* who were apprenticed
in the art and assisted at the performances. The second category of
shamans was made up entirely of females. Such a shaman was called
niang, which meant literally Teacher's Wife, an honorary title for
women. The *niang* did not conduct the ceremony of bleeding and
were more individualistic in their practices. The third category of
shamans known as *hsi po* consisted of those whose specialty was to
pray for rain and to ward off destruction by the God of Fire. Such
shamans inherited their power from their fathers and passed it on to
their sons. Finally, quite apart from these categories, there were a
few lay mediums, or people who did a little private shamaning on the
side, so to speak.

Each school of regular shamans or *tuan kung,* dominated in a
certain aggregate of villages. The cohesion of the school depended
upon the fact that the training of the members was derived from a
common teacher rather than upon any formal organization. A boy
was offered to a master at the age of eleven or twelve for a period of
about six years, after which time if he had not qualified, he could
never become a shaman. The master had to be given thirty or forty
dollars as tuition for the training. Although there was a tendency
for a son to follow in his father's footsteps, any boy might be accepted
as a novice, and observers did not seem to be aware of any physical
or mental peculiarities which distinguished children who were.
They seemed to be normal members of the community. Neither
could the full-fledged shaman be distinguished by speech or dress,
but if he removed his hat, scars might well be discernible on his
shaven head.

The training consisted of learning the formal behavior, or ritual,
of shamanistic practice, and of acquiring the art of spirit possession.
The pupil learned the former primarily by assisting the master at
his performances. The possession of spirits came through the development of a self-induced trance, but as to the actual origin of the
power, as was usual in such matters, there were differences of
opinion. It was said that the teacher passed on his power to his
student or more exactly, shared it with him. On the other hand,

we were told that a shaman during his trancelike communings with
the spirit world saw various deities whom he described to an artist
who painted their likeness on a scroll such as was done for my
benefit. The shaman then worshiped these gods and derived his
power from them. There were stories about dead people whose
ghosts were enlisted as a troop of shaman's soldiers. When possessed, a shaman might give a description of the soldiers and their
horses, as well as commonplace pictures of their daily life which
were extraordinarily similar to what might be observed among the
living in an ordinary village. At a shaman's behest, the ghost army
might fight off evil spirits or recapture a wandering soul. Certain
shamans had the reputation for greater power than others; their
contact with the other world was more far-reaching. This was
clearly indicated by their success in saving lives.

A shaman was called in by a family to restore a sick person to
health. For simple curing services the shaman asked perhaps two,
three, or four dollars. Then the family usually bargained to reduce
the price a little. When the matter had been settled, the shaman
went to the house of the sick person and wrote on a piece of paper
the names of his deities—names of his own creation, the characters
for which he often did not even understand. No real attempt was
made at diagnosis nor was one considered necessary since all sickness
was attributed either to loss of soul or to an attack by evil spirits.
When the injury was visible, the latter explanation was given, when
it was not, the soul was said simply to have wandered away.

What happened while the shaman cured a patient has already
been described from an actual ceremony for a sick child. The performance could take place at any time. It might be carried out in
any room of a house although usually the most spacious one, but
seldom, however, in the open. The shaman always sang, kowtowed,
recited magical words, and sacrificed a chicken—supplied at the
family's expense. Prayers were made to the shaman's deities and
incense was burned. Shamans used a language which was not
understood by their audiences, apparently a distortion of normal
Chinese. They did not practice ventriloquism, however. While in
communication with their deities, the latter demanded payment for
their services, which requests were passed on to the family being
served. The deities asked for money, rice, cloth, or anything else,

all of which the shaman took home. The cost of such articles could double the price which had been agreed upon for the ceremony.

After the soul had been called back, the shaman removed the shell and examined a hard-boiled egg on which he claimed to see an image of the soul—unclear spots on the white surface. He almost certainly announced that the soul had been recaptured in the nick of time, as it was about to proceed elsewhere for reincarnation. Despite all this, the patient might die, but there was no penalty for the shaman. If he had enjoyed other successes, his failures were forgotten. Reputedly there was little or no rivalry among shamans, and no public display of their skill to advertise their prowess other than those which occurred at paid performances.

More elaborate ceremonies, which included the essentially theatrical interludes, and brought not only health but fortune, could be purchased by the wealthy. Few such extravagant performances as we provided had probably ever been witnessed in Kao Yao. The actual proceeding has already been described and a few more details may be added by way of explanation. Of the shaman's assistants, two were novices and the other was the shaman who had been the teacher of the star performer of the evening. The touching of the scroll of the gods with blood from the comb of the sacrificial chicken was necessary to hallow the scroll or, to quote literally, "to make it alive." The actors' costumes were typical of the stage and had no special religious significance. The cutting of the head had nothing to do with the coming or going of spirits and was not done in the ordinary curing ceremony. It pertained rather to bringing fortune to the sponsor of the performance, and the more blood that flowed, the more fortune he should have. According to an informant who was the close friend of another shaman, the cutting did not hurt because of the application of hot water and steam. No one doubted that the shamans actually cut themselves and there was no evidence that they did not do so.

In curing, shamans did not attempt direct hypnosis, neither did they indulge in such a common practice as sucking the body to remove an evil spirit. Apparently the local shamans sought only after good for there was a systematic lack of the negative aspect which one thinks of as sorcery or black magic. Neither was there evidence that black magic was formerly common, which fact, if true, was the more notable since it was still recordable in other parts of China where the outward forms of shamanism had almost disappeared. Shamans seldom indulged in prophecy and then it pertained to some good fortune for those who hired their services. If a crime had been committed, shamans made no pretensions of discovering the perpetrator.

Informants told us there were no shamans among the residents of Kao Yao, but there was evidence to believe this was not so. In either event, Kao Yao had no reputation for shamans, such as was attributed to the village of Yü Wo Yang, or Jade Nest Sheep (exact location uncertain), on the other side of the lake where there were said to be five such practitioners. As a matter of fact, the majority of villages had none and if their services were wanted, a shaman had to be imported. As stated previously, one school of shamans usually dominated in a certain area and met whatever demands there might be. People on the margins of areas selected shamans of any available school without any danger of resentment for their choice, a parallel being given in the lack of competition between lay readers and priests.

Shamans found their clientele primarily among the lower class. The more intellectual people ordinarily despised the shamans, and the schoolteacher said no person of any education would appeal to a shaman for aid. One attribute of shamanism which caused hardship was the expense. Although it has been pointed out that a performance might cost from three to over ten dollars including extra fees, it must be remembered that these figures represented national currency and, in order to gain a proper feeling for the expenditure, they should be multiplied by ten to turn them into local values. Thirty to a hundred dollars for an evening's spiritual assistance could be economically devastating to the poorer people of Kao Yao. Certainly, the practice was on the wane, if for no other reason than that it had been banned by the authorities, and it seemed likely to be soon driven under cover, if not to disappear as it had in many parts of eastern China.

Female shamanism was a private matter, and a woman was said to have no choice about joining the vocation. She was either taken possession of by spirits or she was not. People describing the process of possession said that a woman suddenly went crazy. Then she either accepted the mantle which had fallen over her or she would die.

Female shamans were popular as physicians for women. In so far as we could discover, there was none in Kao Yao, but there was a celebrated practitioner in P'i Chi Kuan, less than two miles away. Theoretically the female shamans were each of equal rank with equal efficacy in curing, but some were more in demand than others. The lady at P'i Chi Kuan, it was said, had so much business that she could not take care of it, and her patronesses sent a horse to bring her to them. She was a barren woman of about forty years of age who supported her husband in luxury, apparently having successfully exploited the whole community. In her home was a roomful of images which were so atypical of the usual religious figures that they frightened the visitors.

In her performances, she used drums and gongs, but no other special paraphernalia. She dressed in ordinary clothes, prescribed no medicine and, like other female shamans, did not gash her head as did the *tuan kung*. She could not cause sickness; only cure it. Besides the regular payments, people customarily gave her rewards when cures had been effected. She offered no public performances of any kind, but on the first and fifteenth of each month, she worshiped her deities at home, chanting and beating on her drums and gongs. There were no professional relationships between the male and the female shamans.

Members of the third category of shamans recognized in Kao Yao had the special function of bringing rain and warding off fire. These *hsi po* were called in when there was a drought or when a "mass of fire" had been seen in the air, a phenomenon widely accepted by the Chinese as representing the God of Fire. There were three such shamans at Ming Lang, five miles in a westerly direction on the road to the city of Tali. They all belonged to the Pi family, which lineage alone was said to possess this power, it being passed down from father to son.

When there was a drought, the people of a village might collectively invite the shaman to bring rain. The fee was about three dollars to which had to be added the cost of a goat to be sacrificed. The shaman performed his ceremony in the hills in the presence of the people who hired him. He set up a paper tablet written in a

secret character which looked like Japanese *kana*. On his back he
wore a wood image of his deity dressed in white cloth and on his
head he had a tall conical hat. As he prayed, he rang a straight-
handled bell. The goat was forced to bow three times to the tablet
and was then killed, skinned, and cooked as an offering to the gods.
Then the shaman, with the people who wanted rain, kowtowed three
times to the tablet. Afterwards the people ate the goat and went
home expecting rain.

The same shaman could be invited to give a performance when
people feared devastation by fire, either because they had seen the
ignis fatuus or because their house had burned and they wish to
prevent another such loss. The cost was also about three dollars
plus a chicken to be sacrificed. The shaman came to the house which
was to be safeguarded and put up a paper tablet. Then he took a
chicken and some straws of grain and fastened both to a bamboo
pole. When all was ready, he took the pole and waved it several
times under the eves of the house, following which he sacrificed the
chicken before the tablet, kowtowing three times. The family likewise kowtowed three times. The chicken was then cooked and
eaten. The same evening the shaman mixed cedar twigs and an
unidentified kind of seed which were then put into the stove and
burned as incense. Quite regardless of any invitation, in full regalia
he carried this incense to every house in the village, and at each he
received a bowl of rice and an egg.

The wood image which was carried on the back during these
ceremonies was kept among the ancestral tablets in the shaman's
home and worshipped daily. New images might be made, but the
old ones from past generations were carefully treasured. These
shamans had no ability to stop rain or to start fires, nor any other
special powers apart from those described. When an informant was
asked if there were any penalty for failure, the answer was no since,
as it was explained, they always succeeded.

The fourth category of shamanism consisted of the type of
medium who communicated with the spirit of a deceased person.
After a death, a family might gather on a certain night with the
help of such a medium to greet the spirit of the departed. This was
done most commonly on the 15th day of the 7th month, which was
the time of the Receiving Ancestors Festival. The performing
medium was blindfolded and his ears stuffed with what was described

as "mint pepper." His hands, holding sticks of incense, were clasped over the knees. In that position the medium began to shake and continued until he entered into a trance.

One night, two days before the Receiving Ancestors Festival, we visited one of the poorer homes in the village. A middle-aged woman was sitting on the floor with her back against a post. The single room was dark except for a clay saucer lamp in an iron frame held by one of the numerous individuals who had come to witness the performance. The medium had a black cloth around her eyes. Her hands, holding incense, shook violently and she was muttering in a way that sounded like groans. Mucus dripped from her nose and was occasionally wiped off by a person sitting nearby. Many women and children surrounded her, and men stood in the darkness of the background.

A woman sitting on the floor next to the medium had lost a son because of a stomach ailment and she was speaking to him through the woman in the trance. She asked if he wanted anything, and the son said he would like some milk but could not get any. This brought laughter from some of the onlookers who apparently took the performance lightly, but others, and especially those asking questions, were completely credulous and insisted that the medium spoke with exactly the same intonation as the dead boy. The performance went on for a considerable time, and apparently some of the onlookers became bored as they did considerable talking and moving about. One woman remarked sarcastically that she did not see how anyone could get in touch with the spirits when so many people were around. We went home through thick mud which had come with the heavy rains.

The role of medium, which could be undertaken by anyone, was very exhausting, and the performer received some payment. The schoolteacher as usual said that he did not believe in the validity of such performances, but our cook said he had communicated with spirits himself. According to his account, he had sat down and shaken as he had seen others do and by this means had made himself completely unconscious. While in this state, however, it was said that he had reported very successfully on behalf of a dead relative.

20

RELIGIOUS IDEAS

AMONG THE conglomeration of ideas which composed religion in Kao Yao, the most formalized were Buddhistic although, as in most Chinese villages, Taoism and Confucianism contributed generously. Any one of the three systems might have dominated by some historical chance, but perhaps it was the very proximity of no less than four famous temples which affected Kao Yao in a way that brought it the reputation of being a comparatively unreligious community. As it turned out, the people could not really distinguish one set of beliefs from another. Pilgrims came from afar to visit the temples, but with characteristic disdain for the familiar, the residents of Kao Yao seldom did so. The small village temple (Pl. 11, p. 76), a stone's throw from our residence, Ho immediately characterized as Taoist since no priest was attached to it, and Pi was apparently ashamed of the structure which was overshadowed by its illustrious neighbors. It lacked the ostentatious display of images which characterized three of the four other temples, but it contained nonetheless a series of elaborate figures placed against the long rear wall of the single room. The run-down appearance of the place with its overgrown courtyard rather appealed to me, and I liked the caretaker who was suffering from a badly infected leg. His scraggly haired dog barked at strangers but quickly became affectionate to the fearless. Perhaps I was prejudiced in favor of the unimposing Kao Yao temple because of its peaceful atmosphere and the quality of the water in its well. The only time I saw any visitors in it was when the women of the Buddhist Club gathered there to make paper boats for the Receiving Ancestors Festival.

The P'u Hsien Temple, however, deserved more attention for various reasons (Pl. 35, p. 320). Only a few hundred feet away and in plain view from the little brook at the south side of Kao Yao where the women washed clothes (Pl. 36, p. 321), it was the home of eight Buddhist priests to whom we paid our respects on several occasions. The temple itself consisted of three halls one behind the other in typical Chinese style with tiled roofs having gracefully upturned corners supported by a series of braces which rested on great round posts of local wood rising from barrel-shaped socles set upon much larger squares of stone. In the first hall one encountered the usual Four Guardians towering over the visitor and providing a sharp contrast to the benign and somewhat obese gilded Buddha seated with his back to the rear wall. In the center hall, or Rear Room as it was called, stood the figure of a large white elephant bearing the Bodhisattva P'u Hsien on its back, the manifestation from which the temple took its name. The third hall, or Great Room, had been in the process of reconstruction since 1935 and contained only the stand for its Buddha.

One of the priests who had heard of our residence in Kao Yao obligingly informed us that the income of the temple was derived from the rental of more than ten *mou* of rice land and from gifts presented by the stream of visitors from Kunming. Money obtained by the sale of incense was no longer available, however, since under the New Life Movement of the National Government, the burning of incense by laymen to supplicate the gods had been banned as a superstitious practice.

We were told that the temple had been founded during the Han dynasty (206 B.C. to A.D. 220), and there was a signboard on a tree declaring that to be fact. "Of course," the priest added, "the buildings have been rebuilt innumerable times." He had come recently from the province of Hupeh and probably doubted the extreme antiquity ascribed to his venerable temple as we did. To me, the historical significance of the P'u Hsien temple came from the fact that it at one time sheltered Yang Shên (1488-1529), a famous scholar of the Han-lin college who was banished to Yünnan by the emperor for protesting the appointment of a mediocre person to those sacred precincts of learning. According to tradition, Yang Shên quietly drank himself to death while writing what has become one of the most important sources of information on the province for the Ming period. In his volumes he has a poem in which he mentions the smoke rising above the houses of Kao Yao, thus proving its existence a hundred years before the founders of the Massachusetts Bay Colony settled at Boston.

35. P'U HSIEN TEMPLE

36. THE VILLAGE LAUNDRY

The schoolteacher stated soon after our arrival that Kao Yao was one hundred per cent Buddhist, but what he meant was that there were no Mohammedans or Christians in the village. Although in Yünnan about one person in three was a Mohammedan, the nearest who praised Allah resided in Ma Chieh about five miles to the north, whereas there were two or three Protestant Christian families in Ch'ih Chia Pi less than two miles away on the road to Kunming. Within Kao Yao, it was both verbalized and apparent that the older people were more concerned with Buddhism than the younger. Certainly the aged had more time for religious matters and a more immediate concern with death, the obsequies surrounding which we have already seen to be tied with Buddhism through lay readers and priests.

It is significant that only two or three men of over two hundred in Kao Yao belonged to the Buddhist Club of lay readers, whereas the Buddhist Women's Club had eighteen members. This was more participation than it might seem since one was supposed to be forty years old to join and there were only seventy-seven females over that age in the village. On the other hand, a few younger widows were included and it is not certain that some of the boat women did not belong. In theory, to be able to read the Buddhist scriptures was a requirement for membership, and to read them, the purpose of the Club, but since only four women in Kao Yao over twenty years of age were reported as literate, we can assume good intentions and regard the organization as a social one. This coterie of ladies met on the 1st and 15th of each month in the P'u Hsien Temple and ate only vegetables and rice on those days. They also had a special meeting at the temple on the 19th of the 2nd month, the birthday of Kuan Yin, which was one of the occasions on which people from Kao Yao set off firecrackers. The Club had no chairman and no dues, but was no doubt guided by the priests at the temple. Clearly the age requirement had some connection with this fact for, although we have not one whit of empirical evidence, the love affairs of the priests were proverbial. Realistically, priests were more often charged with homosexuality and it was taboo to mention the sire of a mule in front of them, priests being called "bald donkeys," in itself an expression with homosexual connotations. Apart from contacts at the meetings of the Buddhist Women's Club and their

occasional appearance at upper class funerals, the priests had little to
do with the residents of Kao Yao.

It was stated that there was little difference in attitudes toward
Buddhism in so far as class or wealth was concerned. In times of
crisis, a priest would be called in if his services could be afforded.
Except for the bimonthly food restriction on the part of the Women's
Club members, there were no religious taboos practiced by the villagers, including lay readers. Only the priests were vegetarian and
celibate. There was very little direct religious education in Kao
Yao. If a child played with a figure of Buddha or a religious picture, its mother would tell it to stop, perhaps making some comments
to indicate the respect due sacred objects. No figures of Buddha
were worshiped in the homes of Kao Yao, but they were common as
decoration. Kuan Yin, the Buddhist Goddess of Mercy, was sometimes supplicated by women on the 19th of the 6th month in matters
concerning childbirth such as the conception of a son. Children were
formerly told to kowtow when in front of a Buddha, but the government prohibited this form of obeisance in 1935. Since then, it was
sometimes done in private, but the custom was apparently disappearing.

Of the abstract concepts of Buddhism, probably the most meaningful to the people of Kao Yao was that of the soul with its ultimate
destination in the Western Heaven where the individual was judged
and punished for his sins by the King of Hell. Our search for sins
produced the following notions. For those who practiced vegetari-
anism on certain days, a relapse was a sin. For a lay reader to ever
eat the flesh of an animal that had died, rather than having been
slaughtered, would be sinful. If a Buddhist woman were to have an
extra-marital sexual relation, it would be a sin—although excusable
for a man. Besides these distinctive behaviors, to murder, steal,
and commit similar crimes was to sin. For the guilty one, there was
no escape, no atonement. Even the act of confession was denied.
Punishment was inevitable and to be beaten or cut up was the least
one could expect.

On the other hand, a good person's soul was sent back to earth
to be reincarnated in the body of some newly conceived child. A lay
reader was expected to be able to ascertain the place where a departed
soul would be reborn, that is, at least to the extent of determining

the general direction of the place and the number of people eating in the family. This could provide comfort to the relatives without any chance of finding the new body. For the dead body, there was no hope of resurrection.

In pursuing our investigation of the soul, we were first told that each individual had only one, called the *hun,* which left the body— the only other aspect of the person—instantaneously at death, and might be reincarnated as previously described. Evidence immediately followed, however, which proved that under certain conditions the *hun* might leave the body without death resulting. For example, if a man became intoxicated, the loss of his mental capacities was attributed to the fact that his *hun* had gone wandering. The solution to this problem was to take an egg and some rice to the place where the individual became drunk on the theory that the *hun* would be attracted to return by this good food. The procedure seems to have proved consistently successful. Sickness also was an indication that the *hun* had departed from the body, in which case more than an egg and some rice was usually required to bring it back.

Walking to the village temple one day, we encountered near the corner of the school a lump of turf which had been curiously treated. The grass on it had been twisted into five wisps, each of which had been surmounted with a paper cap on which a face had been roughly painted. In front of the lump of turf lay an old piece of basket on which it was obvious that both incense and gold-silver paper money for the spirits had been buried. Also there were several peach branches lying nearby. Inquiry brought the information that the five paper-faced wisps represented a collective entity known as the Five Spirits deemed responsible for sickness. The burned offerings were a supplication to the Five Spirits to liberate the wandering soul of a sick person, while the peach branches represented a deterrent to ghosts traditional in Chinese mythology. Such entreaties were made at any time on behalf of an ill person in Kao Yao. With good luck, the *hun,* which was said to be shapeless, returned to the sick person where it normally lodged in the spine. Shamanism, or Bad Religion, could also be resorted to in effecting a recovery of the *hun* by the proceedings previously described.

Our study of the soul ultimately led us to another of its manifestations which we can distinguish as the *p'o,* or ghost. The first lay reader who was invited to a funeral was expected to calculate from a book on what dates—usually three—the ghost of the deceased might be expected to return to its former home. For this service he was paid a half *sheng* of rice and sixteen cents. On an evening when the ghost was expected, the family and friends who came for the purpose retired to bed but kept watch to see what would happen, ashes perhaps having been spread over the table in the ancestral hall to record footprints. Any noise such as the creaking of a door, the rattling of cooking utensils, not to mention a disturbance in the ashes, was interpreted by the pretending sleepers as an indication of the return of the ghost. Such visitations were expected to occur only three times and were called *hui chia,* which was translated as the Returning of the Evil Spirit of the Dead, but literally means simply "to return home."

Actually, the ghost was feared as a potential attacker, although no case was known of one having done so. It was the ghost that made people avoid graveyards at night, corpses when alone, and also caused them to expectorate after mentioning the name of a deceased person. The spittle was regarded as taking the place of wine for the ghost, which would presumably be spilled were the speaker drinking some at the time. Not everyone in Kao Yao was willing to admit the existence of ghosts. Our friend Pi said specifically that he did not believe in the return of ghosts but that a fear of them was innate. As elsewhere in the world, there were undoubtedly exceptional individuals in Kao Yao who demonstrated complete disdain for anything supernatural.

Turning from a direct interest in the body and its two souls to ancestral worship, the weakness of this basic aspect of Confucianism in Kao Yao became apparent. Although a new scroll or vertical strip of red paper was inscribed with the characters "ancestors of every generation" each New Year's, there was no celebration of the birth or death day of one's forbears. Neither was there any particular ceremony at the inauguration of an ancestral hall, and certainly no deification of any particular ancestor. At least once a year the people did visit the ancestral graves.

Coming finally to Taoism in its degenerate or primitive form, we found it manifested in the belief in a multiplicity of gods which we could not find time to pursue over the countryside. Even Pi, who in such matters had both exceptional sophistication and curiosity compared to most villagers, was unable to establish any consistent order or hierarchy among the deities known in Kao Yao. None was supreme. When we mentioned the possibility of that role being given to the Emperor God, he demoted the latter below the City God because the latter could only be invoked in the city whereas the Emperor God could be worshiped anywhere, an interesting deduction insofar as it indicated a respect for urban cultivation. Our lists which usually began with the Kitchen God, were sure to include one or more Dragon Gods associated with water or shamans, and spread out to include various geomorphic deities. A Mountain God was at one time coalesced with an Earth God, and then the two were distinguished. Even various rocks were designated as gods. This aspect of our study was not pushed very far, but we were left with the feeling that given enough informants, gods would accumulate in connection with everything, and that the spirit world was truly multitudinous. For any of these deities, food offerings and incense were appropriate. The schoolteacher said he had a faint recollection of having heard of a place in which porcelain was manufactured where a person with white hair and a fair complexion was sacrificed to a god. We could only be certain that it was not a locality near Kao Yao.

Apropos of superstitions, it was believed that a nameless monster in the shape of a fish more than five feet long, accompanied by two files of smaller fish, might be come upon in any river, but to do so was to die. We did not investigate, as the nearest river was two or three miles away. It was also stated that to see a snake that had feet was a most unfortunate sign, and we were quick to agree. Sometimes during heavy thunderstorms, individuals burned bundles of straw to warn the Thunder God that people were around and, that if he meant to strike some wrongdoer, please to be careful of his aim. Three, ten, and twenty seemed to be numbers that recurred with special significance, as also did sixty.

People in Kao Yao likewise shared the widespread penchant for inscribing their thoughts on toilet walls. The following reflection is a translation of what was written on a piece of red paper and stuck up for patrons to peruse.

> My fate is so bad and troublesome
> It causes me sadness and pain
> Now I write something on this paper
> After some gentleman reads it
> My fate may improve.

This was not intended as a poem, merely as an effort to thin out one's misery. A second example was more pointed.

Our baby always cries at night
This is unfortunate and painful
We think that fastening up words is good
It should make our baby stop crying.

Probably few spiritual concepts are more widespread in China than the belief in *feng-shui,* literally wind and water, a term of reference for the ancient belief in geomancy. It seems strange, therefore, that in all our discussions in Kao Yao, it was brought up by informants only once—the time we learned about choosing the site of a village wall. Neither in respect to the location of graves nor of buildings was it mentioned. On the other hand, we did not pursue the subject, so *feng-shui* may well have been more meaningful in the life of the villagers than our data indicate.

Religion in Kao Yao was said to be simply whatever anyone believed, and it made no difference whether one was religious or not. No one paid attention to disparaging remarks about religion—unless one was gossiping about a monk's liaison with some woman—but impiety was not commonplace. There was not even much cursing in the speech of the villagers. A few individuals were devout, especially among the women and old men, but most people were not interested. With the risk of presenting a misleading cliché, we can state that the residents of Kao Yao were born in the awareness of Confucianism, that they lived out their working lives as Taoists, and finally passed through the valley of shadows to the drumbeats and gong clashing of Buddhism.

21

THE CEREMONIAL YEAR

THE SPIRITUAL life of Kao Yao had many exciting aspects because of the disparate elements which composed the people's religion. Whereas a shaman's performance in the depth of the night could shatter one's emotional serenity, some of the recurrent ceremonial activities represented the gayest occasions of the year. The first of the two festivals in which we participated demonstrated the breadth of the spiritual activities in the village. The Torch Festival took place during the second week of our stay, and it was quite startling to observe the effect of throwing a handful of resin and charcoal through a blazing torch toward some individual who could thus consider himself honored. Most people ran from this treatment, but to do so seemed inconsistent with the dignity of the teacher who received particular attention as the fire-throwers were mostly young adolescents who loved him more or less well.

Perhaps after further thought the children had decided that sufficient appreciation had not been accorded their visiting "scholar," for on the second evening they invaded our home with their flaming branches. We had finished dinner and settled down to an evening of note-taking when the first barrage of fire crossed the stage. Instinct directed my attention to saving our irreplaceable documents and by the time that had been accomplished there was no hope of repelling the attackers who were already being reinforced by more children ascending the ladder. It impressed me that almost all of our visitors were young girls, but it was not clear whether that was so because they reacted more strongly when released from restraint, or because adolescent females had naturally more courage. Perhaps they just enjoyed burning men, but the hour they devoted to us proved not only exhausting but slightly frightening as well. For a few minutes it seemed that they would set the building on fire, and when they had finally squandered their resin, the house was full of smoke and fine ash, while my trousers had been burned beyond usefulness. Fortunately, with no west wall, the air soon cleared, and we could return to work, our eyes stinging for some time afterward.

Most of these annual ceremonies, or festivals, had religious significance, and they provided the only regular vacations from the continuing routine of work. Before considering them, it may be mentioned that in the Province of Yünnan there were also six legal holidays designated according to the Western calendar. These are listed below.

January 1.	New Year's Day
March 12.	Death of Sun Yat-sen
March 29.	Death of the 72 Patriots in Canton
October 10.	Anniversary of the Establishment of the Chinese Republic
November 12.	Birthday of Sun Yat-sen
December 25.	Revolution in Yünnan against Yüan Shih-k'ai's Assumption of the Throne

On these six days all schools were closed and government officials were released from duty. Pi, from whom we learned of them, said that the adult villagers in Kao Yao not only failed to observe these holidays but were not even aware of them. The reverse was true of the annual festivals named below.

1st of 1st month.	New Year's (Hsin Nien) Festival
15th of 1st month.	Flower Lantern (Hua Têng) Festival
3rd of 3rd month.	Western Hill (Yu Hsi Shan) Festival
ca. 5th of 3rd month.	Tree Planting (Chih Shu or Ching Ming) Festival
5th of 5th month.	Dragon Boat (or Tuan Wu) Festival
24th of 6th month.	Torch (Huo Pa) Festival
15th of 7th month.	Receiving Ancestors (Chieh Tsu) Festival
15th of 8th month.	Middle Autumn (Chung Ch'iu) Festival
9th of 9th month.	Ascending the Hill (or Ch'ung Yang) Festival
20th of 11th month.	Winter Arriving (Tung Chih) Festival
8th of 12th month.	Winter (Tung *) Festival

An annual round of festivals was celebrated in all parts of China, but the number and choice of ceremonies was not the same, local cus-

---

* *Chieh* (festival) may or may not be added to the name of a feast. Following Hsin Nien it sounds strange, whereas Tung does without it. To avoid confusion, *chieh* has been eliminated.

tom determining the inclusion of a particular feast and the manner of its presentation. In explaining those of Kao Yao, only information obtained during our residence in the village will be given so as to reflect no more than the people's own conceptions of them. That we may progress toward those in which we participated, we shall begin our comments with the Middle Autumn (Chung Ch'iu) Festival.

On the 15th of the 8th month the people of Kao Yao enjoyed a celebration, the main features of which were the gathering together of the family and the worship of the moon. It was considered essential that a person who was residing away from home in any part of the province return to his native village for this occasion, bringing with him "moon cakes," sugar wheat noodles, pomegranates, and pears. The "moon cakes" which were round and about four inches in diameter were made by professional bakers basically of wheat flour. No one worked on the day of the Chung Ch'iu, or Middle Autumn Festival, the family enjoying their reunion and the eating of the special dishes prepared for it.

After supper when the full moon had risen, a table was set up in the middle of the courtyard—or in a room of a house which was without such an open area—and on it was placed an incense burner with two red candles. The head of the family approached the table with incense sticks in his clasped hands, bowing once before kowtowing three times to the moon. Then each member of the family kowtowed three times in turn, after which gold-silver paper money was burned on the ground. With the obeisance to the moon completed, the table was brought into the house and more food enjoyed. None of our informants could explain the origin of this feast which they obviously enjoyed.

The people of Kao Yao took cognizance of a ceremony on the 9th of the 9th month which they referred to as the Ascending the Hill Festival, or more exactly as the Ch'ung Yang, by eating the steamed corn cakes for breakfast which the women prepared. Except for the homophonic association between the word for high (kao) and that for cake (kao), even Pi could give no explanation of why anyone should climb a hill, and he insisted that none of the old men in the village knew either. This was perhaps to be expected since no one actually did climb any hill or, for that matter, even interrupted his usual pattern of labor.

The Tung Chih, or Winter Arriving Festival, occurred on the 20th of the 11th month and was similarly celebrated by having simply a breakfast of special dumplings which had been prepared on the previous evening. The housewife steamed the rice for two hours and then pounded it in a stone mortar with a large T-shaped pestle. Using this dough, dumplings were formed and placed on a tray, from which they were taken and cooked in the morning as an offering to the ancestors. They were then eaten by the members of the family, some of whom might possibly proceed to the ancestral graves in order to make offerings and obeisance there. Usually, however, the people just went to work as on any other day.

At the Tung, or Winter Festival, on the 8th of the 12th month, the villagers at least refrained from their labors. During the day, the ear lobes of all six-year-old girls were punctured by their mothers who then inserted threads to keep the holes open. The children were said to welcome the process even though it hurt since associated with the act came the promise of a pair of earrings at New Year's. That evening before supper, the women of the house made congee and cooked it with some dried pork, a meal shared by everyone. No explanation of the feast was given except that the special meat porridge served to keep one warm and free of stomach-aches.

New Year's, or Hsin Nien, was so important a festival that the people would not class it with the others. Although technically occurring on the 1st of the 1st month (sometimes between late January and late February of the Western calendar), it not only included New Year's Eve but much of the period between the 15th of the 12th month and the Flower Lantern Festival on the 15th of the 1st. After the middle of the 12th month, people began preparing food and clothing while meeting other requirements for the coming celebration. If a family could afford the cost, they were sure to butcher a pig, afterward salting the pork, and almost everyone would expect to eat chicken. Rice noodles were made, and good things like sugar, sweet stuffed breads, oranges, cookies, and other desserts were purchased. Furthermore, new gate pictures had to be acquired. These cost ten cents a pair, but the head of the family or a grown son had to go to Kunming to obtain them. Neither buyer nor seller could recognize the deities they portrayed, so a choice was made on esthetic grounds. If there had been a death in the family during the year, however, then the pictures selected always had a predominance of blue.

Papers on which to write fresh sayings for the gate posts also had to be acquired, then taken to the schoolteacher who would inscribe them with poetic utterances copied from a special book of pole-paper writings. Also, firecrackers were purchased, usually the local ones that were made in Yünnan, but sometimes those from Canton which, despite the similarity in size, made twice as much noise. Firecrackers, it may be noted, were used likewise at weddings and funerals. On the 27th of the 12th month occurred the special cleaning of the house previously described (p. 108).

Before supper of the last day of the year, the new gate pictures and vertical papers for the posts were pasted in place and then everyone enjoyed a feast in his own home. Guests were never invited to meals during the New Year's festivities. After the meal had been finished, someone in the family put a dish of candy near the ash door of the stove and a red candle on each side of it. Incense also was burned and everyone kówtowed toward the stove three times after which the head of the family, still on his knees with his face down, asked the Kitchen God to report something good about the family, it being believed that this deity gave an accounting to the God of Heaven at the end of each year. Actually, the offering of candy was supposed to make the lips of the Kitchen God sticky so that he would not be able to report too well. After this, the people went to bed early. It may be recorded that, curiously enough, the last day of the year was always referred to as the 30th of the 12th month despite the fact that it was one of the shorter, or twenty-nine-day, months of the Chinese calendar.

On New Year's Day everyone rose at dawn, it being traditionally asserted that if a person remained in bed, the dikes of his rice fields would be apt to collapse. Before breakfast each family sent one son—or a man, if there were no sons—to burn incense and kowtow three times at the village temple in prayer for good fortune during the coming year. Then the boys used sticks of burning incense to light strings of firecrackers tied to the ends of bamboo poles. After the noise had ended, the boys went to their respective homes where everyone had an unusually elaborate breakfast.

The meal over, everyone changed to the new clothes that had been specially prepared for the occasion, a procedure that particularly made the children happy. Then the women went into the hills and spent an hour or two collecting green pine needles which they spread over the ground of the courtyards to indicate cleanliness, the green color symbolizing it. Everyone then sat or lay down on the needles in whatever positions they chose. It was there that the family head brought the candy which had been offered to the Kitchen God and distributed it to everyone, and there that he and every man or woman of fifty years of age or over gave each unmarried child in the family a paper packet containing a gift of money in an amount up to ten cents for which the recipient promptly said "Thank you."

Sometimes families of betrothed children exchanged courtesy visits after the New Year's breakfast but to do so was rare among the residents of Kao Yao. Usually the people occupied themselves in various recreations. Men went to the teahouses to talk or to friends' homes to play mah-jongg. Women turned to their proverbial sewing and children played games. After a festival luncheon some men always erected a swing in the marketplace by suspending ropes from a crosspiece between the notches of paired cypress poles tied firmly in position. All the children in the village were then supposed to swing back and forth, and some adults could not resist participating also. It was explained that this swinging would prevent sickness, but no rationalization was forthcoming as to why.

Again in the evening, the meal was sure to be of exceptional quality. After it, the performers in the coming Flower Lantern Festival, who had been practicing every day during this period, visited a rich family in the village and sang three or four songs which required as many hours. For this performance, which was repeated at different homes during the following fortnight, they were paid three dollars as a contribution to their expenses for face paint, candles, and the other necessities of the Flower Lantern Festival, as well as being served various delicacies plus tea or wine, or perhaps both. Most people went to bed tired but some played mah-jongg, or perhaps cards, all night long.

On the 2nd of the 1st month, married daughters and sons-in-law were invited for a visit of two days and nights. Again, the meals were of the best quality that could be afforded. After dinner, games of chance were usually played. The visiting couple returned to their homes following breakfast of the third day, while the residents of Kao Yao continued to refrain from labor in the fields until the middle of the month. No one even bothered to pull the weeds in the gardens.

It was the Hua Têng, or Flower Lantern Festival, held on the 15th of the 1st month which climaxed the New Year's holidays. The main activity, as has already been indicated, centered on the presentation of one act of some drama, either historical or pertaining to daily life, the choice being essentially up to the special teacher who was employed from the beginning of the 12th month until the day of the feast at a fee of fifty cents a night, plus accommodation and meals in one house after another during the period. This man, basically a musician, chose the performers among the boys who applied, selecting those whom he thought could best pass as girls for the feminine roles. Individuals were motivated to participate, not only for the social pleasures involved, since the group formed a kind of singing society, but because they wanted the satisfaction of wearing the elaborate theatrical costumes which had been accumulated for this annual performance. When a rich man of the village was so moved, he would buy one or more costumes as a contribution to the festivities, or more often a collection was made for the purpose. When not in use, the costumes, worth about fifty dollars in all, and the lantern, a large oval affair with flowers painted on it as decoration, were kept in any house where the owner offered an unused room. The lantern, like the costumes, was used year after year, but when the man who carried it thought it should be replaced, he collected a few cents from a sufficient number of people to buy another for about a dollar in Kunming.

At the beginning of the evening rehearsals each year, someone sacrificed a chicken and burned incense to the Lantern God whose name was then brushed on a piece of paper and fastened to the lantern. The offering was made in an empty house where the lantern was placed on a table with an incense burner in front of it. Of the more than ten participators in the festival play, one was chosen to burn incense and kowtow in front of the lantern three times before breakfast and supper each day. A chicken, however, was sacrificed only on the first evening and on that of the 15th of the 1st month.

The process of sacrificing the chicken which was the same on both occasions, can be described in more detail. The chicken, with a bowl of rice, pieces of pork, and a bottle of wine were placed on the table, the chicken being held by a man who forced it to bow its head three times toward the lantern, then poured some wine down its throat, and put some rice in its mouth. This done, the chicken's throat was cut with a knife, the blood being caught in the rice bowl. Pale and dead, the chicken was taken away and submerged in boiling water in order to remove its feathers and then cut up and cooked in some house by a man, finally being returned to the sacrificial table. There, all the participators kowtowed three times to the Lantern God, afterward eating the chicken and pork, and drinking the wine. On the final evening, the paper with the God's name was removed from the lantern and set on fire in the incense burner, a process which was said to send the God back to heaven.

As the time for the performance on the evening of the 15th of the 1st month approached, the man who was to carry the lantern lighted a candle and put it inside. Then, fastening the lamp to the end of a bamboo pole, he led a parade down the street to the quay and then back to the village temple. Immediately behind him came the actors dressed and painted for female roles, next the other actors, then the musicians recruited among the residents of Kao Yao, and finally the remaining villagers. On reaching the temple, everyone kowtowed to the gods, burning incense in the process, a privilege retained by laymen for this festival. The religious service completed, everyone returned to the school compound for the performance of the play, a festive conclusion to a day, which many of the men had spent gambling.

The Hsi Shan Festival took place on the 3rd of the 3rd month at which time the young people of Kao Yao, both men and women, dressed in their best clothes and set out after breakfast for the temples of the Western Hill, spending the day among them, and then returning home before supper. No purpose was recognized in so doing except to have a good time, the day's activities being unaccompanied by any special ceremony, music, or even the shooting of firecrackers.

On a day determined by the solar calendar, but indicated on the regular lunar ones purchased in Kunming, the Chih Shu, or Planting Trees Festival, was celebrated in Kao Yao. This feast was widely known over China by its alternative name, Ch'ing Ming. Usually it occurred between the 1st and the 6th of the 3rd month and consequently just before or after the Western Hill Feast. On the morning of the festival, everyone in the family kowtowed three times with burning incense before the ancestral "tablet" hanging above a table on which had been placed the usual burner and two red candles.

This done, they ate an elaborate breakfast, after which each individual made and put on a crown of willows which produced amusement and laughter all day long. Once adorned, and bearing various offerings including a chicken, rice, and wine, the family proceeded to the graveyard where an open fire was built in front of the ancestral tomb. Nearby grew the Mu Lu Shu, or Grave Tree, marked by a stone bearing three characters which designated it as such. The tree could be of any species, but it was always the best one adjacent to the tomb. Its marker was about one by two feet in size. Some member of the group with salt on his palm went to the tree carrying the chicken which he fed a handful of rice over which a little wine had been poured. The rice was supposed to signify to the dead that the chicken had been cooked although it was actually alive. The person then kowtowed three times to the tree. This done, the chicken was killed, blood from its cut throat being collected in a bowl and mixed with salt. The blood was afterward sprinkled over the grave mound and the chicken cut up and boiled.

When the chicken had been cooked it was once again taken to the Grave Tree, the person making the offering kowtowing three times. Then all the food was removed to the front of the tomb and each member of the family kowtowed three times before it during which performance the principal worshiper spilled wine and others burned incense and gold-silver paper money. The dead having thus been properly cared for, the food and wine was consumed by the family. This entire ceremony required about two hours, and when it was over, the family returned home and went on with the customary work of the season.

The schoolteacher was unaware of any connection between paying obeisance to the ancestors and to the tree, but he stated that the latter was never cut, and that if it were injured, bad fortune would descend on the family. He also pointed out that a goat might be sacrificed in place of a chicken. This Chih Shu Festival was the principal occasion during the year on which a family visited the ancestral graves, but should it be impossible for a person to participate on that day, he might do so at the time of the Receiving Ancestors Festival in the 7th month or during the Winter Arriving Festival in the 11th.

The Tuan Wu, popularly called the Dragon Boat Festival, was celebrated on the 5th of the 5th month. For the occasion, people purchased pork, chicken, and beans, as well as a wine with an ingredient said to be an antitoxin against poisonous bites. These things were eaten and drunk for breakfast after which people went to their work as usual. Children between the ages of one and six, however, had either red or green string tied around their wrists as a prevention against snake bites. Also they wore a dried water caltrop in an upper button loop of their coats. Everyone was pleased to have eaten especially well, and the children enjoyed playing with their coat ornament. No explanation was offered concerning the origin of the festival.

The Huo Pa, or Torch Festival, was celebrated in Kao Yao on the 24th of the 6th month, and with great enthusiasm at least on the part of the children whose behavior has already been described at the beginning of this chapter. The festival was distinguished by two features, the conspicuous custom of throwing burning resin and the visits of married daughters and sons-in-law. In consequence, a special supper with pork, chicken, fish, or other delicacies was prepared in the evening of the 24th, and all meals on the day following were equally sumptuous. In theory, both were holidays and no unnecessary work done.

In preparation for the feast, people split the middle sections of pine sticks five to ten feet long, inserting bunches of sedge to hold them apart, thus making torches. They also mixed resin with powdered charcoal in equal proportions and put it into bags which could be fastened to the belt on the right-hand side. Then they lighted their torches and chased people, throwing a handful of resin and charcoal through the flame at a person to whom they came close. Most of the flame throwers we saw were adolescents but one mother gave a child less than three years old a torch and he toddled after people with it. Other young children of both sexes participated, attacking their victims with a sizzling streak of fire. Our neighbor, the widow who owned the teahouse near the entrance of the school, was one of the older participants and she, with her usual good humor, seemed to have an excellent time. All down the street one could see the torches and flashes of burning resin which gave a distinctive odor to the air. In the darkness of the night, the torches in neighboring villages appeared as fireflies.

At the beginning of the evening, I was afraid that someone would have their eyes badly burned, but Pi assured us that no one was ever injured. One could either tolerate the prickly sensation of the momentary heat and accept the damage to one's clothing, or a person could run without losing face which was the usual response. Until 1936, the performance was carried into the fields with the purpose of causing destruction to insects, but since that time the activity had been limited almost entirely to the village streets.

The Huo Pa, or Torch Festival, was in large measure a provincial Yünnanese ceremony rather than a national one. A brief origin myth was recounted to explain it. Long ago a king who lived in Tali, the largest city in the west of the province, had six daughters. Seeing political advantage in the act, he invited six princes who held authority in various parts of Yünnan to marry them in one grand ceremony. This was finally arranged and the marriages took place with extravagant feasting. Then, when the exhausted princes had all retired upstairs with their brides, the king took a torch and set fire to his palace, burning them all to death, thereby eliminating potential competition abroad and, no doubt, domestic difficulties at home.

The eleventh and last festival to be described was that known as Chieh Tsu, or Receiving Ancestors Festival, which took place on the 15th of the 7th month and in which we were also fortunate enough to participate during our visit to Kao Yao. From a religious point of view, it was probably the most important ceremonial occasion of the year and in any respect only second to the New Year's festivities as a period of relaxation since people did no ordinary work on the day or on the two which preceded.

On the 13th, each family was busy acquiring food for the elaborate meals that were expected and also buying gold-silver paper money as well as green paper, and red, from which to cut symbolic clothing for the dead. These were of curious shape which can be shown by their outline (Fig. 33, p. 339). People furthermore made what looked like tiny lanterns from paper flowers but were actually representations of sedan chairs only a few inches tall. For the evening meals, the women (or occasionally the men) cooked pork and rice and placed it with pears, pomegranates, and wine on a tray which at sundown the head of the family carried out and put down on the street near the door. Then he burned incense and kowtowed three times, the other members of the family not participating. After that obeisance, he burned gold-silver paper money and prayed to his deceased ancestors, "Grandfathers and grandmothers, father and mother, please return home." Naturally the latter were not named in cases where they were still alive. Then the head of the family picked up the tray with the food and drink offerings and carried it into the house, putting it on a table against the wall on which the symbolic red and green paper clothing had been stuck with some paste made from wheat flour and water. The table had been decorated earlier with an incense holder and two red candles, while two or three chairs had been placed facing it. These were reserved for the ancestors and none of the surviving family sat on them. With

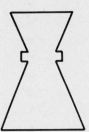

Figure 33. Shape of Symbolic Clothing for the Dead

the offerings deposited, the head of the family again kowtowed three times. Afterward the empty chairs were pushed up to the table, while all the members of the family feasted.

Before breakfast and dinner of the 14th and the 15th, usually a son in the family placed rice on the table under the paper clothing and kowtowed three times. This was never done after eating for such an inversion of the ceremonial order of procedure would show disrespect. During the three days of the Receiving Ancestors Feast, the men gathered in the teahouses and the women sewed. A few families visited the tombs, especially if they missed doing so at the Planting Trees Festival. The delayed rites would then be carried out, but such procrastination was rare. The period was a serious one and not given over to such pleasures as were enjoyed at New Year's.

Finally, after supper on the 15th, the head of the family put a great deal of gold-silver paper money in baskets, covering them with the symbolic red or green paper clothing pulled from the wall as well as the flower sedan chairs, and then carried the baskets into the street and put them down near the door. There he burned everything repeating, "Good-by, go quickly," to his ancestors, afterward kowtowing a final three times.

As an ultimate gesture to the deceased came the floating of burning lamps on the lake, but this finale to the festival had been banned by government authority as superstition and consequently had not been performed for many years. Pi, the schoolteacher, had never seen it. Perhaps because of the presence of "the foreigner," it was adjudged safe to perform the ceremony once more, which happy decision enabled us to include it in the empirical record of the Huo Pa Festival which follows.

When we awoke on the morning of the 13th of the 7th month or, in our terms, the 8th of August, 1938, it was raining. The market was convening outside in the dreariest of circumstances and would not have held my attention except that two men engaged in the only fight we saw in Kao Yao in which the participants came to physical blows. The dispute involved the sale of some grain, and the participants struck at each other with their fists several times and then swung out with their feet but to little advantage. Finally one picked up a stick and all action stopped for a minute until more verbal abuse marked the end of the contest. It was the beginning of our last week in Kao Yao and I planned our departure, figuring out what could be most effectively accomplished in the hours that remained to us. The procedure involved a review of the main aspects of culture in an attempt to record the more important points that had been missed. Also, it had come time to face up to those controversial and intimate aspects of life on which one usually gains more information from an informant the longer one has known him. We worked until late in the afternoon by which time it had fortunately stopped raining. Then we walked down the street to observe the heads of the families kowtowing to their ancestors.

Our friends, the T'aos, had asked us to come in after supper as they knew that we wanted to participate in the holiday pleasures. The T'ao family served us with hot water, peaches, and some doughnut-like cakes. I do not know why I should have been slightly surprised to find the head of the family lying on the curtained bed in his den smoking opium with a friend. On second thought, it seemed as logical a way to celebrate a religious festival as any other, and we took the opportunity to observe the scene more carefully than on previous occasions. A large part of the room was taken up by the bed which extended two feet off the floor and was covered by a mat of the ordinary size, or five feet two inches by three feet eight. At the edge near the wall was a padded headrest about ten inches high, eight inches wide, and two feet long which was shared by both smokers. Between them in the center of the mat was a two-by-three-foot red tray with two opium lamps, two pipes, some extra pipe bowls, scissors, opium boxes, and scrapers among other things. There was even a package of cigarettes.

T'ao's friend removed himself in deference to the special guest and I took his place, smoking the ceremonial number of three pipes with my host. He told us that he had been smoking for two years, but that he had stopped and started again at various periods in his life. T'ao, I noticed, always finished rolling his pill by giving it a few twists on the flat surface of his pipe bowl. Also, when he had finished, he scraped out the ash which he told us he saved for medicinal use. When we finally went home, his son T'ao Hua was mixing water with dry opium in a copper bowl for the holiday customers, but I was not permitted to pay for my pleasure.

The morning of the 14th of the 7th month was clear and pleasant for a change and we were all up at six-thirty since Li An-che and his wife were going to Kunming for the day. Pi came to breakfast and we worked for a while, after which Ho went off to copy signs and I wrote up my notes. After luncheon, we consulted for an hour or two with T'ao Hua on the plan of the village he was trying to complete for us. In his home, the women were still cutting out paper clothes for the ancestors. Nearby, the medium was still carrying on her séance. We saw our neighbor, the widow of the teahouse, setting off to the graveyard with food. Attending her was a boy with a large basket on his back filled with paper clothes. Walking up to the village temple, we found the members of the Buddhist Women's Club making paper boats to set afloat on the lake during the ceremony of the following night. While the others worked, one nice little old lady was chanting and beating a small wood drum, her arm resting on a miniature cloth bolster as she did so.

We had not been home long when Pi arrived from school, and we proceeded to record information on sexual habits with excellent results until the return of Mrs. Li stopped his tongue. This was compensated for by the letters, the roast duck, ham, candy, and other good things that she had brought. Our dinner was unusually elaborate and accompanied by lightning, thunder, and rain. Li did not feel well afterward, so Ho took the former's usual role as interpreter and we worked until ten when our artist came for a visit followed a little later by T'ao Hua with a large basket of paper boats we had asked for. The evening had turned pleasant and cool, and there was a large moon in the sky. Pi went home for his guitar and played it awhile.

It was a relief that Li felt better in the morning and we were able to pursue our regular schedule. Ho was coping with the problem of packing our collection of specimens which had accumulated increasingly as the end of our visit approached and more people had become aware of the opportunity for mutual advantage. When we went out to use up the last of our films, we found a notice posted on our gate that our residence would henceforward be occupied by soldiers. I was somewhat perturbed, but Pi and Li both assured me that we would not be dispossessed before the end of the week.

About four-thirty, the people began burning gold-silver paper money and paper clothing in the street and we went out to watch them. Our neighbor, the teahouse woman, burned hers in a large copper pan. She set fire to whole paper bagsful of money at one time. Then she burned clothing and flower sedan chairs. In a little green bowl, she had water with wheat grains and two kinds of beans. This mixture she dipped out onto the ground with a spoon a few times. Kneeling on a straw cushion, she then kowtowed four times —perhaps she lost count. Finished with her obeisance, she discarded what was left in the green bowl. Finally, she went into the house and threw out some flowers that she had placed in front of her "tablet," or scroll of red paper.

Continuing down the street, we encountered many more offerings to the ancestors. Some were elaborately set out on low tables containing various kinds of food including fruit and cakes. Some had little glasses of water and elaborate bronze candlesticks and incense holders. In almost every case, incense was burning. Also, as a distinction from the widow's performance, most of the offerings were ringed with ashes to indicate that they were intended for the spirit of a particular ancestor, rather than for all. Before we returned home, there seemed to be scores of fires lighting the street, and innumerable people kowtowing.

Pi's close friend, the assistant police chief, and one of the latter's associates were waiting for us to make an apology for the nuisance we had been caused after our public demonstration of shamanism. Some official had thought the séance was a disgrace to China and had ordered the arrest of the performers, whereupon we had been put to the trouble of arranging their release which was easily accomplished. With Pi, we invited our guests up to have a drink, I pressing them on by the proper and courteous setting of an example. Soon T'ao Hua joined us and we ate plate after plate of fried hard sausage with cup after cup of strong wine. Everyone became very friendly and speeches were made by various members of the groups, while T'ao Hua played the guitar, the whole situation being sufficiently comical to attract the attention of people who began to gather in our courtyard. The assistant police chief was most happily intoxicated, and I began to fear that the aftermath of one misunderstanding with the authorities might lead to another. It therefore seemed judicious to announce that our festivities would have to be interrupted while I went down to the street and made obeisance to my ancestors.

Since I had not wanted to be embarrassed by being so conspicuously a non-participating observer, we had acquired the necessary materials. At the last moment, Ho wisely suggested that I change to my Chinese clothes which had been made for me in order that I could record the process of their manufacture. This I quickly did and, dressed in my long gown, cloth shoes, and black skullcap, I descended to the market place followed by the cook carrying great bags of paper which I proceeded to burn with all the dignity I could uphold. I had not anticipated that the whole population of Kao Yao would be on hand to return my curiosity about people's behavior in the village, but apparently few individuals could resist such an opportunity. As I was about to conclude my ceremonial obligations, the teahouse widow rushed up with her straw cushion, thus enabling me to knock my head on the street three times without dirtying my gown. The effect on our audience was most ingratiating as could be seen from their smiles and nods of approval. The propriety of following established custom had not only been acknowledged, but pleasure had been provided as well, and pleasure was an added element which the residents of Kao Yao always liked with their religion. On returning home, we found that Pi and the assistant police chief had gone off to P'i Chi Kuan in search of more entertainment, so we were obliged to sit down to our feast without them.

About seven-thirty we left for the T'aos' house, having invited that family to be our guests at the concluding ceremony of the evening. We had arranged for a boat and soon were aboard it with our basketfuls of lanterns. Slowly we moved out from the quay and proceeded in an arc around the inner shore of the islands which protected the harbor. T'ao's second wife, nursing her baby, sat at a little table under the mat housing with another woman and poured oil into the cuplike paper lanterns and, after lighting them, passed them out to us who took turns in setting them afloat about thirty feet apart. Thus they drifted behind us, a bridge of red and green lamps in the water, with an unbalanced one occasionally flaring yellow as the dry edges of the paper caught fire. Each light promised that a soul would be put to rest. Periodically, someone burned a package of gold-silver paper money and tossed it overboard also. With a woman at the bow oar, we progressed slowly, leaving a trail of "water lily" lanterns curving behind us. It was a clear night with a full moon in the southeast. The outward ring of trees and clumps of bushes, the vague outline of the Kao Yao houses, and the rolling horizon of hills provided a background for floating dots of fire on the water that had magical beauty. We continued our course outside the half circle of tree clumps, still dropping lanterns and gradually approaching another string to the northward set out by a boat filled with members of the Buddhist Women's Club. From it came the sound of bells and the clapping of wood drums across the water. Drawing abeam, we exchanged greetings, each company impressed by the whole bay full of lanterns we had together let loose. Soon the tiny flames began to blink out and we headed for shore, hushed by the fanciful scene.

T'ao Hua invited us to stop at a teahouse, and then sent his ten-year-old niece home for watermelon seeds which I wasted by my inability to bite them open correctly. Everyone rose to greet us, bowing and smiling, while we returned the expected response "Pu tung, pu tung, don't be disturbed." One man was sitting in the corner, naked to his waist. Another had his little daughter with him. The small open saucer lamp in a frame of iron rods above our heads, together with the kerosene lamp in the center of the room and a can with a burning spout on the far wall, conspired to leave the room dim, and I enjoyed the silhouette of the teahouse owner wielding his large copper kettle of boiling water above the seated figures of his patrons.

We stayed half an hour and then went home where we found Pi and the assistant police chief who presented me with a set of three dice, the use of which he said had become illegal. Finally, when Pi and his friend had gone home, our artist arrived and we talked for an hour. I was exhausted by the compounding of events, and concluded the evening by smoking three pipefuls of opium, rolling the pills so deftly that our cook, who considered himself expert, congratulated me. That, I admit, was flattery which I consumed with satisfaction, although I am compelled to admit that the artist insisted that I might have done even better. Thus I went to my rest and peaceful dreams after the excitement of receiving my ancestors in Kao Yao.

22

COMPARISONS AND COMMENT

ALTHOUGH ALMOST everything we had brought to Kao Yao had been given away by the time we said our final farewells on Sunday, August 14, 1938, or exactly five weeks from the date of our arrival, we were even more heavily burdened by the accumulation of specimens destined for the museum at Yale. A wartime curtailment of exports becoming effective that week threatened to prevent the shipment, but with the cooperation of carpenters and officials, we had the material crated and cleared by the customs in readiness to depart for Indo-China on the following Thursday morning, and I was able to leave the collection in the hands of trustworthy compradores in Saigon a few days later.

During the following year, 1939, eight of the chapters (1–4, 6, 17–19) were written essentially in the form they have been printed. Even then it seemed desirable to safeguard the full impact of the descriptive detail derived from personal participation as a necessary complement to the thousands of words typed on four-by-six-inch yellow sheets representing the answers to my myriad of questions. Not until the fall of 1961, however, when all hope of continuing the original field work had been destroyed, was the writing of the final report undertaken. Time had transformed an incomplete account of the commonplace into a record of some rarity, and the temptation to use it as a pillow on which to embroider a much larger picture of Chinese culture had to be overcome. Instead it was decided to present the material as the simple story it seemed to be in historical perspective, for even the brief descriptions of Kunming and the journey thence through Tonkin had taken on new value as fragments of things past. Effort was exerted to infuse into the account as little as possible of information acquired later, although new insights into old data could not be rejected. By conscious intent, a rereading of strictly comparable studies was avoided until the evidence from Kao Yao had been formulated. This done, those not too well remembered volumes were avidly perused with unexpected shocks and surprises. Some comment will be made on them and their authors before considering the cultural comparisons they provide.

Community studies among literate peoples were begun by sociologists in the nineteenth century, but not undertaken by anthropologists with their special techniques until the second quarter of the twentieth. Three monographs have been previously published which are comparable in a general way to this one on Kao Yao in that they deal with specified settlements rather than Chinese culture in general and villages rather than towns, that they purport to cover more rather than less of the total activities in the community, and that they have been written by professional social scientists with Western university training. I am, of course, referring to the works of D. H. Kulp, Fei Hsiao-tung, and M. C. Yang, which have been cited in the bibliography. Each volume for special reasons is a most remarkable contribution, and it becomes increasingly unlikely that any more such works can appear.

Before going on, it would be ungracious not to mention the half dozen predecessors who did much to gather the first broad range of data about contemporary Chinese culture, men such as Doolittle, Johnston, Leong and Tao, Smith, and Werner. It would be even a greater oversight not to take cognizance of the recent anthropologists who, although not providing us with village studies according to the criteria listed, have proved to be of the first importance in formulating or refining the working concepts on which the study of traditional Chinese culture must be based. In this category, recommendation is made to the volumes of Freedman, Fried, Hsu, and Hu. Also C. K. Yang's monograph should be noted as a source for further comparisons, although it is not closely comparable to the studies by Kulp, Fei, and M. C. Yang. In the larger sense, of course, those who have contributed to community studies in China by research on specific problems number in the scores, and only a few have been mentioned in our limited bibliography.

To return to the works by Kulp, Fei, and Yang, it is not intended to present a proper comparative study of all the data that have been made available. We shall try merely to highlight certain aspects of Chinese village culture in the hope that by so doing the situation in Kao Yao may be seen in perspective, while certain problems and inadequacies of our information will thereby be illuminated. Actually, as one proceeds, the differences in the work become exaggerated. To begin with, the men themselves had quite different educations, and collected their data in divergent ways and at various periods. Kulp, a sociologist, who received his graduate training at the University of Chicago, a school probably unmatched for its long-term attention to community studies, undertook his research early in the century utilizing a Chinese student assistant to record information during the summers of 1918 and 1919, only visiting the village himself in the spring of 1923 (Kxvii, xx).* As he once told me in conversation, the distinctive anthropological flavor in his presentation stemmed from the influence of Clark Wissler and wide reading in ethnology, including the work of Franz Boas, although the latter man he never met personally.

Fei was educated at Yenching University in Peking and later at the London School of Economics where Bronislaw Malinowski was a dominant influence on his theoretical approach. His village study was made as the result of a two-month residence (July–August, 1936) in Kaihsienkung, but he himself was a native of the same district (F25–6). This latter fact is, of course, of considerable significance, since it is a questionable point as to exactly how objectively any man can view his own culture. Contrariwise, the inherent richness of such a picture cannot be gainsaid. For our purposes, it is perhaps unfortunate that Fei was more concerned with presenting data pertaining to certain economic problems than he was in giving total coverage of the culture that he presumably knew so well.

Finally, we have to comment on the anthropologist Yang whose book was written under the tutelage of Ralph Linton while the latter taught at Columbia University (Yxii). The community presented was that in which Yang was born, and the sensitive depiction he gives is the result of an extraordinary memory rather than intentionally conducted field work (Yix–xi). It may be noted that despite its less weighty appearance, Yang's book is the most extensive of the three volumes and has the broadest anthropological coverage.

Turning to the villages themselves, we find them to be well dispersed, thus giving us studies from the northern, central, and southern districts of eastern China to compare with Kao Yao in the south-

* References to the source of statements appearing in the works of Kulp, Fei, and Yang will be given in parentheses with the initial of the author's surname followed by the page number.

west (Fig. 1, p. 7). The basic information on their locale and population can quickly be appreciated from the table below.

Village	Province	Families	Population	Reference
Taitou	Shantung	120 (est.)	720 (est.)	(Y2, 10)
Kaihsienkung	Kiangsu	359	1458	(F18, 22, 29)
Phenix	Kwangtung	133	650 (est.)	(K2, 29, 104)
Kao Yao	Yünnan	122	497	

It may be added that Taitou was located across the bay from Tsingtao, whereas Kaihsienkung was situated on the southeast bank of Lake Tai about eighty miles west of Shanghai, while to reach Phenix Village required a two-hour boat ride upstream from Chaochow, an urban center west of Swatow. In each village, some outside or non-participating families were excluded from the population count. By chance, two of our four villages were situated on the banks of small streams (Taitou and Phenix), and two beside lakes.

Comparisons of the material culture are difficult as some of the authors indicate little interest in that aspect of the communities. Nevertheless, from what one can discern there were notable differences. In Taitou, for example, as was commonplace in parts of Shantung, stone appeared as the prominent feature of the walls of buildings, although kiln-fired brick and some pressed earth was utilized, especially in the higher courses (Y38–9). Kulp states that the walls of Phenix Village residences were constructed essentially from a mortar of lime and coarse sand (K274), and wood apparently was used sparingly. Although Fei is not explicit, it is clear from his pictures that stonework such as was typical of Taitou was not characteristic. House walls appear to have been similar to those in Kao Yao, although there seems to have been more use of wood in Kaihsienkung than in the other three villages. Notable is the fact that Yang remembers roofs, except for a row of ridge tiles, as being only of thatch (Y38–9), whereas tile roofs were the only kind used for houses in Phenix Village (K273) and possibly in Kaihsienkung. Also the houses of the latter village and Taitou were seemingly all of one story, thus contrasting with the two-story upper-class residences of Phenix Village and Kao Yao.

An interest in familial relations and ceremonial functions having induced the authors to supply ground plans, it is quite easy to show distinctions in each of the areas insofar as the better homes are concerned, it of course being inevitable that the poorest merge into almost indistinguishable units of one or two rooms. Taitou, in the north, exemplified the notion of three blocks of rooms, one behind the other, a classic Chinese conception with the ancestral hall at the rear (Y39). At Kaihsienkung, on the other hand, the typical plan seems to be U-shaped with the open side, as so often in Kao Yao, paralleling rather than facing the street. The important distinction lies in the fact that it was the front room that contained the ancestral shrine and women had to sleep in the rear room behind the kitchen (F121–2). At Phenix Village in the south, the upper-class residence was a rectangular structure built around a court with a two-story suite of rooms in each corner to house the one or more family units of the compound. Additional courtyards appeared at both front and rear, while one such house had two rows of additional, outside rooms (K153–5). Kao Yao, of course, displayed its typical upper-class residence as a two-story U-shaped house with the ancestral hall at the rear as in Phenix Village and Taitou, and its regular bedrooms in the rear corners.

The description of clothing in the village studies leaves much to be wished for, although Yang made a concentrated effort to be explicit (Y42–3). From what one can discover, the similarities greatly outweigh the differences, but there is one extraordinary exception in the fact that the women of Kaihsienkung regularly wore skirts rather than trousers. Fei states that it is "a characteristic of the region where women do not work on the farm" (F124). Skirts were recorded as ceremonial dress for women in Taitou (Y42) and were used in Phenix Village as part of the bridal costume (K275), but were undoubtedly not otherwise seen in those villages or in Kao Yao. Furthermore, Fei adds that men put skirts over their shorts when meeting visitors (F124). Another noticeable point was the use of bright colors such as red, pink, green, and purple for the costumes of younger women in Taitou (Y43), a style which one suspects was not characteristic of the other villages, although no definitive statements by either Kulp or Fei have been found.

Turning to the matter of transportation, it seems that although Taitou had a stream dividing its land, boats were too insignificant to be mentioned. Phenix Village, on the other hand, had one ferry boat operated and owned collectively by eight men (K5, 7). Among the residents of the lake shore village of Kaihsienkung, nearly every household possessed a boat, and those of agents also provided transport for the populace and served as conveyances of goods (F123, 249ff). Kao Yao, as we have learned, had its separate group of boat people.

Kulp emphasizes the value of the carrying pole and specifically states that there were no wheeled vehicles in either Phenix Village or the surrounding area (K17). The same limitation seems to have characterized Kaihsienkung where animals were not even available for labor (F159). Yang depicts in Taitou the use of the wheel-barrow pulled by a mule or a donkey, but says there were no carts (Y23, 255, 257). Kao Yao, as we have seen, was distinguished by its development of transport facilities, and it may be mentioned that all four villages made use of sedan chairs (K17, 275; F45; Y110).

Although rice was grown in all the villages, only in Kaihsienkung and Kao Yao was it the primary agricultural crop. In the former village Fei, who contributes an illuminating description of rice culti-vation, estimated that ninety per cent of the land was devoted to rice, the remainder being largely in wheat, rapeseed, and vegetables (F15, 159–165). In Taitou, the rice crop was insignificant except for the fact that the planting of any rice was rare in the area where the primary crops consisted of wheat, millet, and sweet potatoes (Y16ff, 32). In Phenix Village, the details of farming remain a mystery, fruit being the principal product grown (Kxiii, 84). Rice cultivation in Kao Yao was of paramount importance.

Among the farm animals of Kao Yao, water buffalo, oxen, horses, mules, donkeys, pigs, chickens, and geese were commonplace. In Taitou, farmers owned all of these except water buffalo, horses, and apparently geese, the ox being especially significant (Y25, 47). At Kaihsienkung, apparently there was not one of these creatures (a Chinese village without chickens?), but there had been a recent introduction of sheep (F126, 159, 236). In Phenix Village, we discovered the existence of water buffalo and pigs in a reference to sanitation, although Kulp later seems contradictory in stating that "the only meat the home produces is from chickens or geese, but the people find it more profitable to sell these and buy bits of pork to eat" (K57–8, 96).

What Kulp failed to do for pigs, he did most generously for school children, devoting a whole chapter to education, thus provid-ing many points on which comparisons may be based. We shall choose only a few. In 1918, there were four schools in Phenix Village, two public and two private, one of the latter being Christian (K222). These were reduced in 1923 to two non-Christian schools each offering a four-year course of instruction (K230). Kulp computed that forty-four per cent of the village children of school age (six to twenty inclusively) were attending classes, but that these pupils were almost entirely boys (K44, 245).

In Kaihsienkung to the north, Fei tells us that there was a single six-year public school with a nominal attendance of more than a hundred students, but that seldom more than twenty of them appeared (F39). Computing on the basis of 387 children in the village between the ages of six and twenty as in Phenix Village gives us a figure for nominal attendance of about twenty-five per cent, but only about five per cent in reality (F22). Fei attributed the poor educational conditions to a series of causes. First of all, he says that "illiterate parents do not take school education very seriously" and then goes on to present the village head man's criticisms which included the maladjustment of the school terms with working periods and the fact that the teacher was a girl who in consequence could not command prestige (F39–40).

Yang relates that there were two schools in Taitou, one a lineage (clan) school that had become public and one a private Christian school (Y137). Writing from memory, Yang could not supply statistics on attendance, but he noted that only a few girls went to the Christian school, and none to the other (Y144).

In the single public school in Kao Yao there were about forty-six children from the village attending which, for sake of comparison with the figures given by Fei, was slightly over thirty per cent of the individuals between the ages of six and twenty. The remarkable thing is that, of these, almost half were girls. This rise in female education undoubtedly may be explained by the fact that the data pertains to a period fifteen years later than Kulp's and probably Yang's.

Fundamental to comprehending Chinese society is a knowledge of the social organization, and to no aspect of the culture has so much attention been given. It is therefore almost surprising that there are still numerous things that one would like to know, subtle points that have not been adequately made explicit. Sophistication develops slowly. First comes the question of the patrilineal descent groups in which the terms family (*chia*), compound (*hu*), branch (*chih*), sub-lineage (*fang*), lineage (*tsu*), and surname (*hsing*) provide a hierarchy of enlarging enclaves.* For centuries the Chinese have structured their society around the notion that the important family relationships were those defined in terms of male descent from father to son. The importance of women rested in their ability to produce males, and in doing so they became attached to the line of their husbands, their ultimate social security depending on their becoming the ancestresses of sons. To a Chinese man, his father's mother was venerable if alive, and worshiped if dead, whereas his mother's mother had no such importance even though he might love her more.

As among English and Americans, a difference in surname set apart those who were not descended in the same male line. In the early studies of Chinese society, the surname group, usually called a clan but occasionally a sib or gens, was considered paramount as the historical, religious, political, social, and economic unit—really an ultimately extended exogamous family within which any inter-marriage was considered incest. At certain periods and places, this ideal had been defended even by the Chinese. Realistically, however, it became obvious that many *hsing* groups were not descendants of a common ancestor, the surname having been appropriated at various times for one reason or another. Thus the lineage (*tsu*) had to be distinguished as the unit representing the true agnatic line, normally recorded in a written genealogical record called a clan book. Since most of the Chinese lived in small villages and since most of the villagers were poor and illiterate, clan books could not always be preserved and continued when they existed at all. Both the prolifera-tion of the population in periods of peace and its decimation during wars destroyed the continuity of the records. Thus the meaningful ancestral groups became the segments of which there were clear records, if not face-to-face knowledge. When these were large, sub-lineages (*fang*) and branches (*chih*) had to be set off to demarcate special roles. These subdivisions existed particularly in villages that were dominated, if not exclusively occupied, by the members of one lineage.

* This alignment has been taken from a translation of a section of an article in Chinese by Lin Yueh-hua which appears in Freedman's *Lineage Organization in Southeastern China* (pp. 36–7). It should be noted that Hu Hsien-chin in her thesis on *The Common Descent Group in China and Its Functions* suggests that *tsu* may be divided into *ku,* or branches, and *ku* into *fang* (p. 30).

Before continuing with our effort to simplify comprehension of
the social structure, let us turn to the actual villages under consideration. Kulp emphasized the point that Phenix Village in southeastern
China was a one-lineage (*sib*) community, fifteen shopkeepers bearing other surnames notwithstanding (Kxxiv, 30, 143). The point
was well made as the shops had only been recently rented to outsiders
who were certainly so considered. We might add that the intrusions
surely were pregnant of change. Kulp also noted, astutely for one in
his day, that the single village sib was subdivided into two large and
a number of small ancestral groups, or branch families, which functioned primarily for religious purposes (K145–6). Whether or not
these properly corresponded to *fang* and *chih* is not clear, but at least
the hierarchy was indicated.

In Taitou, Yang tells us, there were four lineages (clans), as
well as representatives of two more who had lived in the village for
over half a century seemingly without having gained the status of
full membership in the community (Y6, 12). In his opinion, villages
with two to four lineages were typical of north China, although some
comprised only one, as was commonplace in south China (Y134).
Yang speaks of lineages subdividing into branches, each with its own
ground for burial, and reports specifically that the largest of the Taitou
lineages had five or six branches (Y7, 134). From a functional
point of view, however, the whole matter is not clearly presented.
Yang makes the interesting note that one of the smaller of the four
lineages, not having a clan book, had recently acquired one by going
to a neighboring village where a group with the same surname had
a clan book and there copying it, after which they simply added their
own genealogical record insofar as it was known (Y138).

Kaihsienkung, in east central China, was a village of no less than
twenty-nine surname groups (*hsing*), and at least thirty lineages
(*tsu*) as the largest (*hsing*) was known to be divided into two *tsu*
of entirely separate origins. Also a lower level of subdivisions was
clearly implied (F92). To these more inclusive units of the descent
group, however, Fei devoted little attention. We may add that in
Kaihsienkung there were no written genealogical records, or clan
books (F76, 84), but only lists of lineal ancestors to whom sacrifices
should be offered which were kept by local priests (F76, 84).

In Kao Yao we found thirty lineages, a relatively much larger
number than in Kaihsienkung where the population was almost three

times as great. It was made certain that these *tsu* were not confused
with *hsing*, but we do not have positive evidence that the larger of
the *tsu* had no branches although I suspect that they did not. As
tired as my colleague Li An-che may have been, to that sociological
fact he might well have alerted me. It may be added that an informant in one of the leading families stated that he knew nothing of his
ancestors over four generations removed, whereas the schoolteacher
went so far as to say no one cared about anyone over three.

Having considered the larger divisions of the common descent
groups, we can now turn to the smaller ones which are the essence
of the social organization and which have been the focus of most
interest to anthropologists. At the base of our hierarchy is the
family, or *chia*. Exactly what the Chinese term means has never
been agreed upon and perhaps it is a variable which is subject to
local interpretation. Certainly a husband and wife and their children—or the survivors of such a group—are intrinsic to all *chia*, but
this nuclear (natural, conjugal, elementary, etc.) family is only one
kind of *chia*, the latter frequently being categorized as extended
(stem) in consequence of containing a third generation of the patrilineal line, or as joint in having more than one married son included.
Fei provides us with data for the following table to which I have
added the corresponding figures for both the village and boat people
of Kao Yao (F29).

	Kaihsien-kung	Kao Yao (Village)	Kao Yao (Boat)
1. Nuclear *chia*		147	80	15
a. With married couple	85	58	10
b. With one spouse	62	22	5
2. Extended *chia*		200	40	18
a. With one married couple	138	19	9
b. With one spouse	37	8	1
c. With father, mother, son, and son's wife	25	13	8
3. Joint *chia*		12	2	3
a. With father, mother, two sons and their wives	3	2	1
b. With one parent and two sons and their wives	9	0	2
	359	122	36

What is notable from the above table is that the nuclear families, both in Kaihsienkung and among the Kao Yao boat people, approximate forty per cent of each total, whereas among the Kao Yao village group there are about sixty-five per cent of nuclear families.

The term *chia,* however, has not been defined simply with respect to the kinship relations of its members, but according to other factors as well. In most cases, the eating together of food cooked on a common stove has been stated or implied. With this criterion is usually coupled the sharing of a single residence, a condition which leads to the confusions brought about on account of absentee members as well as because of the position of individuals with other surnames who have lived long with the family (Y46, 77). Then there is the question of whether or not the members of the *chia* must be subjected to a common economic control with all important property held in the name of the *chia* head, as most authorities seem to assume.

Considering our several village studies, we find that Kulp in distinguishing the functions of a family was concerned as an outsider not so much with the limiting factors of the Chinese concept of the *chia,* as with the actual workings of the family in the broadest meaning of the word (K158ff). Viewed historically, it is remarkable that he dissected as much as he did. His use of the word *chia,* however, in the form of *chia-chiang* (probably thinking of it as *headman)* apparently was carelessly extended to refer to the leader of the *tsu* and its subdivisions as well (K149). On the other hand, in his only enumeration of *chia,* he is clearly referring to economic families (K104).

Fei, greatly interested in economics, states of Kaihsienkung, "The basic social group in the village is the Chia, an expanded family. The members of this group possess a common property, keep a common budget and co-operate together to pursue a common living through division of labour" (F27). If *expanded* is the equivalent of *extended,* which it seems to be, then his attribution of *basic* must rest on less than sixty per cent of the *chia,* for forty per cent he himself showed to be nuclear. Fei adds that in Kaihsienkung, the average *chia* consisted of only four persons (F29).

Yang likewise makes clear that what he refers to as the family (*chia*) is an economic unit as well as a group of people living and eating together (Y44, 77–8). On the other hand, there is no explicit definition of the term and, working from afar, he could give us neither their number nor the total population, but he estimated the average size of the *chia* at six individuals, a not altogether trustworthy figure.

Certainly we have added little to a resolution of the conceptual problem in our study of Kao Yao. Unfortunately, in 1938 no such sophisticated essay on lineage organization as Freedman's was available, and Kulp's was the only one of the three village studies in print. Clearly, in Kao Yao, the concept of the family involved a common residence and table, but the economic role was more complex. The family of Li Fu, for example, had split up, and the several married brothers and their offspring, being considered economically independent of each other, were counted as separate *chia*. They ate separately but continued to live in the same house which was actually a compound. Most important it would seem, is the fact that the brothers held their residence and their farm land in common.

The notion of a compound itself is infected with difficulties, as the Chinese word *hu* may be translated as household, a term perhaps most reasonably used to refer to all those inhabiting a common home irrespective of their relationship and, in that sense, an aggregate distinguishable from the one or more patrilineal *chia* occupying a building. One of my major regrets about our work in Kao Yao is that, despite having a numbered list of every resident in Kao Yao and a numbered plan of each house and compound, the correlation of the two is missing and no search has produced it. Quite probably, in the confusion of our last few days in the village, it never was made.

As complicated as anything so far discussed in reference to the social structure was a realistic kin group lying somewhere between the *chia* and the larger subdivisions of the *tsu*. Generally termed the *wu fu,* or five mourning grades, it referred to those relatives for whom mourning ideally was carried out. Since, in theory, such an aggregate would vary for almost each individual, the functioning group was somewhat arbitrary. In no village to my knowledge has a complete descriptive empirical study of the *wu fu* been made, but Freedman (pp. 41–5) devotes a summary chapter to the subject.

Only Fei among authors of the village studies mentions the mourning grades beyond a passing reference and, by some vagary, he refers to the *wu fu,* as well as the lineage, by the term *tsu* (F84–6). He does make the interesting point, however, that in reality the average *wu fu* comprised eight patrilineally related *chia* (F85). Furthermore, Freedman (p. 37) has supplied evidence from the previously mentioned article that Lin Yueh-hua published in Chinese, that a *wu fu,* if strong, will embrace a whole *chih,* or branch.

Another question that comes up is the actual relationship of the wife in the descent group into which she has married. Fei states categorically that a woman becomes a member of her husband's *tsu* on marriage, but then adds that "she loses her membership of her father's Tsu when she is married in the sense that she will not join the offerings of sacrifice to ancestors on the father's side and will not be offered sacrifices by them after her death" (F85–6). Is the implication that she retains membership in her father's *tsu* in some other sense? Some authorities seem to think so, and others quite the contrary. Kulp holds that females are members of the lineages into which they are born and that they attain the status of lineage (sib) members in the family into which they marry only by virtue of their potential motherhood; in fact, they are actually adopted (K143–4). Yang suggests an almost opposite point of view when he states, "A girl has no status whatsoever in the family of her own parents. Her father and mother and brothers may love her very much, but it is recognized that she is not a permanent member of the family and can add nothing to the family fortunes" (Y104, 113). In Kao Yao, the impression was given that females were members of the lineage into which they were born, and that this identification was gradually transferred to another lineage between the time of their betrothal and the motherhood of a son. Once a male descendant was assured, the mother's membership in the lineage of the son seemed complete.

A corroboration of the theory of transfer from one lineage to another lies in the adoption of a son-in-law, which device for assuring the continuation of a family line is reported from all four villages, and with in each case a change of surname on the part of the adopted boy (K82, F71–2, Y84). Apparently the custom was more often resisted by the son-in-law in the single-lineage villages of south-eastern China where clan feeling was strongest, for Kulp points out that an adopted son-in-law lost so much face in taking his wife's name that in certain instances he refused after marriage to give up his own, and sometimes he even ran off with his wife (K82, 144).

The fact that there was only a single lineage in a village may have also affected the potential development of social classes, although Kulp does not hesitate to divide up the people of Phenix Village into three groups based on wealth. In fact he says, "the groups would distribute themselves as follows:

Good [upper class?]	18 per cent
Fair [middle class?]	31 per cent
Poor [lower class?]	51 per cent" (K104).

The bracketed insertions are mine.

Yang divides the houses of Taitou into three groups correlated with the wealthiest people, those of average income, and those of the poor, but as usual, not being in the field himself, there are no statistics (Y38–9). In another place, however, he states, "The population of Taitou can be divided roughly into four classes on the basis of food consumption," but this fourfold categorization seems to have been forced by a permutation of the three principal foods, rather than a conception of social strata (Y32). The matter also becomes involved with the concept of "respected laymen" and the gentry (Y181ff). Fei gives us little help, and it is not impossible that he either had a personal block on the subject of class or reserved data for other occasions. He does say in discussing clothing, however, that a long gown was indispensable for persons of distinction (F124). In Kao Yao, a three-class system seemed indigenously Chinese.

Turning to marriage, we find a number of interesting details which supply data for comparisons. For instance, Kulp states that the family of either the girl or the boy could initiate a betrothal through a matchmaker or go-between (K170). Yang's discussion seems to suggest that marriages were initiated by the boy's family, but the situation was not precisely described (Y106–7). Fei writes, "it is improper for a girl's mother to initiate a proposal," although a matchmaker could apparently do it for her in which case, however, the decision to begin joint negotiations rested with the boy's family. Fei continues, "the real factor in the selection is the personal preference of the boy's parents" (F40–2). Yang implies it was the boy's mother who initiated negotiations at the suggestion of the matchmaker, although again the negative point is by no means specific (Y106–7, 113). In Kao Yao both parents of a boy were responsible for inaugurating their son's betrothal, but a girl's parents could not do so for her. In all villages, the betrothal of a son-in-law to be adopted was an exceptional case. Whatever else may be concluded, the role of matchmaker proved to be of fundamental importance.

The question of preferential marriages comes up particularly with respect to the desirability of a boy's marrying his mother's brother's daughter (maternal cross-cousin) or his father's sister's daughter (paternal cross-cousin). Kulp states that marriages to unrelated individuals were preferred, but that a mother's brother's daughter was acceptable, whereas it was taboo to marry a paternal cross-cousin (K167–8). Fei makes clear that for a boy to marry his mother's brother's daughter was highly desirable, but that to marry his father's sister's daughter was disliked, though permissible (F50–1). Yang likewise admits that the latter was a permissible, but not desirable, form of marriage, but any comment by him on the attitude toward the marriage of a maternal cross-cousin has not been found (Y119). In Kao Yao, the marriage of a boy to his mother's brother's daughter was the first choice, and even an alliance with a paternal cross-cousin was considered good. This information can be advantageously summarized in tabular form.

Boy's Marriage to:	Phenix Village	Kaihsienkung	Taitou	Kao Yao
Mother's brother's daughter	Permissible	Desirable	?	First choice
Father's sister's daughter	Taboo	Permissible, but undesirable	Permissible, but undesirable	Desirable

In Phenix Village, since it was occupied by only one lineage, marriage was exogamous (Kxxiv). Kulp adds, however, that "people of the same surname but five generations removed, may intermarry provided they have a name which may be changed and provided a slight change is made" in the character (K167). In Kaihsienkung, most marriages united different villages and sometimes a husband and wife might have the same surname as long as they did not belong to the same *tsu* (lineage or *wu fu?*) (F86). Yang knew of no intravillage marriages in Taitou and reports various reasons for their being disliked (Y115–6). In Kao Yao, most marriages involved two villages, and the same surname was no bar providing the couple represented different lineages.

Kulp indicates that the average age of betrothal for children in Phenix Village was from eight to ten, and that girls were married at an average age of close to nineteen while boys were a little younger (K170, 175). The data were based on a small sample, however. Fei states that betrothals were usually made in Kaihsienkung when a child was six or seven, although it could be done later, and that ninety-two per cent of girls were married by sixteen as were seventy-five per cent of the boys (F40, 52). Most of the wives were younger than their husbands, but many were older and one woman by eleven years (F53). In Taitou, both betrothals and marriages were later than in some other parts of China, as Yang recognized. He indicates that girls were betrothed from twelve or thirteen onward, while boys were perhaps fifteen (Y106). The average age of marriage was about twenty, no cases of boys under nineteen or girls under seventeen being known (Y113). Also, boys were frequently married to girls who were much older because of economic reasons (Y104). In Kao Yao, most betrothals were contracted about the age of ten or eleven but many were settled from the age of five onward. The age of marriage ranged from fourteen to twenty, over fifty per cent of the couples being within two years of the same age, and most of the wives younger.

A point of difference in marriage customs between the four villages was that in Phenix Village and Taitou the bridegroom awaited his bride at home, whereas in Kaihsienkung and Kao Yao, the bridegroom fetched her. Kulp reports that the bride was delivered to her husband's family in a sedan chair accompanied by a man chosen by her father, and that there was a band in the procession if the parties to the marriage were rich (K178). A favorable date for the occasion was determined by the boy's family with the assistance of a diviner, apparently without regard for the season (K177). Yang says that the boy's family sent the chair, but that a band did not accompany it in Taitou or in the villages of the surrounding area (Y110). In Kaihsienkung, the bridegroom went to his bride's house and brought her back in a sedan chair to the accompaniment of a band which did not play while in her village, however (F44-5, 53). The New Year's holiday, or apparently the first fifteen days of the 1st month, was the usual time for marriage (F129). The Kao Yao bridegroom also brought home his bride in a sedan chair with an accompanying band, but in that village the 10th month was preferred for nuptial celebrations.

Another point of difference was the fact that neither Kulp nor Yang knew of any cases of infanticide in Phenix Village or Taitou, while Yang went so far as to add that the practice had never existed in Taitou (K152, Y10). It was likewise unknown in Kao Yao except for the belief that an unmarried mother would kill her newborn child, strangling it with her own hands. Contrariwise, infanticide was extremely common, especially with respect to females, in the economically depressed village of Kaihsienkung (F33–4, 52). Of this, Fei leaves no doubt, and he indicates that the babies were killed by refusing them milk (F64).

Yang reports that there was no concubinage, not to mention cases of plural wives, in Taitou, but attributes the situation basically to the depressed economic conditions of the area (Y114–5). Perhaps for the same reason concubinage was absent from Kaihsienkung where conditions were seemingly even worse, although I can find no mention of it by Fei, an omission which is strange. Kulp reports fourteen cases of concubinage in 182 marriages in Phenix Village which is over seven per cent, and states that to have concubines is "looked upon as a symbol of wealth and honor" (K181). Although concubines might be brought to their homes in sedan chairs—often regarded as a symbol of marriage—Kulp makes clear that there were no plural marriages with more than one wife living in Phenix Village, but he does report them among men who had been overseas (K50–1, 151, 181). In Kao Yao, plural marriage replaced concubinage as was demonstrated by three or four cases in 122 families. This situation, of course, raises the question of what criteria should be used to distinguish a true Chinese marriage. Yang says that the parade of the bridal chair shows a marriage is being properly performed, that homage to the Gods of Heaven and Earth assures their sanction, and that obeisance to the ancestors of the bridegroom informs them that thereafter the bride is of their lineage (Y113). Kulp lays great weight on the betrothal ceremonies and their spiritual sanctions (K171–3, 181). Jamieson (p. 188) concludes that from a legal point of view "it would follow that the numerous ceremonies subsequent to betrothal which are generally practiced at a

Chinese marriage are all superfluous as far as giving validity is concerned, and that the only two things necessary to a complete marriage are a contract between the heads of the two families and the actual transfer or rendition of the woman." In Kao Yao it was assumed that what distinguished a true marriage, in contrast to the taking of a concubine, was the status and privileges of the woman in relation to her husband and his family. It did not impress me that a Chinese villager would try to hide concubinage under the guise of polygyny, and the situation in Kao Yao was recorded without more than ordinary attention on my part. The local position surprised my colleague Li An-che on his arrival, but he soon afterward concurred with it independently of me. I must admit, however, that in 1938, I had no strong reasons to think the situation so unusual, as I have been inclined to do since.

Another peculiarity of Kao Yao was the occurrence of widow inheritance by a younger brother which was regarded as normal when the latter was unmarried and as possible when he was not. The only mention of the levirate in the other village studies is by Kulp who says it was not practiced in Phenix Village (K168). Hsu (237), however, in *Under the Ancestor's Shadow* speaks of the levirate which he believes "very rarely and informally occurs among the poor in some parts of China."

Leaving the subject of marriage, we can interpolate the observation that in Phenix Village and Taitou, land was said to be inherited equally by the sons (K101–2, Y14). In Kaihsienkung and Kao Yao, on the other hand, the eldest son received an extra share (F66). To counter the suggestion that a minor point may have been overlooked, we can refer to a statement in *Lion and Dragon in Northern China* about the people of Weihaiwei, which like Taitou, was also in Shantung. Johnston (153), in speaking of the division of inheritance by lots, states, "The eldest brother is so far from having a claim to a larger or better share than the rest that, as we see, he is not even entitled to draw the first lot." Johnston, a magistrate in the territory, was extraordinarily conversant with both the customary and statutory law of the region.

Moving on to ceremonial procedures connected with death, Fei and especially Yang supply information for a comparison of several features. Kulp's data, on the contrary, is meager, emphasizing avoidance in relation to contacts with a corpse, an attitude which may well have affected his recording of the local customs (K198ff). In Taitou, Yang says that when the end for a dying parent was near, he was washed and dressed in his shroud (Y86). Fei does not cover the point, but in Kao Yao it was stated specifically that this was not done before death. Furthermore in Taitou, after wailing, the corpse was placed in the coffin which was not immediately sealed according to Yang (Y87). He is not specific as to the time, but one judges that this placing of the corpse was done on the day of the death, as in Kao Yao. Fei, on the other hand, states clearly that the corpse was put into the coffin on the second or third day and then closed and moved to the graveyard on the next one (F75). In Kao Yao, the coffin was sealed on the third day and interment immediately followed as in Kaihsienkung, but in Taitou, after being sealed, the coffin was kept in the house from one to three months, in fact, the longer the better (Y87). In all three villages, white mourning clothes were worn and priests read holy books at the funeral ceremony (F75–6, Y86, 88–9). A peculiarity in Kao Yao, it would seem, was the custom of the chief mourners preceding the coffin, at least in the first part of the funeral procession, rather than following it as in Taitou (Y89). It may be added that Yang reports mourners dropping earth on the coffin in the grave, but without specifying any particular relationship of those doing so as was deemed significant in Kao Yao (Y89). Finally, we note that Fei reports the return of the spirit of the deceased to its former residence on the seventeenth or eighteenth day after death (F76). In Kao Yao, the spirit, or ghost, was said to return on three different occasions, the dates being calculated by a lay reader.

In none of the villages was religion covered in such precise detail as to beg comparisons. Clearly in all cases there was a merging of the tenets of Confucianism, Taoism, and Buddhism. Ancestor worship, it seems, was ubiquitous. Christianity had obviously become an important force in Taitou and had also made some impression on Phenix Village, but in neither case was it the dominant religion (Y6–7, 188–9, K309–11). There were no Christians in Kao Yao and none mentioned in Kaihsienkung. Buddhism, probably because of the proximity of great temples, was perhaps a stronger influence in Kao Yao than in the other three villages. Local gods of a Taoist character were common to all, but they seemed to have been particularly meaningful in Kaihsienkung where the role of the Kitchen

God was elaborated upon by Fei (F99ff). A measure of this god's significance is shown in the fact that on seven days of the year, cognizance of his position was demonstrated by special sacrifices or other ceremonial acknowledgments (F152–3).

In our review of the culture of the four villages, three particular annual festivals were mentioned in each one of them. These were New Year's (Hsin Nien), the Ching Ming Festival in the 3rd month, and the Chung Ch'iu on the 15th of the 8th (K301, F129–30, 151–2, Y90–4, 101, 249). Although both Kulp and Fei supply little if any description of these celebrations, it is most probable that, as in Kao Yao and Taitou, New Year's overshadowed the others (Y90ff). It may be noted in passing that Yang recorded the house cleaning on the 27th of the 12th month (i.e., "two days before New Year's Eve") that has been described for Kao Yao (Y92). Yang furthermore gives us a notable description of the Ching Ming Festival. The Hua Têng, or Lantern Festival, on the 15th of the 1st month, only Fei failed to mention. Yang again provides an interesting account which must be read to be appreciated (Y95).

It does seem a little strange that in neither Fei nor Yang have been found any mention of the Chieh Tsu Festival on the 15th of the 7th month, and Kulp merely includes it in his perfunctory list of ceremonies (K301). For those wishing to pursue the subject, informative accounts are provided in two important sources on festivals, *The Moon Year* by Bredon and Mitrophanow (376ff) and *Annual Customs and Festivals in Peking* by Tun Li-chen translated by Bodde (60–2). Neither of these volumes, however, seems to throw any light on the Huo Pa, or Torch Festival in Kao Yao, unless the latter is related to the worship of the Fire God.

In pursuing the comparative data presented above, it must be admitted that more has been done to raise problems than to solve them. This is a defensible procedure insofar as any awareness of a deficiency in knowledge stimulates the acquisition of new data, just as a depression in the earth attracts water until it is filled. With an overwhelming social revolution already a generation past, to secure and preserve an understanding of the great classical culture of China will demand concentrated and immediate effort. May the rains that represent enlightenment flood this field soon.

Appendix A

HISTORICAL NOTE AND ACKNOWLEDGMENTS

It has been intended in the introductory chapters written in 1939, and in those following, to portray the practical problems of field work as well as to present the results thereof, distinguishing in the manner of writing that which was reported by informants from what was visually observed. This latter point but vaguely reflects the interest in epistemology which stimulated the original project, an undertaking which may be briefly explained for the anthropologist and others intellectually curious about the historical processes of research which sometimes lead to unanticipated results. Field work undertaken among the Northern Athapaskans in Alaska during 1931 emphasized the importance of distinguishing what people simply believe to be true in their culture from that which an alien can either verify empirically or otherwise prove. Painfully convinced of the disadvantage of working among people whose traditional culture had to be reconstructed, I concluded that China would be an ideal area for study. After a brief introductory visit to that country in 1935, it was my good fortune to meet Li An-che of Yenching University who, on a year's visit to the United States in 1935–36, settled for the second semester at Yale. With mutual enthusiasm for advancing cultural research, it was not difficult to gain his cooperation for a project which seemed to be as sound as it perhaps was ambitious. It was suggested that we collaborate on two community studies, one to be undertaken in his native village in Hopei, the other in a settlement in southeastern Vermont which came as close as was possible to being comparable from the standpoint of an assumed knowledge of American culture on my part. The plan involved starting our work in China where Li would describe the culture of his village as he conceived it to exist, while I recorded data that would be necessarily more objective, if less sensitive to the nuances of understanding which are only possible to a native. We would then attempt to reverse the procedure in Vermont with the ultimate goal of providing data which could be subjected to a double comparison in terms of its epistemological validity. We agreed to begin work in Hopei in the summer of 1938.

I was concluding my study of the Ingalik Indians on the lower Yukon River in Alaska when I heard of the Japanese invasion of China in the summer of 1937. By the time I had returned to Yale in the fall, work in Hopei had become impossible. Challenged by the difficulties and disturbed by the possibility that I would never have the opportunity to know China before basic changes took place, I decided to go into field despite obstacles. It was the linguist Li Fang-kuei, a former schoolmate and fellow student of Edward Sapir, who suggested that I attempt to reach Yünnan where, in theory at least, I could make use of some knowledge of mandarin. This reasonable proposal was not the obvious one to an American that it proved later. With a plan of action established, I informed Li An-che who had withdrawn into northwest China beyond the reach of the encroaching Japanese of my intentions, admitting to him the necessity for putting off our joint program of research but expressing the hope that we might somehow soon meet again. The realization seemed unlikely as it was a serious question whether I would even be able to reach China. Yünnan was much farther away than Hopei, financial support for the venture was limited, and the U. S. State Department at first refused to provide a passport that was valid for travel in China. Despite these minor complications I arrived in Shanghai aboard the fast trans-Pacific line "Empress of Canada" on June 14, 1938, where to my delight I received word that Li An-che hoped eventually to meet me in Kunming on his way to join his university colleagues in Cheng-tu, Szechwan. If I needed encouragement, that news supplied it, and the remainder of the journey, as it continued a few days later, has been described in the introductory chapters of this volume.

Not until 1946, following the end of the war, was it again possible to undertake community studies in Asia. For reasons unnecessary to elaborate here, Korea was chosen for field work in 1947 and, by 1950, when the report had been completed, China had become effectively barred to Americans. Li An-che, himself, had gone to Tibet. In 1954, a survey of the peripheral regions of Japan and Hong Kong led me to the decision that it would be wise before returning again to the Far East to complete the series of monographs begun many years before on the Northern Athapaskan Indians. This having been done, my activities again concentrated on Chinese culture, and I began the community studies in Hong Kong which have been continued since 1960, interpolating into the time available for writing those reports, this account of the basic study undertaken in 1938.

It is apparent that the above paragraphs give more evidence of perseverance than of accomplishment in the field of oriental studies. Not a sinologue, nor ever one with hope of being, it has been my fundamental goal, in the limited way given to an ethnologist, to document contemporary Chinese culture as it was expressed in the villages of that country by the common people. This desire has been based, not only on the belief that Chinese culture has been one of the greatest the world has ever produced, but that through the study of this cultural sourceland it would be possible to attract more American anthropologists to the realization that a comprehension of great and vital civilization may best reflect the weakness of our own, weaknesses which, remaining uncorrected, loom like signposts on the turnpikes leading to decline.

ACKNOWLEDGMENTS

The obligations of a scholar are widespread and, for the anthropological field worker, they readily multiply in place and time. Inspiration, teaching, and the innumerable favors of casual acquaintances are absorbed as a parched field welcomes the rain. Unfortunately, of necessity, the most important gifts often go unrecorded by name. To the hospitable and helpful villagers of Kao Yao, my thoughts return again and again, and I wonder how many still survive. Most of all, I would like to convey my gratitude to the teacher, Pi Ch'un-ming, and once more hear him play his haunting melodies on the school organ. There is also a sense of obligation to Ho Chia-ping, not only as an interpreter, but for collecting many of the specimens from which the illustrations in this volume have been made. Memory likewise plays obeisance to the rare hospitality of Paul and Harriet Meyer in old Kunming.

The cost of the field study, a mere $1,500 in 1938, was largely defrayed by Yale University. Professor Edward Sapir was responsible for contributing $750 from the anthropology research funds in the Institute of Human Relations and $350 came from the Peabody Museum of Natural History. Perhaps I should thank my wife for her share of our own contribution, but I would prefer to record her much greater gift of toleration and encouragement.

For recent aid, I thank Shirley Glaser Hartman for the maps and line drawings, John Howard for revivifying the plate photographs taken by an amateur cameraman in 1938, Chen Tchaw-ren for identifying fish, and Soo Sui-ling for her assistance in preparing the manuscript including the writing of the Chinese characters in Appendix E. Maurice Freedman has read the text and made helpful suggestions which could but slightly relieve its inherent deficiencies.

In acknowledging my debt to those with whom I worked and lived in Yünnan, men and women with whom war and tragedy have long since cut all contact, none were as significant as Li An-che and his wife. Their deep concern for human beings remains as a bright star in a clouded sky. Whether they have survived the changes in the past fifteen years I do not know, but I happily dedicate this book to my friend with the hope it may find him safe and well.

Appendix B

NEGATIVE DATA

As all ethnologists are aware, the recording of negative data can be extremely important, although such information is usually more difficult to determine with accuracy. A knowledgable and cooperative informant is not likely to offer erroneous positive statements unless he misunderstands a question or is intentionally lying. Furthermore, any such suspicious or inconsistent point in the record is usually easy to check. On the other hand, when an informant states that some object does not exist, that some behavior does not take place, or that some idea does not occur, unless he has had reason to investigate the matter, it usually means only that he has not seen, heard, or thought of it himself. This leaves much room for error—since the several informants from whom one might seek corroboration could, on some subjects, be equally ignorant. Therefore the following list, in which it has not been intended to duplicate negative statements in the text, must be utilized with particular care, even though the errors are probably few.

Food
  No starvation in village
  Animals (horses or dogs) not used in hunting
  Animals not taken in drives
  No hunting ceremonies
  Use of birdlime unknown

Dress, etc.
  No wood buttons on clothes
  No body painting
  No tattooing
  No cranial deformation
  No nose or lip perforations
  No circumcision
  No female genital mutilations

Travel
  No seasonal migrations
  No restriction on travel
  No dugouts
  No lighthouses
  No snowshoes
  No skis
  No skates

Tools
- No cloth weaving
- No dyeing
- Pulleys not used

Arts, Amusements, etc.
- No sundials
- No puzzles
- No contests with animals
- No wrestling
- No boxing
- No ball games
- No distance jumping
- No boat races
- No puppet shows
- No radios
- No telephones
- Never heard of head being seat of soul
- No flight or disguise from epidemics
- No purification ceremonies after sickness
- Frost-bite unknown

Social Organization
- Girls not adopted
- No merchants associations
- No insurance or mutual aid societies
- No monopolies
- No secret societies
- No nose-thumbing
- No ear-thumbing

Social Customs
- Never heard of men urinating in sitting position
- No exchange of wives
- No wife lending
- No ceremonial incest
- Never heard of a concubine having to leave husband before dawn
- Never heard of looking in bride's eyebrows for a red thread (or a hair) as an indication of conception
- Never heard of taboo on sexual intercourse with a pregnant woman to prevent child from having smallpox
- No professional mourners
- No exhumation of corpse

Religion
- No evangelism
- No trickster gods
- No continence for religious purposes
- No religious seclusion
- No concept of dwarfs or fairies
- No totemism

Appendix C

KINSHIP TERMS

SECOND ASCENDING GENERATION

1. *lao tieh* (old father) : FaFa
2. *wai kung* (outside old man) : MoFa
3. *nai* (breast, milk) : FaMo
4. *wai p'o* (outside old woman) : MoMo

FIRST ASCENDING GENERATION

5. *tieh* (father) : Fa, SpFa (m.s.)
6. *lao tieh* (old father) : SpFa (w.s.)
7. *chi fu* (stepfather) : MoHu
8. *mu* or *ma* (mother) : Mo
9. *ma* (mother) : SpMo (m.s.)
10. *ch'in ma* (dear mother) : SpMo (w.s.)
11. *lao ma* (old mother) : FaWi (older than Mo)
12. *niang niang* (girl) : FaWi (younger than Mo)
13. *ta tieh* (great father) : FaBr (older than Fa)
14. *shu shu* (father's younger brother) : FaBr (younger than father)
15. *chiu yeh* (maternal uncle *plus* grandfather) : MoBr (older than Mo)
16. *chiu tieh* (maternal uncle *plus* father) : MoBr (younger than Mo)
17. *ku ma* (elder paternal aunt) : FaSi (older than Fa)
18. *lao niang* (old girl) : FaSi (younger than Fa)
19. *ta yi ma* (great maternal aunt) : MoSi (Mo eldest Si)
20. *erh yi ma* (second maternal aunt) : MoSi (Mo second eldest Si)

EGO'S GENERATION

21. *ko ko* (elder brother) : Br (elder), FaBrSo (older than ego)
22. *hsiung ti* (younger brother) : Br (younger), FaBrSo (younger than ego), SpBr (younger than ego)
23. *chieh fu* (elder sister's husband) : Si (elder) Hu, SpSi (elder) Hu
24. *hsiung ti* or *mei hsü* (younger sister *plus* son-in-law) : Si (younger) Hu
25. *ta ko* (great elder brother) : SpBr (eldest and older than ego)
26. *erh ko* (second elder brother) : SpBr (second eldest and older than speaker)
27. *chieh chieh* (elder sister) : Si (elder), FaBrDa (older than ego), SpSi (m.s.)
28. *mei mei* (younger sister) : Si (younger) FaBrDa (younger than ego)
    No term for direct address of spouse (teknonymy used when possible)
29. *ku ma* (elder paternal aunt) or *lao niang* (old mother) : SpSi (w.s.)
30. *ku t'ai* (husband's sister) : SpSi (w.s. without children)
31. *sao sao* (elder brother's wife) or *chieh chieh* (elder sister) : Br (elder) Wi, SpBr (elder) Wi (w.s.)
32. *sao sao* (elder brother's wife) : SpBr (elder) Wi (m.s.)
33. *ti hsi* (younger brother's wife) : BrWi (younger)

372

34. *shen niang* (father's younger brother's wife *plus* girl) : SpBr (younger) Wi (w.s.)
35. *chiu mu* (maternal uncle *plus* mother) : SpBr (younger) Wi (m.s.)
36. *lao piao* (old first cousin) : MoSiSo (elder or younger), FaSiSo, MoBrSo
37. *piao chieh* (first cousin *plus* older sister) : MoSiDa (older than ego), FaSiDa (older than ego), MoBrDa (older than ego)
38. *piao mei* (first cousin *plus* younger sister) : MoSiDa (younger than ego), FaSiDa (younger than ego), MoBrDa (younger than ego)

FIRST DESCENDING GENERATION

No term for direct address of son or daughter (name is used)
39. *chih erh tzu* (nephew) : BrSo, SiSo
40. *chih nü* (niece) : BrDa, SiDa
41. *erh tzu hsi fu* (daughter-in-law) : SoWi
42. *ku yeh* (son-in-law) : DaHu

SECOND DESCENDING GENERATION

43. *sun tzu* (grandson) : SoSo
44. *sun nü* (granddaughter) : SoDa
45. *wai sun* (outside grandson) : DaSo
46. *wai sun nü* (outside granddaughter) : DaDa

The above list constitutes the common terms of address used in Kao Yao, Yünnan, in 1938, and it should not be confused with the literary set of Chinese relationship terms. It will be noted that the characteristic distinction of differentiating the members of one's lineage is lacking in the case of nephew and niece (39, 40), the usual term *sheng* not being substituted for *chih* in the cases of sister's children. If this is a mistake, it is not likely a slip of the pen as the terms did not follow each other on the original listing. Furthermore they were written down in both Chinese and English by Li An-che who would not be expected to make such a substitution unconsciously. Still, this reduction is difficult to believe. The equally characteristic distinction of differentiating generations fails in the case of a woman addressing her husband's sister (29) by a term belonging to the first ascending generation (18). This, however, is really explainable by the custom of a mother copying the speech of her children.

Much has been written on Chinese relationship terms, yet further analysis is needed with respect to such terms which are used by the common people if their relationship to the social structure is to be completely understood. For those wishing to pursue the subject, a partial list of the pertinent bibliography has been appended.

BENEDICT, PAUL K. "Tibetan and Chinese Kinship Terms," *Harvard Journal of Asiatic Studies,* Vol. 6, No. 3–4, pp. 313–37. Cambridge, 1942.
CHAO, Y. R. "Chinese Terms of Address," *Language,* Vol. 32, No. 1, pp. 217–41. Baltimore, 1956.
CHEN, T. S., and J. K. SHYROCK. "Chinese Relationship Terms," *American Anthropologist,* Vol. 34, No. 4, pp. 623–69. Menasha, Wisconsin, 1932.

DAVIS, K., and W. L. WARNER. "Structural Analysis of Kinship," *American Anthropologist,* Vol. 39, No. 2, pp. 291–13. Menasha, Wisconsin, 1937.

FEI, H. T. "The Problem of Chinese Relationship System," *Monumenta Serica,* Vol. 2, No. 1, pp. 125–48. Peiping, 1936–37.

FENG, H. Y. "The Chinese Kinship System," *Harvard Journal of Asiatic Studies,* Vol 2, No. 2, pp. 141–275. Cambridge, 1937.

———. "Teknonymy as a Formative Factor in the Chinese Kinship System," *American Anthropologist,* Vol. 38, No. 1, pp. 59–66. Menasha, Wisconsin, 1936.

HSU, FRANCIS L. K. "The Differential Functions of Relationship Terms," *American Anthropologist,* Vol. 44, No. 2, pp. 248–56. Menasha, Wisconsin, 1942.

KROEBER, A. L. "Process in the Chinese Kinship System," *American Anthropologist,* Vol. 35, No. 1, pp. 151–57. Menasha, Wisconsin, 1933.

MAY, ALFRED J. "Chinese Relationships," *The China Review,* Vol. 21, pp. 15–39. Shanghai, 1894–95.

RUEY, Y. F. "The Similarity of the Ancient Chinese Kinship Terminology to the Omaha Type," *Bulletin of the Department of Archaeology and Anthropology,* No. 12, pp. 1–18. Taipei, 1958.

SELIGMAN, B. Z. "Review of Feng, H. Y. The Chinese Kinship System," *American Anthropologist,* Vol. 41, No. 3, pp. 496–98. Menasha, Wisconsin, 1939.

WU, C. C. "The Chinese Family," *American Anthropologist,* Vol. 29, No. 3, pp. 316–25. Menasha, Wisconsin, 1927.

Appendix D

WEATHER IN KAO YAO—JULY–AUGUST, 1938

Date	Temperature				Casual Comments from Diary
	8 A.M.	12 A.M.	4 P.M.	8 P.M.	
July 11		70	70	68	Heavy rain in A.M.
" 12	66	71	70	68	A little rain
" 13	68	73	74	70	No rain
" 14	69	70	65	64	
" 15	67	73	70	67	Periodic rain
" 16	63	67	66	63	Rain all day
" 17	62	68	67	64	Cool day
" 18	64	72	72	66	A little rain
" 19	65	71	69	66	A little rain
" 20	65	71	75	72	Warm sunshine
" 21	67	74	75	68	Fair and warm
" 22	65	72	68	67	Rain most of the day
" 23					
" 24	65	65	69	67	Rain all day
" 25	65	69	70	68	Rain in A.M.
" 26	65	74	74	70	Early rain with lightning
" 27	68	75	76	69	Lovely day—rain over hills—many insects
" 28	68	78	77	69	Showers and sunshine—more insects
" 29	67	76	75	71	
" 30	69	75	74	70	Rain with thunder and lightning in P.M.
" 31	66	75	74	71	Heavy rain in early A.M.
Aug. 1	69	77	79	74	Lovely warm day
" 2	68	75	72	68	Heavy rain, thunder, and wind in P.M.
" 3	68	73	76	70	Heavy rain at 6 P.M.
" 4	68	77	78	71	Perfect weather
" 5	66	76	77	72	Overcast but no rain
" 6	68	78	76	69	Very heavy rain with thunder in late P.M.
" 7	67	76	74	70	
" 8	66	68	72	69	Overcast with considerable rain
" 9	66	73	72	66	Nice day
" 10	67	72	70	66	
" 11	66	73	73	68	Nice day with a little rain
" 12	66	74	77	70	Heavy rain in early A.M.
" 13	68	73	74	68	Periodic rain—many insects

The maximum temperature recorded at hours given was 79 degrees at 4 P.M., August 1, and the minimum 62 degrees July 17 at 8 A.M. Higher temperatures may have occurred at other hours in the day, and lower ones certainly did, especially when it rained. Of the thirty-three days on which temperatures were recorded, it rained in Kao Yao during twenty.

Appendix E

A LIST OF CHINESE WORDS IN THE TEXT

(Not included are common terms such as those for the annual festivals, words such as *feng-shui* which can be found in Webster's *New International Dictionary,* and a few names for which the corresponding characters could not be found)

An Ning 安寧

Chang 張

chang 丈

Chang Chia Ts'un 張家村

Chang Ts'eng 張曾

Chao 趙

Chen Tchaw-ren 鄭昭任

Ch'en 陳

Ch'en Ku-i 陳古逸

Chi Chieh 雞街

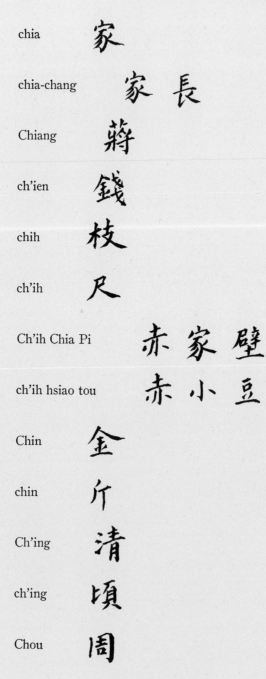

chia 家

chia-chang 家長

Chiang 蔣

ch'ien 錢

chih 枝

ch'ih 尺

Ch'ih Chia Pi 赤家壁

ch'ih hsiao tou 赤小豆

Chin 金

chin 斤

Ch'ing 清

ch'ing 頃

Chou 周

chu 主

Ch'u 儲

Ch'u Hsiung 楚雄

ch'ü 區

fang 房

fên 分

Feng 馮

fu 富

Fu Tien 富滇

Han 韓

hei hsiao tou 黑小豆

hei ma yeh 黑媽葉

ho 合

Ho Chia-ping   何家炳

Ho Hsi   河西

hsi po   西雹

Hsi T'ou Wa Shan   洗頭髮山

Hsia Yao   夏窰

hsiang   鄉

hsiao hsiang   小鄉

hsien   縣

hsien tzu   弦子

Hsin Ts'un   新村

hsing   姓

Hsu   徐

Hu   胡

hu 户

hu ch'in 胡琴

hui chia 回家

hun 魂

ju i 如意

K'ai Hua 開化

K'ai Yüan 開遠

kan-pei 乾杯

k'ang 炕

Kao 高

kao (high) 高

kao (cake) 糕

Kao Ch'iao 高橋

Kao Liu Chia 高六甲

Kao Yao 高嶢

Ku 顧

ku 骨

kuan jên 官人

K'un Yang 昆陽

Kung 龔

kung 工

Kung Chung Shan 公冢山

Kuo 郭

lao pan 老板

Li 李

li (equivalent to ⅟₁₀ fên lineal) 釐

li (equivalent to 360 pu) 里

li (equivalent to ⅒ fên weight) 釐

Li An-che (-chai) 李安宅

Li Chi 李濟

Li Fu 李富

Li Wan-nien 李萬年

liang 雨

Liang Ssu-yung 梁思永

Liu 劉

lu hsiao tou 綠小豆

Lung T'an 龍潭

Lung Wang Miao 龍王廟

Ma Chieh 馬街

Mei   梅

Mei Jên Shan   美 人 山

Mi   米

Mi Ts'ao   米 槽

Miao   苗

Min Chia   民 家

Ming Lang   明 朗

Mo Yü   墨 雨

mou   畝

ni ch'iu sha   泥 鰍 痧

niang   娘

pai chia tou   白 架 豆

Pai Hu Tsa Shan   白 鬍 薩 山

Pai Tzu	白子		
pan	板		
pao	保		
Pi Ch'un-ming	畢	春	明
P'i Chi Kuan	碧	雞	關
P'i Chi Shan	碧	雞	山
p'i-p'a	琵	琶	
p'o	魄		
pu	步		
pu tung	不	動	
P'u Hsien	普	賢	
P'u P'ing Li	普	坪	里
shao	勺		

sheng (equivalent to 10 ho volume) 升

sheng (province) 省

shih 氏

Shih I Tzu Shan 石 椅 子 山

Shih Pai Fang Shan 石 白 枋 山

shui tung kua p'i 水 冬 瓜 皮

Sun 孫

Sun Lo 孫 樂

Ta Hsüeh Shan 大 雪 山

ta lan tu 大 蘭 毒

Ta Ying P'an Shan 大 營 盤 山

Tai 戴

T'ai Hua Shan 太 華 山

tan (eggs)　　　蛋

tan (a measure)　擔

Tang　　　　譚

T'ang　　　唐

T'ao　　　　陶

T'ao Hua　　　陶　華

t'eng　　　　藤

ti　　　　　笛

Tien Ch'i　　　滇　池

Tien Chung　　旬　中

tou　　　　斗

tsu　　　　祖

ts'un (village)　　村

ts'un (a measure) 寸

Tu 杜

Tu Wen-ch'ing 杜文清

Tuan 段

Tuan Huan-chang 段煥章

tuan kung 端公

Tung 董

Tung Chai 董澤

Wang 王

Wang Chia Tui 王家堆

Wu 吳

wu fu 五服

Yang 楊

Yang Chia Ts'un 楊家村

Yang Ma Shan 養馬山

Yang Shên 楊慎

Yeh 葉

Yen 嚴

yin 引

Yu Yün-lung 由雲龍

Yü 余

Yü Ch'i 玉溪

Yü Wo Yang 玉窩羊

BIBLIOGRAPHY

(of books and articles referred to in the text)

BREDON, JULIET and IGOR MITROPHANOW. *The Moon Year: A Record of Chinese Customs and Festivals,* pp. xi, 514 xx. Shanghai, 1927.

DOOLITTLE, JUSTUS. *Social Life of the Chinese: With Some Account of Their Religious, Governmental, Educational, and Business Customs and Opinions with Special but not Exclusive Reference to Fuchau,* 2 vols, pp. xvi, 459, xii, 490. New York, 1867.

FEI HSIAO-TUNG. *Peasant Life in China: A Field Study of Country Life in the Yangtze Valley,* pp. xxvi, 300. London, 1939.

FREEDMAN, MAURICE. *Lineage Organization in Southeastern China,* London School of Economics: Monographs on Social Anthropology, No. 18, pp. xix, 151. London, 1958.

FRIED, MORTON H. *Fabric of Chinese Society: A Study of Social Life in a Chinese County Seat,* pp. xiv, 243. New York, 1953.

———. "Community Studies in China," *The Far Eastern Quarterly,* Vol. 14, No. 1, pp. 11–36, Lancaster, Pennsylvania, 1954.

HOCKETT, C. F. "Chinese Versus English: An Exploration of the Whorfian Theses" in Hoijer, Harry, *Language in Culture,* pp. xi, 286. Chicago, 1954.

HSU, FRANCIS, L. K. *Under the Ancestors' Shadow: Chinese Culture and Personality,* pp. xiv, 317. New York, 1948.

HU HSIEN-CHIN. *The Common Descent Group in China and Its Functions,* pp. 1–204. Viking Fund Publications in Anthropology, No. 10, New York, 1948.

JAMIESON, G. *Chinese Family and Commercial Law,* pp. ii, 188. Shanghai, 1921.

JOHNSTON, R. F. *Lion and Dragon in Northern China,* pp. xiv, 461. New York, 1910.

KULP II, DANIEL HARRISON. *Country Life in South China: The Sociology of Familism: Vol. I, Phenix Village, Kwantung, China,* pp. xxxi, 367. New York, 1925. (Vol. II never published.)

LANG, OLGA. *Chinese Family and Society,* pp. xvii, 395. New Haven, 1946.

LEONG, Y. K. and L. K. TAO. *Village and Town Life in China,* pp. xi, 155. London, 1915.

SMITH, ARTHUR H. *Village Life in China: A Study in Sociology,* pp. 1–360. New York, 1899 (4th ed.)

TUN LI-CH'EN. *Annual Customs and Festivals in Peking as Recorded in the Sui-shih-chi* (Translated and Annotated by Derk Bodde), pp. xxii, 147. Peiping, 1936.

WERNER, E. T. C. (Compiler). Edited by Henry R. Tedder. *Descriptive Sociology; or, Groups of Sociological Facts, Classified and Arranged by Herbert Spencer. Chinese,* pp. 1–312. London, 1910.

YANG, C. K. *A Chinese Village in Early Communist Transition,* pp. ix, 284. Cambridge, Mass., 1959.

YANG, MARTIN C. *A Chinese Village: Taitou, Shantung Province,* pp. xvii, 275. New York, 1945.

INDEX

391